The Yudhoyono Presidency

The **Indonesia Project**, a leading international centre of research and graduate training on the Indonesian economy and society, is housed in the **Crawford School of Public Policy**'s **Arndt-Corden Department of Economics**. The Crawford School is part of **ANU College of Asia and the Pacific** at **The Australian National University (ANU)**. Established in 1965 in response to profound changes in the Indonesian economic and political landscapes, the Indonesia Project has grown from a small group of Indonesia-focused economists into an interdisciplinary research centre well known and respected across the world. Funded by ANU and the Australian Department of Foreign Affairs and Trade, the Indonesia Project monitors and analyses recent developments in Indonesia; informs the Australian and Indonesian governments, business and the wider community about those developments and about future prospects; stimulates research on the Indonesian economy; and publishes the respected *Bulletin of Indonesian Economic Studies*.

ANU College of Asia and the Pacific's **Department of Political and Social Change** focuses on domestic politics, social processes and state–society relationships in Asia and the Pacific, and has a long-established interest in Indonesia.

Together with the Department of Political and Social Change, the Indonesia Project holds the annual Indonesia Update conference, which offers an overview of recent economic and political developments and devotes attention to a significant theme in Indonesia's development. The *Bulletin of Indonesian Economic Studies* publishes the conference's economic and political overviews, while the edited papers related to the conference theme are published in the Indonesia Update Series.

The **Institute of Southeast Asian Studies (ISEAS)** was established as an autonomous organization in 1968. It is a regional centre dedicated to the study of socio-political, security and economic trends and developments in Southeast Asia and its wider geostrategic and economic environment. The Institute's research programmes are the Regional Economic Studies (RES, including ASEAN and APEC), Regional Strategic and Political Studies (RSPS), and Regional Social and Cultural Studies (RSCS).

ISEAS Publishing, an established academic press, has issued more than 2,000 books and journals. It is the largest scholarly publisher of research about Southeast Asia from within the region. ISEAS Publishing works with many other academic and trade publishers and distributors to disseminate important research and analyses from and about Southeast Asia to the rest of the world.

Indonesia Update Series

The Yudhoyono Presidency

Indonesia's Decade of Stability and Stagnation

EDITED BY

Edward Aspinall
Marcus Mietzner
Dirk Tomsa

INSTITUTE OF SOUTHEAST ASIAN STUDIES
Singapore

First published in Singapore in 2015 by
ISEAS Publishing
Institute of Southeast Asian Studies
30 Heng Mui Keng Terrace
Pasir Panjang
Singapore 119614

E-mail: publish@iseas.edu.sg
Website: http://bookshop.iseas.edu.sg

All rights reserved. No part of this publication may be reproduced, translated, stored in a retrieval system, or transmitted in any form or by any means, electronic, mechanical, photocopying, recording or otherwise, without the prior permission of the Institute of Southeast Asian Studies.

© 2015 Institute of Southeast Asian Studies, Singapore

The responsibility for facts and opinions in this publication rests exclusively with the authors and their interpretations do not necessarily reflect the views or the policy of the Institute or its supporters.

ISEAS Library Cataloguing-in-Publication Data

The Yudhoyono Presidency : Indonesia's Decade of Stability and Stagnation / edited by Edward Aspinall, Marcus Mietzner and Dirk Tomsa.
This book emanates from the 2014 Indonesia Update Conference presented by the Indonesia Project, College of Asia and the Pacific, The Australian National University, and held on 19–20 September 2014.

1. Indonesia—Politics and government—1998-—Congresses.
2. Indonesia. President (2004-2014 : Yudhoyono)—Congresses.
3. Indonesia—Foreign relations—1998-—Congresses.
4. Indonesia—Economic conditions—1998-—Congresses.
5. Indonesia—Social conditions—1998-—Congresses.
6. Human rights—Indonesia—Congresses.
7. Yudhoyono, Susilo Bambang, 1949-—Congresses.
I. Aspinall, Edward.
II. Mietzner, Marcus.
III. Tomsa, Dirk.
IV. Australian National University. Indonesia Project.
V. Indonesia Update Conference (32nd : 2014 : Australian National University)
DS644.4 I41 2014   2015

ISBN 978-981-4620-70-3 (soft cover)
ISBN 978-981-4620-71-0 (hard cover)
ISBN 978-981-4620-72-7 (e-book, PDF)

Cover photo reproduced with kind permission of Abror Rizki.

Edited and typeset by Beth Thomson, Japan Online, Canberra
Indexed by Angela Grant, Sydney
Printed in Singapore by Markono Print Media Pte Ltd

Contents

Tables and figures	vii
Contributors	ix
Acknowledgments	xi
Glossary	xiii

1 The moderating president: Yudhoyono's decade in power   1
  Edward Aspinall, Marcus Mietzner and Dirk Tomsa

2 Prologue
  Yudhoyono's legacy: an insider's view   23
  Dewi Fortuna Anwar

PART 1   PERSONAL, COMPARATIVE AND INTERNATIONAL PERSPECTIVES

3 The politics of Yudhoyono:
  majoritarian democracy, insecurity and vanity   35
  Greg Fealy

4 Men on horseback and their droppings:
  Yudhoyono's presidency and legacies in
  comparative regional perspective   55
  John T. Sidel

5 Yudhoyono's foreign policy: is Indonesia a rising power?   73
  Evi Fitriani

PART 2   INSTITUTIONS, POLITICS AND SECURITY

6 A balancing act:
  relations between state institutions under Yudhyono   93
  Stephen Sherlock

7 Professionalism without reform:
   the security sector under Yudhoyono   114
   Jacqui Baker

8 Yudhoyono's legacy on internal security:
   achievements and missed opportunities   136
   Sidney Jones

9 Toning down the 'big bang':
   the politics of decentralisation during the Yudhoyono years   155
   Dirk Tomsa

10 The rule of law and anti-corruption reforms
   under Yudhoyono: the rise of the KPK and the
   Constitutional Court   175
   Simon Butt

PART 3 GENDER, HUMAN RIGHTS AND ENVIRONMENT

11 Yudhoyono's politics and the harmful implications
   for gender equality in Indonesia   199
   Melani Budianta, Kamala Chandrakirana and Andy Yentriyani

12 Human rights and Yudhoyono's test of history   217
   Dominic Berger

13 Religious politics and minority rights during the
   Yudhoyono presidency   239
   Robin Bush

14 Big commitments, small results:
   environmental governance and climate change
   mitigation under Yudhoyono   258
   Patrick Anderson, Asep Firdaus and Avi Mahaningtyas

PART 4 THE ECONOMY AND SOCIAL POLICIES

15 The Indonesian economy during the Yudhoyono decade   281
   Hal Hill

16 The Yudhoyono legacy on jobs, poverty and income
   distribution: a mixed record   303
   Chris Manning and Riyana Miranti

17 Ambitious but inadequate:
   social welfare policies under Yudhoyono   325
   Dinna Wisnu, Faisal Basri and Gatot Arya Putra

Index   345

Tables and figures

TABLES

17.1	Share of national government expenditure by sector, 2005–13 (% of GDP)	329
17.2	Rate of acceleration or deceleration in mean mathematics performance (quadratic term) in the PISA tests, selected countries, 2003–12	336

FIGURES

7.1	Annual budgets of Polri and the TNI, 2006–14 (Rp trillion)	118
10.1	Indonesia's ranking on the Corruption Perceptions Index, 2004–14	178
10.2	Corruption cases handled by general prosecutors and KPK prosecutors, 2004–14 (no.)	183
12.1	Freedom House: civil and political rights in Indonesia, 1998–2014	222
12.2	Survey of human rights activists: what is the biggest challenge to the advancement and protection of human rights?	224
12.3	Survey of human rights activists: how do you rate Yudhoyono's commitment to human rights?	224
14.1	Carbon dioxide emissions of the major emitters by sector (million tonnes)	264
15.1	Growth in GDP and GDP per capita, Indonesia, 1960–2013	287
15.2	Growth in GDP per capita, Indonesia, the Philippines and Thailand, 1980–2012 (%)	288

15.3	Growth in GDP by sector, Indonesia, 1960–2013 (%)	288
15.4	Public debt as a share of GDP, Indonesia, 1991–2013 (%)	290
15.5	Inflation, Indonesia, the Philippines and Thailand, 2000–13 (% p.a.)	291
15.6	Ranking on 'Ease of doing business' surveys, selected Southeast Asian countries, 2013–14	296
15.7	Ranking on Logistics Performance Index, selected Southeast Asian countries, 2007–14	297
16.1	Distribution of agricultural and non-agricultural jobs in the formal and informal sectors, 2004–13 (%)	309
16.2	Poverty rates for urban and rural areas, 2000–14 (%)	312
16.3	Gini index for urban and rural areas, 2000–13	317
16.4	Share of the highest wage decile and lower wage quintiles in the total wage bill, 2004 and 2012 (%)	319

Contributors

Patrick Anderson, Policy Advisor, Forest Peoples Programme; and Research Associate, School of Culture, History and Language, College of Asia and the Pacific, Australian National University, Canberra

Dewi Fortuna Anwar, Research Professor and Deputy Secretary for Political Affairs to the Vice President of the Republic of Indonesia, Jakarta

Edward Aspinall, Professor, Department of Political and Social Change, Coral Bell School of Asia Pacific Affairs, College of Asia and the Pacific, Australian National University, Canberra

Jacqui Baker, Lecturer in Southeast Asian Politics, School of Management and Government, Murdoch University, Perth

Faisal Basri, Senior Lecturer, Faculty of Economics, University of Indonesia, Jakarta; and Chief of Advisory Board, Indonesia Research and Strategic Analysis (IRSA), Jakarta

Dominic Berger, PhD candidate, Department of Political and Social Change, Coral Bell School of Asia Pacific Affairs, College of Asia and the Pacific, Australian National University, Canberra

Melani Budianta, Professor, Department of Literature, University of Indonesia, Jakarta

Robin Bush, Director, Research and Strategic Collaborations – Asia, RTI International, Jakarta

Simon Butt, Associate Professor and Associate Director, Centre for Asian and Pacific Law, University of Sydney, Sydney

Kamala Chandrakirana, Former Chair, National Commission on Violence against Women (Komnas Perempuan), Jakarta

Greg Fealy, Associate Professor and Head, Department of Political and Social Change, Coral Bell School of Asia Pacific Affairs, College of Asia and the Pacific, Australian National University, Canberra

Asep Firdaus, Founder/Board Chair, Impartial Mediator Network, http://imenetwork.org/

Evi Fitriani, Head, International Relations Department, Faculty of Social and Political Sciences, University of Indonesia, Jakarta

Hal Hill, H.W. Arndt Emeritus Professor of Southeast Asian Economies, Arndt-Corden Department of Economics, Crawford School, College of Asia and the Pacific, Australian National University, Canberra

Sidney Jones, Director, Institute for Policy Analysis of Conflict, Jakarta

Avi Mahaningtyas, Policy Advisor, Climate and Land Use Alliance, Indonesia

Chris Manning, Adjunct Associate Professor, Arndt-Corden Department of Economics, Crawford School, College of Asia and the Pacific, Australian National University, Canberra

Marcus Mietzner, Associate Professor, Department of Political and Social Change, Coral Bell School of Asia Pacific Affairs, College of Asia and the Pacific, Australian National University, Canberra

Riyana Miranti, Senior Research Fellow, National Centre for Social and Economic Modelling (NATSEM), University of Canberra, Canberra

Gatot Arya Putra, Economist and Advisor, Indonesia Research and Strategic Analysis (IRSA), Jakarta

Stephen Sherlock, Visiting Fellow, Department of Political and Social Change, Coral Bell School of Asia Pacific Affairs, College of Asia and the Pacific, Australian National University, Canberra

John T. Sidel, Sir Patrick Gillam Professor of International and Comparative Politics, Department of Government and Department of International Relations, London School of Economics and Political Science, London

Dirk Tomsa, Senior Lecturer, College of Arts, Social Sciences and Commerce, Department of Politics and Philosophy, La Trobe University, Melbourne

Dinna Wisnu, Associate Professor and Director, Paramadina Graduate School of Diplomacy, Paramadina University, Jakarta

Andy Yentriyani, Former Commissioner, National Commission on Violence against Women (Komnas Perempuan), Jakarta

Acknowledgments

With the exception of Chapter 1, all of the chapters in this volume are revised versions of papers that were presented at the thirty-second annual Indonesia Update conference held at the Australian National University (ANU), Canberra, on 19–20 September 2014. We are very thankful to the large group of people who contributed to the success of the Update conference and to the preparation of this volume.

Our greatest thanks, of course, go to the authors, who contributed their expertise on the diverse matters discussed in this book in ways that we believe add up to a coherent evaluation of the presidency of Susilo Bambang Yudhoyono. We thank those who made the long trip to Canberra, and all authors for responding so quickly to our editorial input and inquiries during what was a very rapid publication process.

We are also grateful to the institution that organises and hosts the conference, the Indonesia Project at the ANU. Under the leadership of its director, Budy Resosudarmo, the Project was from the start very supportive of our proposal for a conference and book to evaluate the Yudhoyono presidency. Staff members of the Project and a large group of volunteers helped organise a flawless conference, and we are very thankful to them for their hard work. Special thanks go to core team members Cathy Haberle, Nurkemala Muliani and Allison Ley.

At the ANU, we are also thankful for the continuing support of the College of Asia and the Pacific and the Department of Political and Social Change. We also acknowledge the support of the Director of the Coral Bell School of Asia Pacific Affairs, Professor Michael Wesley, who launched the conference.

The Department of Foreign Affairs and Trade has been a long-term supporter of the Indonesia Update, through its grant to the Indonesia Project. We gratefully acknowledge that support, which has helped make the ANU a leading centre for the study of Indonesia's economy and society, and without which the conference and this book would not have been possible.

To create this book we relied on the excellent editorial work of Beth Thomson. It is a pleasure to work with such a highly skilled and efficient editor and we are indebted to her for her professionalism, skill and patience. Our thanks go to Angela Grant for preparing the index.

We are also very grateful for the ongoing support of the Institute of Southeast Asian Studies (ISEAS) in Singapore, which has been publishing the Indonesia Update series since 1994. In particular, our thanks go to Ng Kok Kiong and Rahilah Yusuf for their support through the production process. Finally, we would like to thank Dr Saiful Mujani for arranging for two of the editors of this volume to interview Susilo Bambang Yudhoyono. That interview forms the basis of a large part of Chapter 1.

Edward Aspinall, Marcus Mietzner and Dirk Tomsa
Canberra, March 2015

Glossary

ABRI	Angkatan Bersenjata Republik Indonesia (Armed Forces of the Republic of Indonesia)
adat	custom or tradition; customary or traditional law
AEC	ASEAN Economic Community
AMAN	Aliansi Masyarakat Adat Nusantara (Alliance of Indigenous Peoples of the Archipelago)
AMDAL	Analisis Mengenai Dampak Lingkungan (Environmental and Social Impact Assessment)
ASEAN	Association of Southeast Asian Nations
Bakor Pakem	Badan Koordinasi Pengawas Aliran Kepercayaan Masyarakat (Coordinating Board for Monitoring Mystical Beliefs in Society)
Bappenas	Badan Perencanaan Pembangunan Nasional (National Development Planning Agency)
BIN	Badan Intelijen Negara (State Intelligence Agency)
BKPM	Badan Koordinasi Penanaman Modal (Investment Coordinating Board)
BLHD	Badan Lingkungan Hidup Daerah (Regional Environment Agency)
BLSM	Bantuan Langsung Sementara Masyarakat (Temporary Direct Cash Assistance)
BLT	Bantuan Langsung Tunai (Direct Cash Assistance), unconditional cash transfer program
BNP2TKI	Badan Nasional Penempatan dan Perlindungan Tenaga Kerja Indonesia (National Agency for the Placement and Protection of Indonesian Migrant Workers)
BNPT	Badan Nasional Penanggulangan Terorisme (National Counterterrorism Agency)
BOS	Bantuan Operasi Sekolah (Schools Operational Assistance)

BPJS	Badan Penyelenggara Jaminan Sosial (Agency for Social Security Providers)
BPK	Badan Pemeriksa Keuangan (Supreme Audit Agency)
BPS	Badan Pusat Statistik (Statistics Indonesia)
bupati	district government head
CPP	Communist Party of the Philippines
DPR	Dewan Perwakilan Rakyat (People's Representative Council), also known as the House of Representatives and as parliament
ELSAM	Lembaga Studi dan Advokasi Masyarakat (Institute for Policy Research and Advocacy)
FKUB	Forum Kerukunan Umat Beragama (Religious Harmony Forum)
FPI	Front Pembela Islam (Islamic Defenders Front)
G20	'Group of Twenty' for the governments and central bankers from 20 major economies
GAM	Gerakan Aceh Merdeka (Free Aceh Movement)
GAPKI	Gabungan Pengusaha Kelapa Sawit Indonesia (Indonesian Palm Oil Association)
GDP	gross domestic product
GKI	Gereja Kristen Indonesia (Indonesian Christian Church)
Golkar	originally 'Golongan Karya'; the state political party under the New Order, and one of the major post-New Order parties
hadith	traditions (of the Prophet Muhammad)
HKBP	Huria Kristen Batak Protestan (Congregation of Batak Protestant Churches)
ICC	International Criminal Court
Inpres	Instruksi Presiden (Presidential Instruction)
ISIS	Islamic State of Iraq and Sham
Jamkesda	Jaminan Kesehatan Daerah (Regional Health Insurance)
Jamkesmas	Jaminan Kesehatan Masyarakat (Community Health Insurance)
Jampersal	Jaminan Persalinan (Maternity Insurance)
JKN	Jaminan Kesehatan Nasional (National Health Insurance)
Keputusan Presiden	Presidential Decision/Decree
Kodam	Komando Daerah Militer (Regional Army Command)
Komnas HAM	Komisi Nasional Hak Asasi Manusia (National Commission for Human Rights)
Komnas Perempuan	Komisi Nasional Anti Kekerasan Terhadap Perempuan (National Commission on Violence against Women)

Kompolnas	Komisi Kepolisian Nasional (National Police Commission)
KontraS	Komisi untuk Orang Hilang dan Korban Tindak Kekerasan (Commission for the Disappeared and Victims of Violence)
Kopassus	Komando Pasukan Khusus (Special Forces Command)
Koramil	Komando Rayon Militer (Subdistrict Military Command)
Korpri	Korps Pegawai Negeri (Civil Servants Corps)
Kostrad	Komando Strategi Angkatan Darat (Army Strategic Reserve Command)
Koter	Komando Territorial (Territorial Command)
KPA	Komite Peralihan Aceh (Aceh Transition Committee)
KPK	Komisi Pemberantasan Korupsi (Corruption Eradication Commission)
KPPU	Komisi Pengawas Persaingan Usaha (Business Competition Supervisory Commission)
KUR	Kredit Usaha Rakyat (People's Business Credit)
LGBT	lesbian, gay, bisexual and transgender
LSI	Lembaga Survei Indonesia (Indonesian Survey Institute)
menjadi orang	a high achiever, a person of note
MP3EI	Masterplan Percepatan dan Perluasan Pembangunan Ekonomi Indonesia (Master Plan for the Acceleration and Expansion of Economic Development in Indonesia)
MP3KI	Masterplan Percepatan dan Perluasan Pengurangan Kemiskinan Indonesia (Master Plan for the Acceleration and Expansion of Poverty Reduction in Indonesia)
MPR	Majelis Permusyawaratan Rakyat (People's Consultative Assembly)
MRP	Majelis Rakyat Papua (Papuan People's Council)
MUI	Majelis Ulama Indonesia (Indonesian Council of Ulama)
musrenbang	*musyawarah perencanaan pembangunan* (development planning meeting)
NIE	newly industrialising economy
NPA	New People's Army (Philippines)
NU	Nahdlatul Ulama
OECD	Organisation for Economic Co-operation and Development
OPM	Organisasi Papua Merdeka (Free Papua Organisation)
otsus	*otonomi khusus* (special autonomy)

Pancasila	the five guiding principles of the Indonesian state (belief in God, humanitarianism, nationalism, democracy and social justice)
PD	Partai Demokrat (Democrat Party)
PDIP	Partai Demokrasi Indonesia-Perjuangan (Indonesian Democratic Party of Struggle)
Pelindo	PT Pelabuhan Indonesia (Indonesia Port Corporation)
pemekaran	literally, 'blossoming'; referring to the process of subdivision of administrative units
perda	*peraturan daerah* (regional government regulation)
perppu	*peraturan pemerintah pengganti undang-undang* (government regulation in lieu of law)
pilkada	*pemilihan kepala daerah* (elections for local executive heads)
PISA	Programme for International Student Assessment
PKH	Program Keluarga Harapan (Hopeful Families Program), conditional cash transfer program
PKI	Partai Komunis Indonesia (Indonesian Communist Party)
PKS	Partai Keadilan Sejahtera (Prosperous Justice Party)
PLN	Perusahaan Listrik Negara (the state electricity company)
PNPM	Program Nasional Pemberdayaan Masyarakat (National Program for Community Empowerment)
Polri	Polisi Republik Indonesia (Indonesian National Police)
PPLS	Pendataan Program Perlindungan Sosial (Data Collection for Targeting Social Protection Programs)
PPP	Partai Persatuan Pembangunan (United Development Party)
PSHK	Pusat Studi Hukum dan Kebijakan (Centre for the Study of Law and Policy)
qanun	local (Islamic) regulation (Aceh)
Qanun Jinayat	Islamic criminal code (Aceh)
RAM	Reform the Armed Forces Movement (Philippines)
Raskin	Beras Untuk Keluarga Miskin (Rice for Poor Families)
REDD	Reducing Emissions from Deforestation and Forest Degradation
reformasi	the 'reform' (post-Suharto) period
Sakernas	Survei Angkatan Kerja Nasional (National Labour Force Survey)
Satgas Bom	Anti-bomb Taskforce
SBY	Susilo Bambang Yudhoyono
Seskoad	Sekolah Staf dan Komando Angkatan Darat (Army Staff and Command School)

Setgab	Sekretariat Gabungan (Joint Secretariat)
SKB	Surat Keputusan Bersama (Joint Ministerial Letter)
SMRC	Saiful Mujani Research and Consulting
Susenas	Survei Sosio-Ekonomi Nasional (National Socio-economic Survey)
Tipikor Court	Pengadilan Tindak Pidana Korupsi (Anti-Corruption Court)
TNI	Tentara Nasional Indonesia (Indonesian National Army)
TNP2K	Tim Nasional Percepatan Penanggulangan Kemiskinan (National Team for the Acceleration of Poverty Reduction)
TPF	Tim Pencari Fakta (Fact-finding Team)
UKP4	Unit Kerja Presiden Bidang Pengawasan dan Pengendalian Pembangunan (Presidential Working Unit for Development Monitoring and Oversight)
UP4B	Unit Percepatan Pembangunan di Papua dan Papua Barat (Unit for the Acceleration of Development in Papua and West Papua)
WALHI	Wahana Lingkungan Hidup Indonesia (Indonesian Forum for the Environment)
Wantimpres	Dewan Pertimbangan Presiden (Presidential Advisory Council)

Currencies

$	US dollar
Rp	Indonesian rupiah

1 The moderating president: Yudhoyono's decade in power

Edward Aspinall, Marcus Mietzner and Dirk Tomsa

Susilo Bambang Yudhoyono presided over a critical period in Indonesia's modern history. During his decade in power, between 2004 and 2014, Indonesia's new democracy stabilised. Not only was Yudhoyono able to serve out his two full terms without experiencing any major political crisis or disruption to his government, but he also managed to implement democratic reforms initiated before he took office, such as popular elections of heads of provinces, cities and districts. Democratic elections were generally well run and the military kept out of day-to-day political affairs. The new Corruption Eradication Commission (Komisi Pemberantasan Korupsi, KPK) began to make inroads into the elite-level corruption that had bedevilled the country. While the 1998–2004 transition from the authoritarian rule of long-time president Suharto had been marked by significant ethnic, religious and other forms of violent conflict, the Yudhoyono years were far more peaceful, symbolised by the signing of the Aceh peace agreement in 2005. Indonesia maintained an impressive rate of economic growth averaging over 5 per cent, paid off the debts it had accrued to the International Monetary Fund during the 1997–98 economic crisis and succeeded in reducing the official poverty rate from 16.7 per cent in 2004 to 11.5 per cent in 2013.[1] Moreover, it seemed to be playing a major role in world affairs, with the country gaining entry to the G20 club of major economies, and with the president touting Indonesia's international leadership role as a modern Muslim democracy.

---

1 See the figures by the central statistics agency at http://www.bps.go.id/eng/tab_sub/view.php?kat=1&tabel=1&daftar=1&id_subyek=23&notab=7.

However, Yudhoyono's record of success was far from being unadulterated. As we shall show in this chapter and throughout this book, every time the president or his supporters pointed to an achievement, his critics were ready to identify a contradiction, failing or shortcoming. With regard to his democratic record, for example, some observers have characterised the Yudhoyono period as being marked by stagnation rather than progress (Tomsa 2010; Fealy 2011; Mietzner 2012; McRae 2013). In the economic field, Yudhoyono was widely criticised for being reluctant to push through major structural reforms (such as the full elimination of costly fuel subsidies) that would have freed funds for much-needed investments in infrastructure, education and other fields. Though poverty declined, it did so at a slower rate than during the late Suharto years; the number of the near-poor living on less than $2 a day remained close to half the population; and inequality significantly worsened (see Chapter 16 by Manning and Miranti for details). In international affairs, critics often suggested that the president and his foreign policy apparatus appeared unable to enunciate a set of clear and precise goals and did not seem to know quite what to do with Indonesia's newfound global profile. Thus, much controversy surrounds how best to interpret the Yudhoyono presidency and its legacy.

It should not surprise us that assessments of the personal role played by Yudhoyono in Indonesia's stabilisation and transformation have been highly divergent. While controversy is to be expected in assessments of any head of state, they have been unusually polarised in the case of Yudhoyono. Internationally, the president has been lauded as a visionary democratic leader. In 2014, for example, he was feted at UN headquarters in New York and praised by US President Barack Obama for his 'leadership which has succeeded in leading Indonesia toward democratic transition' (Cabinet Secretariat 2014). In contrast, large parts of Indonesia's commentariat and the politically engaged public became increasingly disillusioned with the president, especially as the end of his second term neared. The most consistent line of criticism was that Yudhoyono was a *peragu*—a hesitator or vacillator—who took such care to avoid political controversy that he was rarely able to take decisive policy action. In the place of the authoritative and firm leader many Indonesians had expected when they first elected him, by the end many saw him as incurably hesitant and compromising.

How do we make sense of these very divergent assessments of Yudhoyono, his presidency and his legacy? Our fundamental proposition in this chapter is that Susilo Bambang Yudhoyono might be thought of first and foremost as a *moderating president*. By this, we mean more than that Yudhoyono saw himself as politically moderate or centrist, though this was indeed an important element of his political philosophy. More fundamentally, Yudhoyono viewed himself as leading a polity and a society characterised by deep divisions, and he believed that his most important role was to moderate these divisions by mediating between the conflicting forces and interests to which they gave rise. This interpretation of the president's main function as that of a moderator — rather than a decision-maker — differs significantly from what scholars have typically described as visionary, effective and agenda-setting presidencies (Edwards 2012). Of course, Yudhoyono had his own policy priorities and goals, but in practice he often subordinated these to his desire to forestall political confrontation, safeguard stability and avoid alienating public opinion, important interest groups or his own coalition partners. Thus, instead of pursuing a coherent presidential agenda and using his powers to defend it, his overriding goal was to avoid inflaming division.

Yudhoyono's moderating style was apparent in his approach to forming and maintaining oversized government coalitions, where he sought to maximise participation by the major parties represented in Indonesia's parliament, the People's Representative Council (Dewan Perwakilan Rakyat, DPR). In these broad coalitions, he was reluctant to discipline coalition partners even when they opposed his policies. But his habit of always seeking the middle ground was also visible in his responses to a host of controversial policy issues. When Yudhoyono encountered entrenched interests or political controversy, his deepest instincts told him to avoid hostility. The result was that he repeatedly cancelled, deferred or modified policy reforms, or otherwise put them in the too-hard basket. This approach accounts for most of the hesitations, shortcomings and failures that critics have identified in Yudhoyono's government. While many political leaders, including in advanced democracies, have routinely been forced into compromises, few of them have rationalised risk avoidance and the need to balance rival forces as a virtue of governance in the way Yudhoyono did. The obvious weaknesses of this approach notwithstanding, it also helps to explain the much-praised stability of his presidency.

The rest of this chapter elucidates this argument and provides a guide to help readers navigate through the remainder of the book. In the first section, we describe Yudhoyono's political background and his rise to the presidency, highlighting his identity as both a product of the New Order and as a reformer. In the second section, we analyse Yudhoyono's view that Indonesia has in effect adopted a 'semi-presidential' system, which supposedly forced him into building large government coalitions. We also place his notion of semi-presidentialism in a comparative context. In the third section, we further deconstruct Yudhoyono's philosophy of presidential rule, advancing our proposition that he was above all a moderating and arbitrating leader. The fourth section presents the implications of our analysis for the study of Indonesia's democratic transition and consolidation. We argue that viewing Yudhoyono as a mediating president helps us to reconcile the starkly conflicting assessments of his decade in office, with his tenure emerging as a period of both democratic stability *and* stagnation. Finally, we look briefly at the first few months of the presidency of Yudhoyono's successor, Joko Widodo, to see what light they throw on the nature and legacy of Yudhoyono's presidency. We also briefly explain the structure of the rest of the book.

YUDHOYONO'S RISE TO POWER

Yudhoyono's ascent to the presidency was by no means accidental. While born into a relatively humble East Javanese family, his studies at the military academy between 1970 and 1973 made him part of the upper echelons of the New Order elite. He was educated alongside many other soldiers who would later play key political roles, including the defeated presidential candidate of 2014, Prabowo Subianto. Yudhoyono's marriage in 1976 to the daughter of the academy's governor, Sarwo Edhie Wibowo, further advanced his social and political fortunes. In addition to his network in the military and his growing prominence in Jakarta elite circles, Yudhoyono was increasingly known for his sharp intellect, strict discipline and organisational capability. Importantly, this reputation set him apart from many other New Order generals, who were notorious for their crude rhetoric, open hostility to intellectual debate and unashamedly extravagant lifestyles. Between the late 1980s and the mid-1990s, Yudhoyono developed a solid public image as a moderate reformer, in terms both of rethinking the military's political role and of discussing changes to the overall polity. Suharto appointed him to the crucial post of chief-of-staff for social and political affairs in February 1998, hoping that he would be able to moderate the protesters' demands and save his crumbling regime. After Suharto fell, Yudhoyono managed the early phase of the military's extraction from politics, proposing significant changes to its doctrine while at the same time trying to protect some of its privileges.

Yudhoyono's entry into politics came in October 1999, when President Abdurrahman Wahid recruited him into his cabinet as minister of mining and energy. Initially Yudhoyono was reluctant to agree to the appointment, hoping that he would be allowed to complete his military career by climbing to the position of commander. But he relented, and was rewarded in August 2000 with promotion to the senior role of coordinating minister for political, social and security affairs. His years in the Wahid cabinet were decisive in shaping his view of the internal machinations of politics, and what is needed to survive them. He observed at close range how Wahid self-destructed by alienating almost the entire political elite, including his allies. Yudhoyono himself was eventually fired from his position, and Wahid was impeached shortly afterwards. The spectacle of Wahid's downfall had a tremendous impact on Yudhoyono's political thinking, convincing him that a president needed to accommodate rather than confront Indonesia's myriad interest groups. Yudhoyono's defeat in the vice-presidential election of July 2001, at a time when the Constitution still required the president and vice-president to be elected by the members of the People's Consultative Assembly (Majelis Permusyawaratan Rakyat, MPR), consolidated his view that he needed his own political vehicle to seek higher office. Hence, in September 2001, two months before the MPR approved direct presidential elections, Yudhoyono's supporters formed the Democrat Party (Partai Demokrat, PD). Over the next two years Yudhoyono was reluctant to publicly endorse the party, because he was uncertain whether it was the right time for him to run for the presidency. Megawati Sukarnoputri, who had succeeded Wahid and reappointed Yudhoyono to his old (but renamed) post of coordinating minister for political and security affairs, seemed difficult to beat, so Yudhoyono hoped to be named her running mate (Honna 2012: 475).

Yudhoyono only decided to declare his candidacy for the 2004 presidential elections when his relationship with Megawati soured in early 2004. Megawati had grown suspicious of her minister and his (till then) undeclared ambitions, and had begun to isolate him from government business. In response, Yudhoyono resigned in March 2004, fully endorsed PD and offered himself as an alternative to Megawati. In designing his campaign, Yudhoyono proved far more adept than his competitors at recognising the potential of direct presidential elections. He created the acronym 'SBY' for himself, suggesting a level of informality and familiarity that he did not necessarily enjoy, but which he knew voters would find appealing. He was also skillful at identifying, articulating and embodying the core ambiguity felt in the Indonesian electorate after six years of chaotic transition: he stood for both reform *and* stability. In the campaign, 'He presented himself, above all, as a professional and modern politician who could restore efficiency and competence to government' (Aspinall 2005: 131-2). This strategy led him to victory in the second round of the presidential election, in which he roundly defeated Megawati by a margin of 61 per cent to 39 per cent. When he ran for re-election in 2009, he achieved an even more decisive victory. This time he defeated the competition (Megawati once more, as well as Yudhoyono's first-term vice-president and head of the Golkar party, Jusuf Kalla) with an almost identical result of just under 61 per cent, but this time in the first round (Mietzner 2009). Indeed, though his popularity fluctuated over the course of his ten years in power, for much of the decade Yudhoyono maintained approval ratings that would have been the envy of most democratically elected leaders. In May 2014, shortly before his retirement, 51.4 per cent of Indonesians declared they were either 'satisfied' or 'very satisfied' with Yudhoyono.[2]

However, success and popularity were not the only features of Yudhoyono's electoral campaigns and his presidency. Almost immediately after he came to office, media commentators, political opponents and others began to criticise him for indecisiveness. Two years into his first term, one seasoned observer was already concluding:

> Yudhoyono's presidency was also defined by his naturally cautious political instincts. The methodical manner in which he went about making decisions was calculated to alienate as few constituencies and organised interests as possible. He intervened in political struggles only when he absolutely had to (as in the case of the fuel price hikes) or if he was confident of a positive outcome (as in the Aceh peace process). These defining features of the SBY presidency resulted in a strong tendency for the government to engage in political compromise and prefer stability over unsettling political and economic change (McGibbon 2006: 322).

These perspicacious remarks might have been written at the end of the Yudhoyono presidency rather than its birth. They not only identified core features of Yudhoyono's style of government, but also point us towards the political and ideological controversies that were to surround his presidency. In the following, we examine the shape and roots of Yudhoyono's particular philosophy of governance, which was centred on moderating, rather than guiding, the political process.

YUDHOYONO AND INDONESIA'S 'SEMI-PRESIDENTIALISM'

In a December 2014 interview with two of the authors of this chapter, Yudhoyono explained how his experiences during the transition to democracy had shaped his approach to government during his own presidency.[3] In particular, he recalled pleading with Wahid (popularly known as Gus Dur) on many occasions to avoid conflict with parliament. During various night-time meetings, he frequently told Wahid, 'We are not really strong enough to confront parliament. We are not strong

---

2 'Survei PDB: 50 persen lebih masyarakat puas akan pemerintahan SBY' [PDB survey: more than 50 per cent of the people are satisfied with the Yudhoyono government], *Kompas*, 14 May 2014.
3 Any unattributed quotes in this section are taken from Edward Aspinall and Marcus Mietzner's interview with Susilo Bambang Yudhoyono, Cikeas, 2 December 2014.

enough, Gus'. Though his pleading ultimately fell on deaf ears, Yudhoyono learned valuable lessons from these events. The chief one was that it was critical to maintain 'continuity of this government' and ensure that 'it doesn't collapse halfway through'. Only by securing the government's survival, and ensuring its stability, would Yudhoyono be able to achieve his other goals, including economic development. 'I *love* stability, I *love* order', he said. Perhaps most tellingly of all, he concluded from his experience under Wahid that Indonesia's multi-party democracy was, in effect, 'a semi-parliamentary, semi-presidential system'.

With these remarks, Yudhoyono connected to a longstanding debate among democracy scholars about the stability and effectiveness of presidential systems with multi-party landscapes, as in Indonesia. As early as 1990, Scott Mainwaring (1990: 2) had pointed out that presidentialism with multi-party systems was likely to produce 'immobilism, weak executive power and destabilizing executive/legislative conflict'. This is because few popularly elected presidents have a majority in parliament, and if they put together an alliance that delivers one, it is typically difficult to manage. In Mainwaring's view, there were only a handful of presidential systems with multi-partyism that worked well — presidentialism, he contended, is much more compatible with two-party systems such as the United States. While the remarkable democratic consolidation of Latin American countries has since delivered a number of examples in which presidentialism and multi-partyism do successfully coexist (Pereira and Melo 2012), an influential stream in the literature still maintains that presidentialism is a much riskier path to democracy than parliamentarism (Linz 1990; Stepan and Skach 1993). Indeed, Mainwaring suggested that even semi-presidentialism (that is, a system in which both a president and a parliament-supported prime minister run government) is a more effective system of government than pure presidentialism constrained by multi-partyism. Reflecting on his presidency, Yudhoyono also suggested that Indonesia should start a discussion about a more suitable political system, although he offered no specific details about how he would like to see it reformed, that is, whether he wanted the restoration of what he would consider pure presidentialism with an institutionally engineered reduction in the number of parties or the formal entrenchment of semi-presidentialism (or, for that matter, parliamentarism).

Yudhoyono's experience with and analysis of the pitfalls of Indonesia's political system instilled an extreme sense of caution in him. This caution, in turn, became a hallmark of his presidency, notable in particular in his attitudes to coalition building (see Chapter 6 by Sherlock). Like his two predecessors, Yudhoyono chose to create large 'rainbow coalition' cabinets that included not only former military officers, bureaucrats and professionals, but also representatives of a large majority of the parties holding seats in parliament. His first cabinet (2004–09) included members of seven parties holding 402 (73 per cent) of the 550 seats in the DPR, while the second (2009–14) contained members of six parties representing 421 (75 per cent) of the 560 seats. Such broad coalitions have been the subject of much scrutiny in scholarship on post-Suharto politics. In some assessments, these arrangements constitute a form of 'party cartel' in which the major political parties collude to strip contestation from the body politic and share access to state power (Slater 2004; Ambardi 2008; Slater and Simmons 2013).[4] Even scholars who do not work within the cartel theory framework agree that such inclusiveness undermines the effectiveness of governments by bringing parties with widely varying interests into cabinet—a point Mainwaring had already raised. They also concur that it reflects the centrality of patronage in the polity, with parties eager to participate in cabinet primarily to gain access to the programs and funds that ministries provide, rather than to identify opportunities to steer policy (Diamond 2009; Sherlock 2009; Aspinall 2010; Tomsa 2010).

Certainly, intracoalition conflicts and lack of policy direction were evident throughout Yudhoyono's reign. The breadth of party representation in cabinet meant that it included ministers who sometimes adopted stances that contravened the president's own policy preferences. For example, during his second term, when Yudhoyono was emphasising internationally his credentials for religious tolerance, his minister of religion, Suryadharma Ali, the head of the Islamist United Development Party (Partai Persatuan Pembangunan, PPP), was a major voice of intolerance, inflaming community tensions targeting minority groups such as the Ahmadiyah and the Shi'a (see Chapter 13 by Bush). Though Yudhoyono was not entirely averse to replacing cabinet ministers who underperformed or who contravened his policies, he was generally reluctant to do so—he only replaced Suryadharma after he was declared a suspect by the KPK towards the end of his term. Between 2005 and 2011, Yudhoyono reshuffled his cabinet four times, replacing a total of 19 ministers; he also had to replace three when they were charged with corruption offences. While Yudhoyono was conservative in removing ministers, the parties in his coalition often quarrelled openly over individual appointments. In late 2009, Golkar leader Aburizal Bakrie engineered a campaign against the respected finance minister, Sri Mulyani Indrawati, after she took decisions that adversely affected his companies; this conflict ended with Mulyani leaving cabinet.[5]

---

4 For a critique of the cartelisation argument, see Mietzner (2013).
5 See, for example, 'Golkar bantah dongkel Sri Mulyani' [Golkar denies ousting Sri Mulyani], *Koran Tempo*, 19 January 2010.

The conflicts within the Yudhoyono government also extended into the legislature. Leaders of coalition parties frequently criticised government policy and worked within the DPR to amend or reject bills proposed by government ministers. In fact, negotiations over bills generally occurred in the DPR committees without clear distinctions between government and opposition parties (Sherlock 2010). Occasionally, coalition parties actually voted against government initiatives in DPR plenary sessions. The most habitual offender in this regard was the Islamist Prosperous Justice Party (Partai Keadilan Sejahtera, PKS), which was particularly vehement in its rejection of Yudhoyono's attempts to reduce fuel subsidies. The debate on reducing wasteful fuel subsidies was a critical but controversial issue that bedevilled government policy-making throughout the Yudhoyono years, as Hal Hill demonstrates in Chapter 15 of this book. As late as June 2013, PKS still voted with the opposition against a reduction, even when all other government parties supported it. In the end, the knowledge that he would face parliamentary opposition from his own coalition partners made Yudhoyono very reluctant to move on sensitive issues. He did not make another effort to reduce fuel subsidies in 2014 when the government faced a severe fiscal squeeze, for example, opting instead to cut other spending programs.

However, Yudhoyono was sanguine about these outcomes. As he explained to the authors in December 2014, the 'semi-parliamentary, semi-presidential' nature of the system meant that even if a presidential candidate won 80 per cent of the vote in a direct election, but was opposed by a majority of parties in the parliament, 'Then nothing will work. That's why in my view, despite all the trouble, it is much better to have a coalition'. While such a coalition forced him to make compromises, he claimed that he got most of his policies through (a claim that many of his critics would dispute):

> I always had to convince my own coalition about the importance of this policy, the importance of this decision, the importance of this option. And sometimes it was not easy. Sometimes it took great effort. But, at the end, I can calculate that I achieved 70 per cent of my goals, and for 30 per cent I had to accept the reality.

As for aiming for a narrower and more disciplined coalition, for example one representing just 55 or 60 per cent of the parliament, this had never entered into his calculations:

> I never designed how big my coalition would be from the beginning ... and that is not Indonesian political culture. What happened was that when I became president in 2004, a number of parties [approached me and asked] 'Can we join?' Yes, of course they were welcome.

Asked why he did not remove parties from cabinet when they refused to support important government policies, Yudhoyono pointed to the example of PKS. After it rejected his policy of reducing fuel subsidies in parliament in 2012 and 2013, Yudhoyono seriously considered removing its ministers, but decided against it. He felt residual loyalty to PKS because it had been the first significant party, after PD, to back his presidential aspirations. More importantly, however, he feared that 'If PKS was expelled, perhaps politics would become more noisy, more unstable'. Getting rid of PKS might have given rise to more 'tumult in parliament', but in the end that was not what the people would judge him on; what they really wanted, according to Yudhoyono, were results in terms of improved per capita income, education, health, small business activity and internal security.

THE MODERATING PRESIDENT

A fear of political turmoil and a determination to avoid it lay at the heart of Yudhoyono's political philosophy. More than other compromise-wielding politicians in new and advanced democracies, Yudhoyono refrained from advancing his own ideas (if he had them) in a debate—instead, he saw his primary task as being to shepherd through an outcome in which everyone could 'save face'. In his descriptions of how policy was made under his government, he exhibited visible disdain for conflict but also pride in having routinely neutralised it. He recalled that these policy-making processes often followed a similar pattern: a reform proposal would be introduced (rarely by Yudhoyono himself), there would be consultation on it, but then there would be conflict, controversy or 'tumult' (*kegaduhan*), with the result being a compromise in the form of a watered-down version of the reform or its postponement—often for an indefinite period.[6] This occurred not just when the president was dealing with his cabinet and parliament, but also in interactions with other potential opponents of reform, both within the bureaucracy and among interest groups outside it. On other occasions, commentators observed that the president simply refused to get involved in the negotiations, failing to direct his ministers on key policy issues and intervening only when public pressure had become too great to resist or where polling or other means of gauging public reaction allowed him to choose 'a course of action exactly in accord with the majority view' (Fealy 2011: 335).

This book gives many examples of Yudhoyono either failing to intervene decisively on a major issue or backing off from reform after encountering resistance from ministers, political parties, bureaucrats or interest groups. For instance, in Chapter 9 Dirk Tomsa describes the president's

---

6   Interview with Susilo Bambang Yudhoyono, 2 December 2014.

remarkable failure, late in his second term, to set a course that would have protected the system of direct elections of local government heads (*pemilihan kepala daerah, pilkada*) from repeal. Despite proclaiming that popular elections had been a highpoint of democratic performance under his presidency, he allowed members of his own government to develop plans for their abolition, and let his own party connive in a DPR decision to replace them with the previous system of indirect elections by local legislatures (a system that had been notoriously corrupt). Typically, Yudhoyono only took action to reverse this outcome when prompted to do so by a popular outcry. A similar example, discussed by Simon Butt in Chapter 10, was the president's reluctance to vigorously defend the KPK when it came under attack from elements in parliament and the police who were threatened by its anti-corruption drive. This was despite the fact that Yudhoyono himself had acquired much public credit from the commission's work during his first term. Similarly, in Chapter 12 Dominic Berger shows how Yudhoyono stalled any attempts to deal with past human rights abuses, despite having promised victims and their families that there would be credible investigations. Once more, Yudhoyono had avoided conflict with vested interests (in this case, powerful ex-generals) in order to maintain overall stability.

Yudhoyono's instinctive habit of detecting possible sources of conflict early, and then avoiding them, also contributed to his government's low productivity in the drafting of government regulations. For example, while the 2005 Aceh peace accord has rightly been praised as one of Yudhoyono's great achievements (Morfit 2007), his government failed to produce several crucial implementing regulations (Aspinall 2014). Resistance from central government ministries reluctant to cede power to Aceh meant that the province's 'special autonomy' was still incomplete in some areas a full seven years after the deal was signed (Aspinall 2014). Indeed, such failure to enact government regulations that were required to give teeth to a law—sometimes for many years—became something of a hallmark of the Yudhoyono presidency. Often, the relevant government ministries or the president's office would drag their feet in issuing implementing regulations—or produce watered-down versions of the regulations—because full implementation would have harmed either their own interests or those of their cronies. One example discussed in this book is Law 32/2009 on Environmental Protection and Management. As Patrick Anderson, Asep Firdaus and Avi Mahaningtyas explain in Chapter 14, only one of the 19 required implementing regulations had been issued by the end of Yudhoyono's presidency, reflecting 'Yudhoyono's failure to push through reform efforts against resistance from sectoral ministries and associated industries' (page 259). In Chapter 7, Jacqui Baker identifies similar failings in the security sector, as do

Dinna Wisnu, Faisal Basri and Gatot Arya Putra in their account of social welfare policies (Chapter 17).

Yudhoyono's love of stability and concomitant reluctance to court conflict led him to position himself not so much as a political leader trying to persuade the elite and the public of his chosen course of action. Rather, he defined himself as Indonesia's main political conciliator—someone who was willing to ensure that every party felt accommodated regardless of the rationality or constitutionality of its demands. A good illustration of this is found in Yudhoyono's account of his position with regard to the protection of religious minorities such as the Ahmadiyah sect. As Robin Bush demonstrates in Chapter 13, attacks against such groups increased during Yudhoyono's presidency and he was often accused of adopting an equivocal position in response. For Yudhoyono, however, this was not the nub of the issue. As he explained in his December 2014 interview with the authors, he located himself between 'two extremes, two poles': on the one hand, the human rights activists who 'pressured me' to protect Ahmadiyah on the grounds of religious freedom and the Constitution, and on the other, 'a number of Islamic leaders' who also 'pressured me', but this time to ban Ahmadiyah and arrest and jail its followers. A purist interpretation of the constitutional right of religious freedom as urged by the activists would have given rise to 'clashes'; banning Ahmadiyah would have breached the Constitution. Thus, Yudhoyono chose a middle path: 'we only regulated how they could conduct their worship'. In other words, Yudhoyono adopted a utilitarian view of the presidential duty to protect the Constitution; the prospect of a particular decision leading to 'clashes' carried, for him, the same weight as the Constitution's guarantee of religious freedom.

Hence, while many public figures criticised Yudhoyono for his inability to take strong stands on controversial issues, the president himself saw his predilection for the 'middle way' as a positive attribute.[7] For Yudhoyono, who was acutely aware of the criticisms, it was crucial that an Indonesian president was not only a moderate, but a moderator. This image of a president establishing 'balance' between a myriad of quarrelling forces was central to his political philosophy:

> It's like this. Indonesia is diverse. We have a multi-party democracy, decentralisation is rolling out but is not fully mature, there are many interests. So my role and my mission is to safeguard balance, to ensure that it doesn't happen that some win too much while others lose too much ... So maintaining balance is perhaps the most challenging task for whoever would be the leader of Indonesia—balance. There were times when my choice was the middle

---

7   See, for example, President Yudhoyono's comments in an interview with US journalist Charlie Rose in April 2011, available at http://www.charlierose.com/watch/50143491.

way, but there were times when, no, I had to say A is right, B is wrong. So it doesn't mean that for every issue I did not have a position; of course there were some where A was wrong, or B was wrong. But in a broader context, in my opinion, it is better to maintain balance. It shouldn't be a winner-takes-all situation because that, in my opinion, will cause harm in a pluralist nation, in a multi-party democracy. Whenever the winner takes all, it's harmful, there will be losers, and losers generally like to hit back, and if that then gets out of control, then it can be terrible. Ya, I must admit that *I love* to maintain balance, yes, the balance in life, in our country.[8]

Whereas studies of presidential leadership highlight the capacity for persuasion as the most important attribute of an incumbent (Edwards 2012), Yudhoyono arguably did not want to persuade; he wanted to be a mediator in or facilitator of policy-making processes. His lack of ambition to lead by persuasion, however, contrasted sharply with his general ambition to be president and, as Evi Fitriani shows in Chapter 5, his desire to be viewed as a strong leader by his international peers.

What were the sources of Yudhoyono's obsession with creating balance? Any student of Indonesia's modern history will immediately recognise strong traces of the political thinking that flourished under the New Order regime. An emphasis on harmony and balance and an overriding commitment to stability and order were central features of the 'Pancasila ideology' promoted by that regime (Bourchier 2015). Regime leaders used such ideas to legitimate a highly repressive system of rule, and to justify state action against persons who challenged it. As we have already demonstrated, despite his relatively humble origins, Yudhoyono became an important figure in Suharto's New Order, marrying into an important New Order family and rising to near the top of the military; his experience of the transition from Suharto's rule reinforced his predilection for political order. All this is not to say that Yudhoyono was undemocratic — on the contrary, we will argue below that his commitment to constitutional democracy was another core attribute of his political character. But observing the vestiges of New Order thinking in Yudhoyono's outlook does help us to locate him in key respects as a strongly conservative figure who did little to fundamentally challenge the power structures that existed in Indonesia when he came to office.

From a more institutional perspective, scholars of presidential systems argue that Indonesia's political regime — presidentialism combined with multi-partyism — leads to the kind of conflict-mediating leaders that Yudhoyono took pride in being. For Mainwaring (1990), for instance, weak presidents administering the status quo amidst a host of opposing interests are the norm rather than the exception in presidentialist polities with a fragmented party landscape. But in contrast to many of his

---

8 Interview with Susilo Bambang Yudhoyono, 2 December 2014.

counterparts in Latin America or Asia who started out trying to implement their agendas but then got frustrated by the political realities surrounding them (such as a succession of Philippine and South Korean presidents), Yudhoyono embraced his reduction to a moderating role very early on in his presidency. In fact, by his own admission, his view of his role pre-dated his coming to power and had its roots in his experiences during the Wahid government. Accordingly, while institutionalist explanations are powerful, they need to be contextualised by an analysis of Yudhoyono's background and thinking. Another, more structuralist explanation is that advanced by John Sidel in Chapter 4 of this book. He argues that Yudhoyono (like Thailand's Prem Tinsulanonda and Fidel Ramos of the Philippines) was the product of a political transition in which moderate military officers were tasked by the political establishment and an anxious electorate with safeguarding stability. Yudhoyono's moderating approach, then, was a reflection of the ruling elite's interest in avoiding social upheaval that could threaten its privileges. And as mentioned above, this longing for stability was also prominent in the regime that Indonesia's 1998 transition had brought to an end.

An alternative source of Yudhoyono's relentless search for the middle way may be found in deeper-seated features of his personality, especially his much-remarked-upon fixation with his personal image. Fealy (2011: 334), for example, reported that

> Every morning, he and his wife, Ani, are said to pore over the newspapers at breakfast, paying particular attention to critical coverage of the palace or the government. Personal attacks on SBY in the media will often agitate him for hours, if not days.

Strikingly, Yudhoyono's 2014 book, *Selalu Ada Pilihan* [There Is Always a Choice], an 800-page-long explication of his thinking on diverse matters, is to a large degree structured as a series of responses to public or private criticisms of him. In the same vein, he had staff whose job it was to compile the SMS messages sent to his official feedback number; he then used those data in making important decisions. For example, Yudhoyono recalled that 60 per cent of the messages he received after Suharto's death in 2008 favoured providing a state funeral for the late ruler, 20 per cent urged him to go further and grant Suharto 'national hero' status and another 20 per cent were against official displays of respect to Suharto. 'I chose the 60 per cent', Yudhoyono said.[9] Later in his presidency, Yudhoyono became an avid user of social media, not only taking pride in his high number of Twitter and Facebook followers, but also paying close attention to critical remarks and responding to them. Finally, Yudhoyono

---

9   Interview with Susilo Bambang Yudhoyono, 2 December 2014.

was Indonesia's first truly poll-driven national politician; he regularly commissioned polls to track his own popularity, and he used surveys to guide his actions on issues of importance, such as who would be his designated successor or, when he failed to groom someone from his own party, which candidate to support in the 2014 presidential election.

In Chapter 3 of this volume, Fealy locates the source of Yudhoyono's concern with his public image in his abiding sense of personal insecurity. In terms of what this insecurity meant for his moderating presidency, two contrasting political effects stand out. On the one hand, as many critics have argued, Yudhoyono's constant poring over polls and his thin skin for criticism often had a paralysing effect on him. They helped drive his constant search for a middle way, which he believed would prevent individuals or groups from turning against him. We have already described the stultifying effects this had on policy-making and reform. On the other hand—and this point has been insufficiently emphasised in evaluations of Yudhoyono's presidency—his concern for public opinion was part of what made Yudhoyono a democratic leader. Despite having risen to prominence under an authoritarian regime whose ideology had lingering effects on his thinking, he was serious about representing majority views. While he shared the New Order's stress on stability, he did not want to create balance by force, but by mediation and by heeding the popular will. His desire to be popular may have made him highly cautious, but an ability to express mainstream opinion is, to risk stating the obvious, a core quality of democratically elected leaders. His wish to avoid antagonising majority opinion also often acted as a check when he or other members of his government were considering measures that would have seriously undermined democratic institutions. Yudhoyono's pursuit of the mainstream, in short, helps explain why democracy both stagnated *and* was protected under his presidency, a topic to which we now turn.

YUDHOYONO AND INDONESIAN DEMOCRACY

The evaluations in this book of Yudhoyono's achievements in diverse policy fields not only provide a detailed picture of his presidency but also feed into the debate on his overall contribution to democracy. Indeed, when asked to name the greatest achievement of his presidency, Yudhoyono did not hesitate:

> I would mention the consolidation of democracy. I would not say it's already perfect; we still have to perfect it. But I must say that in 2004 when I began as president, our democracy was not yet really fully mature. It was not yet stable, not yet strong. At the very least, over the following ten years we were able to safeguard the transition to democracy so that it experienced no setbacks,

no changes of direction. As a result, I can say that my successor can now actually further continue this democratic consolidation.[10]

Some scholars agree with this judgment. Liddle and Mujani (2013), for example, argue that Indonesian democracy was consolidated during Yudhoyono's tenure. But we challenge this assessment, arguing instead that Yudhoyono merely stabilised Indonesia's fragile democracy without ensuring that democracy became the 'only game in town' (Linz and Stepan 1996: 5).

Of course, it is difficult to dispute that Yudhoyono presided over a period of remarkable democratic stability. Despite his New Order background, he preserved the democratic system he had inherited, motivated both by his political moderation and by his respect for majority opinion. As global democracy expert Larry Diamond (2009: 338) put it at the end of Yudhoyono's first term, the president 'stands out as a conciliatory and unifying figure, one willing to share power, to compromise and to build broad coalitions'. By adopting such a posture, Yudhoyono helped Indonesia maintain democracy at a time when many countries that had become democratic in the 1980s and 1990s were sliding back towards authoritarianism (Diamond 2010, 2014). Often, it was popularly elected heads of government — such as Vladimir Putin in Russia and Thaksin Shinawatra in Thailand — who were the leading forces of democratic rollback in these countries. In contrast to such autocratic figures, Yudhoyono did not personally initiate any significant attempt to wind back major democratic reforms, nor did he attempt to concentrate power in his own hands or try to engineer his entrenchment in power.

But although Yudhoyono did not reverse Indonesia's democratic trend, he also did nothing to help democratic attitudes, institutions and practices become so entrenched that we can now speak of Indonesia as a consolidated democracy. As many chapters in this book show, democracy is *not* the only game in town in Indonesia. It is therefore important to emphasise that, despite the overall stability, the Yudhoyono presidency was also an era of missed opportunities to deepen democracy further. Indeed, it is essential to note that Indonesia had already strengthened significantly when Yudhoyono took power in 2004. Most of the political and communal conflicts that had destabilised the transition to democracy had subsided, and institutional reforms were taking root. It is striking, then, that when asked to elaborate on his claim to have overseen a period of democratic consolidation, Yudhoyono pointed to the existence of institutions — such as direct presidential elections and direct elections of regional government heads — that were actually the result of constitutional or legislative changes under his *predecessors*. Similarly, the KPK,

---

10 Interview with Susilo Bambang Yudhoyono, 2 December 2014.

whose investigations into high-level corruption helped burnish Yudhoyono's reputation in his first term, was a product of the Megawati presidency—albeit one that began to function fully only under Yudhoyono.

Most of these important democratic institutions survived, and in some cases flourished, under a combination of positive support and benign neglect from Yudhoyono. Direct local elections and the KPK, however, only narrowly escaped serious attempts to destroy them during the Yudhoyono presidency—and only after public outrage prompted the president to defend them. And as we have already argued, Yudhoyono's reluctance to antagonise powerful entrenched interests meant that reform efforts either failed or produced only partial and ambivalent success in a whole host of second-order areas where it would have been important to build on early gains of the *reformasi* period. Some of these areas are discussed in detail in this book, including internal security (Chapter 8 by Jones), gender equality (Chapter 11 by Budianta, Chandrakirana and Yentriyani) and human rights protection (Chapter 12 by Berger).

A verdict of stagnation is supported by agencies that produce ratings of global democracy. Freedom House, for example, upgraded Indonesia's status from 'partly free' to 'free' in 2006, at the outset of Yudhoyono's presidency, largely on the basis of the country's implementation of direct elections of local government heads in 2005 (based on a 2004 law passed under Megawati). At the end of Yudhoyono's presidency in 2014, however, it relegated the country once again to 'partly free' status, mainly in response to the passage of a new law on social organisations that restricted the freedom of association. In its view, therefore, Indonesian democracy ended the Yudhoyono decade more or less where it had begun. In the *Economist*'s Democracy Index, Indonesia increased its overall score only slightly, from 6.41 in 2006 to 6.95 in 2014, ranking it below Timor-Leste, Panama and Trinidad and Tobago in Yudhoyono's final year in office. In our view, such judgments are justifiable and apt: while Indonesian democracy did not go into reverse during Yudhoyono's tenure, neither did it make dramatic forward progress.

In sum, democratic stability does not necessarily amount to democratic consolidation. While the decade of stable rule under Yudhoyono gave key democratic institutions time to bed down, it is far from clear that they became so strong that they were no longer under serious threat. On the contrary, the near-death of direct elections of local government heads and the attacks on the KPK demonstrate that the reverse was the case. The failure to more thoroughly reform institutions such as the police and military, meanwhile, meant that reservoirs of authoritarian thinking remained powerful in the key security institutions, as they did in the parties (Mietzner 2012). These problems did not pose any immediate threat to the democratic system—precisely because of Yudhoyono's personal commitment to democracy and his reluctance to oversee dramatic change—but they left open the real possibility of future piecemeal erosion. Indeed, the sense of drift that evolved in Yudhoyono's second term, and the public's growing disillusionment with their irresolute leader, came close to propelling an outright authoritarian figure, Prabowo Subianto, into the presidential palace during the 2014 presidential election (Aspinall and Mietzner 2014; Mietzner 2015). Overall, then, the Yudhoyono years should not be interpreted *only* as a period of democratic stability; it was also a decade of democratic stagnation that actually exacerbated the long-term threats to Indonesia's democratic consolidation.

CONCLUSION AND STRUCTURE OF THE BOOK

While there is much to criticise in Yudhoyono's record (and the contributors to this book certainly do not hold back in this regard), early insights into the presidency of his successor, Joko Widodo (Jokowi), suggest that history may treat Yudhoyono rather generously. Jokowi ran his campaign on the promise of being more decisive, less dependent on elites and cronies, and more effective in overcoming bureaucratic resistance to policy implementation than Yudhoyono. But the first few months of his presidency have demonstrated just how difficult it is in Indonesia's multilayered democratic polity to realise such promises. Rather than being more decisive, Jokowi has displayed visible desperation when having to make tough calls, such as the decision to cancel the appointment of Budi Gunawan as police chief in February 2015. Rather than being less dependent on patronage networks, he has come under strong pressure from his own party and the oligarchs who supported him during his campaign. And rather than achieving legislative and bureaucratic breakthroughs, he has postponed key initiatives because they were deemed too 'controversial' (with the exception of cutting fuel subsidies, which he was able to do in late 2014 and early 2015, aided by collapsing international oil prices). At the same time, Jokowi has exhibited none of Yudhoyono's ability to communicate the difficulties of presidential decision-making—where Yudhoyono gave lengthy speeches or uploaded YouTube videos to explain his stance, Jokowi has resorted to reading a few wooden sentences from a prepared script. To a certain extent, Jokowi's less than impressive start provides evidence for Yudhoyono's argument that Indonesia's socio-political arena is a minefield through which one must tread carefully rather than with a false sense of dynamism.

Indeed, as John Sidel points out in Chapter 4 of this book, Yudhoyono's presidency left his successor an artificially domesticated polity that is unlikely to serve as a strong foundation for coherent and decisive governance. Yudhoyono's tendency of bottling up rather than resolving tensions has handed Jokowi a political system in which the country's longstanding patronage practices persist and, consequently, limit the new president's room to manoeuvre. In addition, Jokowi has inherited a host of other problems, from Indonesia's continued dependence on natural resources to debilitated infrastructure, which any new leader would need many years to tackle.

Hence, Yudhoyono will most likely be remembered as a president who used democratic means to bring Indonesia stability for the decade he governed—which is a better record than any of his predecessors can claim. Yudhoyono's rule was longer than that of any other democratic leader in Indonesian history; in fact, it was longer than that of all seven democratic prime ministers in the 1950s combined, and longer than the combined terms of all three of his post-Suharto predecessors. But Yudhoyono will also go down in history as a president who did little to lift Indonesia to the next level of institutional sophistication, democratic quality and economic maturity. In short, while Yudhoyono ensured that Indonesian democracy did not break down, his name will not be tied to any major reform that could have made the democratic system more resilient beyond his own presidency.

The structure of the remainder of this book is straightforward. It begins with a brief prologue by Dewi Fortuna Anwar, who was a government insider during the Yudhoyono presidency. The remaining chapters are grouped in four themed segments: personal, comparative and international perspectives (Part 1); institutions, politics and security (Part 2); gender, human rights and environment (Part 3); and the economy and social policies (Part 4). Within these segments, the various chapters explore different topics that were vital policy areas in the Yudhoyono years. In each case, they endeavour to provide an overall assessment of achievements and failings in the area covered, to assess Yudhoyono's personal contribution to those outcomes and, where possible, to compare Indonesia's experience to those of relevant comparator countries. While a range of views are expressed, and not all of the authors share our assessment of Yudhoyono's legacy, overall we believe that the analyses presented in the book furnish a significant body of evidence to support our fundamental contention that the Yudhoyono decade was a period of *both* remarkable democratic stability *and* underlying democratic stagnation.

REFERENCES

Ambardi, K. (2008) 'The making of the Indonesian multiparty system: a cartelized party system and its origin', PhD thesis, Ohio State University, Columbus OH.
Aspinall, E. (2005) 'Elections and the normalization of politics in Indonesia', *South East Asia Research*, 13(2): 117–56.
Aspinall, E. (2010) 'The irony of success', *Journal of Democracy*, 21(2): 20–34.
Aspinall, E. (2014) 'Special autonomy, predatory peace and the resolution of the Aceh conflict', in H. Hill (ed.) *Regional Dynamics in a Decentralized Indonesia*, Institute of Southeast Asian Studies: Singapore: 460–81.
Aspinall, E. and M. Mietzner (2014) 'Indonesian politics in 2014: democracy's close call', *Bulletin of Indonesian Economic Studies*, 50(3): 347–69.
Bourchier, D. (2015) *Illiberal Democracy in Indonesia: The Ideology of the Family State*, Routledge, Abingdon.
Cabinet Secretariat of the Republic of Indonesia (2014) 'In Bahasa Indonesia, Obama praises President SBY', press release, 29 September. Available at http://setkab.go.id/en/in-bahasa-indonesia-obama-praises-president-sby/
Diamond, L. (2009) 'Is a "rainbow coalition" a good way to govern?', *Bulletin of Indonesian Economic Studies*, 45(3): 337–40.
Diamond, L. (2010) 'Indonesia's place in global democracy', in E. Aspinall and M. Mietzner (eds) *Problems of Democratisation in Indonesia: Elections, Institutions and Society*, Institute of Southeast Asian Studies, Singapore: 21–49.
Diamond, L. (2014) 'Democracy's deepening recession', *Atlantic*, 2 May. Available at http://www.theatlantic.com/international/archive/2014/05/the-deepening-recession-of-democracy/361591/
Edwards, G.C. (2012) *The Strategic President: Persuasion and Opportunity in Presidential Leadership*, Princeton University Press, Princeton NJ.
Fealy, G. (2011) 'Indonesian politics in 2011: democratic regression and Yudhoyono's regal incumbency', *Bulletin of Indonesian Economic Studies*, 47(3): 333–53.
Honna, J. (2012) 'Inside the Democrat Party: power, politics and conflict in Indonesia's presidential party', *South East Asia Research*, 20(4): 473–89.
Liddle, R.W. and S. Mujani (2013) 'Indonesian democracy: from transition to consolidation', in M. Künkler and A. Stepan (eds) *Democracy and Islam in Indonesia*, Columbia University Press, New York: 24–50.
Linz, J.J. (1990) 'The perils of presidentialism', *Journal of Democracy*, 1(1): 51–69.
Linz, J.J. and A. Stepan (1996) *Problems of Democratic Transition and Consolidation: Southern Europe, South America, and Post-communist Europe*, Johns Hopkins University Press, Baltimore MD.
Mainwaring, S. (1990) 'Presidentialism, multiparty systems, and democracy: the difficult equation', Working Paper No. 144, Kellog Institute for International Studies, University of Notre Dame, Notre Dame IN, September.
McGibbon, R. (2006) 'Indonesian politics in 2006: stability, compromise and shifting contests over ideology', *Bulletin of Indonesian Economic Studies*, 42(3): 321–40.
McRae, D. (2013) 'Indonesian politics in 2013: the emergence of new leadership?', *Bulletin of Indonesian Economic Studies*, 49(3): 289–304.
Mietzner, M. (2009) 'Indonesia's 2009 elections: populism, dynasties and the consolidation of the party system', Lowy Institute for International Policy, Sydney.

Mietzner, M. (2012) 'Indonesia's democratic stagnation: antireformist elites and resilient civil society', *Democratization*, 19(2): 209–29.
Mietzner, M. (2013) *Money, Power, and Ideology: Political Parties in Post-authoritarian Indonesia*, Hawaii University Press, NUS Press and NIAS Press, Honolulu, Singapore and Copenhagen.
Mietzner, M. (2015) 'Reinventing Asian populism: Jokowi's rise, democracy and political contestation in Indonesia', Policy Studies 72, East West Center, Honolulu.
Morfit, M. (2007) 'The road to Helsinki: the Aceh agreement and Indonesia's democratic development', *International Negotiation*, 12(1): 111–43.
Pereira, C. and M.A. Melo (2012) 'The surprising success of multiparty presidentialism', *Journal of Democracy*, 23(3): 156–70.
Sherlock, S. (2009) 'SBY's consensus cabinet—*lanjutkan?*', *Bulletin of Indonesian Economic Studies*, 45(3): 341–3.
Sherlock, S. (2010) 'The parliament in Indonesia's decade of democracy: people's forum or chamber of cronies?', in E. Aspinall and M. Mietzner (eds) *Problems of Democratisation in Indonesia: Elections, Institutions and Society*, Institute of Southeast Asian Studies, Singapore: 160–78.
Slater, D. (2004) 'Indonesia's accountability trap: party cartels and presidential power after democratic transition', *Indonesia*, 78(October): 61–92.
Slater, D. and E. Simmons (2013) 'Coping by colluding: political uncertainty and promiscuous powersharing in Indonesia and Bolivia', *Comparative Political Studies*, 46(11): 1,366–93.
Stepan, A. and C. Skach (1993) 'Constitutional frameworks and democratic consolidation: parliamentarism versus presidentialism', *World Politics*, 46(1): 1–22.
Tomsa, D. (2010) 'Indonesian politics in 2010: the perils of stagnation', *Bulletin of Indonesian Economic Studies*, 46(3): 309–28.
Yudhoyono, S.B. (2014) *Selalu Ada Pilihan* [There Is Always a Choice], Kompas Gramedia, Jakarta.

2 Prologue
Yudhoyono's legacy: an insider's view

Dewi Fortuna Anwar

As an insider in both the Habibie and Yudhoyono–Boediono administrations, and an academic who does not shy away from expressing candid opinions, I have been asked to evaluate the performance of the Yudhoyono government from both an internal and a comparative perspective. It is indeed difficult to get a clear picture of what is happening in Indonesia if one simply relies on media reports. Reading news or commentaries in Indonesian newspapers, or watching talk shows on Indonesian television, would give one the impression that the country is a basket case. Indonesia is at times portrayed as a failed state, or one that is very close to failing, with a huge number of people still living in poverty, crumbling infrastructure, widespread social conflict and a high level of corruption.[1] Moreover, many Indonesians are critical of the government's perceived weakness *vis-à-vis* the outside world. Listening to the rhetoric during the 2014 presidential race between Joko Widodo and Prabowo Subianto, one would be left with the impression that Indonesia is a weak state, powerless in the face of external machinations bent on controlling the country's natural resources; an object rather than a subject in international relations; and a country lacking the wherewithal to stand up for itself and, by implication, be counted in an increasingly competitive and uncertain global era.[2]

---

1 'Indonesia negara gagal? Ini alasannya' [Indonesia a failed state? Here are the reasons], *Sorot News*, 20 June 2012.
2 'Prabowo: negara kita lemah, saya patriot' [Prabowo: our state is weak, I am a patriot], *Tempo*, 2 April 2014.

In contrast, reporting in the foreign media has mostly been complimentary towards Indonesia in recent years. Differing sharply from the negative image projected onto the world stage in the immediate post-Suharto years, Indonesia is now generally seen as a success story.[3] The country's success in peacefully managing its democratic transition has received international plaudits, particularly when so many other countries have failed dismally.[4] Indonesia's economic recovery, its status as a newly emerging economy and its constructive role in the Southeast Asian region have drawn praise. Far from being regarded as a failed or failing state, Indonesia is regarded as a model for countries embarking on a democratic transition, whether in the predominantly Muslim countries in the Middle East and North Africa or within Southeast Asia.

Obviously, official speeches by Indonesian government officials have emphasised this favourable narrative while glossing over Indonesia's many remaining shortcomings. As is so often the case, however, the truth lies somewhere in between. Indonesia is neither a failed state nor an unmitigated success story. As I show below, the Yudhoyono administration chalked up a number of significant achievements, while failing to meet expectations in other areas.

SEVEN KEY ACHIEVEMENTS OF THE ADMINISTRATION

Whatever one thinks of Susilo Bambang Yudhoyono's overall record, one cannot deny that his administration notched up considerable achievements. To begin with, Yudhoyono will go down in history as Indonesia's first directly elected president. Moreover, he served two full terms (2004–09 and 2009–14), the maximum allowed by the amended 1945 Constitution. Yudhoyono's election as president in 2004 with Jusuf Kalla as vice-president, and his re-election in 2009 with Boediono as vice-president, marked the end of Indonesia's democratic transition and the beginning of an early phase of democratic consolidation. As most of the fundamental enabling legislation for reform had been passed during the administrations of Presidents B.J. Habibie, Abdurrahman Wahid and Megawati Sukarnoputri (Crouch 2010; Horowitz 2013), Yudhoyono was charged with overseeing the implementation of the various reform measures in order to consolidate Indonesia's hard-won democracy. He was popularly elected as president twice to rule over new institutions created to ensure greater political participation, improved government account-

---

3 'In Southeast Asia, Indonesia is an unlikely role model for democracy', *New York Times*, 4 September 2014.
4 'The Indonesian success story', *Manila Standard*, 28 March 2014.

ability, a more empowered civil society, a truly independent judiciary and stronger rule of law. Thus, his presidency needs to be judged according to the degree to which it succeeded in moving Indonesia forward to embrace the next level of reform, as envisaged in the ideals of the reform (*reformasi*) era.

An objective observer would acknowledge that Indonesia was stronger, more democratic, more united and more prosperous in 2014 than it had been ten years earlier. While this was a result of the collective efforts of various stakeholders, the government must be given a large part of the credit. In the following, I mention seven key achievements of the Yudhoyono administration. They are by no means the only ones, but they are the legacies that had the greatest influence on the shape of post-authoritarian Indonesia 16 years after the fall of Suharto.

The first and arguably most important marker of Yudhoyono's ten years in power is Indonesia's relatively successful democratic political transformation, which has brought about political stability and normality. After the first few tumultuous if not chaotic years of *reformasi*, which many blamed on the rapid pace of political liberalisation, democratic processes seem to have taken root in Indonesia. While democracy in Indonesia still has many shortcomings, it has on the whole been endorsed as the most acceptable way of governing the nation. Direct elections have become a prominent feature of Indonesia's democracy. Most Indonesians believe that this is the only legitimate way of choosing their presidents and vice-presidents. The same goes for the selection of governors, district heads and mayors, who have been directly elected since 2005. While direct elections for regional leaders have a number of weaknesses, notably a tendency to encourage money politics (Erb and Sulistiyanto 2009), attempts to return to the earlier practice of allowing local parliaments to elect regional heads have met with widespread public opposition (Mietzner 2012). Notwithstanding the argument that regional legislators are themselves directly elected, thus making their subsequent election of regional government heads 'democratic', most Indonesians refuse to give up their right to choose their leaders directly. Although elections have often led to disputes, under Yudhoyono it became commonplace to bring such cases to the Constitutional Court or the Supreme Court, where those conflicts were settled.

Thus, during Yudhoyono's presidency, political changes — and changes in national and local government — became regular events, not a matter of life and death that would merit prolonged disagreement, let alone open, violent conflict. With rare exceptions, elections at the national, provincial and local levels were peaceful. At the same time, the possibility that the losers of today might win in five years' time reduced the need for people power or other unconstitutional means to try to remove politicians from office. For Indonesia, the democratic experience has therefore been a virtuous circle resulting in greater legitimacy of the state as well as greater political and government stability.

Second, decentralisation truly flourished in Indonesia during Yudhoyono's decade in office, moving the country a long way from the centralised and Java-centric polity of the New Order era (Hill 2014). Indonesia's wide-ranging regional autonomy program, with districts and towns as its locus, has brought about both positive and negative changes in terms of democratic participation, governance and development outcomes. Some regions have excelled under decentralisation, introducing new initiatives, lifting the standard of public services and enhancing welfare, while others have lagged behind due to corruption, mismanagement or a lack of capacity. It is important to note, however, that regional autonomy has realised the ideal of 'Unity in Diversity' (*Bhinneka Tunggal Ika*). The possibility for each region to showcase its unique characteristics and capitalise on its competitive advantages has made Indonesia a more complex and challenging place. Political and economic action no longer takes place exclusively in the big cities in Java—rich opportunities to participate in politics and business are now available across the archipelago. Lack of connectivity remains a major constraint in developing the regions, but post-decentralisation Indonesia can no longer be described as being strictly compartmentalised into Java on the one hand and the Outer Islands on the other.

Importantly, the advent of regional autonomy has also transformed the political landscape at the national level. Direct elections have made it possible for new leaders to emerge outside of the major political parties. The success of many district heads and mayors in developing their regions in innovative ways has increasingly been noted by the country at large. Until quite recently, Indonesia's national political elites—mainly with military or bureaucratic backgrounds, or strong political pedigrees—used to congregate in the capital (Poczter and Pepinsky 2015). But since the election in 2012 of a former mayor of Solo, Joko Widodo (Jokowi), as governor of Jakarta and a former district head of Belitung, Basuki Tjahaja Purnama (Ahok), as vice-governor, a very different pattern of political recruitment of national leaders has developed. The election of Jokowi and Ahok (and the emergence of similar figures in the cities of Surabaya and Bandung) has given rise to a much larger pool of potential leaders, no longer limited just to the old elites in the Greater Jakarta area, but increasingly including politicians with experience of governing in the regions.

Third, by the end of his presidency Yudhoyono ruled over a country that was more united, more secure and more capable of dealing with crises than when he came to office in 2004. Between 2004 and 2014, Indonesia was able to recover from a series of major natural disasters (including a devastating tsunami in Aceh soon after Yudhoyono assumed office), end a long separatist insurgency in Aceh through a negotiated peace agreement and deal successfully with terrorist threats. Indonesia's increased ability to deal with natural disasters such as earthquakes, volcanic eruptions, tsunami, landslides and floods was largely due to special agencies that the Yudhoyono government had established at the national and regional levels. After the 2005 Aceh peace accord, no other major conflicts arose to strain national unity, with the exception of simmering tensions in Papua. The country's capacity to fight terrorist threats improved considerably in the early to mid-2000s with the establishment of a special anti-terrorism police unit (Detachment 88) and a national counterterrorism agency (Badan Nasional Penanggulangan Terorisme, BNPT) (see Chapter 8 by Jones).

Fourth, the conducive political and security climate under Yudhoyono facilitated uninterrupted economic growth. The economy recovered fully from the devastation the Asian financial crisis had wrought in the late 1990s, though growth did not regain the high levels reached during the New Order period. The economy also became more resilient, allowing Indonesia to record positive growth even during the global financial crisis of 2008–09. The country's economic competitiveness improved considerably between 2004 and 2014. Indonesia's ranking on the World Economic Forum's Growth Competitiveness Index rose from 69 out of 104 countries in 2004, with a score of 3.72 (WEF 2004: xiii), to 54 out of 134 countries by the end of Yudhoyono's first term in 2009, with a score of 4.26 (WEF 2009: 13). By the end of his presidency in 2014, Indonesia's ranking had improved further to 34 out of 144 countries, with a score 4.57 (WEF 2014: 13). The national economy expanded nearly four-fold during Yudhoyono's presidency. In terms of GDP, Indonesia had the world's sixteenth-largest economy in 2013. Based on purchasing power parity, its economy was the world's tenth largest (World Bank 2015).

Fifth, the combination of political stability and economic development made it possible for the Yudhoyono government to carry out ambitious social welfare, education and health programs. While sustained economic growth produced a rapidly growing middle class and led to widening inequality, the government's wide-ranging and targeted welfare measures reduced absolute poverty. For much of the Yudhoyono period education spending rose, though it rarely reached the formally constituted 20 per cent of the national budget that had been mandated by the Constitution. In June 2013, the government also extended compulsory education to 12 years. In early 2014, Indonesia launched one of the world's most ambitious national health-care systems, aimed at providing health coverage to most of Indonesia's 250 million citizens. However, the budget provided for this effort is still insufficient to meet the huge demand.

Sixth, under Yudhoyono Indonesia became an active player in regional and international affairs (Reid 2012). The president took a strong interest and role in foreign policy. Fully recovered from the setbacks of the immediate post-Suharto period, Indonesia became—under Yudhoyono's leadership—an acknowledged leader of ASEAN, while ASEAN itself gained recognition as a driver of wider regional community-building in East Asia (see Chapter 5 by Fitriani). Indonesia also tried to strengthen its democratic credentials internationally by promoting the spread of democracy through the Bali Democracy Forum, held annually from 2008 until the end of the Yudhoyono presidency. Globally, Indonesia contributed regularly to international peacekeeping efforts, especially under the auspices of the United Nations. In this context, one of the missions of the Indonesia Peace and Security Center, established in Sentul, West Java, in April 2014, is to support the country's ambition to be among the top ten countries contributing troops to UN peacekeeping missions.

Seventh, the period 2004–14 witnessed the rise of civil society to become a force to be reckoned with in Indonesia. Aided by a revolution in information and communication technology, citizens deployed their resources to galvanise support for causes that had grabbed public attention. The goals of such campaigns included protecting the Corruption Eradication Commission (Komisi Pemberantasan Korupsi, KPK) from attempts by the police to discredit it in 2009; defending and collecting money for an individual indicted in 2009 for a justified complaint against a hospital (called the 'Coin for Prita' movement); organising a large rock concert to support the 2014 presidential campaign of Joko Widodo when his popular support began to slip; and, in September 2014, opposing the proposed termination of direct elections of regional heads. During Yudhoyono's rule, Indonesians became avid users of social media, and the most prominent user was none other than the president himself. He often posted several tweets daily, and he also occasionally uploaded messages to the public on YouTube. For instance, after the parliament abolished direct local elections, he posted a video explaining why his party had abstained from voting on the bill and outlining his plan to reintroduce the direct elections regime. (He eventually issued a government regulation in lieu of law to do so.)

SERIOUS SHORTCOMINGS OF THE ADMINISTRATION

While Yudhoyono and his government should be lauded for the remarkable progress Indonesia made under his leadership, the administration's record was also marred by a number of serious shortcomings. For instance, while the promotion and protection of human rights is now enshrined in the amended 1945 Constitution and the human rights environment improved considerably under Yudhoyono, his government failed to deliver on its promises or to carry out its responsibilities in a number of prominent cases. Most importantly, the perpetrators of the 2004 murder of human rights activist Munir Said Thalib have still not been brought to justice (see Chapter 12 by Berger). The government also failed to protect religious freedom in several serious cases in which religious minorities had been attacked by intolerant groups claiming to protect the purity of Islam (Mietzner 2012). In addition, the police's anti-terrorism taskforce, Detachment 88, at times used excessive force in dealing with suspects, and human rights violations continued to take place with distressing frequency in Papua.

The second area in which shortcomings must be noted is that of corruption. Yudhoyono and his Democrat Party (Partai Demokrat, PD) pledged to fight corruption during the 2004 and 2009 election campaigns, and made some progress in this field. Under Yudhoyono, the KPK was ruthless in going after corrupt public officials, even high-ranking ones. The public became disenchanted with the president and his party, however, when it became clear that one of the worst offenders was PD itself. Two PD ministers — the minister for youth and sports, Andi Mallarangeng, and the minister for mining and energy, Jero Wacik — were forced to resign, with the former sentenced to four years in prison in 2014 and the latter declared a suspect by the KPK in the same year. Just weeks before Yudhoyono's presidency ended, the former chair of PD, Anas Urbaningrum, was sentenced to eight years in jail for corruption. As a result of these cases, PD's share of the vote dropped by around half in the 2014 elections. Outside of PD, in May 2014 the chair of the United Development Party (Partai Persatuan Pembangunan, PPP), Suryadharma Ali, was forced to resign from his position as Yudhoyono's minister for religious affairs after being accused of embezzling funds intended for the pilgrimage (*haj*), while the chair of the Prosperous Justice Party (Partai Keadilan Sejahtera, PKS), Luthfi Hasan Ishaaq — also a member of Yudhoyono's coalition cabinet — was jailed for 16 years in late 2013 for money-laundering and corruption. Nearly 300 regional heads of government or their deputies were also investigated for corruption. Thus, while the fight against corruption intensified, the level of corruption remained unacceptably high.

Despite the government's considerable achievements, at the end of the Yudhoyono presidency there was a general feeling that the president could have achieved much more. Decision-making is clearly more challenging and time-consuming in a democracy than in an authoritarian system. But especially during Yudhoyono's second term, many Indonesians hoped that he would move faster and make bold decisions to push through unpopular but necessary measures, such as reducing, if not ending, fuel subsidies. After all, Yudhoyono had been re-elected in a single round with a convincing majority and remained personally popular. Moreover, his party controlled the largest number of seats in the 2009–14 parliament. Indeed, including the members of the five other parties forming the ruling coalition, Yudhoyono theoretically had the support of over 75 per cent of the members of parliament. The reality, however, was somewhat different. The unwieldy coalition cabinet more often than not became a liability as ministers from different political parties openly disagreed with the president; the expected support in parliament for unpopular measures such as cutting the fuel subsidy also did not materialise (see Chapter 6 by Sherlock).

Finally, I need to say a few words about Yudhoyono's two vice-presidents, who had such contrasting styles but who each, in his own way, skilfully assisted the president. The businessman, politician and social activist Jusuf Kalla, Yudhoyono's first deputy, had an outgoing personality and was not shy about putting himself forward or claiming credit where it was due. He was good at finding innovative solutions to intractable issues, and among other things, was responsible for the peaceful settlement of the Aceh conflict in 2005. As the chair of Golkar, which had the most seats in parliament in the 2004–09 legislature, Kalla was also an effective political broker who could ensure that parliament supported the government on key issues. Towards the end of their term, however, there was clear rivalry for the limelight between the president and vice-president, and their partnership was not renewed for the 2009 presidential elections. Indeed, Kalla ran for president, against Yudhoyono, in that election.

For his second tilt at the presidency, Yudhoyono chose Boediono as his vice-president. Boediono's background, personality and style could not have been more different from Kalla's. He was a highly respected economist and technocrat with no political base of his own. He had been a minister in the Habibie, Megawati and Yudhoyono governments but had never belonged to a political party or developed any other patronage network. While not exactly self-effacing, Boediono deliberately kept such a low profile as Yudhoyono's deputy that the public was often left in the dark about what exactly the vice-president was doing during his five years in office. In reality, Yudhoyono entrusted Boediono with the task of supervising and coordinating several key government policies. The planning and execution of bureaucratic reform efforts, the improved targeting of poverty alleviation measures, the acceleration of development in Papua and the executive supervision of major infrastructure projects, including the building of new ports, airports, toll roads, double-track railways and power plants—all were done under the personal direction of the vice-president.

In sum, the Yudhoyono years laid down a solid foundation for following governments to build on. Despite continuing weaknesses and problems, Indonesia's political and economic foundations stabilised under Yudhoyono. In 2014 Indonesians opted to chart a new course for the country and make a clear break with the past. The man they chose as Yudhoyono's successor, Joko Widodo, represents a new type of political leader. His deputy, however, is an old hand—Jusuf Kalla, Yudhoyono's vice-president during his first term. Thus, the lessons learned from the Yudhoyono presidency are likely to have a strong influence on the new administration as well.

REFERENCES

Crouch, H. (2010) *Political Reform in Indonesia after Soeharto*, Institute of Southeast Asian Studies, Singapore.

Erb, M. and P. Sulistiyanto (eds) (2009) *Deepening Democracy in Indonesia? Direct Elections for Local Leaders (Pilkada)*, Institute of Southeast Asian Studies, Singapore.

Hill, H. (ed.) (2014) *Regional Dynamics in a Decentralized Indonesia*, Institute of Southeast Asian Studies, Singapore.

Horowitz, D.L. (2013) *Constitutional Change and Democracy in Indonesia*, Cambridge University Press, Cambridge.

Mietzner, M. (2012) 'Indonesia's democratic stagnation: anti-reformist elites and resilient civil society', *Democratization*, 19(2): 209–29.

Poczter, S. and T.B. Pepinsky (2015) 'Authoritarian legacies in post-New Order Indonesia: evidence from a new dataset', unpublished manuscript, Cornell University, Ithaca NY.

Reid, A. (ed.) (2012) *Indonesia Rising: The Repositioning of Asia's Third Giant*, Institute of Southeast Asian Studies, Singapore.

World Bank (2015) 'Gross domestic product 2013, by PPP', Washington DC. Available at http://databank.worldbank.org/data/download/GDP_PPP.pdf

WEF (World Economic Forum) (2004) 'Excerpt from global competitiveness report 2004/2005', World Economic Forum in collaboration with IESE Business School, Geneva. Available at http://www.ieseinsight.com/casos/study_0035.pdf

WEF (World Economic Forum) (2009) 'Global competitiveness report 2009-2010', Geneva. Available at http://www3.weforum.org/docs/WEF_GlobalCompetitivenessReport_2009-10.pdf

WEF (World Economic Forum) (2014) 'Global competitiveness report 2014-2015', Geneva. Available at http://www3.weforum.org/docs/WEF_GlobalCompetitivenessReport_2014-15.pdf

PART 1

Personal, comparative and international perspectives

3 The politics of Yudhoyono: majoritarian democracy, insecurity and vanity

*Greg Fealy**

In the twilight of his presidency, Susilo Bambang Yudhoyono spoke reflectively to his personal staff about his place in Indonesian history and on the world stage. He saw himself as holding the exalted position of one of his nation's great presidents, if not *the* greatest. Moreover, he was convinced that he bore comparison with other leading contemporary international figures, such as Barack Obama, Tony Blair, David Cameron and Angela Merkel. He saw these leaders as peers because, like them, he had not only had a major impact on his own country but also become a significant player in global affairs.[1]

Yudhoyono's lofty opinion of his own attainments stands in contrast to the widespread opinion of scholars and political commentators that he was a good, but not a great, president (Bachelard 2014; Howes and Davies 2014). His achievements have often been referred to and it is only necessary to refer briefly to them here. He is credited with stabilising and consolidating democracy in Indonesia; facilitating the fight against corruption; overseeing the peace process in Aceh; providing policies that led to high economic growth; and supporting law enforcement agencies in their counterterrorism operations.

---

* I would like to thank Ken Ward, Angus McIntyre, Adi Abidin, David Jenkins and Marcus Mietzner for their assistance in preparing this chapter. Their stimulating observations on Yudhoyono and their comments on draft versions of the text have proven very helpful.
1 Much of the information in this article comes from confidential interviews in Jakarta in January, May and August 2014. Unless otherwise stated, the material in this chapter comes from sources that cannot be disclosed.

Arguably, the principal reason that Yudhoyono was not a better president was that he was too hesitant and indecisive—in a position that required the very opposite of these traits. One of the most common terms used by Yudhoyono's detractors to describe him was *'peragu'*, a waverer or doubt-ridden person. And indeed, he lacked the gumption to take bold decisions that is the mark of a great leader. A vivid early illustration of Yudhoyono's indecisiveness comes from 2002 when, as coordinating minister for political and security affairs in Megawati Sukarnoputri's government, he was tasked with overseeing peace negotiations with the Free Aceh Movement (Gerakan Aceh Merdeka, GAM). A senior diplomat on the Indonesian negotiating team recalled that the initial discussions with Yudhoyono went well: 'We presented him with a quite complex brief but were surprised at how quickly he grasped the details. He was very impressive intellectually'. The problems began, however, when the team asked for guidance on their negotiating position. Yudhoyono requested a succession of option papers over the following weeks but repeatedly failed to give instructions. Matters came to a head as the negotiators were about to depart for meetings with GAM in Geneva. The exasperated team leader called the minister from Jakarta airport and told him he needed his negotiating directions without further delay. Yudhoyono then asked, 'Which option do you think is best?' The team leader told him and Yudhoyono immediately replied with relief, 'Yes, I agree. Use that option'. In recounting this story, the senior diplomat concluded that 'Yudhoyono just can't make a decision. He understands, but he can't decide. That's his big problem'. Indeed, dithering on big decisions was a hallmark of Yudhoyono's political career, and there are a great many anecdotes from his time as president that make the depth of his irresolution clear.

To explain Yudhoyono's political behaviour, it is necessary to reflect not only on the societal context in which he operated (see Chapter 4 by Sidel), but also on the personal reasons for both his chronic hesitancy and the vanity that led him to ascribe greatness to himself. I will argue that the key to understanding both of these traits is insecurity. Throughout his life, Yudhoyono has suffered from corrosive self-doubt, which he seeks to manage by limiting the risk of criticism while attempting to cloak his emotional fragility in grandiosity. But why would a man who had won two handsome popular mandates as president, risen to the rank of general, gained a PhD and won international plaudits for his statesman-like qualities want for self-regard? To answer this I will draw on psychoanalytical literature, which offers tools to explore the origins and nature of Yudhoyono's insecurity and vanity. Some caveats need to be stated before I proceed to the substantive discussion. I am not a political psychologist and have no training in this discipline; my background is in history and political science. Nonetheless, I hope that this chapter will foster a scholarly discussion on Yudhoyono's character as a politician. To date, I have been unable to find any academic articles that deal with Yudhoyono's personality and inner thinking.

This chapter is divided into seven sections. The first analyses Yudhoyono's formative years. This is followed by a description of his social and professional rise—or, in Yudhoyono's words, the process that led him to 'become someone' (*menjadi orang*). The third section discusses his entry into politics, and the fourth and fifth deal with his two markedly different presidential terms. Against this backdrop, the sixth section illuminates how Yudhoyono's insecurity and vanity shaped his presidency, especially in its later years. The final part reviews his last months in office—a period in which many of Yudhoyono's narcissistic personality traits became pronounced.

FORMATIVE YEARS

Yudhoyono's insecurity is almost certainly a product of his childhood and his relationship with his parents. Researching Yudhoyono's early life is difficult because he has revealed little of his formative years in either interviews or his own writings, or in the works of others with whom he has collaborated. No one who knew him as a child or teenager has written anything, either. The main source of information about his childhood is *SBY: Sang Demokrat* [SBY: The Democrat], a 1,000-page book produced in the run-up to the 2004 presidential election by former journalist and politician Usamah Hisyam and a team of five writers (Hisyam 2004). Yudhoyono oversaw the preparation of the book and the text includes many direct quotes from him. The account of his childhood is patchy at best, and sometimes the absence of information is as revealing as the provision of it. Much of the biographical material found in later books, such as the biography of his wife (Endah 2010) and the *Pak Beye* series written by *Kompas* journalist Wisnu Nugroho (2010a, 2010b, 2011), draws heavily on *Sang Demokrat*.

Yudhoyono was born into a humble and unhappy family in the hardscrabble district of Pacitan, East Java, on 9 September 1949. Both his parents and his hometown were to have a powerful negative effect on his development. His father, Soekotjo, was a soldier and a man of rigid views and low attainment.[2] He had joined the army in 1945 but through-

---

2 In *Sang Demokrat*, Soekotjo is described, somewhat unattractively but quite possibly on the basis of Yudhoyono's own account, as having a 'stiff personality and hard attitudes' (Hisyam 2004: 35–6).

out Yudhoyono's youth he would rise no further than the rank of first sublieutenant (*peltu*), the lowest level of officer, and he would never progress beyond holding subdistrict military commands (Komando Rayon Militer, Koramil) within Pacitan district.³ This was despite his claiming aristocratic descent from the Majapahit dynasty and kinship with the Hamengkubuwono sultanate in Yogyakarta. Indeed, he used the nobleman's title, 'Raden', before his name. Even less is known about Yudhoyono's mother, Habibah. *Sang Demokrat* tells us that she was part of the 'extended family' that founded the famous Tremas Islamic boarding school (*pesantren*) in Pacitan. Nothing else of substance is said about her, almost as if Yudhoyono sought to deny her any meaningful place in his life (Hisyam 2004: 36–7, 829; Endah 2011: 170–71).

Life was difficult for Soekotjo, Habibah and their only child. Soekotjo's salary was low, and the family is described as living from day to day (Hisyam 2004: 35). By some accounts, Yudhoyono's parents often squabbled and there was tension and rancour in the household. Towards the end of Yudhoyono's primary school years, Soekotjo entrusted his son to his sister and her husband, Sastro Suyitno, the head of Ploso village in Pacitan.⁴ The reason given was that Soekotjo's constant postings to new military subdistricts were disrupting Yudhoyono's education, but a more likely explanation is that the parents' marriage was failing and they wanted to spare their son further turmoil. Conditions in Ploso were spartan, and Yudhoyono was given a tiny, plain bedroom near the village offices. Sastro already had two sons, and there is a sense in *Sang Demokrat* and *Pak Beye* that Yudhoyono largely had to fend for himself (Hisyam 2004: 40–41; Nugroho 2011: 7–24).

Accounts of Yudhoyono's childhood offer some early insights into his personality traits. He is said to have enjoyed ceremonies and pageantry at school and in the village, and would often ask to be given a prominent role in such events. He was a strapping boy, tall for his age, but he objected strongly to violence and harsh or uncompromising views (*bersifat keras*), to the point that he avoided contact sports such as soccer and the game *kasti*, where teams try to hit their opponents with a ball.

---

3 Only later in his career did Soekotjo enjoy success. After leaving the army in 1971, he became a Golkar member of the Pacitan legislature and head of the district's *haj* association (Hisyam 2004: 37). Some of the success he achieved in later life may have been due to his son's growing reputation and influence within the armed forces.

4 *Sang Demokrat* records that Habibah wanted Yudhoyono to have an Islamic education at her family's Tremas *pesantren* but that Soekotjo rejected this in favour of a state schooling. This may have been one source of tension between the parents, and it is notable that Soekotjo alone accompanied Yudhoyono when he went to live with his aunt and uncle (Hisyam 2004: 41).

One anecdote in *Sang Demokrat* has it that a student punched Yudhoyono in the school grounds but he refused to strike back, even though he was much bigger and stronger than his assailant; the following day Yudhoyono is said to have become a good friend of the boy (Hisyam 2004: 42-3). Yudhoyono was sociable and readily joined organisations such as the scouts. Above all else, he was highly intelligent and hardworking. He did well at school and was popular with both his teachers and his peers.

Yudhoyono's parents eventually divorced when he was about 15 or 16. This was a heavy blow for him, and he is quoted in *Sang Demokrat* as saying, 'That was the saddest experience of my life'. Indeed, this event is described as a turning point, one that led to a steely resolve to escape the adversity of Pacitan and become a success in life. 'I have to fight. I have to be different', he told the *Sang Demokrat* authors, recalling his feelings at the time. 'I have to become someone. I don't want to experience what happened to my parents. I have to leave Pacitan and survive[5] so that I can become someone' (Hisyam 2004: 56-7; Nugroho 2011: 7-8).

The expression 'become someone' (*menjadi orang*) is found repeatedly in accounts of Yudhoyono's early life, and it conveys the sense that he felt untended and inconsequential in Pacitan, despite his good academic performance at school and his wide range of social activities. It is likely that he regarded his father and mother as failures, both in their careers and as parents. They had been unable to provide a stable and financially secure family life for him, and judging by the detached way in which Yudhoyono speaks of them, they also seem to have aroused little sense of affection in him. Yudhoyono makes only dutiful statements about his parents, such as that they cared for him to the best of their abilities. He also seeks, rather unpersuasively, to give the impression that his father's lowly position was not a hindrance to his career, writing in *Sang Demokrat*: 'If my father had been a minister, a general, a president or a king, then that would have been okay. But, we shouldn't lose hope if we're not descended from people of [high] status' (Hisyam 2004: 57). This seems intended to emphasise Yudhoyono's achievement in surmounting his humble origins, and it also shows how sensitive he is about his background. As will be discussed later, there is much psychological literature linking insecurity and narcissism in adults to poor relations with one's parents. Ultimately, Yudhoyono conveys an impression of disengagement from and disappointment with his parents, such that he resolved to leave Pacitan and the unsettled environment they had created for him there.

---

5 Although speaking in Indonesian, Yudhoyono uses the English word 'survive' here.

'BECOMING SOMEONE'

Yudhoyono graduated from senior high school in mid-1968 with good grades and impatient ambition. From an early age, he planned to become an army officer. His father had taken him to the Armed Forces Academy in Magelang when he was a boy and the parades, the uniforms and the elite nature of the institution had made an indelible impression on him (Hisyam 2004: 77). In Suharto's New Order, a career as a military officer offered bright prospects given the extensive role that the armed forces played in political, social and economic affairs. One wonders also whether becoming an officer may have held particular attraction for Yudhoyono in that it would allow him to eclipse his father's own modest army career. He was late submitting his application to the academy, however, and had to wait till the following year to apply again.

Determined nonetheless to leave Pacitan, Yudhoyono went to East Java's capital city, Surabaya, and enrolled in a machine technology degree at the well-regarded Surabaya Institute of Technology. This field of study proved not to his liking, so he transferred to an education degree at a teachers' college in Malang, presumably so that he would have a fall-back career should he fail to gain admission to Magelang (Hisyam 2004: 78). Eventually Yudhoyono was accepted into the military academy and commenced training in 1970. He excelled in both the scholarly and physical aspects of his officer course and graduated dux of his year in 1973. Perhaps as important for his career prospects was the growing favour he found with the academy's governor, Sarwo Edhie Wibowo, and his family. Sarwo Edhie was a revered commander within army ranks and was especially well known for his role in overseeing the killing of tens of thousands of communists in Central Java in late 1965. He became governor of the academy in the same year as Yudhoyono began his training at Magelang, and the young cadet soon came to Sarwo Edhie's attention, not only for his impressive academic results but also for his polite and obliging manner. With Sarwo Edhie's blessing, he began courting Kristiani (commonly known as Ani), one of the general's three daughters. The couple became engaged soon after Yudhoyono graduated and, at Sarwo Edhie's urging, married in 1976 (Endah 2010: 176; Hisyam 2004: 883).

Sang Demokrat recounts an interesting story of Yudhoyono's father opposing the nuptials on the grounds that his son would be marrying above his station. 'Isn't there an imbalance between your status and that of the daughter of a governor who holds the rank of major-general?', Soekotjo asked his son. Yudhoyono pressed his father repeatedly not to feel 'inferior' or 'fearful', and in time Soekotjo relented and gave the marriage his blessing. The authors, perhaps at Yudhoyono's suggestion, then chide Soekotjo for feeling this way given his own aristocratic heritage

(Hisyam 2004: 883–4). The inclusion of this account in *Sang Demokrat* is significant for two reasons. First, it reveals Yudhoyono's irritation at his father's objections to the marriage to Ani. Just as he is on the threshold of elevating himself, his father is seeking to drag him back down. Second, it serves the political purpose of declaring that Yudhoyono's family has no need to feel inadequate given its noble heritage. There is thus a tension in Yudhoyono's family story between that of lifting himself out of straitened circumstances and that of belonging to a privileged class.

Marrying into the Sarwo Edhie clan was a breakthrough for Yudhoyono. His wife's family was everything that his own was not. It was stable, tight-knit, well-to-do and politically powerful, and it boasted a pedigree on the distaff side that made Soekotjo's putative nobility look threadbare. Sarwo Edhie dominated the family until his death in 1989; his legacy is still evident at the Yudhoyono residence in Puri Cikeas on Jakarta's southern outskirts, which came to resemble a shrine to him, with large portraits of the patriarch on the walls, cabinets filled with memorabilia and a life-size bronze bust of Sarwo Edhie atop a two-metre-high column in the rear yard. As if to symbolise and perpetuate this veneration of Sarwo Edhie, photographs of the extended family are regularly taken in front of this bust, with the general looking commandingly down on his brood.[6] There were mutual benefits for Yudhoyono and the Sarwo Edhie family in the marriage. For Yudhoyono, being the son-in-law of the great Sarwo Edhie could accelerate his rise through the ranks and maximise his chances of becoming a general, a long-held dream. It was also probably the case that Ani's family gave Yudhoyono a sense of belonging and support that he had lacked in his own family. For Sarwo Edhie, Yudhoyono was a far more broadly gifted officer than his own son, Pramono, and therefore more likely to achieve the kind of high rank that could advance the family's military and political interests.

Nevertheless, Yudhoyono did not enter the family as an equal but as a subordinate. For all his achievements as a young officer, he still came from a broken family with a lowly background. Some sense of this can be gained from Ani's biography, which is subtitled *A Soldier's Daughter* rather than *A General's Wife*, let alone *A President's Wife*. Her adoration for her 'Papi', as she calls her father, is evident throughout the book, whereas her attitude towards her husband is affectionate and respectful but not glorifying. For her, Yudhoyono would always remain in Sarwo Edhie's shadow, and he could never attain the august status of his father-in-law, even upon becoming president. There is also considerable anecdotal evidence that Yudhoyono felt obliged to defer to the wishes of Ani and his

---

6 See, for example, the photographs in Hisyam (2004: 918) and Endah (2010: 490–91).

mother-in-law, Sunarti Sri Hadiyah, on important decisions, especially relating to the family and politics. On occasion he would admit to advisors that it was difficult for him to disregard the wishes of Ani and her family, even when he was of a strongly differing opinion. Thus, while joining the Sarwo Edhie family helped Yudhoyono's career, it may also have fed his sense of inadequacy.

Yudhoyono's military career progressed apace after he graduated. Over the next 23 years he would hold 18 positions, ranging from battlefield commands and peacekeeping operations to desk jobs, such as teaching and advisory positions. He began his career as an officer in the Army Strategic Reserve Command (Komando Strategi Angkatan Darat, Kostrad) and served as a platoon commander in an airborne battalion. He did three tours of duty in East Timor, the last, in 1986–88, as a battalion commander. He became one of the youngest heads of a military region (Komando Daerah Militer, Kodam) when he was appointed to lead the Sriwijaya command in south Sumatra in 1996–97. His penultimate position in the armed forces was as chief-of-staff for social and political affairs in 1998, the year in which Suharto's New Order regime was toppled. As chief-of-staff, he played an important part in revising the armed forces' doctrine redefining the military's role in the new democratic system.[7]

Yudhoyono was especially proud of two aspects of his military career. The first was the reputation he gained as an armed forces intellectual, and he particularly liked the sobriquet 'thinking general' that was sometimes applied to him. He completed eight military training courses abroad and obtained a master's degree in management from Webster University in the United States, making him the most internationally credentialed officer of his generation.[8] He also read widely on history, strategic issues and global politics, and enjoyed discussing such matters with scholars and officials. Second, he found his role as Indonesia's chief military observer to the United Nations peacekeeping mission in Bosnia-Herzegovina in 1995–96 to be very gratifying. It brought him into contact with senior officers from numerous countries, and Yudhoyono's own performance was widely lauded. This experience no doubt consolidated his belief that he had become someone—that is, that he had left the depressing remoteness of Pacitan behind and arrived on the international stage.

---

7 For a full list of Yudhoyono's military appointments and awards, see Hisyam (2004: 973–81).
8 In 2004, some years after he had retired from the military, Yudhoyono went on to obtain a PhD in agricultural economics from Bogor Agricultural University (Institut Pertanian Bogor).

INTO POLITICS

Yudhoyono claimed to be a reluctant politician and said that he would happily have remained a military officer till the end of his career. Nevertheless, his rise to political prominence was steep and rapid. He gained some direct experience of politics when he became chair of the armed forces' faction in the People's Consultative Assembly (Majelis Permusyarawatan Rakyat, MPR) in 1998, but his substantive entrance into political life came the following year when President Abdurrahman Wahid chose him to be his minister of mining and energy. Yudhoyono was loath to take the position but relented when Wahid pressed him to do so. Aware that Yudhoyono would have preferred the post of army commander, the president made him a four-star general as compensation (Hisyam 2004: 20; Daves 2014). In March 2000, Wahid appointed him coordinating minister for political, social and security affairs, but he was sacked in June 2001 after objecting to the president's plans to declare a state of emergency to save his presidency.

Yudhoyono portrayed his acceptance of these cabinet appointments as a simple case of a soldier obeying the instructions of his president and commander-in-chief, rather than him actively seeking high civilian office. This is probably correct. Although he had been involved in the military's social–political operations as well as the MPR, Yudhoyono was not a natural politician. He lacked the guile and tenacity required for the parry and thrust of practical politics. He didn't like cutting deals and he preferred not to be directly involved in raising the large funds necessary for political campaigning. While he coveted the prestige that high political office could bring, he wanted to remain above the grime and grind of day-to-day politics.

There was more to Yudhoyono's decision to join the Wahid cabinet than merely following orders, however. The Sarwo Edhie family undoubtedly played a large part in his decision—especially Ani and her mother, who saw their role as securing the family's future. Ani was much more politically savvy than her husband. Whereas he was preoccupied with attaining high military rank and burnishing his intellectual credentials, her focus was on power and the family's advancement. Ani appears to have been central to all of Yudhoyono's major political decisions, including the formation of the Democrat Party (Partai Demokrat, PD) in 2001, his nomination for the presidency in 2004 and the appointment and dismissal of cabinet ministers. After he became president, senior advisors felt that when Yudhoyono was agonising over decisions, he paid greater heed to his wife's opinions than to those of his staff. Despite Yudhoyono's misgivings, Ani also insisted on the appointment of family members such as their son Edhie Baskoro, her brother-in-law Hadi

Utomo and her brother Pramono to top positions within PD. Given this later pattern of behaviour, it is very likely that Ani pressed Yudhoyono to accept a ministerial position, as this opened up the prospect of greater power and opportunity.

After Wahid's impeachment in July 2001, the incoming president, Megawati Sukarnoputri, reinstated Yudhoyono as coordinating minister for political and security affairs, a position he occupied until resigning in March 2004 to run for the presidency. As coordinating minister, Yudhoyono gained a high public profile and by 2003 was securing sufficiently strong approval ratings to be ranked as a serious presidential contender. Voters liked his dignified bearing, his worldliness and his apparent decency and freedom from corruption. He seemed to offer both the stability that Indonesia had enjoyed during the Suharto era as well as a concern for human rights and rule of law needed in a consolidating democracy. Yudhoyono's popularity continued to grow throughout early 2004. Amid growing speculation that he would nominate for the presidency, Yudhoyono reportedly assured Megawati that he would not do so, only to renege on this in March. Megawati has never forgiven Yudhoyono for what she regards as a perfidious act, though Yudhoyono has denied that he made such an assurance.

In the first round of the presidential election in July 2004, he emerged as the leading candidate with 34 per cent of the vote to Megawati's 27 per cent. In the second round of voting in September, Yudhoyono was triumphant with 61 per cent support. Not only had he won Indonesia's first direct presidential election, but he had also secured a generous mandate from the electorate. He would record an equally emphatic victory in 2009, winning in a single round with roughly the same percentage of the vote. He may initially have been a reluctant politician, but the magnitude of his success in politics must have been immensely satisfying to him.

FIRST-TERM PRESIDENT

Yudhoyono's two five-year presidential terms were markedly different. The contrasts reveal much about his changing view of himself and his evolving political priorities. The first term was far more productive and successful than the second, and the main achievements of Yudhoyono's presidency took place before 2009, not afterwards.

When he assumed the presidency in October 2004, Yudhoyono's personality traits were well known in elite political circles. As a senior military officer and then a minister, he had acquired a reputation for being highly intelligent, hard-working and upright. But it was also clear to many that he was a vacillator. Those who had worked closely with him as coordinating minister under Wahid and Megawati knew of his tendency to agonise at length over matters, to call repeatedly for more information as a means of postponing a decision, to shift responsibility for decision-making to others and to reverse earlier positions if he came under concerted pressure to do so. From the outset, many of his cabinet ministers knew that they would need to manage these propensities if the government was to be effective.

The successes of the first term owed much to those whom Yudhoyono chose to fill key positions in his cabinet. Like all of the post-1999 governments, Yudhoyono's first cabinet was something of a rainbow coalition, containing representatives from seven parties as well as technocrats filling many of the main economics portfolios. But three members in particular would play a critical role: Vice-President Jusuf Kalla, Coordinating Minister for Social Welfare Aburizal Bakrie and presidential spokesperson Andi Mallarangeng. Kalla and Bakrie were both millionaire businessmen with can-do, cut-through approaches to government. Kalla was the more important of the two. Aware of Yudhoyono's cautious nature, he worked closely with key economics ministers to get their policy proposals accepted by the president. For example, he hosted regular gatherings of ministers at his residence where they would discuss strategies to win Yudhoyono's agreement on a particular matter and then hold him to that decision. Kalla also played a critical role in overseeing the peace negotiations in Aceh. His impatience with the president's dilatory nature often led him to make brusque remarks directly to Yudhoyono, which both offended the president and impelled him to act.

Bakrie, a longstanding Golkar politician, was the political fixer in the Yudhoyono government. He and his staff had an intimate understanding of practical politics and how to achieve a desired outcome, particularly with regard to the parliament. They were expert in working out which parliamentarians needed to be paid or cajoled or threatened in order to have bills passed.

Andi Mallarangeng, finally, was much more than Yudhoyono's spokesperson. He was the president's favourite among a group of bright, capable, articulate young intellectuals and officials who worked at the palace. By all accounts, Yudhoyono found Andi stimulating and genial company and he came to trust him more than he did most other members of his staff. Andi had the knack of reading the president's mood and was able to present information, including information of an unpalatable nature, in a way that was acceptable to Yudhoyono. In addition to explaining the president's decisions to the public, Andi served as a trouble-shooter, detecting emerging problems and liaising between ministers, palace staff and the media to defuse them. As a result, the government was able to avoid major political controversies for much of the term.

Each of these three figures was, in different ways, able to ensure that the government not only made good progress on policy issues but also could keep its legislative program on track. Kalla and Andi were especially pivotal because of their ability to manage Yudhoyono and his personal foibles. In effect, they saved him from himself. By the end of the first term, many of the government's key policy goals, such as peace in Aceh, economic growth of at least 5 per cent, decreasing poverty and rising investment, had been realised. There were relatively few policy reversals, with a notable exception being Yudhoyono's backdown on the planned revisions to the 2003 Labour Law (Law 13/2003) after large protests in Jakarta in 2006. Many ministers from the 2004–09 period liked working with Yudhoyono, despite their frustrations at his indecisiveness. Particularly in the first half of the term, Yudhoyono met regularly with ministers to discuss policy issues. He solicited advice and was prepared to countenance views contrary to his own. Cabinet meetings involved genuine discussion of pending decisions. One minister commented: 'I enjoyed cabinet meetings. Yudhoyono was engaging and open-minded. He would go around the room asking ministers for their views. I felt that this was precisely how a cabinet should function'.

PRESIDENT REGNANT

Yudhoyono's resounding win in the 2009 presidential election, in which he gained 34 per cent more of the vote than his nearest rival, Megawati, had a powerful effect on his thinking.[9] After the election, he boasted to palace staff that his victory had elevated him to a unique position in Indonesia's history: not only was he the first president to be popularly re-elected but he had won in a single round. None of Indonesia's preceding five presidents had faced the voters, let alone secured such a ringing endorsement in an election. This was a source of deep and cossetting self-satisfaction to him. In his own mind this victory must have indisputably proved that he had 'become someone' — *menjadi orang*.

Ministers and staff noted that Yudhoyono became more aloof and vain. He had much less contact with ministers, communicating with many of the less important ones largely through trusted lieutenants, such as Secretary of State Sudi Silalahi, Coordinating Minister for Economic Affairs Hatta Rajasa and Cabinet Secretary Dipo Alam. Halfway through the second term, numerous ministers had yet to have a one-on-one meeting with the president and saw little of him outside cabinet meetings and

---

9 Yudhoyono gained 61 per cent of the vote, Megawati 27 per cent and the third contestant, Jusuf Kalla, 12 per cent.

formal ceremonies. Cabinet meetings were no longer forums for open exchanges of views and decision-making among ministers but rather became stiffly formal, Yudhoyono-centred events. He and a small coterie of ministers and advisors developed pre-determined positions on most policy matters and these were conveyed to cabinet largely as *faits accomplis*. Debate was rare and ministers had to listen to long-winded and often tedious disquisitions from the president. Some ministers ruefully nicknamed Yudhoyono 'The Professor' for his tendency to deliver boring lectures to cabinet (Fealy 2011: 334–6). Yudhoyono also became increasingly unhappy when ministers or staff expressed opinions contrary to his own. Ministers who openly disagreed with him would often be 'punished' by being temporarily denied access to the president or would receive a phone call from Sudi, Hatta or Dipo admonishing them for upsetting the president; Yudhoyono almost never confronted a minister or staff member personally.

Yudhoyono's new cabinet was also less effective than its predecessor, not because it lacked good ministers, but rather because it lacked the political operators who had been so important between 2004 and 2009. Jusuf Kalla had been replaced as vice-president by Boediono, arguably Yudhoyono's single biggest mistake of his second term. The president had been irritated by Kalla's blunt manner, high public profile and propensity to claim credit for key initiatives. Of the numerous options available to Yudhoyono for his next vice-president, he chose an eminent but reserved technocrat with no party base or political skills. In Boediono, he had a deputy who would be compliant and would not vie for attention in the way that Kalla had done. This was an act of political complacency by Yudhoyono, reflecting his failure to recognise that he was incapable of driving policy- and decision-making processes without an assertive senior figure in cabinet. In Bakrie's place as the government's point man in dealing with parliament, Yudhoyono put the veteran Golkar politician Agung Laksono, but he proved incompetent, and relations between the executive and legislature deteriorated as a result. Finally, Andi Mallarangeng, who had become a minister, was replaced with another political scientist, Daniel Sparingga. Although well liked by Yudhoyono, he lacked Andi's problem-solving and networking skills.

It was during the second term that Yudhoyono became increasingly reliant on opinion polling to inform his decision-making. He and Ani had always been highly attentive to public attitudes and media reporting. They religiously read the leading newspapers, including *Kompas, Jawa Pos* and the *Jakarta Post*, every morning, following editorial commentaries and published survey results. During his first term, Yudhoyono had quietly begun to use Indonesia's leading opinion surveyor, Lembaga Survei Indonesia (LSI), to conduct targeted polling on specific issues. Data from LSI, for example, had persuaded him that he could win the 2009 presidential election with Boediono as his running mate. But in his second term, Yudhoyono's dependence on polling became an open secret. On thorny issues, he would privately commission surveys to gauge the electorate's mood. Almost invariably he would decide on a policy only after being assured that he was in step with majority opinion.

A telling example of this was the so-called Cicak–Buaya (Gecko–Crocodile) controversy in late 2009, involving a showdown between the police and the Corruption Eradication Commission (Komisi Pemberantasan Korupsi, KPK). The police arrested two KPK commissioners who had approved phone taps that had yielded evidence of high-level police corruption, and charged them with extortion and abuse of power. The KPK, for its part, asserted that the commissioners had done nothing wrong and the police were simply trying to intimidate them. The crisis acquired its name when one of the police generals involved in the case described the KPK as a 'gecko' and the police as a 'crocodile' in order to emphasise the superior size and strength of the police.

As the crisis grew, Yudhoyono came under intense pressure to intervene. Despite weeks of briefings and recommendations from a highly regarded and independent fact-finding committee, the president seemed no closer to making a decision. He eventually turned to the LSI to survey public attitudes. Its data revealed that a majority of respondents did not want the KPK commissioners prosecuted. Yudhoyono expressed relief upon learning of the findings and immediately told the police to drop the charges against the commissioners. What is instructive about this case is that Yudhoyono did not make his decision based on legal advice or as a matter of principle—indeed, the fact-finding team had recommended, many days before he received the LSI results, that the charges against the KPK commissioners be dropped. Rather, the president lacked the courage to act until he knew where the weight of public opinion lay.

A more glaring case can be found in the dying months of his presidency, when opinion polling persuaded Yudhoyono to change from a neutral position in the July 2014 presidential election to belatedly backing Prabowo Subianto. He had long told those close to him that he believed Prabowo was unfit to be president, based largely on what he knew of the candidate's temperament and his record in the armed forces.[10] He reversed this stance upon receiving polling halfway through the campaign from Saiful Mujani Research and Consulting (SMRC) showing

---

10 Confidential interviews in Jakarta, August and September 2014. Yudhoyono was a member of the Armed Forces Honour Council when it discharged Prabowo in August 1998 for being involved in the disappearance of several anti-Suharto activists.

that Prabowo had drawn level with Joko Widodo (Jokowi) and now had a serious prospect of winning the election. Although he refrained from personally declaring his support for Prabowo and forbade publication of the SMRC results for fear it would undermine Jokowi, Yudhoyono instructed his party, PD, to join Prabowo's coalition.[11] In short, Yudhoyono's desire to be on the winning side overrode his conviction that Prabowo would make a bad president. His decision also seems to have been swayed by survey data showing that he was more popular with Prabowo's than with Jokowi's supporters.

Far from seeing a preoccupation with public opinion as a weakness, Yudhoyono regarded it as epitomising democratic behaviour. He argued that a democrat should know and be guided by what the majority wanted. In his view, democracy was not just about upholding citizens' rights and ensuring free and fair elections, it was also about respecting the wishes of the population when it came to government decision-making. He regarded this majoritarian approach as essential to keeping society stable and prosperous. If too much weight was given to minority views or black-letter law, then large sections of society could become restive, leading to tension and disorder. Though Yudhoyono portrayed his thinking as being driven by democratic principles, it was also heavily influenced by Javanese concepts that prioritised community harmony and political order. Much like Suharto, who had also been raised in rural Java, Yudhoyono was influenced by traditional cultural norms that greatly shaped his thinking on personal interactions and socio-political arrangements.

It is also probable that Yudhoyono's casting of himself as a majoritarian democrat was making a virtue of a psychological necessity. Polling allowed him to overcome his chronic indecisiveness. When in a quandary as to how to decide a difficult issue, Yudhoyono turned to the views of the majority as captured in opinion surveys. In effect, the public made the decision for him. This was also a means for him to deal with his sense of insecurity. It allowed him to take refuge in the weight of public opinion. Despite his seemingly increased self-regard, he still lacked the inner confidence to hold views that ran counter to those of his peers or the masses and hence derived comfort from polling that showed that he was in step with public opinion — a feature discussed further below. Repeatedly, when justifying a particular action, Yudhoyono would refer approvingly to his view being in keeping with the majority — unaware

---

11 The largest party in Joko Widodo's coalition was Megawati's party, the Indonesian Democratic Party of Struggle (Partai Demokrasi Indonesia-Perjuangan, PDIP). Yudhoyono's initial plan for PD to join Jokowi's coalition fell through when Megawati refused to deal with him.

that this rendered him a follower, rather than a leader, of community opinion.

Another aspect of Yudhoyono that became far more pronounced during his second term was his vanity. This took various forms. One was a preoccupation with his status as a world leader. On the one hand, he sought and delighted in praise from international leaders. On the other hand, he constantly compared himself to world leaders to identify ways in which he could be seen as being in their circle. Both tendencies were evident in what palace staff called Yudhoyono's 'Obama fever'. Of all the world leaders, it was the US president whose opinion and style the Indonesian president most sought to cultivate. Staff were instructed to tell Yudhoyono whenever Obama praised him, and he would beam with satisfaction at any such acknowledgment. He copied some of Obama's outreach methods, such as using Twitter and Facebook. Twitter, in particular, became something of a fixation for Yudhoyono. He regularly checked his number of followers and was delighted whenever it rose sharply.

Yudhoyono also became obsessed with awards and titles. He insisted, against convention, that the *State Gazette* (*Berita Negara*) include all his pre- and post-nominals, including 'Professor', 'Dr', 'General' and 'President', when referring to him. He established a special unit, known as the Honours Staff (Staf Penghargaan), to seek out international awards for him. The further his second term progressed, the more time he spent abroad at award ceremonies. Among the honours that he accumulated were at least seven honorary doctorates, the Knight Grand Cross of the Order of the Bath from Queen Elizabeth II, the Honorary Companion of the Order of Australia, the United Nations Global Champion Trophy for Disaster Risk Reduction and the Key to the City of Lisbon — most of which were awarded after 2009. Such were his aggrandising tendencies that staff complained that it was increasingly difficult to get Yudhoyono to concentrate on serious matters of state. As one staffer commented, 'Ceremony topped substance'.

INSECURITY AND VANITY

Yudhoyono's later years as president provide the best insights into the inseparable link between his indecisiveness, his insecurity and his vanity. Even after almost a decade in power, Yudhoyono was still unable to bring himself to make difficult or controversial decisions because he feared disapproval, and because such decisions would have provoked a backlash from sections of the community. He wanted endorsement and affirmation, not criticism or ridicule. He lacked the strength of character and self-confidence to make a decision and hold to it. In this regard, he compares unfavourably with Megawati, another president who was often accused of dilatory decision-making. Although slow to decide, once Megawati had made up her mind, she adhered steadfastly to that stance. Several ministers who worked under both Megawati and Yudhoyono admitted that they preferred Megawati because she was resolute. With Yudhoyono, they recalled, one could never be sure that he would not reverse a decision in the face of elite or public pressure.

As noted above, this vacillation and hesitancy was a product of Yudhoyono's gnawing insecurity, which in turn could be traced to his childhood and family circumstances. There is a large, and admittedly contested, psychological literature on the nexus between insecurity and poor relations with one's parents. Kernberg (1985), for example, has written of perceived parental rejection or lack of nurturing as a major cause of vulnerability in later years. Children who experience loveless or disrupted formative years often exhibit a fragile sense of self (Morf and Rhodewalt 1993: 668). This would appear to be the case with Yudhoyono. His family life was unstable and unhappy. His lack of warmth in describing his parents, or, indeed, the uncle and aunt with whom he stayed during his teenage years, suggests that he felt that he was on his own in the world and could not rely on others. Insecure individuals often see their lives as a battle against adversity, and Yudhoyono conforms to this mould. Much of his life story as told in *Sang Demokrat* is of his overcoming the many obstacles he faced in his early life.

Many psychoanalysts argue that insecurity is closely tied to narcissism. The insecure person is forever striving to manage their brittle self-esteem. They have a low tolerance for criticism because it compounds their insecurities, and they seek to regulate their interactions with others in ways that reduce the possibility of their shortcomings being exposed (Morf and Rhodewalt 1993: 689). Yudhoyono's acute sensitivity to criticism is apparent throughout the book he wrote in 2014, *Selalu Ada Pilihan* [There Is Always a Choice] (Yudhoyono 2014). The tone of the book is defensive, and he frequently casts his critics as emotional, poorly informed or irrational while characterising his own decisions as rational, just and balanced. Yudhoyono's strategy for regulating interactions is evident in his preference for formality during meetings and his refusal to reveal his private thoughts and anxieties to any but a handful of family members and trusted colleagues. In the last years of his presidency, he increasingly refused to do media interviews or answer questions at press conferences, preferring instead tame interviews with palace or PD officials that were then uploaded to YouTube. He was wary of showing spontaneity and familiarity, as this might reveal aspects of his inner life that could give the lie to his carefully cultivated outward expression of confidence and competence. As president, then, Yudhoyono adhered strictly to protocols and rules that helped to control the environment in which he worked.

Vulnerable people tend to compensate for their lack of self-regard by seeking the attention and admiration of others, and by validating themselves through shows of grandiosity. Emotionally secure individuals feel less need to impress others and are content to stand by their own decisions, whether popular or not (Bushman and Baumeister 1998: 219). Yudhoyono's love of pageantry, his desire to take prominent roles in ceremonies and his resentment of people who stole the spotlight from him (as Jusuf Kalla did when vice-president) are symptomatic of narcissism. Rosenfeld (1987: 275) identifies two types of narcissism that are relevant to the discussion of Yudhoyono: thin-skinned narcissism and thick-skinned narcissism. The thin-skinned narcissist is hypersensitive and overreactive to perceived slights; the thick-skinned narcissist tends to be uncaring or disdainful of criticism. Yudhoyono is undoubtedly of the thin-skinned variety — the sort of narcissist given to timidity and anxiety. His displays of vanity can be seen as a response to self-doubt and an attempt to provide a psychological buffer against threats to his self-esteem. His ceaseless quest for plaudits, awards and titles has been part of proving to himself, and the wider world, that he is a successful and admirable person.

Yudhoyono would probably have imagined that rising to the rank of general or being elected president would have banished his insecurities, but the extravagant vanity of his final years as head of state shows that there has been no escape. Indeed, as Fast (2009: iv, 3) points out, far from assuaging feelings of vulnerability, occupying high office can actually increase ego-defensive behaviour because it can heighten the fear of failure. The higher and more public the position held, the greater the prospect of shame and ridicule should one not succeed. Thus, occupying the presidency only sharpened the contradictory elements in Yudhoyono's personality: it provided unimagined opportunities for self-aggrandisement but it also exposed him to unprecedented risk of failure and humiliation.

SELF-DEFEAT

The final months of his presidency provide the most graphic evidence of how Yudhoyono unwittingly sabotaged his own plans to be remembered as a great president. Just as he was seeking to engineer a triumphant closing chapter on his rule in which there would be resounding acclaim at home and abroad for his achievements, he allowed ego to lead him into damaging miscalculations. Much of this concerned his response to the efforts of the Prabowo-led 'opposition' to push through democratically regressive legislation to abolish direct elections for district heads, mayors and governors. Yudhoyono had expressed his opposition to the bill but had failed to ensure that PD's parliamentary faction would vote against it. While he was basking in praise at the United Nations General Assembly in New York, his party abstained from the vote, thereby allowing the bill to pass. The ensuing torrent of media and civil society criticism shocked him into returning home early and attempting to rescind the law. His wounded indignation at the criticism he received served only to sharpen ridicule of him in many sections of society (Parlina and Nurhayati 2014). He then compounded the problem by launching competitions with prizes for those who offered the best encomiums for his presidency, once more exposing his habit of insulating himself from widespread criticism by engineering praise of his achievements from more loyal and, in his view, 'reasonable' segments of society.

Ultimately, then, Yudhoyono left office not to rousing applause but to disparagement. Through his own vain actions, he had drawn attention to his weaknesses rather than highlighting his strengths. The Indonesian people were not ungrateful for the stability and increased prosperity that he had brought to their nation, but many appeared relieved that an increasingly self-absorbed and ineffectual president had gone. The greatness that he so fervently hoped for had eluded him, leaving him a victim of his own flawed personality.

REFERENCES

Bachelard, M. (2014) 'Susilo Bambang Yudhoyono's legacy', *Sydney Morning Herald*, 18 October.
Bushman, B.J. and R.F. Baumeister (1998) 'Threatened egotism, narcissism, self-esteem and direct and displaced aggression: can self-hate lead to violence?', *Journal of Personality and Social Psychology*, 75(1): 219–29.
Daves, J.H. (2014) *The Indonesian Army from Revolusi to Reformasi – Volume 3: Soeharto's Fall and the Reformasi Era*, Amazon-Kindle Edition.
Endah, A. (2010) *Ani Yudhoyono: Kepak Sayap Putri Prajurit* [Ani Yudhoyono: Spreading Wings of a Soldier's Daughter], PT Gramedia Pustaka Utama, Jakarta.
Fast, N.J. (2009) 'Power, incompetence and hubris', PhD thesis, Graduate School of Business, Stanford University, Stanford CA.
Fealy, G. (2011) 'Politics in Indonesia in 2011: democratic regression and Yudhoyono's regal incumbency', *Bulletin of Indonesian Economic Studies*, 47(3): 333–53.
Hisyam, U. (ed.) (2004) *SBY: Sang Demokrat* [SBY: The Democrat], Penerbitan Dharmapena, Jakarta.

Howes, S. and R. Davies (2014) 'Assessing SBY's second term', *New Mandala*, 7 August. Available at http://asiapacific.anu.edu.au/newmandala/2014/08/07/assessing-sbys-second-term-the-president-and-the-parliament/

Kernberg, O.F. (1985) *Borderline Conditions and Pathological Narcissism*, Jason Aronson Inc., Lanham MD.

Morf, C.C. and F. Rhodewalt (1993) 'Narcissism and self-evaluation maintenance: explorations in object analysis', *Personality and Social Psychology Bulletin*, 19: 668–76.

Nugroho, W. (2010a) *Pak Beye dan Kerabatnya: Tetralogi Sisi Lain SBY* [Pak Beye and His Relatives: The Other Sides of SBY Tetralogy], Penerbit Buku Kompas, Jakarta.

Nugroho, W. (2010b) *Pak Beye dan Politiknya: Tetralogi Sisi Lain SBY* [Pak Beye and His Politics: The Other Sides of SBY Tetralogy], Penerbit Buku Kompas, Jakarta.

Nugroho, W. (2011) *Pak Beye dan Keluarganya: Tetralogi Sisi Lain SBY* [Pak Beye and His Family: The Other Sides of SBY Tetralogy], Penerbit Buku Kompas, Jakarta.

Parlina, I. and D. Nurhayati (2014) 'Civil society groups boycott Yudhoyono's Democracy Forum in Bali', *Jakarta Post*, 8 October.

Rosenfeld, H. (1987) *Impasse and Interpretation: Therapeutic and Anti-therapeutic Factors in the Psychoanalytic Treatment of Psychotic, Borderline and Neurotic Patients*, Tavistock, London.

Yudhoyono, S.B. (2014) *Selalu Ada Pilihan* [There is Always a Choice], Kompas Gramedia, Jakarta.

4 Men on horseback and their droppings: Yudhoyono's presidency and legacies in comparative regional perspective

John T. Sidel

Conventional understandings of the Yudhoyono years have long been framed in terms of personal leadership. This focus on personal leadership has been abundantly evident in journalistic treatments of Indonesian politics, and in everyday commentaries, comparisons and counterfactual musings about the strengths and weaknesses of Susilo Bambang Yudhoyono's presidency. There is also a long history of academic preoccupation with questions of leadership in Indonesian politics, dating back to Herbert Feith's account of the tensions and conflicts between 'solidarity-makers' and 'problem-solvers' in the decline of constitutional democracy in the 1950s and extending into the writings of William Liddle over the long rule of the Suharto regime (Feith 1962; Liddle 1996). Recent years, moreover, have seen a wide range of institutions and authors in the so-called development industry emphasising and extolling leadership as a (if not *the*) crucial ingredient in enacting economic reforms, enhancing good governance and otherwise promoting development (see, for example, Grindle 2007).

This tendency to emphasise—and essentialise—leadership as a personal quality of individuals has almost always served as a substitute, rather than a starting point, for serious analysis of Indonesian politics. It is often said that Presidents B.J. Habibie and Abdurrahman Wahid were mercurial and erratic; President Megawati Sukarnoputri was staid and standoffish; and President Yudhoyono was indecisive and conflict-averse. In lieu of references to traditional Javanese culture and jargon from the heyday of modernisation theory, today's political analysis simply uses the language of personality tests, pop psychology, pulp fiction and the tabloids. Indonesian presidents, it is assumed, have different personalities that explain the different politics they pursue and produce. Thus, after the July 2014 presidential elections, leading commentators on Indonesian politics breathed a collective sigh of relief that the hot-headed, ill-tempered, violence-prone Prabowo Subianto had lost his presidential bid and would not be subjecting Indonesian society to his authoritarian personality disorder and childish antics for the next five years, and that the appealingly approachable, earnest, easygoing and apparently incorruptible Joko Widodo (Jokowi) had been cast in the leading role in Indonesia's political drama instead (Mietzner 2014).

If this kind of individualised 'great man'/personality-based approach to Indonesian politics is ultimately unhelpful, inaccurate and obfuscatory, a comparative perspective on presidential leadership in Indonesia may prove more illuminating instead. Indeed, Stephen Skowronek has shown how a longitudinal analysis of presidential leadership in the United States reveals striking patterns suggestive of structural logics exceeding the personal foibles and fortes of individual national executives.

> Certainly it is no accident that the presidents most widely celebrated for their mastery of American politics have been immediately preceded by presidents generally judged politically incompetent. John Adams and Thomas Jefferson, John Quincy Adams and Andrew Jackson, James Buchanan and Abraham Lincoln, Herbert Hoover and Franklin Roosevelt, Jimmy Carter and Ronald Reagan—this repeated pairing of dismal failure with stunning success is one of the more striking patterns in presidential history, and accounting for it forces us to alter the ways we have been thinking about that history. In the first place, we are prompted to think about what incumbents in very different historical periods have in common with one another and not with their immediate predecessors or successors. What conditions for leadership did the latter presidents in each of these pairs share; what could they do that their predecessors could not? Conversely, what conditions for leadership did the first presidents in each pair share; what did they do to open the door to greatness for their successors?
>
> Note further that by accounting for the pattern in this way, we place the leaders themselves in a different light. A search for the typical effects that presidential action has in differently structured political contexts takes us behind the familiar portraits of individual incompetence and mastery. If it turns out that the 'great' political leaders have all made the same kind of politics and if that politics is only made in a certain kind of situation, then our celebration of their extraordinary talents and skills will be seen to obscure more than it clarifies (Skowronek 1997: 8–9).

But while Skowronek could identify recurring patterns over more than 200 years and 40-odd presidents in the American context of uninterrupted institutional continuity, it is hard to see the intellectual benefits of a comparison among six presidents so varied in terms of style, substance and circumstances of rule in Indonesia over the tumultuous 70 years of dramatic change since independence in 1945. How then can we think comparatively about presidential leadership in Indonesia in a way that helps to illuminate the Yudhoyono era?

Here, a comparative historical perspective on democratisation across Southeast Asia may prove more illuminating than a narrowly Indonesia-centric view. For much as Skowronek was struck by the recurring pairings of presidential losers and winners in American history, observers of political change across Southeast Asia since the 1970s are likely to have experienced a sense of *déjà vu* as they witnessed the ascendance and entrenchment of Susilo Bambang Yudhoyono in the early years of the twenty-first century. In particular, Yudhoyono's decade-long presidency (2004–14) recalls the eight-year prime-ministerial stint of Prem Tinsulanonda in Thailand (1980–88) and the six-year presidency of Fidel V. Ramos in the Philippines (1992–98). In all three countries that have experienced transitions from authoritarian rule to democracy in Southeast Asia, we find striking parallels in the profiles of national executives at similar stages of political transformation.

This chapter is offered as a complement and corrective to analyses of Yudhoyono's two-term presidency that focus on presidential leadership in narrowly individualistic terms. I argue that the style and substance of Yudhoyono's personal leadership and the long-term significance of his presidency can be further illuminated through a more comparative, historical and structural mode of analysis. By highlighting parallels between the Yudhoyono era and earlier periods in the recent histories of Thailand and the Philippines, this chapter suggests a new way of understanding the Yudhoyono years. Like his counterparts in Thailand and the Philippines, Yudhoyono should be understood as deeply implicated in conservative efforts to constrain the nature and extent of political change during the transition from authoritarian rule to democracy. As with corresponding periods in recent Thai and Philippine history, the Yudhoyono era should be viewed as a period during which underlying structural problems and tensions in Indonesian society and politics were sublimated and suppressed, deferring and distorting tensions and conflicts that have already begun to emerge and escalate in the early post-Yudhoyono era.

In developing this argument, the chapter first provides an overview of the parallels between the Prem, Ramos and Yudhoyono periods, highlighting the similar political profiles of these three 'men on horseback' (Finer 2002) and the regimes over which they presided.[1] It then deals

---

1 First published in 1962, Finer's book has long served as a foundational text for academic study of the role of the military in modern politics. Hence the allusion in the title of this chapter.

with the 'droppings' they left behind: underlying social tensions, escalating political conflict and resurfacing challenges to the parameters of democracy. The chapter concludes by reconsidering the Prem, Ramos and Yudhoyono periods as preludes to significant political upheaval in Thailand, the Philippines and Indonesia, much as the tumultuous late 1960s and early 1970s followed the 'Era of Good Feeling' under Eisenhower and a period of apparent political consensus under Kennedy and Johnson in the United States in the 1950s and early–mid 1960s.

THREE MEN ON HORSEBACK: PREM, RAMOS, YUDHOYONO

The parallels between Thailand's Prem in the 1980s, the Philippines' Ramos in the 1990s and Indonesia's Yudhoyono over the past decade are manifold. In all three cases, we find recently retired (or retiring) senior military officers serving out lengthy terms in office, having dominated national politics for the better part of a decade and enjoying continuing influence for years to come. In all three cases, we find that these former army generals enjoyed largely cooperative and consensual relations with national legislatures, fairly consistent popular appeal among the electorate at large and abiding support from powerful international audiences and institutions, their democratic credentials seemingly confirmed by both their conduct in office and their willingness to cede power to unanointed successors. In all three cases, these national executives were acknowledged and applauded not only as protectors of constitutional rule, but also as promoters of economic development and avowed supporters of initiatives broadly understood under the rubric of 'reform'. In all three cases, moreover, the rise to power of 'professional soldiers' was widely celebrated as a welcome relief from the more divisive and 'dirty' forms of politics that preceded their administrations, and in all three cases, their departures from power were met in many quarters with a measure of regret or disquiet.

Overall, then, looking at the three countries in Southeast Asia where transitions from authoritarianism to democracy have unfolded, it seems that there is invariably a phase of democratisation that involves a protracted period of rule by a consensus-oriented, avowedly reformist and internationally credible ex-general such as Prem, Ramos or Yudhoyono. Thus, we might conclude that if Burma were to continue along a trajectory of democratisation in the years ahead, we should expect a presidency along similar lines in due course. In the Indonesian case, therefore, the Yudhoyono presidency was not an idiosyncratic historical contingency. If Yudhoyono didn't exist, we would have had to invent him, or some other retired army general, to fit the structural niche that he occupied in Indonesia's ongoing political transformation between 2004 and 2014.

How can we explain this pattern, understand it historically and appreciate its meaning and significance? In all three cases, the broader historical context within which these professional soldiers or 'men on horseback' emerged, ascended and entrenched themselves was one of protracted authoritarian rule—a succession of military-led governments in Thailand from 1947 to 1973, Marcos's martial law regime in the Philippines from 1972 to 1986, and the Suharto dictatorship from 1966 to 1998. Under all of these authoritarian regimes, the armed forces occupied key positions in national and local politics, enjoying considerable insulation from civilian oversight and impunity with regard to the commission of large-scale human rights abuses. In all three cases, moreover, the *raison d'être* of the armed forces was not external defence, but rather internal security, defined in ways that helped to circumscribe opposition to authoritarian rule. Thus, crucially, in all three cases, transitions from authoritarian rule to democracy necessitated the emergence and activism—and the disaffection and defection—of senior military officers willing to engage with opposition forces, abstain from efforts to repress protests in the streets, and aid and abet in the forced removal of entrenched dictators and the often impromptu arrangements enabling transitions to democracy. Without General Krit Sivara's intervention in Bangkok in October 1973, without the coup attempt by the Reform the Armed Forces Movement (RAM) in Manila in February 1986 and, it is worth recalling, without Wiranto's quiet but effective role in Jakarta in May 1998, these transitions to democracy would not have unfolded—if not at all, then at least not in the remarkably orderly and peaceful manner in which they occurred (Lee 2014).

In all three cases, however, the seemingly progressive role of putative softliners in the military establishment during the fall of these dictatorships was soon complemented by the regressive role of assertive hardliners who worked to undermine if not overthrow early civilian-led transitional governments as they struggled to establish their authority. Avowedly concerned about security threats of various kinds and alarmed about the supposedly growing dangers of disorder and subversion that civilian rule and democracy allegedly enabled, senior military officers resisted efforts to reduce the insulation and impunity of the security forces, criticised civilian leaders for their policy failings and political leanings, and asserted their own prerogatives in terms of control over policy, personnel and political power. In all three cases, moreover, the early years following the fall of long-time authoritarian regimes witnessed forms of both violent and non-violent mobilisation that prompted armed interventions by the security forces, thus involving senior military officers in matters of internal security in ways that inevitably enhanced their public prominence and political authority. Finally, in all three cases these developments impelled vulnerable civilian leaders of transitional governments (Kukrit and Seni Pramoj in Thailand, Corazon Aquino in the Philippines, Abdurrahman Wahid in Indonesia) to forge alliances with senior military officers whose influence in the armed forces could potentially offset that of the hardliners and thus provide much-needed protection from military foot-dragging, mischief and coup attempts (and from civilian opposition as well).

Beyond the narrow logic of military involvement in the demise of dictatorships and the stabilisation of provisional civilian-led governments under conditions of ongoing transitions to democracy, there are other, broader parallels in the political and ideological transformations that helped set the stage for the rise of Prem in the late 1970s in Thailand, Ramos in the late 1980s and early 1990s in the Philippines, and Yudhoyono at the turn of the twenty-first century in Indonesia. The final years of authoritarian rule in Thailand, the Philippines and Indonesia had seen the emergence of independent oppositional forces in civil and political society that claimed to articulate the broad aspirations and grievances of the Thai, Filipino and Indonesian people against the narrowly personalistic interests of long-time dictators, their families and their cronies. But with the shift to civilian rule, competitive elections and unfettered media coverage of politics, such notions of unified electorates, universal interests and unselfinterested politicians inexorably faded away, even as the fractiousness of democratic politics and the failings of elected political figures inevitably came into sharp focus. Against this backdrop, in all three cases, a palpable sense of disillusionment led to a growing sense of nostalgia and yearning for something and someone above politics, a resurrection of that ideological notion of an Archimedean point, a 'view from nowhere' from which the national interest and the popular will could be represented, much as preceding authoritarian regimes had claimed to do.

At the same time, the transitions from authoritarian rule to democracy had effected a reconfiguration of what political scientists often simple-mindedly call 'state–society relations', altering pre-existing boundaries between state and society, expanding opportunities for state capture by powerful interests and undermining established notions of the state *qua* state. In all three cases, this development had also provoked a counter-reaction, with efforts made to reassert not just state power but also notions of stateness. In this vein, the cause of reform was most effectively championed not by figures and forces emanating from society, but by elements within the state itself, as seen in the pronounced trend towards the judicialisation of politics over the years following the initial transition from authoritarian rule to democracy in all three countries (Dressel 2012). Thus, while the political exigencies of the transitions to democracy required the services of softliner senior military officers to secure the ouster of entrenched dictators and counter the dangers posed by hardliners in the military establishment, the deeper, underlying tectonic shifts accompanying political change following the end of authoritarian rule continued to support the rise of professional soldiers or 'men on horseback' over subsequent years as well (Bungbongkarn 1986; Hedman 2001; Mietzner 2009).

It was in this context that the ascendancy of men like Prem, Ramos and Yudhoyono was not only possible but arguably inevitable. Indeed, their individual personal histories and public profiles fit to a tee the available roles and job descriptions of professional soldiers or 'men on horseback' outlined above. All three men literally grew up in the shadow of the state: Prem's father was a senior civil servant; Ramos's father helped found the Philippine Foreign Service; Yudhoyono's father was a low-ranking army officer. All three embarked on their military careers during periods of expanding roles for the armed forces in public life: Prem in the 1940s on the eve of the 1947 coup that ushered in more than 25 years of uninterrupted army rule; Ramos in 1950 amidst the counterinsurgency campaign against the Huks and Philippine involvement in the Korean War; Yudhoyono in 1973 against the backdrop of the consolidation of the Suharto regime and on the eve of the Indonesian invasion of East Timor. All three established their credentials in terms of combat and counter-insurgency operations: Prem in the northeast against the Communist Party of Thailand; Ramos in the campaign against the Huks and in the Korean War in the early 1950s, and as founder of the Special Forces in the early–mid 1960s; Yudhoyono with the Army Strategic Reserve Command (Komando Strategi Angkatan Darat, Kostrad) in East Timor.

But all three men were also drawn into roles that enhanced their contacts, prominence and presentational skills in arenas of civilian public life: Prem as a member of the legislature, aide-de-camp to King Bhumibol Adulyadej and deputy interior minister; Ramos as presidential assistant on military affairs and as vice chief-of-staff of the Philippine armed forces; Yudhoyono as a lecturer at the Army Staff and Command School, as personal assistant to armed forces commander-in-chief Edi Sudradjat and as chief-of-staff for social and political affairs. In the final years of authoritarian rule, all three found themselves in positions that enabled if not impelled them to mark some distance between themselves and the dictatorships they had long served: Prem was affiliated with General Krit Sivara rather than the entrenched duumvirate of Thanom Kittikachorn and Praphat Charusathian in 1973, and he was safely 'up-country' and thus not directly involved in the violence in Bangkok leading up to the coup of October 1976; Ramos served as vice chief-of-staff and then acting chief-of-staff in the early–mid 1980s, when real power rested with Marcos's cousin, Chief-of-Staff General Fabian Ver; and Yudhoyono's links to

Edi Sudradjat (who was sidelined in 1993) disqualified him from sensitive army command positions in Jakarta in the final years of Suharto's rule.[2]

Hence, all three men were well positioned and well suited to play crucial roles as softliners during the critical years of transition from authoritarian rule to democracy. They were all consummate insiders with seemingly impeccable credentials as professional soldiers within the military establishment, yet they also conveniently occupied 'safe' positions outside the line of command of coup-making colonels and generals. Prem had commanded the 2nd Army Division in the distant northeast rather than the coup-prone 1st Army Division in Bangkok; Ramos had long occupied an essentially ceremonial post; Yudhoyono's position as chief-of-staff for social and political affairs left him with oversight of the military's contingent in the legislature during the student demonstrations of February and March 1998, rather than command over boots on the ground. As paper-pushers, parliamentarians and pretty faces for the military establishment, these three men had more to gain from a gradually stage-managed disengagement of the armed forces from politics than from a full-blown *coup d'état*.

Consequently, all three men attracted the support of key civilian figures in national politics during the transitional periods when more assertive, aggressive and adventurous officers undertook or threatened efforts to seize power directly, or otherwise tried to consolidate effective power as military strongmen. Prem was recruited as prime minister as an effective palliative and alternative to the coup-prone 'Young Turks' and 'Democratic Soldiers' in the Thai military. Ramos, for his part, provided a bulwark of support for Corazon Aquino against a succession of coup attempts launched by Marcos loyalists and RAM officers backed by Defence Minister Juan Ponce Enrile. Yudhoyono was drawn into Wahid's cabinet in 1999 as a counterweight to the more conservative Wiranto, and was enlisted in Wahid's manoeuvres to dislodge Wiranto from his position of pre-eminence within the military establishment. As coordinating minister for political and security affairs under Megawati (2001–04), he counterbalanced the influence of ultraconservative army chief-of-staff Ryamizard Ryacudu in the conduct of military operations in Aceh and elsewhere. In all three cases, these men appeared to serve their patrons in an unselfinterested, inconspicuous and self-effacing manner, unless and until their patron stood in the way of their ascendancy to higher office. Therefore, Prem won strong backing from King Bhumibol and Queen Sirikit throughout the 1980s; Ramos was grudgingly anointed by Aquino as her successor in 1992; and Yudhoyono eventually fell out with Mega-

---

2   For biographical details of these three leaders, see the hagiographical accounts by Warren (1997), Crisostomo (1997), Purwadi (2004) and Hisyam (2004).

wati only in the months leading up to the 2004 presidential election, in which he would beat her in a landslide.

In all three cases, these 'men on horseback' presented themselves as consensus candidates behind whom diverse business and political interests could unite, forging coalition governments and adopting a style of leadership variously celebrated as 'consultative' and derided as 'indecisive'. With prominent civilian figures disqualified, discredited or defined by overly narrow partisan interests, these professional soldiers presented themselves as honest brokers for diverse interests, who in turn deemed them safe bets in elections, bankrolled their campaigns and otherwise bandwagoned behind their ascendancy and entrenchment in office. Prem, Ramos and Yudhoyono reconciled former enemies and recruited into their administrations major representatives from business and finance, old military associates and machine politicians as key cabinet ministers, heads of state agencies and personal advisors. They pursued fairly conventional macroeconomic policies that enabled economic growth and won qualified praise from local business communities, international financial institutions, foreign investors and the bond markets. They pursued ceasefires, amnesties and peace deals to settle armed insurgencies within national borders while improving their countries' international profiles and strengthening relations with the sole remaining global superpower, the United States.

Living up to their reputations as softliners, Prem, Ramos and Yudhoyono paid lip-service to the cause of 'reform' without disrupting the status quo. In sharp contrast to the fragmentation and fractiousness, and the conflict and drama, of preceding prime ministers' and presidents' terms in office, these three 'men on horseback' represented re-equilibration, restabilisation, reconciliation and a measure of recentralisation of power under the veneer of a seemingly more professional and less political form of national leadership. In an era of globalisation and democratisation, these three former military officers thus appeared if not as knights in shining armour, then as officers and gentlemen who could combine the Feithian functions of both problem-solvers *and* solidarity-makers in ways that none of their predecessors had managed to do.[3]

DROPPINGS: THE LEGACIES OF THE MEN ON HORSEBACK

As the terms in office of these professional soldiers drew to a close, it quickly became apparent that the legacies of their years in power

---

3   For a careful chronicling of these manoeuvres in the ascent of Yudhoyono, see Mietzner (2009).

included deep-seated socio-political conflicts and problems that not only had remained essentially unresolved but had been exacerbated to the point of virtual crisis. In Thailand, Prem's eight years in office were followed by the short-lived, scandal-ridden premiership of Chatichai Choonhavan, who was overthrown in a coup in February 1991, only to be followed by a succession of similarly ephemeral governments that set the stage for the economic crisis of 1997–98 (Ockey 1994, 2001). In the Philippines, Ramos was succeeded as president in 1998 by Joseph 'Erap' Estrada, whose quasi-populist appeal failed to save him from corruption scandals, urban middle-class protests, impeachment proceedings and a 'People Power' rebellion that led to his ouster in January 2001 and the equally problematic nine-year presidency of Gloria Macapagal-Arroyo (Hedman 2006). In Indonesia, the 2014 elections proved to be extremely divisive, narrowly averting a Prabowo presidency and portending more conflict in the years ahead, if post-Prem Thailand and the post-Ramos Philippines provide any hints as to Indonesia's post-Yudhoyono future.

How can we explain the seemingly sudden (re)irruption of conflict in the early aftermath of these placid periods of ostensibly stabilised, consensual politics under Southeast Asia's softline generals? In mid-2014, the temptation was to reach for the readily available language of idiosyncratic individual leadership and express relief that Indonesia's new president, Jokowi, would be neither as venal as Chatichai, nor as habitually inebriated as Estrada, nor as hot-tempered and violence-prone as Prabowo. But if personality, as F. Scott Fitzgerald famously quipped, is merely 'an unbroken series of successful gestures', then the success and sustainability of political personality and leadership rest on the broader contexts within which they are embedded.

We therefore need to step back and consider the shared contexts within which our 'men on horseback' emerged, ascended and entrenched themselves in power. As many scholars have argued, the polities that crystallised in Thailand, the Philippines and Indonesia in the Prem, Ramos and Yudhoyono eras were (and, with the exception of Thailand, still are) oligarchical democracies, in the sense that competitive elections are embedded within societies characterised by glaring social inequalities, exceptionally easy access for businesspeople and bankers to state power, and the endemic use of elective offices as bases for personal pecuniary advancement. Yet over the years, these oligarchical democracies have experienced significant change, with established modes of voter mobilisation and interest aggregation increasingly attenuated in the face of demographic trends, the expanding circuitries of the mass media and the rise of public opinion (Hedman 2010). The general trends in these polities seem clear: they have witnessed increasingly direct forms of popular and quasi-populist political appeals to the electorate—what some call 'political branding' (Pasotti 2010) — rather than narrowly machine-based forms of voter mobilisation; anti-corruption campaigns; and efforts to expand the provision of subsistence guarantees and improve access to public education and health care. In other words, in Thailand, the Philippines and Indonesia, we have seen the crystallisation and (except, it seems, in Thailand) consolidation of democracies that are both oligarchical and contested (Quimpo 2008; Walker 2012; Ford and Pepinsky 2014). Invariably, the disjunctures haunting these democracies have given rise to contestation over the meanings and parameters of democratic citizenship — a trend also evident in the oligarchical, contested democracies of Latin America (Caldeira 2000; Holston 2008).

Accordingly, we might reconsider the prevailing contemporaneous and retrospective understandings of Prem, Ramos and Yudhoyono as simply occupying the moderate centre ground and embodying the natural 'new normal' of democratic politics in Thailand, the Philippines and Indonesia, against which oddball outliers — Thaksin Shinawatra, Joseph Estrada, Subianto Prabowo — should be distinguished (and, indeed, defended). For the oligarchical foundations (and the terms of contestation) of democracy in these three Southeast Asian countries were secured through the effective, if artificial, disqualification or dislodging of left-wing movements and parties from the positions in society and roles in democracy that they had previously struggled to attain.

In Thailand, the gradual, fitful shift to parliamentary democracy that unfolded over the 1970s, 1980s and 1990s proceeded only once the left-wing forces that mobilised between 1973 and 1976 (and that were forced to join the Communist Party of Thailand after the violent military coup and crackdown of 1976) had been marginalised from political life (Haberkorn 2011; Lertchoosakul 2012). In the Philippines, the consolidation of democracy in the late 1980s and early 1990s transpired alongside the US-backed anti-communist vigilante campaign and counterinsurgency effort that drastically reduced the considerable strength of the Communist Party of the Philippines (CPP), of its military wing, the New People's Army (NPA), and of the allied labour, peasant, urban poor and student organisations in the countryside and the cities (Lawyers Committee for Human Rights 1988; May 1992). In Indonesia, the transition from authoritarian rule to democracy unfolded after 1998 without official recrimination, or reversal, of the anti-communist pogroms of 1965-66 and the manifold restrictions on political activities associated, however tangentially, with the long-banned Indonesian Communist Party (Partai Komunis Indonesia, PKI) (Heryanto 2006). Even the one party with residual traces of a left-wing mass-mobilisational repertoire in 1998-99 — Megawati's Indonesian Democratic Party of Struggle (Partai Demokrasi Indonesia-Perjuangan, PDIP) — was rendered suitably safe for Indonesian democracy by the recruitment into its ranks of conservative machine politicians, businesspeople and retired army officers (Ziv 2001; Mietzner 2012). In all three countries, left-wing parties were, at best, effectively relegated to marginal positions in electoral politics, and leftist organisations and activists were confined to minor, supporting roles in public life. Thailand, the Philippines and Indonesia, it was clear, were only safe for democracy if and when communist parties and serious left-wing politics were — forcibly, violently — excluded from the realm of the politically possible.

In all three cases, our proverbial 'men on horseback' were profoundly implicated in the violent suppression and evisceration of left-wing movements, parties and politics. To begin with, Prem led counterinsurgency operations in the northeast as the deputy commander and then commander of the 2nd Army Division. He subsequently acquiesced in the right-wing military coup and violent crackdown of October 1976, and he incorporated into his administration military and civilian elements who had been prominently involved in atrocities against left-wing activists. Ramos, for his part, participated in the anti-Huk counterinsurgency campaign in the early 1950s, founded the Special Forces, acquiesced in Marcos's proclamation of martial law in 1972, and supervised the mobilisation of anti-communist vigilantes and the counterinsurgency campaign that decimated the CPP–NPA as well as its allied front organisations in the latter half of the 1980s. While Yudhoyono himself was not directly involved in military operations against the Indonesian left, his famous father-in-law, Lieutenant-General Sarwo Edhie Wibowo, had played a crucial role in the anti-communist pogroms of 1965–66. As commander of the precursor to the Special Forces, Sarwo Edhie had led anti-communist operations in the crucial PKI stronghold region of Central Java, where tens of thousands of PKI activists were butchered (Jenkins and Kammen 2012). In other words, all three of our 'men on horseback' were closely associated with the suppression of left-wing political movements and parties, and clearly endorsed the use of violence to effect the elimination of the left from the political field.

In this regard and more generally, these three 'men on horseback' were profoundly shaped by the Cold War and by the efforts of the US national security state to maintain American hegemony in Southeast Asia. Prem's military career in Thailand was dramatically enhanced by the scholarship he won to study at Fort Knox and by his subsequent years of service as an instructor in the US Military Assistance Program. As deputy commander and then commander of the 2nd Army Division in northeast Thailand, he was intimately involved in the implementation of American counterinsurgency doctrine against the Communist Party of Thailand and in US covert operations across the border in neighbouring

Laos. Similarly, Ramos's army career began after his graduation from the US Military Academy at West Point, with service in anti-Huk counterinsurgency operations in Central Luzon under the guidance of the legendary CIA officer Colonel Edward Lansdale and the Joint US Military Assistance Group. Moreover, he served in the Philippine contingents in the Korean War and the Vietnam War. In the early–mid 1980s, his close relations with the US Embassy earned him a widespread reputation as an 'Amboy', and in the late 1980s he closely coordinated with American intelligence and military agencies while overseeing counterinsurgency operations and the broader anti-communist campaign as armed forces chief-of-staff and secretary of national defence. Finally, Yudhoyono's career in the Indonesian armed forces was distinguished by early, extensive and recurring stints of training at various US military facilities, such as Fort Benning in the 1970s and Fort Leavenworth in the 1980s and early 1990s. Consequently, all three 'men on horseback' were deeply imbued with distinctly American, Cold War conceptions of what it meant to be a professional soldier.

In short, the era of the 'man on horseback' in Thailand in the 1980s, the Philippines in the 1990s and Indonesia in 2004–14 has in each and every case represented the ascendancy of US-trained anti-communist 'Cold Warriors'. The representation of these three professional soldiers as honest brokers, moderate centrists and consensus-builders has thus masked both their acquiescence and their active involvement in the violent elimination of left-wing movements and parties. Equally, it has camouflaged their historical roles in the construction, preservation and legitimation of narrowly construed, deeply conservative forms of democracy in Thailand, the Philippines and Indonesia. In the 1970s and 1980s (and in various ways since that time), Prem worked to create a form of politics in Thailand in which parliamentary politics would be dominated by provincial businesspeople and Bangkok-based bankers, the economy would be opened to foreign investment and organised around export-oriented industrialisation and agro-business production, and the military, national security and foreign relations would continue to be insulated from civilian interference. In the late 1980s and 1990s, Ramos similarly strove to secure the reconstitution of oligarchical democracy and to promote economic liberalisation in the Philippines. At the same time, he actively supported suppression of the countervailing power and policy critiques articulated by the activists and organisations of the left. In the early twenty-first century, Yudhoyono likewise played a crucial role in the consolidation of an Indonesian democracy in which powerful banking, business, civilian and military interests from the Suharto era were successfully preserved and promoted under democratic auspices (Hadiz and Robison 2014). Pressures for reform, therefore, were largely left unheeded and challenges from below kept at bay. In other words, all of these 'men on horseback' rode into power not simply as part of a natural process of selection, in which the failings and foibles of fickle, factionalised civilian politicians left power, willy-nilly and by default, in the hands of professional soldiers, but also as part of the active construction of artificial, undemocratic and in some measure American-style, externally imposed constraints on the very parameters of democracy itself.

Viewed from this perspective, we can make much more sense of the problematic legacies of the eras of the 'men on horseback' in Southeast Asia and the otherwise seemingly odd and inexplicable (re)lapse into open political conflict in Thailand, the Philippines and Indonesia as these three horsemen rode off into the proverbial sunset, in 1988, 1998 and 2014 respectively. After all, if in all of these democracies left-wing movements and parties, unions, peasant movements and urban poor groups have been effectively excluded or marginalised from the field of politics, then we should hardly be surprised when calls for a more equitable redistribution of the fruits of growth and counterhegemonic challenges to the established parties and entrenched interests of administrations such as those of Prem, Ramos and Yudhoyono inevitably surface in other, putatively populist forms. When the champions of such countervailing power are avaricious businesspeople, alcoholic action-film stars or psychotic ex-army officers, it is easy to demonise and deride their emergence and appeal as evidence of irrational pathologies among the population at large, in the face of the eminently reasonable likes of Prem, Ramos and Yudhoyono. But a proper aetiology of the problem suggests that it was the very construction of artificially constrained forms of democracy—by these 'men on horseback'—that explains the strange symptoms represented by a Thaksin, an Estrada or indeed a Prabowo in the first place. The pathology, then, lies in the very normality effected and embodied by the likes of Prem, Ramos and Yudhoyono, and in the political displacements and distortions this normality has produced. Prabowo may have lost the 2014 election, but Indonesia will remain haunted for years to come, if not by Prabowo then by what he represents—and for this Indonesians have the likes of Yudhoyono to thank and blame.

CONCLUSION

What can we conclude at this juncture with regard to the significance and legacy of the Yudhoyono era? Viewed in comparative perspective, Yudhoyono's substantive, structural achievements seem essentially nugatory. Prem, it must be noted, helped to oversee structural adjustment and a shift to export-oriented industrialisation amidst the global recession of the early–mid 1980s (Doner and Laothamatas 1994). In a similar vein, Ramos successfully promoted banking and tax reform, and the partial opening of telecommunications and interisland shipping, in an era of global financial and trade liberalisation (Hutchcroft 1998: 206–31; Austria 2003; Salazar 2007). Yudhoyono, by contrast, oversaw stagnation in Indonesian manufacturing while banking heavily on a commodities boom (World Bank 2010; Rahardja and Winkler 2012). In political terms, he also defended the status quo rather than initiating structural reforms. Like observers speaking of China's years of rapid economic growth but political stagnation under Hu Jintao and Wen Jiabao (Johnson 2012), we might speak today of a 'lost decade' in Indonesia under Yudhoyono.

But in years to come, we may view the Yudhoyono period in a somewhat different light—if not as the calm before the storm, then as a prelude to, or part of a process of, political change. Democratisation, after all, is a process in which conflict serves as catalyst, as seen in the repeatedly cyclical pattern of crisis, reform and re-equilibration in the Philippines in the nearly six decades since independence. Arguably, similar dynamics are still unfolding in Thailand, as reflected in a striking zig-zag pattern of expanding and contracting electoralisation of state power in the country. Thus, the era of apparent consensus under a 'man on horseback' represents if not an illusion then a sublimation and deferral of the inevitable return of the repressed. Democracy, it needs to be said, is not about consensus; it is about the management of conflict through electoral competition. The win–lose, zero-sum logic inherent in democratic politics inexorably produces not only regression towards the mean but also opportunistic outbidding as politicians and parties work to respond to and reinforce existing cleavages and tensions in society. As Rick Perlstein notes in the second of his epic, multi-volume study of the rise of the conservative movement in American politics:

> Politicians, always reading the cultural winds, make their life's work convincing 50 percent plus one of their constituency that they understand their fears and hopes, can honor and redeem them, can make them safe and lead them toward their dreams (Perlstein 2008: xi–xii).[4]

Perlstein chronicles the 'unmaking of consensus' and the 'fracturing of America' in the years following the 'Era of Good Feeling' under the two-term presidency of the professional soldier par excellence, Dwight D. Eisenhower (1952–60). He shows how deepening tensions and conflicts in American society and politics in the 1960s enabled the rise of

---

4 Perlstein's study begins by tracing the rise of Barry Goldwater in the 1950s and continues beyond Nixon (Perlstein 2001, 2008). His most recently published volume covers the rise of Ronald Reagan to national prominence over the course of the 1970s (Perlstein 2014).

that awkward oddball and perennial loser, Richard Nixon, to the presidency in 1968 after a succession of political defeats and humiliations. It was, Perlstein suggests, precisely Nixon's embitterment, sense of entitlement and outsider status that eventually enabled so many Americans to identify themselves with him amidst the controversies and cleavages opened up by the civil rights movement, the Vietnam War and the rise of the counterculture during the 1960s. Perlstein thus calls the America that Nixon inherited and oversaw during his presidency 'Nixonland':

> [I]t is the America where two separate and irreconcilable sets of apocalyptic fears coexist in the minds of two separate and irreconcilable groups of Americans. ... 'Nixonland' is what happens when these two groups try to occupy a country together. By the end of the 1960s, Nixonland came to encompass the entire political culture of the United States. It would define it, in fact, for the next fifty years (Perlstein 2008: 46–7).

Leaving aside the implications of Thai, Philippine and American parallels and precedents for a moment, it might be tempting to view — in isolated, idiosyncratic terms — the election of Joko Widodo to the Indonesian presidency in July 2014 as a basis for unbridled optimism about the country's future. In sharp contrast to Prabowo, after all, Jokowi embodies many of the most promising features of development and democratisation in Indonesian society and politics: private, small-scale, productive entrepreneurship rather than monopoly capital and natural resource extraction; origins in local society and experience with decentralised governance; distance from the New Order era, the military establishment and the 'deep state', as well as the so-called party cartels of the post-Suharto period; an ecumenical approach to the role of religion in society and politics; and reliance on popular appeal rather than machine-based forms of voter mobilisation.

Thankfully, in historical terms, Jokowi in 2014 compares favourably to Chatichai in 1988 and Estrada in 1998, in being an eminently more worthy successor to Indonesia's 'man on horseback'. Indeed, Jokowi is a breath of fresh air in Indonesian politics akin to that ascribed to John F. Kennedy when he succeeded America's professional soldier par excellence Dwight D. Eisenhower to the presidency in January 1961, having narrowly defeated Richard Nixon at the preceding election. But we should consider the implications of both Perlstein's account of the post-Eisenhower years in America and the pattern of politics following the 'men on horseback' in nearby Thailand and the Philippines. Someday in the not-too-distant future, Indonesians may find themselves living in 'Prabowo-land'. If so, at least in part, they will have their 'man on horseback' to blame.

REFERENCES

Austria, M.S. (2003) *Philippine Domestic Shipping Transport Industry: State of Competition and Market Structure*, Philippine Institute for Development Studies, Makati City.
Bungbongkarn, S. (1986) *The Military in Thai Politics, 1981–86*, Institute of Southeast Asian Studies, Singapore.
Caldeira, T.P.R. (2000) *City of Walls: Crime, Segregation, and Citizenship in São Paulo*, University of California Press, Berkeley CA.
Crisostomo, I.T. (1997) *President Fidel V. Ramos: Builder, Reformer, Peacemaker*, J. Kriz Publishing Enterprises, Quezon City.
Doner, R.F. and A. Laothamatas (1994) 'The political economy of structural adjustment in Thailand', in S. Haggard and S. Webb (eds) *Voting for Reform: Democracy, Political Liberalization, and Economic Adjustment*, Oxford University Press, Oxford: 411–52.
Dressel, B. (ed.) (2012) *The Judicialization of Politics in Asia*, Routledge, Abingdon and New York.
Feith, H. (1962) *The Decline of Constitutional Democracy in Indonesia*, Cornell University Press, Ithaca NY.
Finer, S.E. (2002) *The Man on Horseback: The Role of the Military in Politics*, revised edition, Transaction Publishers, New Brunswick, NJ.
Ford, M. and T.S. Pepinsky (eds) (2014) *Beyond Oligarchy: Wealthy, Power, and Contemporary Indonesian Politics*, Cornell University Southeast Asia Program Publications, Ithaca NY.
Grindle, M.S. (2007) *Going Local: Decentralization, Democratization, and the Promise of Good Governance*, Princeton University Press, Princeton NJ.
Haberkorn, T. (2011) *Revolution Interrupted: Farmers, Students, Law, and Violence in Northern Thailand*, University of Wisconsin Press, Madison WI.
Hadiz, V.R. and R. Robison (2014) 'The political economy of oligarchy and the reorganization of power in Indonesia', in M. Ford and T.B. Pepinsky (eds) *Beyond Oligarchy: Wealth, Power, and Contemporary Indonesian Politics*, Cornell University Southeast Asia Program Publications, Ithaca NY.
Hedman, E.-L. (2001) 'The Philippines: not so military, not so civilian', in M. Alagappa (ed.) *Coercion and Governance: The Declining Political Role of the Military in Asia*, Stanford University Press, Stanford CA: 165–86.
Hedman, E.-L. (2006) *In the Name of Civil Society: From Free Election Movements to People Power in the Philippines*, University of Hawaii Press, Honolulu: 167–76.
Hedman, E.-L. (2010) 'The politics of "public opinion" in the Philippines', *Journal of Current Southeast Asian Affairs*, 4(1–2): 97–118.
Heryanto, A. (2006) *State Terrorism and Political Identity in Indonesia: Fatally Belonging*, Routledge, London.
Hisyam, U. (ed.) (2004) *SBY: Sang Demokrat* [SBY: The Democrat], Penerbitan Dharmapena, Jakarta.
Holston, J. (2008) *Insurgent Citizenship: Disjunctions of Democracy and Modernity in Brazil*, Princeton University Press, Princeton NJ.
Hutchcroft, P.D. (1998) *Booty Capitalism: The Politics of Banking in the Philippines*, Cornell University Press, Ithaca NY.
Jenkins, D. and D. Kammen (2012) 'The Army Para-commando Regiment and the reign of terror in Central Java and Bali', in D. Kammen and K. McGregor (eds) *The Contours of Mass Violence in Indonesia, 1965–68*, NUS Press, Singapore: 75–103.
Johnson, I. (2012) 'China's lost decade', *New York Review of Books*, 27 September.

Lawyers Committee for Human Rights (1988) *Vigilantes in the Philippines: A Threat to Democratic Rule*, New York.
Lee, T. (2014) *Defect or Defend? Military Responses to Popular Protests in Authoritarian Asia*, Johns Hopkins University Press, Baltimore MD.
Lertchoosakul, L. (2012) 'The rise of the Octobrists: power and conflict among former left wing student activists in contemporary Thai politics', PhD thesis, London School of Economics and Political Science, London.
Liddle, R.W. (1996) *Leadership and Culture in Indonesian Politics*, Allen & Unwin, Sydney.
May, R.J. (1992) *Vigilantes in the Philippines: From Fanatical Cults to Citizens' Organizations*, Center for Philippine Studies, University of Hawaii, Honolulu.
Mietzner, M. (2009) *Military Politics, Islam, and the State in Indonesia: From Turbulent Transition to Democratic Consolidation*, Institute of Southeast Asian Studies, Singapore.
Mietzner, M. (2012) 'Ideology, money, and dynastic leadership: the Indonesian Democratic Party of Struggle, 1998–2012', *South East Asia Research*, 20(4): 511–31.
Mietzner, M. (2014) 'Indonesia's 2014 elections: how Jokowi won and democracy survived', *Journal of Democracy*, 25(4): 111–25.
Ockey, J. (1994) 'Political parties, factions, and corruption in Thailand', *Modern Asian Studies*, 28(2): 251–77.
Ockey, J. (2001) 'Thailand: the struggle to redefine civil–military relations', in M. Alagappa (ed.) *Coercion and Governance: The Declining Role of the Military in Asia*, Stanford University Press, Stanford CA: 187–208.
Pasotti, E. (2010) *Political Branding in Cities: The Decline of Machine Politics in Bogotá, Naples, and Chicago*, Cambridge University Press, New York.
Perlstein, R. (2001) *Before the Storm: Barry Goldwater and the Unmaking of the American Consensus*, Hill and Wang, New York.
Perlstein, R. (2008) *Nixonland: The Rise of a President and the Fracturing of America*, Scribner, New York.
Perlstein, R. (2014) *The Invisible Bridge: The Fall of Nixon and the Rise of Reagan*, Simon and Schuster, New York.
Purwadi (2004) *Wahyu Keprabon: Susilo Bambang Yudhoyono, Sang Piningit dari Pacitan* [Radiance of the Throne: Susilo Bambang Yudhoyono, the Noble Knight from Pacitan], Gelombang Pasang, Yogyakarta.
Quimpo, N.G. (2008) *Contested Democracy and the Left in the Philippines after Marcos*, Ateneo de Manila University Press, Quezon City.
Rahardja, S. and D. Winkler (2012) *Why the Manufacturing Sector Still Matters for Growth and Development in Indonesia*, World Bank Office, Jakarta.
Salazar, L.C. (2007) *Getting a Dial Tone: Telecommunications Liberalization in Malaysia and the Philippines*, Institute for Southeast Asian Studies, Singapore.
Skowronek, S. (1997) *The Politics Presidents Make: Leadership from John Adams to Bill Clinton*, Harvard University Press, Cambridge MA.
Walker, A. (2012) *Thailand's Political Peasants: Power in the Modern Rural Economy*, University of Wisconsin Press, Madison WI.
Warren, W. (1997) *Prem Tinsulanonda: Soldier and Statesman*, Eastern Printing, Bangkok.
World Bank (2010) 'Boom, bust, and up again? Evolution, drivers, and impact of commodity prices: implications for Indonesia', World Bank Office, Jakarta, December.
Ziv, D. (2001) 'Populist perceptions and perceptions of populism in Indonesia: the case of Megawati Soekarnoputri', *South East Asia Research*, 9(1): 73–88.

5 Yudhoyono's foreign policy: is Indonesia a rising power?

Evi Fitriani

When Susilo Bambang Yudhoyono became president of Indonesia in 2004, he took charge of a country whose international reputation had been shaped primarily by political instability, economic hardship and security threats such as terrorism and secessionism. In addition, Indonesia's foreign policy had been devastated by the separation of Timor-Leste and the loss of the Sipadan and Ligitan islands to Malaysia following a decision in the International Court of Justice in 2002. Restoring the country's badly tarnished image became a key priority of Yudhoyono's presidency. At the same time, he aspired for Indonesia to play a more prominent role in international organisations such as the United Nations, the G20 and ASEAN. By the time he left office in 2014, it appeared that Indonesia had indeed defied the inauspicious circumstances at the beginning of Yudhoyono's term in office and re-emerged as a respected player on the global map of international affairs. This remarkable transformation has prompted some observers to describe Indonesia as a rising or emerging power.

This chapter seeks to assess the merits of these claims and analyse Yudhoyono's role in shaping Indonesia's foreign policy during the ten years of his presidency, paying particular attention to an apparent paradox. On the one hand, Indonesia's growing international reputation as a rising or emerging power is often attributed to its successful democratisation and its image as a model Muslim democracy (Acharya 2014). Western governments in particular have not tired of praising Indonesia's achievements under Yudhoyono's leadership (Leahy 2014; Santi 2014). On the other hand, however, both the media and academic observers of Indonesian domestic politics have increasingly questioned whether the country really deserves this praise (Harsono 2012). In this chapter, I argue that this seeming paradox is explained in part by Yudhoyono's approach to foreign policy. As I will demonstrate, the president's personality heavily shaped Indonesia's approach to foreign affairs, especially during his second term when he made the narrative of a successful Muslim democracy a cornerstone of his foreign policy. Building on the appeal of this narrative, Yudhoyono brought Indonesia back into the community of nations, restoring its visibility in the eyes of the international community. It would be premature, however, to consider Indonesia a rising power.

A number of studies have examined Indonesian foreign policy under Yudhoyono. Tan (2007) and Novotny (2010) analysed the early years of his presidency, outlining the difficulty of navigating a fragile country through an era of significant global change. Others have highlighted how Yudhoyono took Indonesia closer to the United States by signing the United States–Indonesia Comprehensive Partnership and other, more specific agreements in 2010 (Murphy 2010; Stone 2010). Poole (2014) examined Yudhoyono's efforts to promote and project democratic identity through Indonesia's foreign policy. Most of the existing studies focus on particular foreign policy issues during Yudhoyono's presidency. This chapter aims to provide a more comprehensive assessment of Yudhoyono's foreign policy legacy and to enrich our understanding of the role of a country's leader in shaping contemporary international relations.

The chapter uses actor-specific theory to understand Yudhoyono's role in and contribution to Indonesia's foreign policy. Actor-specific theory helps us to study the processes and results of a leader's role in decision-making, the consequences of those decisions for foreign entities and the standing of the leader in his or her own country. In actor-specific theory, it is imperative to investigate the motivations, emotions and processes of problem representation of the leader. Hudson (2005: 6), for example, suggests looking at the 'psycho-milieu' around a leader to understand 'the international and operational environment or context as it is perceived and interpreted' during decision-making processes. The perceptions of a leader and of stakeholders may differ such that this creates differing expectations of foreign policy. At this critical juncture, a leader may opt for less satisfactory foreign policy choices (Hudson 2005: 6). Thus, actor-specific theory would prescribe close observation of the individual characteristics of a president such as Susilo Bambang Yudhoyono to understand the approaches to foreign policy he chose during his presidency.

This chapter evolves in five stages. The first section examines the notion that Indonesia is a rising power. The second focuses on Yudhoyono's foreign policy principle of making 'a million friends and zero enemies'. The third section summarises his key foreign policy achievements. This is followed by an analysis of the apparent disconnect between domestic and international assessments of those achievements. Finally, the article analyses the relationship between Yudhoyono's personality and Indonesia's foreign policy during his presidential term.

IS INDONESIA RISING?

In recent years it has become fashionable to describe Indonesia as a country on the rise. Various studies have discussed the peculiar facets of a rising Indonesia and the potential implications for regional and global politics (Laksmana 2011; Reid 2012; White 2013). President Yudhoyono and some Indonesians took pleasure in the notion that the country was rising, especially the prediction by Oberman et al. (2012) that Indonesia would become the world's seventh-largest economy by 2030. While the perception that Indonesia has become a middle power with the potential to play a more important role in international affairs is understandable, the idea that it is a rising power requires critical assessment.

In the international relations literature, a rising power is usually marked by steady growth in economic and military power. The rise and fall of great powers in world history shows that these two kinds of power, as well as political stability at home, are the essential ingredients for a country's position in the world to rise. Soft power in the form of appealing and widely accepted socio-cultural and political values is also often regarded as a key source of power held by rising states, as well as great powers and middle powers (Nye 2004). Thus, to establish whether Indonesia under Yudhoyono can be placed in the category of a rising power, we need to examine whether it had these attributes.

In terms of economic power, Indonesia did indeed progress steadily during the Yudhoyono years, with annual growth rates of around 5–6 per cent. This was not enough, however, to meet the country's need for infrastructure, research and innovation, and human development. As Hal Hill shows in Chapter 15 of this volume, economic growth over the last decade has been driven primarily by a commodity boom and domestic consumption rather than innovation and sustainable development. In short, although the economy has been growing steadily, to claim this as an indicator of a rising Indonesia is problematic in light of the numerous structural problems left untouched by Yudhoyono during his presidency.

Indonesia's military strength has also improved in the last few years, with an increase in the defence budget and the modernisation of defence equipment. But given the gap between what the country possesses in terms of military capability and what it needs to defend its vast territory, it is clear that the improvements have been far from sufficient. The navy still lacks the capacity to patrol the country's extensive maritime borders. During the Yudhoyono years, military vessels and illegal fishing boats from neighbouring countries repeatedly entered Indonesia's territorial waters without fear of being stopped or apprehended, especially in remote areas. Similarly, the air force has yet to develop sufficient fighter capability to guard Indonesia's vast air space. The state apparatus has also shown itself unable to halt the trafficking of drugs, arms, people and fuel across Indonesia's land and sea borders. Given the lack of military capability and the frequent failure to prevent foreign incursions into the country's territory, it seems inappropriate to call Indonesia a rising power.

Indonesia's ability to exercise soft power also remains limited. The country's successful democratic transition may have won the support of many Western leaders, but Indonesia still has little actual capacity to influence political developments beyond its borders or to serve as a model from which countries in ASEAN or the Arab world can learn about democratisation. It has become apparent that socio-political values such as a commitment to democracy, dialogue and peaceful transformation do not really matter when it comes to solving disputes in the South China Sea or resolving border conflicts between ASEAN states, not to mention advancing the prospects for a Palestinian state. Indonesia's limited resources clearly hinder the country's capacity to shape regional and global affairs (McRae 2014: 3).

In short, the notion that Indonesia is a rising power is not supported by the reality of a country that has limited economic and political influence. Although Indonesia has undergone significant processes of political transformation, economic development and military modernisation, it does not yet meet the criteria for a country on the rise. Nevertheless, the view that Indonesia is rising is widely shared and not entirely without reason. As the following section will show, Indonesia acquired a remarkably high global profile under Susilo Bambang Yudhoyono, not least because the president himself dedicated enormous energy to lifting Indonesia's international reputation, especially during his second term.

A MILLION FRIENDS AND ZERO ENEMIES

Perhaps the most distinctive phrase used by Yudhoyono to describe his approach to foreign policy was his principle of 'a million friends and zero enemies'. The president often propagated this principle during his overseas trips in a bid to endear Indonesia (and himself) to his hosts. In a speech before the Australian parliament in 2010, for example, he said: 'We are passionate about our independence, moderation, religious freedom and tolerance. And far from being hostile, we want to create a strategic environment marked by "a million friends and zero enemies"' (Yudhoyono 2010). Serious scholars of international relations would find this principle highly problematic in an anarchical world. In the real world, foreign policy cannot be constructed on an aspiration to remain friends with everyone, without ever taking sides. In fact, Yudhoyono's aspiration sometimes put him, and the country, in an awkward position when dealing with other international actors.

For example, as a key country in Southeast Asia and an important player in the Asia-Pacific, Indonesia was automatically dragged into the complicated relationship between China and the United States. The re-emergence of China as a power that (in contrast to Indonesia) clearly was rising and challenging US dominance forced Indonesia to be prudent in, as Yudhoyono liked to put it, 'navigating a turbulent ocean' (Tan 2007). While China's assertive territorial claims and unilateral occupation of disputed areas in the South China Sea prompted some countries in Southeast as well as Northeast Asia to strengthen their alliances with the United States (Goh 2013; Zheng and Lye 2013), Indonesia shied away from taking sides. Instead, driven by Yudhoyono's desire to make his country, and perhaps himself, more visible on the global stage, Indonesia sought to actively shape regional geopolitics and geo-economy through a hedging strategy that kept both great powers at an equal distance. According to Sukma (2012: 46), this strategy could be interpreted as a 'reflection of a sense of regional entitlement' that made Indonesia feel 'that it deserves to exercise a leading role in shaping not only the future course of ASEAN but also the directions of regional politics'.

Positioning Indonesia carefully on the global stage was challenging not just in relation to the rivalry between the United States and China; it also attracted scrutiny from some members of the Non-Aligned Movement (NAM), who quietly expressed their disappointment in the direction the country was taking. During the Sukarno and Suharto eras, Indonesia had been considered a leader in the developing world through its role in the NAM. Under Yudhoyono, however, the country appeared to be distancing itself from the NAM and instead engaging more actively with high-profile organisations such as the G20 that many NAM members regarded as representing the interests of the United States and other Western countries.

These were but two of the challenges faced by Indonesia in international affairs. They showed that Yudhoyono's dictum of having a million friends and zero enemies was somewhat naive. A far more acceptable principle would have been that foreign policy starts at home. During his first presidential term, Yudhoyono was mainly preoccupied with domestic politics, leaving international affairs primarily to the creativity and initiative of his first foreign minister, Hassan Wirajuda.

Domestically, Yudhoyono relied on the help of his vice-president, Jusuf Kalla, and others in the cabinet to strengthen the country's economy and handle conflicts in Aceh and Poso (Central Sulawesi). He also accepted the assistance of several foreign countries to tackle terrorism and pursue a policy of deradicalisation. The early Yudhoyono years were notable for the relative stability of communal relations between different religious and ethnic groups, despite the widespread violence in places such as Maluku and Kalimantan in the years preceding his election (van Klinken 2007). The fact that these communal tensions were brought under control and the country did not lose any additional territory after the separation of Timor-Leste also has to be credited to the Yudhoyono administration.

As the country became more stable the economy also revived, giving Yudhoyono another source of confidence. A World Bank report reviewing economic conditions in East Asia ten years after the Asian financial crisis included Indonesia in its list of success stories (World Bank 2007). When the global financial crisis hit the United States and the Euro zone in 2007–08, Indonesia was only mildly affected. By the time Yudhoyono's first term ended in 2009, few observers disputed that Indonesia was an exemplary case of successful political transformation from an authoritarian regime to a stable democracy. Moreover, Indonesia had shown that democracy could be developed in a Muslim-majority country, countering the widely held view that democracy and Islam were incompatible.

YUDHOYONO'S FOREIGN POLICY ACHIEVEMENTS

When Yudhoyono was re-elected in 2009, he used his domestic achievements as important underpinnings of his foreign policy. Determined to take advantage of Indonesia's image as a functioning Muslim democracy, he began to redefine the country's foreign policy priorities to move beyond the confines of ASEAN. While he pledged to continue to uphold the 'free and active' principle of foreign policy pursued by his predecessors, he was also determined to make the voice of Indonesia heard more clearly internationally (Bandoro 2014). To achieve this, he asked Indonesian diplomats to focus on improving the country's image and restoring its dignity (Yudhoyono 2014). To a significant extent these efforts were successful. After ten years, the highlights of Yudhoyono's foreign policy can be listed as follows.

First, despite the new global outreach, ASEAN remained the primary focus of and platform for Indonesia's foreign policy. Under Yudhoyono, Indonesia devoted significant energy, time and resources to the ambitious project of creating an ASEAN Community by 2015. The president issued a raft of legislation to prepare his own country for regional economic integration under the ASEAN Economic Community (AEC), including Presidential Instruction 5/2008 on economic development, Presidential Instruction 11/2011 on AEC implementing commitments, Presidential Instruction 6/2014 on Indonesian competitiveness in the AEC, and Presidential Decree 37/2014 establishing a national committee for the AEC. He also played an instrumental role at ASEAN summits, using his personal influence with other leaders to advance AEC projects and preparedness. He visited Myanmar in 2006 and again in 2013, for example, in an effort to demonstrate not only ASEAN's 'real constructive engagement' with Myanmar (Bandoro 2014: 145) but also his personal encouragement for Myanmar's military regime to trust the neighbouring countries in ASEAN. In visiting Myanmar, extending a hand of friendship and treating the military regime as an equal partner, Yudhoyono was employing tried and tested ASEAN principles rather than harsh Western-style diplomacy (Bandoro 2014). However, the Myanmar visits also exposed the limits of Yudhoyono's foreign policy, as the military junta showed few signs of yielding to Yudhoyono's subtle pressure to open the country and trust other ASEAN countries.

Unfazed by his lack of success in Myanmar, Yudhoyono paid close personal attention to another problem that was occupying ASEAN's energy and attention: competing claims over the South China Sea by China, Taiwan and four ASEAN countries, namely the Philippines, Vietnam, Malaysia and Brunei. In June 2012, the ASEAN Ministerial Meeting in Phnom Penh failed to reach agreement on the South China Sea conflict. This 'spectacular failure' marked the first time in ASEAN's 45 years of existence that the group had failed to issue a joint communiqué following its annual meeting (Bower 2012). In response, a furious Yudhoyono summoned Foreign Minister Marty Natalegawa, who had replaced Hassan Wirajuda in 2009, and instructed him to fix the problem immediately. After 36 hours of shuttle diplomacy across key ASEAN member states, Natalegawa emerged with a common position on the South China Sea that reiterated ASEAN's adherence to the 2002 Declaration on the Conduct of Parties in the South China Sea and to the 1982 United Nations Convention on the Law of the Sea (Saragih 2014).

As well as taking an active role in ASEAN's internal affairs, Yudhoyono expanded the organisation's reach into global affairs, and used it and related institutions to lift Indonesia's global profile. It was during Indonesia's time as chair of ASEAN in 2011 that the 19th ASEAN Summit produced the third Bali Concord, a declaration setting out a common platform for the ASEAN countries' engagement with global political, security, economic and socio-cultural issues. Yudhoyono also participated in regional organisations such as ASEAN+3 and the East Asia Summit, two forums that have contributed significantly to the contemporary regional architecture in the Asia-Pacific region. The United States and Russia joined the East Asia Summit in 2011 while Indonesia was the chair of ASEAN. Keen to engage with the leaders of the most influential countries in the region, Yudhoyono always attended the two forums' annual summits.

The G20 was another forum where Yudhoyono could showcase his country's achievements. Indonesia has been a member of the G20 since its inception in 1999 and is the only Southeast Asian country in this influential economic forum. In 2008, the G20 upgraded its meetings to the leaders' level to deal more effectively with the global financial crisis. Yudhoyono never failed to attend any of the G20 summits for political leaders during his two terms in office. Although critics questioned whether Indonesia would gain any real benefits from its involvement in the G20 (Hadi 2009), Yudhoyono frequently said, with some justification, that the Indonesian president's presence at G20 summits reflected the world's recognition of his country's progress and achievements (Yudhoyono 2014). More than any other forum, the G20 summits suited Yudhoyono's intention to mingle with the world's most powerful leaders and strengthen Indonesia's, and his own, global profile.

Yudhoyono also pursued his policy of greater international engagement through the United Nations. In 2013 he became co-chair of the United Nations' High-level Panel of Eminent Persons on the Post-2015 Development Agenda, alongside President Ellen Johnson Sirleaf of Liberia and Prime Minister David Cameron of the United Kingdom. The panel consisted of 27 dignitaries from around the globe who had been asked to set a path for the United Nations' post-2015 Millennium Development Goals (United Nations 2013). Yudhoyono believed that his participation in the panel and his role as co-chair helped to highlight Indonesia's position in the world community (Yudhoyono 2014: 78).

Other UN-related initiatives undertaken by Indonesia during Yudhoyono's presidency included hosting the United Nations Climate Change Conference in Bali in 2007 and finalising the Comprehensive Partnership between ASEAN and the United Nations in 2011. Yudhoyono also repeatedly voiced his support for a democratisation of global governance. In his opening address to the Bali Democracy Forum in 2012, for example, he called for 'reform of the UN Security Council so multilateralism rather than unilateralism could be strengthened' (as quoted in Weatherbee 2013: 31).

In fact, the Bali Democracy Forum was an important instrument for Yudhoyono to pursue his ambition of Indonesia becoming a respected entrepreneur of normative change. Yudhoyono believed that, as a functioning Muslim democracy, Indonesia could help spread the concept of democracy, so when Hassan Wirajuda floated the idea of establishing a forum dedicated to discussing all aspects of democracy, he was quick to lend his support. Yudhoyono never failed to attend and lead the Bali Democracy Forum, highlighting the success of Indonesia's democratisation process and disseminating his conviction that democracy could be spread without the need for hard power, sanctions and condemnation (Yudhoyono 2014). Promoting democracy through dialogue was one of the norms that Indonesia wanted to contribute to the world. Through the Bali Democracy Forum, Indonesia was able to promote its belief that democracy had to be home-grown, that there was no single standard of democracy (Ministry of Foreign Affairs 2012) and that it could not be injected into a country from abroad, but rather had to be nurtured based on the socio-cultural traditions and norms embraced by each nation.

Some scholars agree that Indonesia is in a position to become a norm entrepreneur. Acharya (2014), for example, argues that 'Indonesia matters' because it can project a positive image based on its democratic identity, its capacity to maintain political stability while concurrently undertaking economic development, its non-conflictual approach to its neighbours and its active engagement with international organisations. Indonesia's actual achievements as a norm entrepreneur are limited, however. Indonesia's promotion of respect for human rights on the international stage, especially in ASEAN and among Islamic countries, met with resistance, not least because its own human rights practices deteriorated under Yudhoyono (see Chapter 12 by Berger). Although Indonesia championed the inclusion of an article on human rights in the ASEAN Charter in 2007, the establishment of the ASEAN Intergovernmental Commission on Human Rights in 2009 and the ASEAN Human Rights Declaration in 2012, ASEAN appeared unwilling to advocate actively for these democratic norms or to challenge member states that had poor human rights records (Weatherbee 2013; McRae 2014). In the case of Myanmar, for example, Yudhoyono chose the soft diplomatic route of writing and talking to the leader of Myanmar's military government on the issue of its treatment of the Rohingya (Yudhoyono 2014: 712), even though this strategy had little tangible success. Similarly, Yudhoyono and Foreign Minister Natalegawa tried to spread 'strategic trust' in great power relations in the belief that Indonesia could act as a bridge between contending parties from East and West. Many scholars have questioned this strategy, however, arguing that Indonesia does not have the capability to play an effective role as a mediator in international disputes (Weatherbee 2013; McRae 2014).

Despite some setbacks, Yudhoyono clearly managed to re-establish Indonesia on the global map. Visibly comfortable in the company of world leaders and adept at communicating in English, he was successful in constructing a positive image of Indonesia as a country that was tolerant, moderate and increasingly confident in its ability to play a more prominent role in international affairs. By the end of his first term the message was getting through, with Murphy (2009) declaring that Indonesia had returned to the international stage and that this was 'good news for the United States'. Weatherbee (2013: 97) later wrote that 'the Indonesian phoenix, in fact, has climbed out of the ashes and is in flight. This is a very visible Indonesia'. A senior Japanese diplomat echoed this sentiment, saying 'We are happy; Indonesia is back' (personal conversation, 2014).

Yudhoyono was obviously successful in reviving the international reputation of a country that had suffered years of economic and political turbulence. Yet, Indonesia's forward-looking foreign policy and Yudhoyono's international leadership aspirations were viewed very critically at home in Indonesia. As Habir, Gunawan and Andika (2014: 56) point out, 'the image of tolerance, burnished by President Yudhoyono, has increasingly been viewed as paradoxical with the reality of Indonesian domestic dynamics'.

PRAISED ABROAD, CRITICISED AT HOME

As Indonesia's president during an era of democratic transition, Yudhoyono faced many delicate tasks, not only with regard to maintaining good relations with China and the United States and promoting Indonesia's role on the international stage, but also in terms of adjusting the country's foreign policy in line with domestic demands. Throughout his presidency, Yudhoyono was criticised by his constituents at home for his indecisiveness in handling controversial issues involving neighbouring states, his failure to bring Indonesia's rocketing foreign debt under control, his inability to deal effectively with other domestic problems, his tendency to focus on personal image building (*pencitraan*) and so on. The impression that the president and his state apparatus were often 'missing in action' domestically only strengthened during his second term.

Yudhoyono was particularly severely condemned for his lack of action to protect religious minorities, his unwillingness to push for legal solutions to resolve previous human rights cases and his failure to prevent rapid deforestation of the country's remaining tropical rainforests. He was also blamed for being indecisive and weak in defending Indonesia's territorial integrity. Some Indonesians expected him to be more assertive in responding to perceived violations of Indonesia's sovereignty or slights on Indonesia's dignity by neighbouring countries. Yudhoyono was obviously disturbed by these criticisms; in his book published in early 2014, he bemoans the fact that a day never went by without some public condemnation of him (Yudhoyono 2014: 121–241). The most serious criticism was yet to come, however. Less than a month before his term in office ended, his commitment to the most basic principles of democracy was called into question when he failed to prevent the passage of a bill that abolished the direct election of district heads and governors (see Chapter 9 by Tomsa).

In contrast to these domestic criticisms of the president, Yudhoyono's international reputation was high. Global leaders praised him for his numerous initiatives and for his distinctive approaches to regional and global issues. Numerous overseas institutions and universities bestowed awards and honorary doctorates on him. He mentions many of these international acknowledgments in his book, including the praise he received from political leaders at the 2012 East Asian Summit in Phnom Penh and the 2013 UN General Assembly, and from many distinguished scholars.

The dichotomy between Yudhoyono's high international standing and his declining popularity at home was striking, as the president himself was aware (Yudhoyono 2014: 265). To assess this phenomenon, it is useful to return to the narrative of Indonesia as a rising power, a notion frequently raised by those praising Indonesia for its achievements under President Yudhoyono.[1] In his book, for instance, Yudhoyono frequently mentions the numerous compliments he received from political leaders and international institutions for Indonesia's successful democratisation and its initiatives to respond to international issues. It is no surprise that these compliments came primarily from Western countries or institutions associated with Western interests, and from those who had obtained benefits from Indonesia's political transformation and economic development.

One could argue that those compliments were intended as positive encouragement for Indonesia to stay on the 'right track' — a track that suited the interests and values of those who were showering Yudhoyono with praise. In this sense, the repeated statements that Indonesia was rising can be perceived as a form of appeasement of both the country and the president. In other words, given the personality of the president, the best way for international partners to keep him doing what they wanted him to do was to compliment and praise him. To explain Yudhoyono's need for praise and his propensity to focus his attention where he could receive that praise, it is now useful to take a closer look at the personality of the president.

---

1 See, for example, Reid (2012), Weatherbee (2013), Bandoro (2014), McRae (2014) and Roberts, Habir and Sebastian (2014).

YUDHOYONO'S PERSONALITY AND INDONESIA'S FOREIGN POLICY

One useful framework to analyse the role of leaders in foreign policy is actor-specific theory. This approach relies on the agent as the primary focus of the analysis. It concentrates on people—especially the chief decision-makers in foreign policy—rather than on structures or institutions. The underlying assumption is that foreign policy concerns 'human decision making with reference to or having known consequences for foreign entities' (Hudson 2005: 2). With the human decision-maker as the prime mover of foreign policy, actor-specific theory examines agency-oriented concepts such as motivation, emotion and problem representation (Hudson 2005). This chapter therefore delves into Yudhoyono's motivations, emotions and processes of problem representation to investigate his influence on Indonesian foreign policy during 2004–14. These three psychological dimensions of foreign policy analysis are explained through Yudhoyono's own statements and writings, and through the observations of others.

Motivation

Yudhoyono's proactive engagement with international society reflected his personal drive to be a high achiever and to 'become someone' (*menjadi orang*). Coming from a humble background and a broken family, the young Yudhoyono strove for excellent performance throughout his army career and aimed for high social mobility (see Chapter 3 by Fealy). His determination to escape an unhappy childhood and emerge as a socially important person is very clear in the book he wrote in 2014. Significantly, though, he wanted to do more than occupy the top political position in Indonesia; he also wanted to make the voice of Indonesia—and presumably his own voice—heard regionally and internationally. His penchant for high personal targets was also evident in his ambition to prepare Indonesia to become 'one of the world's most dynamic economies' by 2030 (Yudhoyono 2014: 74).

With his simple background, it is no wonder that Yudhoyono always felt the need to be the best and to impress others. His actions and behaviour were driven by a desire to please the people most important to him, especially his wife, who came from a family of high social status. So, to be accorded respect within his own family, he needed to 'catch up' on the social ladder. Becoming a successful president and an internationally respected leader was his key strategy to meet his immediate family's expectations and make himself a strong focal point within his extended family.

Beyond the members of his own family, Yudhoyono's referent people included several world leaders, especially those from Western countries and institutions. In his book, Yudhoyono writes about his feelings of happiness and comfort when he received accolades or awards from the international community. For example, he expresses satisfaction when told that several world leaders and the UN secretary-general had praised his 'middle-way approach' to resolving the crisis in Syria (Mulyana 2014; Yudhoyono 2014). He also notes with pleasure that he is mentioned twice in a speech by the Russian president (Yudhoyono 2014: 717). Yudhoyono expresses the view that, in stark contrast to the frequent criticisms he encountered at home, his work and achievements were valued and understood by international society (Yudhoyono 2014: 267–9). Significantly, he counts several world leaders as his good friends—*sahabat baik saya*—indicating that he believed he had close personal relations with them as friends, not merely as colleagues. This inclination to see international relations through a highly personalised lens also helps to explain why Yudhoyono was so deeply hurt by the Australian spying scandal in 2013, which he regarded as a stab in the back by a perceived friend.

Emotion

Yudhoyono's emotional personality strongly influenced his approach to international relations and the formulation of foreign policy. He was known to be passionate about foreign affairs, and for using his international engagements to pursue the country's interests. He was aware that, as a statesman, he had to represent and fight for his country, but he refused to be compared to Sukarno or Suharto (Yudhoyono 2014: 90). He says in his book that whatever the perception of him and his work, he simply aimed to work for the betterment of Indonesia and its people (Yudhoyono 2014: 96). The one characteristic of Yudhoyono's psyche that arguably left the deepest impact on Indonesia's foreign policy was his tendency to avoid conflict at all costs. Clearly Yudhoyono preferred not to become involved in conflict if he could avoid it, but if that was not possible, then he would choose peaceful rather than confrontational means to resolve it. His famous dictum of 'a million friends and zero enemies' as the guiding principle for Indonesia's foreign policy needs to be seen through this lens.

For Yudhoyono, conflict resolution always had to take into account the interests of all parties to a dispute. But the constant need to consider a broad range of opinions often made it impossible for him to make decisions, which in turn led to him being seen as indecisive or absent from his responsibilities as president. International relations suited him in this regard, because decision-making processes in international bodies such as ASEAN or the United Nations tend to be slow and, especially in ASEAN, non-conflictual. Because key characteristics of his personality that harmed him domestically were actually valued internationally, he naturally felt more at ease in international forums. Of course, as one of the chief decision-makers in international politics, there were times when Yudhoyono had to make difficult decisions. However, rather than taking pride in this aspect of his position as president, he says that it often made him feel lonely (Yudhoyono 2014: 277).

Problem representation

It is likely that Yudhoyono defined the problems he faced domestically and those he faced internationally in very different ways. This process of developing a 'problem representation' (Sylvan and Voss 1998) was shaped by his beliefs, knowledge and perceptions of other actors' interests, objectives and motives. On the one hand, it seems that Yudhoyono perceived many domestic problems—for example, the rise of religious intolerance or the need to fix the institutional framework for decentralisation—as being so difficult and divisive that he believed proactive intervention would entail unpredictable political risks for him. Feeding into this angst was his perception that much of the domestic criticism directed at him was irrelevant, disproportional or subjective (Yudoyono 2014: 272). On the other hand, the international community rarely if ever criticised Yudhoyono, even if his initiatives failed to achieve results. In fact, the leaders of powerful states often praised Indonesia, so it was not surprising that Yudhoyono felt that they appreciated his work much more than his domestic constituency did (Yudhoyono 2014: 265). The most obvious example of the gap between Yudhoyono's domestic and international reputations relates to the World Statesman Award he received from the New York-based Appeal of Conscience Foundation for his achievements in promoting religious tolerance in Indonesia. While Yudhoyono proudly accepted the award, the foundation's decision was greeted with severe criticism in Indonesia where activists pointed out that, under Yudhoyono, intolerance and discrimination against minority groups had actually risen.

The frequent praise he received from international actors bolstered Yudhoyono's self-esteem and arguably fostered another disconnect in his process of problem representation: his overly confident belief that Indonesia was a capable international actor with the potential to shape regional or even global politics. In reality, as discussed earlier, Indonesia had only a limited capacity to assess international problems and devise solutions. But Yudhoyono genuinely seemed to believe that, under his leadership, Indonesia could not only safeguard its own national interest

but also play an important role on the international stage. His determination to put the country's foreign policy on a new footing is demonstrated in his book, where he writes:
> We must undertake smart and creative diplomacy. Everything we do we devote to our national interest. The doctrines that we have followed in the last nine years — the 'all-direction foreign policy' and 'a million friends and zero enemies' — must be preserved. Our foreign policy must remain in line with the free and active foreign policy outlined by the founders of our republic. However, history shows that, in the past, our foreign policy has also leaned towards the left or the right. I am determined to prevent a repeat of such a situation (Yudhoyono 2014: 708).

In a state address to parliament on 16 August 2013, Yudhoyono affirmed that 'Indonesia resolves always to be a part of the solution to global problems'. His belief that Indonesia could play an active role in international affairs was underpinned by his perception that Indonesia, and he himself, had obtained the trust of the international community. As he writes in his book:
> [T]he world's trust in Indonesia is growing. We remember that not too long ago our international image and the world's trust in us had lapsed. It had collapsed. Nowadays, we have regained that trust as the world has observed the achievements of our country in various fields. We would not have obtained such trust if we had failed to maintain stability and solve our own problems. Finally, in my opinion, the world also acknowledges that Indonesia has been very active in undertaking its international roles. We care [about the world's problems]. We are not passive and apathetic (Yudhoyono 2014: 79).

It seems likely that Yudhoyono's belief in Indonesia's and his own capacity to play an important role on the world stage was driven by his perception that the country had performed well during the decade under his leadership. Also, in his own assessment, Indonesia had been 'smart' in pursuing its interests in global forums (Yudhoyono 2014: 701).

CONCLUSION

The various facets of Yudhoyono's distinctive personality significantly influenced Indonesia's foreign policy during his two terms in office. His drive to be a high achiever, his non-conflictual approach to problem-solving and his tendency to take both criticism and praise personally shaped his way of representing problems and resulted in an active but ultimately inconsequential foreign policy. Especially in his second term, Yudhoyono was a frequent contributor to discussions about some of the world's most pressing problems, including climate change, global governance and conflict in the Middle East. But although the president's contributions were duly noted and occasionally praised, Indonesia's capacity to impose its suggested solutions on other states remained very limited. Thus, although Indonesia clearly enhanced its global profile during Yudhoyono's presidency, it would be premature to describe it as a rising power.

Nevertheless, Yudhoyono should be given due credit for raising Indonesia's global profile. Not only was he adept at highlighting the country's successful political transformation and economic recovery since 1998 (and especially since 2004 when he became president), but he also won the personal respect of many world leaders. This must have been enormously gratifying for a man who felt that he was often unfairly criticised at home. As is evident from his writings, he believed that the international community understood the value of his work much better than did his domestic constituency in Indonesia. As a consequence, whenever possible he preferred to attend to international rather than domestic affairs, perceiving the latter to be potentially damaging to his personal prestige. Ironically, the more criticism he received at home, the more he retreated from the domestic sphere, thereby exacerbating many of Indonesia's most pressing problems, such as growing religious intolerance, corruption and environmental destruction. By the end of his time in office, a remarkable gap had opened up between the largely positive image of Indonesia in the international community and the increasingly pessimistic assessments of Indonesian politics by academic observers and the media.

Despite these contradictions, Yudhoyono left an important legacy in Indonesian foreign policy. Having come to power in 2004 after years of political and economic turbulence in Indonesia, he presided over a period of domestic stabilisation that served as an important backdrop to the growing international perception that Indonesia was a rising power. While this chapter has argued that this notion overstates the country's actual capabilities, there can be no doubt that Yudhoyono made Indonesia much more visible internationally. His successor, Joko Widodo, should be able to use this newly enhanced global profile as a platform from which to craft his own administration's foreign policy. Early indications suggest that he will abandon Yudhoyono's motto of 'a million friends and zero enemies' and pursue a firmer and more assertive foreign policy. Meanwhile, Yudhoyono's global commitments look likely to continue after the end of his presidency. He has accepted a position as chair and president of the Global Green Growth Institute, a South Korea-based international environmental organisation.

REFERENCES

Acharya, A. (2014) *Indonesia Matters: Asia's Emerging Democratic Power*, World Scientific, Singapore.
Bandoro, B. (2014) *States' Choice of Strategies*, Graha Ilmu, Yogyakarta.
Bower, E.Z. (2012) 'China reveals its hand on ASEAN in Phnom Penh', *East Asia Forum*, 28 July.
Goh, E. (2013) *The Struggle for Order: Hegemony, Hierarchy, and Transition in Post-Cold War East Asia*, Oxford University Press, Oxford.
Habir, A.D., A.B. Gunawan and M.T. Andika (2014) 'Normative priorities and contradictions in Indonesia's foreign policy: from Wawasan Nusantara to democracy', Issue Brief No. 7, National Security College, Australian National University, Canberra, May. Available at http://nsc.anu.edu.au/research-and-publications/indonesias-ascent-project
Hadi, S. (2009) 'Arsitektur baru ekonomi global' [New architecture of the global economy], *Kompas*, 29 September.
Harsono, A. (2012) 'No model for Muslim democracy', *New York Times*, 21 May.
Hudson, V. (2005) 'Foreign policy analysis: actor-specific theory and the ground of international relations', *Foreign Policy Analysis*, 1: 1–30.
Laksmana, E.A. (2011) 'Indonesia's rising regional and global profile: does size really matter?', *Contemporary Southeast Asia*, 33(2): 157–82.
Leahy, P. (2014) 'SBY: Abbott says farewell to a friend of Australia', *Interpreter*, Lowy Institute for International Policy, Sydney, 6 June.
McRae, D. (2014) 'More talk than walk: Indonesia as a foreign policy actor', *Analysis*, Lowy Institute for International Policy, Sydney, February.
Ministry of Foreign Affairs (2012) *Diplomasi Indonesia 2011, 2012* [Indonesian Diplomacy 2011, 2012], Jakarta.
Mulyana, Y. (2014) 'Assessing President Yudhoyono's foreign policy in 2013', *Jakarta Post*, 3 March.
Murphy, A.M. (2009) 'Indonesia returns to the international stage: good news for the United States', *Orbis*, 53(1): 65–79.
Murphy, A.M. (2010) 'US rapprochement with Indonesia: from problem state to partner', *Contemporary Southeast Asia*, 32(3): 362–87.
Novotny, D. (2010) *Torn between America and China: Elite Perceptions and Indonesian Foreign Policy*, Institute for Southeast Asian Studies, Singapore.
Nye, J., Jr. (2004) *Soft Power: The Means to Success in World Politics*, Public Affairs, New York.
Oberman, R. et al. (2012) 'The archipelago economy: unleashing Indonesia's potential', McKinsey Global Institute, September. Available at http://www.mckinsey.com/insights/asia-pacific/the_archipelago_economy
Poole, A. (2014) 'The foreign policy nexus: national interests, political values and identity', Issue Brief No. 6, National Security College, Australian National University, Canberra, May. Available at http://nsc.anu.edu.au/research-and-publications/indonesias-ascent-project
Reid, A. (ed.) (2012) *Indonesia Rising: The Repositioning of Asia's Third Giant*, Institute for Southeast Asian Studies, Singapore.
Roberts, C., A.D. Habir and L. Sebastian (2014) 'Indonesia's ascent: power, leadership and Asia's security order', public seminar, National Security College, Australian National University, Canberra. Available at http://nsc.anu.edu.au/research-and-publications/indonesias-ascent-project
Santi, N. (2014) 'Obama, heads of states, speak highly of SBY in New York', *Tempo Online*, 28 September.

Saragih, B. (2014) 'RI: a regional troubleshooter struggling with its missions', *Jakarta Post*, 16 October.
Stone, R. (2010) 'U.S. effort to reach out to Muslim-majority nations begins to bear fruit', *Science*, 328(5,984): 1,339.
Sukma, R. (2012) 'Indonesia and the emerging Sino–US rivalry in Southeast Asia', London School of Economics and Political Science, London. Available at http://www.lse.ac.uk/IDEAS/publications/reports/pdf/SR015/SR015-SEAsia-Sukma-.pdf
Sylvan, D.A. and J.F. Voss (eds) (1998) *Public Representation in Foreign Policy Decision Making*, Cambridge University Press, Cambridge.
Tan, P. (2007) 'Navigating a turbulent ocean: Indonesia's worldview and foreign policy', *Asian Perspective*, 31(3): 147–81.
United Nations (2013) 'A new global partnership: eradicate poverty and transform economies through sustainable development', New York.
Van Klinken, G. (2007) *Communal Violence and Democratization in Indonesia: Small Town Wars*, Routledge, London and New York.
Weatherbee, D. (2013) *Indonesia in ASEAN: Vision and Reality*, Institute of Southeast Asian Studies, Singapore.
White, H. (2013) 'What Indonesia's rise means for Australia: northern exposure', *Monthly*, June. Available at http://www.themonthly.com.au/issue/2013/june/1370181600/hugh-white/what-indonesia-s-rise-means-australia
World Bank (2007) 'East Asia & Pacific update: 10 years after the crisis', East Asia and Pacific Region, World Bank, April.
Yudhoyono, S.B. (2010) 'Stereotypes do our peoples an injustice', *Sydney Morning Herald*, 11 March.
Yudhoyono, S.B. (2014) *Selalu Ada Pilihan* [There Is Always a Choice], Kompas Gramedia, Jakarta.
Zheng, Y. and L.F. Lye (2013) 'China's foreign policy: coping with shifting geopolitics and maintaining stable external relations', in Y. Zheng and L.F. Lye (eds) *East Asia: Developments and Challenges*, Series on Contemporary China, World Scientific, Singapore: 49–72.

PART 2

Institutions, politics and security

6   A balancing act: relations between state institutions under Yudhyono

Stephen Sherlock

When Susilo Bambang Yudhyono was sworn into office in October 2004, he was stepping into a set of constitutional arrangements and political circumstances that was without historical precedent in Indonesia. Following the constitutional reforms of 1999–2002, Yudhoyono faced the task of managing new and untested relationships among the major institutions of state, especially between the presidency and the parliament (Dewan Perwakilan Rakyat, DPR). But while Yudhoyono was Indonesia's first directly elected president, popular and elite views of the office of the presidency were characterised by a sense of continuity rather than difference. There was a widespread, if unspoken, assumption that Yudhoyono was occupying the same office as his predecessors, just doing so in a democratic environment. Echoing this default view, Anies Baswedan (2007: 232) explained that 'an important and enduring feature of Indonesian politics has been the dominance of the president. ... Indonesia's first two presidents set a precedent for the role and stature of their successors'. Clearly, the towering figures of Sukarno and Suharto had stamped an indelible impression on the minds of Indonesians that the president was the most powerful personage in the land.

This left a legacy of expectations for Yudhoyono about the supposedly superior role and power of the presidency. Thus, when the parliament, with its new constitutional powers and popular legitimacy, asserted itself on a number of occasions during his presidency, some observers believed that the relative powers of the executive and legislative branches had become unbalanced and, even more importantly, that the DPR was attempting to usurp the powers of the president (Susanti

2006; Indrayana 2008: 274–5). Common arguments were that Indonesia had moved from an 'executive-heavy' system under Suharto to a 'legislative-heavy' system in the democratic era and that Yudhoyono's reform agenda had been obstructed by reactionary forces in the DPR (Perdana and Friawan 2007: 19; Purnomo 2008). However, there have been few scholarly studies to test such assumptions.

This chapter discusses the ways in which Yudhoyono managed the relationships between key state institutions in Indonesia's reformed presidential system. The first section shows that Yudhoyono inherited a presidency whose relationships with other parts of government, especially the legislature, were still in the process of redefinition. The second illustrates how Yudhoyono, like Abdurrahman Wahid and Megawati Sukarnoputri before him, attempted to build an all-inclusive governing coalition, following a pattern of 'promiscuous power-sharing' that some scholars view as characteristic of democratising governments following extended periods of authoritarianism and political uncertainty (Slater and Simmons 2013). In the third section, however, I argue that Yudhoyono's grand coalition strategy could only have succeeded under an interventionist president prepared to lead and discipline his cabinet—which Yudhoyono was not. The fourth section explores claims that Yudhoyono's administration was stymied by an obstructionist parliament, arguing that—in fact—the DPR had little effective capacity to exercise its new powers. In the fifth section, I show that the reform-resistant civil service was a much bigger factor than the DPR in determining the content and level of implementation of policy. The sixth section demonstrates how Yudhoyono occasionally attempted to circumvent the power of the bureaucracy by establishing special units, although, in practice, a lack of clearly defined powers and inconsistent political support from the president himself eroded their effectiveness. In the conclusion, I consider the legacy of Yudhoyono's uncompleted tasks for future Indonesian governments.

YUDHOYONO'S STARTING POINT: CONSTITUTIONAL AND POLITICAL LEGACIES

It has often been overlooked that the 1945 Constitution actually described a president whose powers were potentially circumscribed by the People's Consultative Assembly (Majelis Permusyawaratan Rakyat, MPR), a quasi-legislative body. According to the underlying doctrine of the Constitution, it was the MPR, not the president elected by it, who 'exercised in full' the sovereignty of the people. More concretely, the elucidation to the Constitution stated that the president was to be 'subordinate and accountable' to the MPR (section 6(IV)). Therefore, the MPR—as the highest institution of state with the powers to appoint and dismiss the president and set the 'guidelines of state policy'—could have greatly constrained the president's effective power. In the final consequence, the president could have been made answerable to a representative assembly in a manner akin to a parliamentary rather than a presidential system. However, this did not stop one prominent constitutional commentator, Mahfud MD (1999: 66), from arguing that the 1945 Constitution was intrinsically 'executive-heavy' because it ostensibly gave wide powers to the presidency with few checks and balances.

Given this ambiguity in the respective powers of the branches of government, Lindsey (2008: 25) concluded that the 1945 Constitution 'did not clearly establish either a parliamentary or a presidential political system but instead created a blended and vague hybrid'. The system was 'not conventionally presidential ... [but] neither [was] it a conventional parliamentary system, or even a recognised hybrid or semi-presidential system' (Ellis 2002: 120, 2007: 23). In practice, of course, any debate about the meaning of the 1945 Constitution was rendered irrelevant by the realities of power politics. When reimposing that Constitution in 1959, Sukarno emasculated the potentially pivotal MPR by the simple expedient of hand-picking all its members, because the Constitution was silent about the chamber's method of election. Suharto, for his part, stacked the institution with hand-picked regional and social-group representatives, while DPR representatives were elected in stage-managed elections.

It was only when the shackles imposed by a controlling president were undone in 1998 that relations between the executive and legislative branches began to work freely as described in the 1945 Constitution. As stated by Crouch (2010: 60), the 'quasi-parliamentary character of the formal constitution had been disguised by Suharto's authoritarian rule but became very apparent in both the election and downfall of President Abdurrahman Wahid'. The hybrid configuration enshrined in the Constitution produced not only a president in 1999 whose party had only a small minority representation in parliament, but also, in Wahid, an individual whose erratic personal and political styles made him uniquely incapable of managing the delicate balancing act between a now mutually dependent executive and legislature. Had a more adroit and accommodating figure presided during this time, the history of constitutional reform might have been different. But with Wahid driving the relationship between the executive and the legislative to the brink of constitutional breakdown, the system was revealed as impractical and possibly unworkable.

The tumultuous experience of the Wahid interregnum from 1999 to 2001 helped ensure that the MPR resolved to separate the powers of the two branches of government more clearly. In its first rounds of constitutional reform in 1999 and 2000, the MPR had already taken one step in that direction by removing the president's dominance over law-making powers and shifting the balance considerably—though not entirely—away from the presidency and towards the DPR. As a result, legislation had to be drafted and passed jointly by the executive and the legislature. After the MPR resumed its deliberations in November 2001—its work had been postponed during the turmoil of Wahid's removal—it amended the Constitution to provide for direct election of the president, thus creating a more conventional presidential system. Hence, the constitutional reforms of 1999–2002 eliminated the quasi-parliamentary character of the Constitution and took away the power of the parliament (through the mechanism of the MPR) to appoint the president. While the MPR retained the power to impeach the president, it could do so only for constitutional breaches, following a lengthy process involving the Constitutional Court. But although parliament lost some powers through the constitutional amendments, its authority to make, or contribute to, decisions on a range of other matters was increased. For instance, it was given the authority to appoint members of the Supreme Audit Agency (Badan Pemeriksa Keuangan, BPK) and to approve the appointment of outgoing and incoming ambassadors.

Consequently, whereas the Wahid and Megawati administrations had been obliged to deal with the uncertainties of an 'undisguised' quasi-parliamentary system within a new electoral democracy, Yudhoyono stepped into a set of circumstances that were historically unprecedented. This novel environment was marked by the continuing maturation of democracy and a reformed presidential system with a clearer separation of executive and legislative powers. Yudhoyono faced a parliament that could no longer remove him from office, but in which parties giving voice to both powerful interests and popular aspirations could nevertheless challenge his program for government. In other words, while no longer quasi-parliamentary, the reformed system continued to equip the legislature with significant powers.

Other elements of the post-2004 institutional environment also complicated the challenges facing the new president. Most importantly, Yudhoyono inherited a machinery of government that was little changed since the time of Suharto. As president he naturally had the right to appoint his own cabinet, and his ministers were served by departments and other agencies that theoretically executed presidential and ministerial decisions. But in fact, the civil service had developed tremendous independent power during the Sukarno and Suharto years. It was convinced of its capacity and right to make and implement policy, and was adept at resisting or subverting ministers' intentions if they ran counter to the interests of the bureaucracy. Democracy was bringing greater demands for scrutiny and accountability, but the president's personal authority over the bureaucracy as exercised by Suharto was greatly diminished. This unreformed civil service would be a challenge to the effective power of any incoming president or minister (Blunt, Turner and Lindroth 2012).

YUDHOYONO'S RAINBOW CABINET STRATEGY

How did Yudhoyono interpret the institutional arrangements he inherited in 2004? He adopted a strategy that was fundamentally informed by the presidencies of his two post-1999 predecessors. Hence, when he named his cabinet, he acted as if political realities had not changed at all as a result of the constitutional reforms. Indeed, Yudhoyono has himself confirmed that the experience of Wahid's impeachment in 2001 — he was a minister in the Wahid cabinet for much of its duration—was crucial in his decision to build a highly inclusive, or 'rainbow', cabinet.[1] In such 'oversized' coalitions, a president forms a government with more parties than would be numerically necessary to have a majority in parliament (Slater and Simmons 2013). Wahid had started out with such a cabinet in 1999 (Liddle 2000: 38–9; Gorjao 2003: 15), but then began firing ministers at will and took a hostile attitude to both the legislature and most of the parties represented in it (Slater 2004). As a result, parliament turned against him and eventually brought him down (Liddle 2001: 209–10). Megawati, learning from this, restored the rainbow coalition Wahid had built at the beginning of his term, simply changing its composition slightly. Although she received praise for emphasising the technocratic capacity of her ministers over their party affiliation, her cabinet had around the same number of party-connected figures as Wahid's initial coalition and, with 33 members, was almost the same size (ICG 2001: 3–5).

Yudhoyono followed suit, embracing the now familiar device of offering cabinet posts to all the major parties in the DPR, as well as to some of the minor ones. Remarkably, his first 'national unity cabinet' had even more party representatives than either Wahid's early government or Megawati's—about 20 of the 35 members were party politicians or had close connections with parties. This was despite—or perhaps because of—the fact that Megawati's party, the Indonesian Democratic Party of Struggle (Partai Demokrasi Indonesia-Perjuangan, PDIP), had declined to join the government and decided to position itself as an opposition

---

1 Marcus Mietzner and Edward Aspinall, interview with Susilo Bambang Yudhoyono, Jakarta, 2 December 2014.

party. He emulated previous cabinets by generally preserving the foreign affairs, defence, economic policy and coordinating ministries for technocrats, or party figures with recognised credentials, while keeping lucrative ministries such as state-owned enterprises, forestry, religion and public works as the special domain of party figures. Thus, 'in truth, Yudhoyono's cabinet did not look very different from its predecessors' (Liddle 2005: 332).

Notably, Yudhoyono persisted with this rainbow cabinet strategy through two terms of government, and through a number of cabinet reshuffles. As explained above, in constitutional terms, Yudhoyono did not need a parliamentary majority to keep him in the presidential palace, as had Wahid and Megawati. Yet the experience of Wahid's presidency continued to haunt him throughout his years in office. According to a leaked confidential report, figures close to Yudhoyono told US diplomats in 2008 that he 'takes serious [sic] the possibility of impeachment ... [He] remembers that President Wahid was impeached in 2001' (US Embassy 2008). Yudhoyono's fears were also probably heightened by his early experience of the behaviour of parties in the DPR before and after his first inauguration in October 2004. At that time, a loose grouping calling itself the National Coalition (led by Golkar and PDIP) excluded Yudhoyono's Democrat Party (Partai Demokrat, PD) from the leadership of the all-important DPR committees, and threatened to block many of the government's policies. The situation was only resolved when Yudhoyono's vice-president, Jusuf Kalla, became chair of Golkar in 2004, bringing that party from opposition into government. Nevertheless, Yudhoyono's fear of impeachment seemed rooted as much in a lack of understanding of the presidency's post-amendment strengthening as it was in his famous tendency to avoid controversy.

Along with fears about the fate of his own presidency, Yudhoyono had concerns about a repeat of the danger of civic violence that had marked Megawati's loss to Wahid in 1999, and the confrontation between Wahid and the parliament in 2001.[2] Thus, at least in the early years of his first administration, Yudhoyono's consensus-style government probably supplied an antidote to the effects of recent traumas. These observations find strong resonance with Slater and Simmons' (2013) argument that post-authoritarian governments frequently resort to 'promiscuous power-sharing' among the political elite in order to ensure the government's longevity during periods of transition and uncertainty. The authors go on to argue that such practices become self-reinforcing beyond the uncertainty of the immediate post-authoritarian era, as their

---

2 Marcus Mietzner and Edward Aspinall, interview with Susilo Bambang Yudhoyono, Jakarta, 2 December 2014.

persistence through four administrations in post-1998 Indonesia attests. But according to Slater and Simmons, promiscuous power-sharing is not only inherently undemocratic in that it ignores voters' wishes and undermines accountability, it also has 'self-undermining' tendencies because it provokes voter backlash and gives rise to renewed political uncertainty. Their critique does not, however, raise the issue of the quality of such coalition governments in terms of their capacity to continue structural reform of government and produce changes in the policy realm. Extending Slater and Simmons' critique to questions of capacity, I argue below that while promiscuous power-sharing brought uncertainty to an end in Indonesia, it also produced stasis in terms of the development of legislation and policy.

YUDHOYONO'S CABINET IN PRACTICE: LEADERSHIP OR MEDIATION?

The strategy of inclusion and power-sharing clearly did not work. As I have argued elsewhere (Sherlock 2009), the attempt to win the loyalty of parties through cabinet posts was based on the assumption that, in return for a place at the table, the parties would sign on to the administration's policy program. But as Baswedan (2007: 325) points out, 'party representatives in cabinet had to serve two principals: the president and their own party leaders'. The parties' main objective was often simply to get control of the financial and political resources of a ministry, with all its opportunities for patronage. The question of loyalty to one's 'own' administration rarely entered into the equation. The concept of cabinet solidarity, under which ministers and affiliated DPR members would defend the administration's policies, never developed. The 'arrangement failed to guarantee the level of political support that [Yudhoyono] might have expected on the basis of the representation of the coalition parties in the DPR, thus rendering the coalition less effective in relation to policy making' (Baswedan 2007: 325). Whether they would take the president's side on any issue depended on the parties' calculations of their immediate interests. After Kalla took control of Golkar in December 2004, he said that the party's allegiance to the oppositional National Coalition had been 'temporary and situational' — a comment that raised the question of how lasting the party's commitment to its new government alliance would be (quoted by Liddle 2005: 335).

Given the opportunism of most of the putative allies in Yudhoyono's cabinet, the inclusive strategy required a very strong guiding hand from the president or from the presidential office in order to carry out a coherent policy agenda. This, in turn, required the president to take a strong lead on cabinet decisions and, if necessary, override ministers. The government's legislative agenda needed to be guided through parliament and made consistent across the various ministerial portfolios. Similarly, it was necessary to intervene at the official level to ensure that senior bureaucrats embraced the administration's policy position and did not subvert its intentions at the level of implementing regulations and execution. In other words, the president had to enforce his mandate within the cabinet, the civil service and the government alliance in parliament.

Yudhoyono, however, did none of these things. It appears that he saw his role as president as being to preside over the policy-making process rather than lead it. Especially in his second term, cabinet was not used as a decision-making mechanism, ministers found it difficult to arrange face-to-face meetings with the president and 'substantive discussion of policy issues rarely occur[red]' (Fealy 2011: 335). Yudhoyono's approach to policy development and implementation was infused with the same spirit that informed the structure of his cabinet—a search for compromise solutions that would include all interested parties and exclude none. In circumstances where there was a clash of interests among competing players, whether among his ministers or among groups in wider society, Yudhoyono repeatedly adopted the role of mediator rather than leader or decision-maker.

Two examples illustrate this point. On the issue of defence of minority religious rights, Yudhoyono declined to adopt a clear stance (see Chapter 13 by Bush). While making general statements of support for traditional Pancasila values of tolerance, he rarely intervened on concrete policy questions, even when they related to controversial decisions made by his long-time and deeply conservative minister for religious affairs, Suryadharma Ali. Tellingly, Yudhoyono declined to respond to calls to pressure the local administrations in Bekasi and Bogor to abide by Supreme Court and ombudsman rulings that there were no grounds for the compulsory closure—or 'sealing' (*menyegel*), as it was euphemistically called—of church sites in those cities. Instead, he argued that this was a matter for local governments. In the case of the minority Islamic sect Ahmadiyah, it seems that Yudhoyono initially opposed plans by three of his ministers to issue a joint ministerial decree (*surat keputusan bersama*) restricting the activities of the controversial group, but eventually agreed not to intervene (Fealy, forthcoming). US diplomats reported that nine of the ten members of the Presidential Advisory Council (Dewan Pertimbangan Presiden, Wantimpres) had advised against issuing the ministerial decree, but that Yudhoyono opted not to oppose it because he wanted 'to save face for the three ministers who had publicly promised some sort of decree' (US Embassy 2008). The decree was eventually issued in June 2008.

A similar pattern was visible in Yudhoyono's approach to the reform of labour regulations. In 2006, Yudhoyono issued a presidential instruction announcing legislative changes to the Labour Law (Law 13/2003), with the aim of increasing investment. When the changes were opposed by a number of unions, including in the form of mass demonstrations, the president quickly backed down and cancelled his plans to amend the legislation. His change of mind occurred despite the fact that the opposition to the proposed legislation was not particularly united or fierce, at least if compared to international experience on reform in this area. Moreover, some unions had appeared willing to accommodate certain changes (Manning and Roesad 2006: 163–9). For Yudhoyono, however, any sign of discontent or even just unhappiness in politically important constituencies was enough to warrant a fundamental revision of his stance.

During his decade in office, Yudhoyono adopted various devices to enforce discipline within his cabinet, but none came to any practical effect. Upon the appointment of his first rainbow cabinet in 2004, for instance, he promised that he would review the performance of his ministers after the first year and replace any underperformers. Despite this promise and widespread public criticism of many ministers, Yudhoyono carried out only very limited reshuffles during his first term. These had no effect on the way the cabinet worked, and perhaps the only major change was to increase Golkar representation after Kalla became chair of the party. But a larger number of Golkar representatives in cabinet did not guarantee the party's support for Yudhoyono's policies in the DPR. Consequently, at the start of his second term in 2009, Yudhoyono insisted that all parties represented in the cabinet sign a vaguely worded coalition 'contract'. After the manifest failure of the agreement to maintain coalition unity during the Bank Century crisis (discussed below), Yudhoyono created a joint secretariat (Sekretariat Gabungan, Setgab) in 2010, with the stated aim of coordinating policy-making among the coalition parties. Setgab's working procedures were never clarified and parties were not censured when they ignored the mechanism. A re-signing of the coalition contract in 2011 was again unable to ensure either cabinet solidarity or loyalty to the administration in the DPR (Mietzner 2013: 156–8).

Given Yudhoyono's presidential style as a conciliator and mediator, it was especially important for him to delegate authority. In this way, he hoped to make progress on policy reforms while safeguarding what many commentators saw as his first priority—his own image and popularity (Fealy 2011). Indeed, this appeared to be his objective in his first term when he chose Jusuf Kalla as vice-president and Aburizal Bakrie as coordinating minister for economic affairs—individuals whose powerful networks could compensate for the weak formal authority of their offices. Kalla was instrumental in effecting one of Yudhoyono's most important achievements, the resolution of the Aceh conflict (see Chapter 8 by Jones). But Yudhoyono increasingly viewed these high-profile figures as overshadowing himself, and as his relationship with Golkar went sour, the powerful roles of both men within the party became a liability. Thus, in his second term, Yudhoyono appointed a senior academic, Boediono, as vice-president. While Boediono had strong technocratic qualifications and was of unimpeachable character, he had no political power base and saw himself as a deputy providing intellectual substance to the president's instructions, rather than as a separate source of authority.[3] This absence of effective political deal-makers in Yudhoyono's second administration was one of the reasons that it had an even weaker record of achievement than the first.

AN OBSTRUCTIONIST PARLIAMENT?

Following the 1999 election, the DPR was infused with new democratic legitimacy and the subsequent constitutional amendments gave it new powers and a changed relationship with the presidency. From the beginning of Yudhoyono's rule, the parliament played an assertive role in appointments to key state institutions, criticised various government initiatives and sometimes differed with the government over legislation. However, some analysts read a much darker political script into the rocky government–DPR relationship, concluding that Yudhoyono's program was being systematically stymied by an obstructionist parliament.[4] The most common explanations for this alleged obstructionism were that DPR members were corrupt, lazy and unproductive, represented their parties rather than 'the people' and were tools of vested interests opposed to reform.[5] Another common claim was that the DPR was exceeding its constitutional authority by intruding into executive decision-making (Haris 2009). Some leading public figures even asserted that the country

---

3 This observation about Boediono's perception of his role as vice-president was made by Dewi Fortuna Anwar at the Indonesia Update conference, Australian National University, Canberra, 19 September 2014.
4 'DPR bantah disebut penghambatan agenda pendidikan' [DPR denies allegations of obstructing education agenda], *Sindonews.com*, 1 April 2013.
5 See Purnomo (2008) and also the newspaper editorial, 'Shameless legislators', *Jakarta Post*, 5 March 2009. NGOs such as Community Forum for the Care of the Indonesian Parliament (Forum Masyarakat Peduli Parlemen Indonesia, Formappi) and the Centre for the Study of Law and Policy (Pusat Studi Hukum dan Kebijakan, PSHK) have repeatedly made accusations of this kind. See, for example, PSHK (2012).

was drifting away from genuine presidentialism into some kind of parliamentary system.[6] But an examination of the record of the Yudhoyono administration shows that the picture is far more nuanced than this.

While there were undoubtedly grounds to criticise the DPR's effectiveness, it has to be remembered that the Constitution mandates that laws are to be passed by 'joint agreement' of the president and the DPR (article 20(2)). Problems in law-making, therefore, are at least as much the responsibility of executive government as of the parliament (Sherlock 2010). Legislative deliberations take the form of discussions between ministerial representatives and the relevant DPR committee. The great majority of laws are drafted in the ministries, whose specialist expertise far exceeds anything available to the party politicians in the DPR committees. The latter are frequently overwhelmed by the mass of detail in highly technical legislation and defer to the experts from the ministries. During interviews over the last decade, the author has repeatedly heard statements such as the following by a DPR committee member (in this case responsible for forestry) that 'there are only two forest specialists in our committee, while the government has a whole ministry to give advice', and by another that 'the ministry gives orders and expects us to follow' (confidential interviews, February 2014). Accordingly, the image of the legislature overpowering the executive is often overdrawn, with the former generally struggling to match the capacity of the latter.

Given the internal weaknesses of the DPR, and the parliament's centrality in Yudhoyono's strategy for the stability of his administration, it should have been an important but manageable task for the president to draft, coordinate and implement his legislative agenda. The respected commentator Jusuf Wanandi, for example, reminded Yudhoyono in 2006 that 'In the US, the president often deals directly with Congress. It would be good if SBY could also do this' (Wanandi 2006). However, Yudhoyono's understanding of the executive–legislative relationship appeared to focus almost exclusively on keeping majority support in the DPR. This was the same strategy he had chosen to manage cabinet, and as in the case of the cabinet, it did not work. Even more seriously, it did not take account of how the DPR operated at the level of its own internal organs, or of how legislators behaved within them. Individual DPR committees made most decisions on legislation and conducted investi-

---

6   Such views existed at the highest levels of Yudhoyono's circle. Hassan Wirajuda, a senior minister in the first Yudhoyono government and a member of Wantimpres, clearly subscribed to the view that the DPR's conduct was inappropriate in a presidential system and constituted a drift towards a parliamentary system, making this assertion on a number of occasions during a visit to Australia in 2012.

gations into policy issues, with each of the committees having its own internal balance of power among the party caucuses (*fraksi*). Even if the head offices of parties in the coalition had wanted to consistently support the administration, they would not have been able to do so because their authority over caucus members in the DPR was weak and incoherent (Sherlock 2008). Thus, the idea of a party 'cartel' exercising rigid control and dividing resources among themselves (Slater 2004) was not borne out by the reality of parliament's 'cacophonic' decision-making (Mietzner 2013: 161).

It was not surprising, then, that members of Yudhoyono's coalition, and even of his own party, PD, were prominent among those opposing the government in the parliament. This included opposing initiatives of key importance to his administration, such as cuts to oil price subsidies and a relaxation of the ban on rice imports. However, the most glaring example of Yudhoyono's poor management of parliamentary relations occurred in September 2014, during the dying days of his administration. The issue at hand concerned a bill that eliminated the direct election of regional executive government heads. Yudhoyono was opposed to the bill, and it would not have passed if his party had voted against it when, unusually for the DPR, it came to a vote in a plenary session of the parliament (see Chapter 9 by Tomsa). The caucus leader of PD, however, directed party members to walk out of the session, thus effectively abstaining from the vote and handing victory to the bill's proponents (which, of course, included parties that were part of Yudhoyono's coalition). A few days later, either because he disagreed with his party's action or because he was swayed by the strongly negative public response, Yudhoyono made the extraordinary decision to declare that he would issue a government regulation in lieu of law (*peraturan pemerintah pengganti undang-undang, perppu*) countermanding the law.

The area in which Yudhoyono had the most difficult relationship with the DPR was the legislature's power of oversight of executive government policy and expenditure. Given the parliament's institutional incapacity to make effective use of its law-making powers in the face of superior executive resources, the politicians found it much easier to exercise their oversight authority by summoning ministers and other senior officials to committee hearings. There, they questioned the actions of ministries and, directly or indirectly, the policies of the president. The most well-known example of this was the Bank Century case, in which a DPR special committee queried the government's 2008 decision to expend large amounts of public funds bailing out the private Bank Century, while also impugning the motives of the then finance minister, Sri Mulyani Indrawati, and of Vice-President Boediono, who had been head of Bank Indonesia during the bailout.

While the Bank Century scandal cannot be discussed in detail here, the case provides valuable insights into executive–legislative relations under Yudhoyono. First, it is possibly the clearest example of the failure of Yudhoyono's 'rainbow cabinet' strategy of maintaining the stability of the administration by relying on a nominal majority in parliament. In the face of DPR pressure (which, once again, was also exercised by members of the government coalition), Yudhoyono left his most vulnerable minister, Sri Mulyani, to deal with the problem alone. After months of hostile interactions with the DPR, Sri Mulyani resigned in May 2010 — reportedly much to Yudhoyono's relief. It is noteworthy that this low point of executive–legislative relations was reached during Yudhoyono's second term when, according to the idea of the rainbow cabinet, the relationship with the DPR should have worked most effectively. Between 2009 and 2014, Yudhoyono's own party, PD, was the largest caucus in the parliament while also controlling the position of DPR Speaker. But in the face of political pressure on his government, Yudhoyono sacrificed his minister rather than take the risk of alienating parliament, which (in his view) might lead to impeachment proceedings against him.

Whatever might be thought about the motives of the special committee members (which varied greatly), the DPR's investigation was not, as has often been alleged, a usurpation of executive powers by the legislature (McLeod 2010). Questions about the Bank Century bailout were first raised by the state audit agency, the BPK, and were passed on to the DPR in accordance with the agency's constitutional role to work with the DPR on oversight of the expenditure of public funds. The issue was then taken up by the DPR in a legitimate use of its oversight powers. And indeed, the DPR's investigative committee revealed a number of significant irregularities in the bailout — not necessarily in relation to Sri Mulyani's or Boediono's role, but in terms of the overall justification for the government's decision, the role of the bank's owner and the involvement of a number of lower-ranking officials. The permanent reality of the post-Suharto, post-constitutional-amendment world is simply that the Indonesian president will have to be prepared to respond to questioning from a powerful DPR, and that such questioning will always be flavoured by partisan political manoeuvring on both sides.

There are wider reverberations for future Indonesian politics. It seems that the political class as a whole has not yet come to terms with the implications of the MPR's amendments to the Constitution in 1999–2002. At the time, a foreign observer recorded that 'fundamental changes' had occurred, although 'almost nobody noticed it happen … in political circles, and even more so among media and other commentators' (Ellis 2007: 28). Hence, even today, after a decade of operating under a reformed system with a clear separation of powers between the branches of government, there is widespread misunderstanding about the role of the legislature. Claims that Indonesia is moving towards a 'parliamentary system' or a 'legislative-heavy system' have been made in apparent ignorance of the fact that disagreements between the branches of government are a normal, not an aberrant, feature of the separation of powers in presidential systems. Impeachment of the president by the DPR is unlikely to occur because the constitutional reforms have made it too difficult, but stand-offs of the kind experienced by President Obama and the United States Congress in 2013 may well be a feature of Indonesian politics in the future.

THE CONTINUING POWER OF THE BUREAUCRACY

Given the institutional weakness of the parliament and Yudhoyono's failure to coordinate cabinet and get his legislative agenda passed, the vacuum in policy was filled by the civil service. The bureaucracy, both at the centre and in the regions, is a key unreformed centre of power remaining from the Suharto years. A number of bills passed by the DPR illustrate the way in which the bureaucracy continued to dominate policy-making and legislation under the Yudhoyono administration. The Civil Service Law (Law 5/2014) was formally an initiative of the DPR, but not because of an institutional position emerging from the parliament as a whole or from a particular party or committee. Rather, it began life as the idea of a number of key individuals in the DPR committee on home affairs, Commission II (Komisi II), who had become frustrated by the obstacles to progress on bureaucratic reform they had encountered in their previous positions in executive government. These politicians even included Yudhoyono's former minister for bureaucratic reform, Taufiq Effendi. On his election to the DPR in 2009, Taufiq Effendi called on the support of a group of reformist academics, oversaw the drafting of a bill and persuaded first his committee and then the parliamentary leadership to accept the draft as an initiative of the DPR (Mietzner 2014).

The broad-ranging proposals in the first draft were, however, strongly opposed by elements within the bureaucracy, especially the Ministry of Home Affairs. The ministry led the government's side of the deliberations with the DPR committee, supported by the Civil Servants Corps (Korps Pegawai Negeri, Korpri). The ministry demanded changes that would effectively have neutralised the bill (Mietzner 2014). As was frequently the case when consensus (*mufakat*) could not be reached in the DPR, the bill was put aside and languished for many months. This was despite the fact that Yudhoyono had nominally deputised Boediono—who strongly opposed the proposed changes to the draft—to take the lead for the government on the bill. Initially Yudhoyono did not intervene to support Boediono. According to one of the academic drafters of the bill, Sofian Effendi, it was only when Sofian published a media article questioning Yudhoyono's failure to act that the president took up the issue.[7] A compromise law was eventually passed that included many of the initial reform ideas, but in a greatly weakened form.

Law 17/2011 on State Intelligence Agencies similarly exemplified the institutional power of the bureaucracy and the pivotal importance of powerful former members of the executive government in making use of the enhanced authority of the DPR. It also revealed a president responding to, rather than leading, policy debate. There had been a number of proposed bills on intelligence since the 9/11 attacks in the United States and the terrorist bombings in Indonesia, designed to define (and increase) the powers of the State Intelligence Agency (Badan Intelijen Negara, BIN), and mostly drafted by BIN itself. For various political reasons, these drafts had not succeeded in entering parliament. But a draft was adopted by the DPR in 2009 because of 'the election in that year of several first-time legislators with intelligence backgrounds', including two prominent former generals (ICG 2011: 8). This draft incorporated most of BIN's objectives, including granting it the power to arrest and to tap electronic communications. A range of human rights NGOs and academics strongly opposed these controversial provisions, and in the context of intense media coverage, the bill became deadlocked in the DPR committee on intelligence and security, Commission I (Komisi I).

Unlike in the case of the stalled Civil Service Law, the president played no role in breaking the impasse. A final version was agreed on largely because the then head of BIN, Sutanto, produced a compromise formula that, in formal terms at least, relinquished the demand for arrest and phone-tapping powers. Sutanto, a former police chief, was widely seen as a reformer in the largely military-controlled agency. Subsequently, however, he was removed from the leadership of BIN and replaced by an active military general, even though he had, in the words of a close observer, 'handed Yudhoyono an intelligence bill on a platter'.[8] Apparently Sutanto was dismissed because the military and the Ministry of Defence opposed his efforts to restructure the agency and increase civilian control of intelligence-gathering. Thus, Yudhoyono once again showed his tendency not to support reformers in the face of entrenched opposition. The end result was that conservatives in the BIN bureaucracy achieved their objective of a stronger legislative basis but with the military still largely in control.

---

7   Interview with Sofian Effendi, 14 July 2014.
8   Interview with Achmad Sukarsono, Habibie Centre, 3 September 2014.

The strong influence of the bureaucracy was also visible in the area of economic reform, especially during Yudhoyono's second term, when Indonesia saw a substantial regression towards economic nationalism. Laws on the horticulture industry (Law 13/2010), the protection and empowerment of farmers (Law 19/2012), the production and importation of food (Law 18/2012), industry (Law 3/2014) and trade (Law 7/2014) all 'either mandate[d] or authorise[d] a protectionist approach to economic policymaking' (Howes and Davies 2014: 160). While some commentary suggested that the laws showed that 'Indonesia's parliament has become a key player in policymaking' (Howes and Davies 2014: 162), the passage of legislation through the DPR did not necessarily make it the product or initiative of the parliament. Instead, most laws were driven by elements in the bureaucracy. The bills were drafted in the respective ministries, with civil servants dominating both the policy direction and the technical detail of the bills. Once again, this reflected the powerful interests close to ministers and their senior officials, and pointed to Yudhoyono's lack of involvement in policy-making.[9]

REFORMING OR CIRCUMVENTING THE BUREAUCRACY?

In the face of an ineffective and divided parliament, a fractious cabinet and a self-interested bureaucracy, Yudhoyono's preferred tactic for implementing his administration's policies was to form special units to coordinate the government's policy agenda or to lead particular programs. The most notable examples were the Presidential Working Unit for Development Monitoring and Oversight (Unit Kerja Presiden Bidang Pengawasan dan Pengendalian Pembangunan, UKP4), set up in 2009, and the National Team for the Acceleration of Poverty Reduction (Tim Nasional Percepatan Penanggulangan Kemiskinan, TNP2K), established in 2010. A major factor behind the creation of such units was the structural weakness of the presidential office. As Baswedan (2007: 327) points out, Yudhoyono was 'obliged to work with an inefficient and sometimes obstructionist bureaucracy within the presidential office', mostly career officials inherited from previous presidents who may or may not have been sympathetic to implementing the new incumbent's policies. The weakness of the presidential office was a legacy of the personalised Suharto regime, in which the president preferred an informal network of confidantes to a structured office. Subsequently, recruitment regula-

---

9 These conclusions are based on extensive interviews with ministry officials, DPR members and staff, and international advisors in a number of ministries, particularly the Ministry of Trade.

tions limited the capacity of post-Suharto presidents to structure their personal staff according to their own priorities.

Problematically, however, Yudhoyono's newly created units added to existing executive agencies rather than replacing them. Therefore, they could be seen as yet another example of the president's tendency to avoid confrontation with vested interests—he chose to establish new agencies he could work with rather than deal with obstruction from existing ones. Instead of being instruments to enforce the presidential will on ministers and senior bureaucrats, Yudhoyono's teams were duplications (or agencies for the circumvention) of ministries and the civil service. At best, they had an ill-defined relationship with the established ministries and agencies; at worst, they were resisted and subverted by bureaucrats who saw them as a threat to their position. Although strong presidential support for the teams was critical in such circumstances, Yudhoyono gave them only limited or episodic backing. Early in his first term, he retreated from his first attempt to create a presidential coordination and oversight unit when he faced strident opposition from his own vice-president, Jusuf Kalla, in concert with Golkar and powerful bureaucrats associated with the party (Baswedan 2007: 327–8; Scharff 2013: 2). He had to content himself with the Presidential Advisory Council (Wantimpres), made up of retired ministers and other public figures who acted in a largely individual capacity and thus could not exercise any power within the bureaucracy or other state institutions.

When Yudhoyono revived the idea of a coordinating presidential unit in his second term, he again encountered the issue of how to deal with existing agencies. The head of UKP4, Kuntoro Mangkusubroto, reportedly asked the president to abolish the coordinating ministries because they would duplicate the new unit's work. Yudhoyono rejected the proposal, at least in part because it would have required the reassignment of the civil servants who worked in these ministries, a difficult task under the existing rigid civil service regulations (Scharff 2013: 6). More importantly, the high-profile ambitions originally held for the unit were gradually eroded when Yudhoyono progressively wound back its activities in the face of predictable opposition from ministers and bureaucrats. The initial approach of publicly announcing the unit's assessments of ministries was quickly dropped when, in 2010, it caused embarrassment to a wide range of agencies, including those headed by Yudhoyono's allies. Later findings were confidential and released only to the president and the relevant minister. One observer of the process concluded that 'UKP4 and Kuntoro are no longer as intimidating to the ministers as they had originally been when the unit was first set up' (quoted by Sharff 2013: 15). At the same time, the unit was overloaded with other responsibilities that the president presumably did not want to entrust to the civil service.

This included leading a taskforce to oversee Indonesia's ambitious targets to reduce greenhouse gas emissions, and supporting the president's role as co-chair of a United Nations panel on the Millennium Development Goals.

CONCLUSION: A LEGACY OF ABSENCES

Given the peaceful transfer of power from one directly elected president to another in 2014, it is easy to take democratic transitions of authority in Indonesia for granted. But it should not be forgotten that when Yudhoyono assumed power in 2004, the country was still bruised and nervous about its future. His election undoubtedly gave the country a needed period of quiet and stability. But beyond that early period of stabilisation, the institutional legacy Yudhoyono has left for future presidents and for governance as a whole is marked by a series of absences. In other words, there were no obvious disasters, but not many obvious achievements either.

As a result of democratisation and the constitutional reforms of 1999–2002, Yudhoyono had inherited a presidency embedded in a historically unprecedented relationship between the branches of government. But the strategy he adopted to manage that relationship was precisely the same as that of the early Wahid and the Megawati presidencies, whose constitutional situation was markedly different. Yudhoyono persisted with the old idea of inclusive, grand coalition-building in the face of its manifest failure either to build cabinet solidarity or to maintain a base of support in the legislature. Had the DPR had a greater capacity (as distinct from the constitutional authority) to develop its own alternative policy agenda, Yudhoyono's administration may have had many more confrontations with the DPR than the relatively few that did actually occur. While there was a need for president and parliament to forge a new understanding about the daily operation of government in a presidential system with a strong separation of powers, Yudhoyono was able to sidestep this task simply because his lack of a strong policy agenda allowed him to avoid deep and regular negotiations with the DPR. His presidency, then, was perhaps paradoxically saved by its own passivity.

Yudhoyono's disengagement from the DPR was replicated in his distant relations with most of his cabinet ministers and his failure to exercise leadership or maintain discipline and policy coherence. Accordingly, a further absence in Yudhoyono's legacy is indicated by the lack of mechanisms to make cabinet work as a coherent and effective decision-making body rather than a forum of disparate ministers largely absorbed in the affairs of their own individual agencies. In the Suharto days, the ultimate executive power of an omnipotent president could compensate for a deficiency of process and accountability. Post-Suharto Indonesia has thus far still not seen a president who can assert his or her authority over ministers and their agencies, and do so in a manner appropriate to a democratic polity.

Finally, the experiments of the Yudhoyono government with new coordinating mechanisms such as UKP4 may provide lessons for future administrations on how, and how not, to enhance the effective authority of the office of the presidency. The most important of these lessons is the need to develop clear lines of authority in the relationships with existing agencies and, especially, the critical importance of presidential support for ministers when they encounter resistance or subversion. Indeed, this is one of the main elements of Yudhoyono's legacy of absences: the continuing need to confront the entrenched power of those in the bureaucracy, both civil and military, who act as independent sources of power rather than as servants of the executive. Yudhoyono played his presidency as a balancing act, but the economic and social progress of Indonesia will depend on the emergence of a president who can rebalance and remake the institutions of state.

REFERENCES

Baswedan, A. (2007) 'Indonesian politics in 2007: the presidency, local elections and the future of democracy', *Bulletin of Indonesian Economic Studies*, 43(2): 323–40.
Blunt, P., M. Turner and H. Lindroth (2012) 'Patronage's progress in post-Soeharto Indonesia', *Public Administration and Development*, 32(1): 64–81.
Crouch, H. (2010) *Political Reform in Indonesia after Soeharto*, Institute of Southeast Asian Studies, Singapore.
Ellis, A. (2002) 'The Indonesian constitutional transition: conservatism or fundamental change?', *Singapore Journal of International and Comparative Law*, 6(1): 116–53.
Ellis, A. (2007) 'Indonesia's constitutional change reviewed', in R.H. McLeod and A. MacIntyre (eds) *Indonesia: Democracy and the Promise of Good Governance*, Institute of Southeast Asian Studies, Singapore: 21–40.
Fealy, G. (2011) 'Indonesian politics in 2011: democratic regression and Yudhoyono's regal incumbency', *Bulletin of Indonesian Economic Studies*, 47(3): 333–53.
Fealy, G. (forthcoming) 'The politics of religious intolerance in Indonesia: mainstreamism trumps extremism?', in T. Lindsey and H. Pausacker (eds) *Pluralism, Intolerance and Democracy in Indonesia: Law, Religion and Conflict*.
Gorjao, P. (2003) 'Abdurrahman Wahid's presidency: what went wrong?', in H. Soesastro, A.L. Smith and H.M. Ling (eds) *Governance in Indonesia: Challenges Facing the Megawati Presidency*, Institute of Southeast Asian Studies, Singapore: 13–43.

Haris, S. (2009) 'Dilema presidensialisme di Indonesia pasca-Orde Baru dan urgensi penataan kembali relasi presiden-DPR' [Dilemmas of presidentialism in post-New Order Indonesia and the urgent need for restructuring of president-DPR relations], in M. Nurhasim and I.N. Bhakti (eds) *Sistem Presidensial dan Sosok Presiden Ideal* [The Presidential System and the Ideal Presidential Figure], Pustaka Pelajar, Yogyakarta.

Howes, S. and R. Davies (2014) 'Survey of recent developments', *Bulletin of Indonesian Economic Studies*, 50(2): 157–83.

ICG (International Crisis Group) (2001) 'The Megawati presidency', Asia Briefing No. 8, Jakarta/Brussels, 10 September.

ICG (International Crisis Group) (2011) 'Indonesia: debate over a new intelligence bill', Asia Briefing No. 124, Jakarta/Brussels, 12 July.

Indrayani, D. (2008) *Indonesian Constitutional Reform 1999–2002: An Evaluation of Constitution-making in Transition*, Kompas Book Publishing, Jakarta.

Liddle, W. (2000) 'Indonesia in 1999: democracy restored', *Asian Survey*, 40(1): 32–42.

Liddle, W. (2001) 'Indonesia in 2000: a shaky start for democracy', *Asian Survey*, 41(1): 208–20.

Liddle, W. (2005) 'Year one of the Yudhoyono–Kalla duumvirate', *Bulletin of Indonesian Economic Studies*, 41(3): 325–40.

Lindsey, T. (2008) 'Constitutional reform in Indonesia: muddling towards democracy', in T. Lindsey (ed.) *Indonesia, Law and Society*, second edition, Federation Press, Sydney: 23–47.

Mahfud, M.D. (1999) *Amandemen Konstitusi menuju Reformasi Tata Negara* [Amendment of the Constitution towards Reform of State Structures], UII Press, Yogyakarta.

Manning, C. and K. Roesad (2006) 'Survey of recent developments', *Bulletin of Indonesian Economic Studies*, 42(2): 143–70.

McLeod, R.H. (2010) 'Economic and political perspectives on the Bank Century case', presentation to the Indonesia Project, Australian National University, Canberra, 19 May. Available at https://crawford.anu.edu.au/acde/ip/pdf/seminars/2010_McLeod.pdf

Mietzner, M. (2013) *Money, Power and Ideology: Political Parties in Post-authoritarian Indonesia*, Hawaii University Press, NUS Press and NIAS Press, Honolulu, Singapore and Copenhagen.

Mietzner, M. (2014) 'The president, the "deep state" and policymaking in post-Suharto Indonesia: a case study of the deliberations on the Civil Service Act', report for the Partnership on Governance Reform (Kemitraan), Jakarta.

Perdana, A. and D. Friawan (2007) 'Economic crisis, institutional changes and the effectiveness of government: the case of Indonesia', CSIS Working Paper Series No. WPI 102, Centre for Strategic and International Studies, Jakarta, June.

PSHK (Pusat Studi Hukum dan Kebijakan) (2012) *Catatan Kinerja DPR 2011. Legislasi: Aspirasi atau Transaksi?* [Notes on the Performance of the People's Representative Council 2011. Legislation: Aspiration or Transaction?], Jakarta.

Purnomo, A. (2008) 'Era legislative heavy, DPR cenderung korupsi' [Legislative-heavy era: DPR prone to corruption], *detikNews*, 25 April.

Scharff, M. (2013) 'Translating vision into action: Indonesia's delivery unit, 2009–2012', Innovations for Successful Societies, Princeton University, Princeton NJ. Available at http://successfulsocieties.princeton.edu/publications/translating-vision-action-indonesias-delivery-unit-2009-2012

Sherlock, S. (2008) 'Parties and decision-making in the Indonesian parliament: a case study of RUU APP, the anti-pornography bill', *Australian Journal of Asian Law*, 10(2): 159–83.
Sherlock, S. (2009) 'SBY's consensus cabinet—*lanjutkan?*', *Bulletin of Indonesian Economic Studies*, 45(3): 341–3.
Sherlock, S. (2010) 'The parliament in Indonesia's decade of democracy: people's forum or chamber of cronies?', in E. Aspinall and M. Mietzner (eds) *Problems of Democratisation in Indonesia: Elections, Institutions and Society*, Institute of Southeast Asian Studies, Singapore: 160–78.
Slater, D. (2004) 'Indonesia's accountability trap: party cartels and presidential power after democratic transition', *Indonesia*, 78(October): 61–92.
Slater, D. and E. Simmons (2013) 'Coping by colluding: political uncertainty and promiscuous powersharing in Indonesia and Bolivia', *Comparative Political Studies*, 46(11): 1,366–93.
Susanti, B. (2006) *Menyoal Kompetisi Politik dalam Proses Legislasi di Indonesia* [Problems of Political Competition in the Legislative Process in Indonesia], Pusat Studi Hukum dan Kebijakan (PSHK), Jakarta.
US Embassy (2008) 'President Yudhoyono's re-election chances dip', confidential cable from US Embassy, Jakarta, to Washington and US diplomatic posts, released by Wikileaks. Available at https://wikileaks.org/plusd/cables/08JAKARTA1377_a.html
Wanandi, J. (2006) 'Two years of the Yudhoyono presidency', *Jakarta Post*, 20 September.

7 Professionalism without reform: the security sector under Yudhoyono

Jacqui Baker

In October 2014, the Indonesian National Army (Tentara Nasional Indonesia, TNI) held the biggest military parade in the nation's history, complete with F16s whistling overhead, battleships and hundreds of military vehicles. This display of force was a farewell to Susilo Bambang Yudhoyono, who left behind a legacy of military modernisation and an emphasis on professionalism (Faridz 2014). From the podium Yudhoyono declared:

> We have witnessed together advancements that make us proud: our defence posture is increasingly strong, our heavy weaponry is increasingly comprehensive and modern, the capacity and professionalism of the TNI is increasingly heightened, and we have finished and completed the reform of the TNI. We are thankful for the last ten years, and we have developed strength and modernisation well (Rizki 2014).

A few months earlier, on 1 July 2014, the anniversary of the founding of the Indonesian National Police (Polisi Republik Indonesia, Polri), the president spoke of his hopes to transform Indonesia's police into a 'world-class' force. Modernisation of equipment and technology was crucial to developing that professionalism. Apart from terrorism, he said, 'your job is to bust criminals. Protect the community. That's it' (Firdaus 2014). Professionalism through modernisation was the cornerstone of Yudhoyono's ten-year governance of the security sector.

Military professionalism was a longstanding theme in the president's intellectual history. But what did he mean by it? In 1990, on the precipice of the New Order's long decline, Yudhoyono presented a paper on military professionalism to the Army Staff and Command College (Sekolah Staf dan Komando Angkatan Darat, Seskoad) (Yudhoyono 1990). In it he rejected the liberal preoccupation with civilian supremacy over the military as a Western import. He argued that officers of the Indonesian Armed Forces (Angkatan Bersenjata Republik Indonesia, ABRI) should be professional, not liberal-democratic, and that ABRI's professionalism did not limit the force to one neat category, 'soldier', 'nation-builder', 'leader' or 'state functionary'. ABRI was all these things and as long as it adhered to professionalism, morality, security expertise, solidarity, leadership, unity and closeness to the people, then it would remain the only institution able to deliver security and stability amidst development. Honna (2003: 77-9) described Yudhoyono's idea of professionalism as a catch-all concept directed against the threat of social change. Yudhoyono's later writings in the hothouse of the New Order's breakdown urged ABRI to embrace a new paradigm of 'professionalism, effectiveness, efficiency and modernity' (Yudhoyono 1998). If ABRI wanted to survive in the face of national crisis and social 'judgment', the institution had to strengthen its capacity and adopt a professional posture.

The idea of Yudhoyono as a military conservative suggested by this record belies his role in modern Indonesian history. In accounts of Indonesia's early transition from authoritarian to democratic rule, he appears as a reformer and military moderate (Rinakit 2005: 110). During the student riots that precipitated Suharto's overthrow in 1998, Yudhoyono toured campuses advocating dialogue over repression. Within days of Suharto's resignation, Yudhoyono called for revision of the military's political role, and in subsequent years he promoted a 'New Paradigm' for ABRI that would see it withdraw from civilian politics (Honna 2003: 163-5).

When Yudhoyono became president in 2004, he inherited a security sector that had undergone, albeit imperfectly, a series of reforms. These included the separation of the police from the military and the construction of a new legislative framework for the TNI and Polri. In the literature on security sector reform, such changes are known as first-generation reforms. It fell to Yudhoyono to take up the challenge of second-generation reform: deepening democratic oversight and accountability. Yet, Yudhoyono's two terms in office were marked by the absence of serious structural reform of the security sector. Instead, they were characterised by a seemingly uncontroversial drive for professionalisation and modernisation in the form of greater budgetary allocations, procurement, recruitment and personnel specialisation.

In this chapter, I argue that Yudhoyono's emphasis on professsionalisation might be thought of as a third-generation reform that came prematurely for a sector still largely lacking in institutional and sectoral oversight, accountability and transparency. By leaping to third-phase professionalisation, Yudhoyono avoided more substantive second-generation reforms that should have occurred during his tenure. This was assisted by the slippery semantics of a term like 'professionalism'. Calling for 'professionalism' does not explicitly imply antipathy to reform. But, Yudhoyono's avoidance of second-generation reforms resonated with his pre-1998 understanding of professionalism wherein the military stood above the norms of democratic governance. For Yudhoyono, the security sector could be professional without being accountable.

This chapter advances the argument in four steps. In the first section, I outline the framework of generational reform, adopting an analysis advanced by Mietzner (2009) but including professionalisation and illustrating the relevance of the framework to the police. In the next three sections I examine the progress of reform in three areas: fiscal accountability, institutional oversight and sectoral reform. I show that in each of these sectors, Yudhoyono's concern with professionalisation—third-generation reform—allowed important second-generation reforms to be neglected. I conclude not only that Yudhoyono avoided reform of the security institutions, but also that the absence of reform in this sector, a sector where he wielded unique authority, revealed a president who held deeply conservative ideas and whose commitment to democracy was tempered by the sanctified position he granted security institutions within the Indonesian state.

THREE GENERATIONS OF SECURITY SECTOR REFORM

To analyse Yudhoyono's approach to the security sector, I draw on a comparative model of democratic military reform described by Mietzner (2009: 27). He adapted to Indonesia a framework first proposed by Cottey, Edmunds and Forster (2002), who argued that democratic security-sector reform after transition from authoritarian rule involves a two-step process. First-generation reforms concentrate on the institutional framework. Countries dismantle coercive institutions associated with the old regime and establish new ones. The powers of civilian institutions such as parliaments and ministries are strengthened to ensure oversight of security bodies. Second-generation reforms address the capacity of the newly created institutions to bring about democratic civil–military relations through repetitive institutional practice. In particular, they furnish

> the democratic substance to the institutional structures established by political decisions. Thus the challenge of second-generation reforms is centred around building the capacity of both state institutions and civil society in exercising democratic civilian control over the military (Mietzner 2006: 4).

However, for military and defence scholars such as Schreer (2014), the two-generation framework omits pressing issues of institutional capacity necessary to produce effective security institutions. Military effectiveness, not democratic oversight, should be the end goal of security sector reform. Schreer proposes a three- rather than two-step process. Third-generation reforms focus on military functionality and defence capability built through institutional modernisation, professionalisation and specialisation. By this argument, Yudhoyono's drive for professionalisation is in keeping with the norms of security sector reform. However, I argue that the way Yudhoyono used 'professionalism' smothered public debate about the need for deeper democratic reforms.

To this framework, I advance two caveats. First, like democratisation itself, security sector reform is rarely effected in discreet, sequential steps. Reform is typically partial and often haphazard, with sensitive reforms put off to await greater political support. The boundaries between the first, second and third generations of reform are frequently blurred. Yudhoyono inherited many enduring problems in the sector from the Megawati Sukarnoputri administration, and legislative reform was hardly complete. Nevertheless, a legal structure was in place that offered not just weaknesses and gaps, but also opportunities to deepen reform.

A second point is that, although the democratisation literature has largely used 'security sector reform' as shorthand for the normalisation of civil–military relations, this framework is equally suited to studying the police. Mietzner's and Schreer's 'generational reforms' framework references the TNI exclusively but it makes sense to include Polri within the framework. The military was not the only actor in the security sector. For 32 years Polri was subsumed within ABRI and enjoyed the same political and economic privileges, forming part of the ABRI faction in successive parliaments and establishing off-budget businesses. As such, in many respects, Polri is a kind of 'military-lite'.

Democratisation in Indonesia privileged the police by separating them from the military and amplifying their role in national security. This meant that Polri, unlike the military, was unlikely to reject regime change. Moreover, civilian leaders were heavily reliant on the police to ensure the day-to-day stability necessary for democratic reform. Thus, the police played a critical role in democratic consolidation.

But the police are not just an instrument of civilian policy. Like the military, they wield enormous coercive power, making them a political force to be reckoned with. Similarly, police typically guard their institutional autonomy jealously and sabotage civilian attempts to curtail it (Hinton 2006). As with military reform, democratic governance of the police is frustrated by a lack of civilian expertise. For these reasons, the three-stage model of democratic security-sector reform is equally relevant to the police. Including the police also widens the scope of analysis to the sector as a whole and draws attention to the necessity of reforming the inter-relationships between the police and the military.

Figure 7.1 Annual budgets of Polri and the TNI, 2006–14 (Rp trillion)

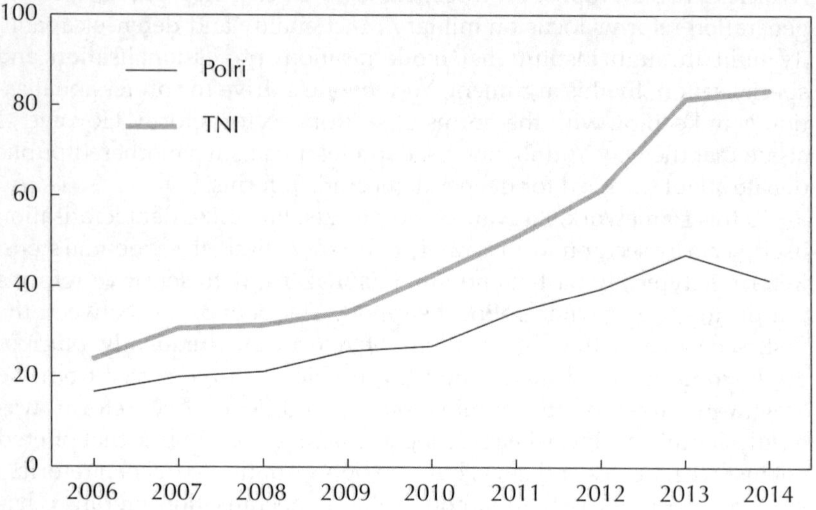

[Line chart showing Polri and TNI annual budgets from 2006 to 2014, y-axis 0–100 Rp trillion]

Source: Ministry of Finance (2014).

PROFESSIONALISM AND THE BUDGETARY BOOM

Yudhoyono's drive for security sector professionalism rested significantly on increased budgetary allowances. As Figure 7.1 shows, Polri's budget almost tripled under Yudhoyono, from Rp 16.61 trillion ($1.78 billion) in 2006 to Rp 47 trillion ($5.03 billion) in 2013. In 2014, a national budget deficit meant that the government cut this allocation by some Rp 5 trillion, the first cut to the police budget since the beginning of the Yudhoyono presidency (Haryanto 2014). Military and defence funding also increased dramatically, more than tripling during Yudhoyono's presidency. Figure 7.1 shows that from just under Rp 24 trillion in 2006, the defence budget (shared between the Ministry of Defence, the army, the navy and the air force) rose to Rp 83 trillion in 2014. Although the TNI was also threatened with cuts in 2014, in fact, no cuts occurred.

Budgets are important to democratic security-sector reform. They are a means for elected governments to exert control over security institutions, by providing greater revenues in exchange for institutional reform. Autonomous revenue-raising has been a privilege enjoyed by security forces across authoritarian regimes. In Indonesia, too, budgetary deficiencies historically allowed the police and the military to raise revenue independently. They did this, first, by establishing legal business entities, mostly subsumed beneath foundations and cooperatives; second, through informal or privately owned businesses run by retired and active officers; and finally, through illegal means, extracting rents and protection money from the criminal economy. Off-budget revenue-raising not only promotes a corrupt environment and undermines professionalism but also, as Mietzner and Misol (2013: 101–2) observe, allows security bodies to plan and fund policies and operations that run counter to the objectives of democratically elected leaders. Bringing funding on-budget is therefore essential to civilian control of the security sector.

In Indonesia, first-generation reforms prioritised ending the military's off-budget economy. As will be discussed below, Law 34/2004 on the Indonesian National Army laid the groundwork for Yudhoyono to dismantle the military's vast octopus of businesses. Although the police also maintained off-budget financing, similar provisions were not made in Law 2/2002 on the Indonesian National Police. Even so, Yudhoyono's persistent prioritisation of TNI and Polri funding was in keeping with necessary second-generation reforms.

But were the budget increases enough? In 2010, Yudhoyono pledged to raise the defence budget to 1.5 per cent of GDP by 2014, but it never reached even 1 per cent of GDP, well below the amount experts argued that the TNI needed to achieve its plan for 'Minimum Essential Force' within 30–40 years (Schreer 2013: 18) and consistently below the amounts requested by defence planners (Sebastian and Iisgindarsah 2013: 42). Although police officers acknowledged that more money was flowing through police territorial commands, operational funds were still well below law enforcement needs. Hence, despite the huge increases in the military and police budgets, observers often accused Yudhoyono of 'benign neglect'.[1]

How fair were such accusations? Yudhoyono identified multiple budget priorities during his two terms, including in other important sectors such as health, education and public works, leaving little fiscal room for the promised 1.5 per cent of GDP for defence (Howes and Davies 2014: 180). A more revealing question is whether, in the face of budgetary limitations, Yudhoyono attempted to increase value by demanding that the security institutions rationalise their on-budget spending through greater fiscal accountability. Simultaneously closing down off-budget revenue-raising while deepening budgetary oversight would have been in line with second-generation reforms.

The end of the casino economy

Paradoxically, Yudhoyono's boldest reform to security sector financing was his least evident. In 2005, he nominated General Sutanto as national

---

1 Benjamin Schreer, personal communication, 5 August 2014.

police chief. Upon taking office, Sutanto declared a nationwide war on gambling. Astonishingly, within a few months, across the country, everything from cockfights to the powerful illegal casinos that had operated for well over 40 years in North Jakarta had largely been eradicated. The anti-gambling crusade was largely credited to the fact that Sutanto had clashed with gambling kingpin Olo Panggabean over his longstanding gambling ventures in Medan.

But closing down Indonesia's vast illegal gambling industry took more than the vendetta of a single cop. Gambling funds had long found their way into every element of state life, from political campaigns to civil servant seminars. Casino revenues were crucial to the security sector's criminal economy, received in the form of routine monthly paycheques to police and military officers through the national and regional commands (Baker 2012). Ostensibly 'protection money', the payments had become a predictable staple of police and military off-budget financing. Thus, while the media speculated on the personal reasons for Sutanto's anti-gambling crusade, in fact, gambling revenues were so important to the security and political elites that the effort required presidential-level clout. By negotiating to shut the casinos, Yudhoyono sought to close an important source of off-budget revenue that had corrupted the police and military and to make the security sector more dependent on formal budgetary allocations (Baker 2012: 280).

Money without accountability?

The bold way in which Yudhoyono tackled gambling at the start of his presidency never rematerialised as a broader push to rationalise budgetary spending by security institutions. The president was reluctant to pressure TNI or Polri leaders to make internally unpopular decisions. For instance, spending on the TNI's 395,000-strong personnel continued to represent the biggest drain on the military budget, yet Yudhoyono never advocated downsizing, despite numerous recommendations to do so. Reducing troop numbers would not merely have been cost-effective, it would have tallied with second-generation reforms by reorienting the military away from domestic security (Sebastian and Iisgindarsah 2013: 37).

Military procurement was also highly problematic. Under Yudhoyono, around $8 billion was spent on modernisation (Bandoro 2014). However, doubts were expressed about the ad hoc nature of procurement and budget planning processes. Indonesia purchased weaponry from over 20 different countries, raising questions about the compatibility of multiple operating systems. Some specific purchases also raised eyebrows. For instance, Yudhoyono's fourth TNI commander, Agus

Suhartono, acquired 100 German Leopard tanks that were of questionable utility given Indonesian terrain and infrastructure. A leaked document suggested that the Ministry of Defence had spent $134.9 million more than budgeted on the 2012 purchase of a multi-launcher rocket system, with multiple violations of the procurement system (Witular 2014). Meanwhile, in 2013, Indonesia was ranked in the second-lowest band of Transparency International UK's Government Defence Anti-Corruption Index.[2]

Polri exhibited similar problems in budget planning and prioritising. Spending was allocated disproportionately to personnel and infrastructure rather than law enforcement. This was partly because expanding personnel numbers was a major priority for Polri as the force attempted to reduce its police-to-population ratio to the international standard of 1:450. In 1998, Polri's personnel numbered around 250,000 (Clark 2014: 68). In 2014, that number stood at around 400,000, bringing the ratio to 1:575.[3]

Unsurprisingly, the focus on personnel meant that Polri's primary budgetary expense was salaries. The projected budget for 2013, for example, devoted 61 per cent to personnel and 20 per cent to procurement (Ismanto 2012). The flow-on effect was significant; it meant that the budget allocated for criminal justice functions such as investigation and prosecution was very low.[4] Other problems included the fact that Polri headquarters in Jakarta routinely ate up around 50 per cent of the budget allocation. Interviews indicate that regionally based criminal investigation officers lacked the money to investigate cases and that the national investigation agencies were prioritised over the 4,000-plus stations at the provincial, district and subdistrict levels.

A second issue was budgetary transparency and accountability. First-generation reforms in public finance management produced several laws designed to increase budgetary oversight, including the State Finance Law (2003), Treasury Law (2004), State Audit Law (2004), National Development Planning Law (2004) and Supreme Audit Agency Law (2006). This meant that the Yudhoyono years saw the implementation of a set of new accountability measures, such as performance-based accounting systems and routine public audits. On paper, the reforms were reasonably successful; from 2007, security institutions performed better in pub-

---

2 See http://government.defenceindex.org/results/countries/indonesia#more.
3 Police chief Sutarman continued Polri's recruitment drive, arguing that a ratio of 1:300 was needed in Java's cities; see 'Rasio polisi dan masyarakat 1:575' [Ratio of police to people is 1:575], *Kompas*, 11 March 2014.
4 'Dana penindakan Polri sangat rendah' [Polri's enforcement funds are very low], *Berita Satu*, 12 October 2011.

lic audits, moving from disclaimer verdicts on audits conducted by the Supreme Audit Agency (Badan Pemeriksa Keuangan, BPK) to clean bills of health in the form of unqualified opinions.[5]

However, serious questions remained about the implementation of these laws. Although its reports were widely seen as credible, the BPK itself was not free of political influence (Peterson 2014), tending towards self-censorship or 'win–win' outcomes for it and the agency being audited (Dwiputriani 2011: 161). The lack of qualified accountants in the public service raised serious doubts about the capacity of the police and the military to implement new accounting standards (Harun 2007). Parliament's ability to respond to audit results was extremely limited (Dwiputriani 2011: 147), and became worse when Yudhoyono's Democrat Party (Partai Demokrat Party, PD) joined forces with pro-Prabowo parties in June 2014 to dissolve the parliament's State Finance Accountability Committee.

Reform failures on military and police businesses

What about efforts to improve government control over military finances by stripping it of businesses? The Megawati administration bequeathed to Yudhoyono Law 34/2004 on the Indonesian National Army (the TNI Law), with article 76 stipulating that 'within five years, the government must take over all business activities that are owned and operated by the military, both directly and indirectly'. This article tasked Yudhoyono with the job of outlining by presidential regulation which businesses would be subject to government takeover, and of effecting such a takeover by 2009. Over the following five years, no such decree was produced. Instead, in the face of repeated statements by senior TNI officers defending the businesses, Yudhoyono dithered. He allowed the TNI to conduct an independent inventory of its businesses, then lost more time vacillating over the formation of an interministerial team to manage the takeovers. The team subsequently reinitiated the inventory, with the TNI using the delay to quietly sell off its shares in the few remaining businesses that remained lucrative in the newly competitive post-*reformasi* business environment (Mietzner and Misol 2013: 116). The sales were not approved by the government and the profits were not returned to the state, instead either returning to military coffers or siphoned off by officers.

By 2009, the year of the deadline, little had been accomplished. Yudhoyono had ignored key recommendations made by the takeover team in 2008. In October 2009, he produced Presidential Regulation 43/2009,

---

5 See the BPK's biannual summaries of audit reports for 2008–14 at http://www.bpk.go.id/ihps.

which established another takeover team. The decree was characteristically vague. The team's work was not circumscribed by time limits and the order to take over businesses did not necessitate government ownership of them. The team also had no authority over TNI personnel, making the takeover dependent on processes internal to the TNI. Ultimately, the decree pushed the team towards a narrow definition of TNI businesses, excluding not only criminal and grey-area, informal businesses, but also foundations, cooperatives, businesses that were listed under the names of individual officers, and those that were nominally independent, contributed to troop 'welfare' or did not use state assets. The main effect was to prompt restructuring of TNI businesses into the more politically palatable category of 'cooperatives'. Despite announcements in 2013 by Finance Minister Chatib Basri that 900 TNI businesses would be taken over, including foundations and cooperatives both directly and indirectly owned, no such takeover took place.[6] As Mietzner and Misol (2013: 114) observe, the 'definitions set out in the 2009 decree helped TNI maintain control over its co-operatives, foundations and associated businesses'.

Yudhoyono's evasion of the legal mandate of the 2004 TNI Law suggests that the president had little interest in reining in the military's economic privileges. In 2012, he argued that the tasks of business and war mirrored each other, emphasising that a good TNI officer usually succeeded in business because the two trades required similar skills (Pratomo 2012). Like many of the military appointees who protested the takeover of TNI businesses, Yudhoyono apparently shared the view that soldiers were persons with unique leadership qualities, that the TNI was an institution with a special history and needs, and that it needed to be allowed to raise revenue autonomously.

Mietzner and Misol (2013) argue that despite the failure of reform, the value of military businesses had been reduced by the free market competition of the post-1998 era. Another reason for the fall in value was that the military faced increasing business competition from Polri. Indeed, competition between the security institutions for business opportunities has been a defining characteristic of the post-authoritarian era.

Although police businesses were listed in academic inventories of military businesses published in the early years of *reformasi*, little is known about them beyond the main foundation owned by Polri headquarters, Yayasan Brata Bhakti. Like military money-raising, police revenue-raising traverses the full spectrum of illegal, grey-area and legal

---

6 'Pemerintah akan ambil alih 900 perusahan milik yayasan TNI' [Government will take control of 900 businesses owned by TNI foundations], *JaringNews*, 9 July 2013.

activities. Many police officers personally own businesses that they use, at least in part, to finance their police work. The idea that officers are entitled to do business in order to secure the welfare of the rank and file is as entrenched within the police as it is within the military. Despite the similarities, Yudhoyono never seriously addressed the question of what to do with police businesses.

The failure to reform police and military businesses not only bolstered the two institutions' fiscal independence but also countered Yudhoyono's ambition to create a more coherent and unified security sector. Despite the president's show of force against casino gaming at the start of his tenure, Mietzner (2008) argues that grey-area and criminal activity actually expanded as a means of revenue-raising. With two security forces plying the same territory for protection rents, competition led to sporadic physical clashes, often resulting in injuries or death. Interagency firefights began almost as soon as the two institutions were separated in 1999, continuing throughout the Yudhoyono decade. The Habibie Center's National Violence Monitoring System counted 54 such clashes between 2005 and 2014.[7] Yudhoyono expressed concern about the clashes and called on Polri and TNI leaders to form joint 'fact-finding' teams to investigate them. However, he never called for third-party investigators or proposed bringing culprits to criminal trial. Instead, the president allowed the issue to be managed in-house, reinforcing TNI/Polri impunity, undermining calls for greater civilian oversight and failing to address the entrenched problem of off-budget financing that underlay the conflicts.

In sum, the Yudhoyono decade saw hugely increased budgetary allocations for both Polri and the TNI. Had these been combined with a commensurate push to eradicate police and military businesses, tighten budgetary oversight and reprioritise spending towards more cost-effective goals, they would have been good policy. But, except for vague exhortations to be 'professional', Yudhoyono failed to leverage the carrot of budgetary increases into substantive reform.

DEMOCRATIC OVERSIGHT OF THE SECURITY INSTITUTIONS

Civilian governance and oversight is a central pillar in security sector reform. Democratic oversight of the security sector begins from the principle that coercive institutions should be accountable to the public,

---

7 See the tweet by Vidya Hutagalung (Habibie Center) to David McRae (Asia Centre, University of Melbourne) dated 21 November 2014, available at https://twitter.com/_DaveMcRae_/status/535760111155687425.

the law and the state. The precise forms of oversight differ between the military and the police and across differing governance systems. Ideally, however, the police and the military should be accountable to (1) the judiciary and subject to criminal law; (2) the public—through parliament, civil society and independent complaints boards; and (3) the state, in the form of control by the executive and the bureaucracy.

Unclear oversight of the military

Indonesia's first-generation reforms outlined oversight structures in legislation for Polri (Law 2/2002 on the Indonesian National Police) and the TNI (Law 34/2004 on the Indonesian National Army and Law 3/2002 on State Defence). The Police and State Defence laws passed with little public scrutiny, but the TNI Law was delayed by two years and involved extended compromises. Article 3 of the TNI Law specifies that on matters of deployment and use of force, the TNI 'sits below the president'; however, in matters of defence policy, strategy and administration, the TNI is 'under the coordination' of the Ministry of Defence. Why the legislation uses different phrases to outline executive accountability is unclear, as is the precise meaning of 'coordination'. Parliamentary oversight is similarly scrappy; although Commission I oversees the military and has powers of approval over the selection of the TNI chief, use of force and the defence budget, Sebastian and Iisgindarsah (2013: 40) note that it is unclear what constitutes 'approval' and what role parliament has in supervising defence policy.

The legislative haze meant that the TNI commander continued to occupy a seat in cabinet alongside the defence minister; although the Ministry of Defence issued policies and decisions that pertained to the military, by and large these were of a routine strategic or administrative nature and had prior TNI approval. Yudhoyono showed interest neither in increasing the responsibility of the ministry over the TNI nor in entrusting the wider project of democratic security-sector reform to civilian ministry officials. On the whole, the TNI remained accountable to itself alone.

Legal impunity for the TNI

The president's lack of interest in enhancing democratic oversight was also evident in the pressing issue of legal accountability. The TNI Law contained several relevant provisions, notably article 65, which stated that 'soldiers must obey the military courts in the case of violations of military law and the civilian courts in the case of violations of criminal law'. Previously, Law 26/1997 on Military Discipline had allowed the

TNI to discipline its own personnel by maintaining the supremacy of the military courts. Article 65 of the TNI Law stated that military obedience to the law would be outlined in subsequent legislation, which fell squarely in Yudhoyono's court.

Accordingly, during the president's first term, a special parliamentary commission drafted a military tribunal bill that sought to affirm soldiers' equality before the law in criminal and civil matters. However, the TNI and the Ministry of Defence dragged out the discussions. Even though Yudhoyono expressed support for the bill in 2006, a coalition of parties, including the president's party, PD, abandoned deliberations before the 2009 elections. It was rumoured that the president engineered this outcome, fearing the bill would threaten TNI support for his re-election campaign. The bill's failure meant that the military courts maintained their supremacy, and had other flow-on effects—for instance, making military personnel effectively exempt from investigation by the Corruption Eradication Commission (Komisi Pemberantasan Korupsi, KPK).

The president's position on civilian trials for criminal violations was further tested when, on 23 March 2013, 11 soldiers from the army's Special Forces (Komando Pasukan Khusus, Kopassus) conducted a raid on Cebongan jail in Yogyakarta, killing four detainees charged with murdering a fellow soldier. Given the failure of the military tribunal bill, Yudhoyono was besieged with calls to issue a government regulation in lieu of law (*peraturan pemerintah pengganti undang-undang, perppu*) to ensure that the perpetrators would be tried in a civilian criminal court. Yudhoyono shrugged off such demands. He condemned the killings, demanded that the police and military 'disclose and arrest the perpetrators in a professional manner' and called on the public to 'give them [the military and the police] ample room to work professionally'.[8] He also labelled the perpetrators 'noble' (*kesatria*) for their willingness to accept 'responsibility' for their actions.[9] Yudhoyono's brother-in-law, General Pramono Edhie Wibowo, established a military team to investigate the killings. Three low-ranking non-commissioned officers were sentenced in a military court to periods of six to eleven years in jail for premeditated murder, and five others were given sentences of 21 months.

The Cebongan case renewed calls from civil society to revive the military tribunal bill and transfer authority for criminal cases involving soldiers to civilian courts. In October 2014, however, during the last

---

8 'Lesson should be learned from Cebongan prison attack: president', *Antaranews.com*, 5 April 2013.

9 'SBY bilang pelaku penyerangan LP Cebongan kesatria' [SBY says that the perpetrators of the LP Cebongan attack are noble], *Tempo*, 5 April 2013.

sitting of the year, parliament passed amendments to the 1997 Military Discipline Law that reframed criminal offenses as disciplinary issues to be dealt with in-house by the military, thereby ensuring that the military would continue to be protected from the wider criminal justice system and rule of law.

Politicisation of the police

In 1999, the dissolution of ABRI moved Polri under the president. At the time, the country's law-makers were clear: this was a temporary governance arrangement pending further consideration about which ministry — probably Home Affairs or Justice — would best house the institution. In 2002, however, the Police Law shored up the move to place Polri below the president, despite commentary that the police would be better served by ministerial supervision. Polri submits to parliamentary oversight, but police frequently argue that the further step of ministerial control would result in their 'politicisation' and demean attempts to professionalise the institution. However, Hills (2007: 407) argues that in African states, it is the relationship of the police to the president that is political:

> Presidents do not want an effective or efficient police answerable to parliamentary committees or judicial enquiries ... they value the police as a tool for enforcing political decisions, maintaining order, regulating activities and regime representation.

But did Yudhoyono use the police to further his political interests? There is little evidence that he politicised the police, compared to his predecessors, Megawati Sukarnoputri and Abdurrahman Wahid. Wahid sacked General Bimantoro when he refused to protect him from impeachment. In 2004, Megawati's presidential campaign was supported by national police chief Da'i Bachtiar, who ordered police families to vote for her party. In contrast, under Yudhoyono, there was no suggestion of overt abuse of police authority to support presidential power. Certainly, Yudhoyono ignored repeated calls from government and civil society to place the police under a ministry, but this simply seems to have been a part of his wider predilection for status quo outcomes.

For Polri, maintaining a close structural relationship with the president served interlinked objectives. First, it amplified the police's sense of self-importance, helping them in their ongoing power struggle with the military. Second, although presidential supervision appeared to be the most concentrated form of institutional control, in reality the president had little time or inclination to supervise day-to-day police affairs, leaving policy, strategy and reform to the police themselves. Like the TNI, Polri was effectively given free rein to control its own institutional reform, impeding efforts to increase accountability and transparency, improve service delivery and promote respect for human rights. Presidential rule was effectively self-rule.

This is the nub of politicisation. Rather than outright politicking, by neglecting his managerial brief and allowing the police to self-govern, Yudhoyono ensured that the police remained corrupt, divided and subject to influence. The president further weakened the prospects for reform through his nominations of national police chiefs, especially in the latter part of his rule. The deeply contested appointment of Timur Pradopo in 2010 and the bland option of Sutarman in 2013 passed over more senior officers with better reformist credentials. Bereft of strong leadership and safeguarded from meaningful public or state oversight, Polri made only weak reforms to its bureaucratic procedures while barely touching police corruption, abuses of authority and human rights abuses. Polri officers have no interest in serious structural reform of the oversight framework of a sort that would end police impunity and bring about a more professional force.

Kneecapping the National Police Commission (Kompolnas)

In lieu of an independent complaints board and a dedicated ministry for Polri, the 2002 Police Law established a national police commission — Komisi Kepolisian Nasional, or Kompolnas — that answered to the president. Two of its main tasks were to advise on police reform and to handle complaints about the police (though the law gave the commission no powers to investigate or prosecute). The commission is something of an institutional hybrid, a strained amalgam of an independent public complaints board and a bureaucratic body with some of the functions of a ministry. Kompolnas has nine commissioners, three of whom are cabinet ministers. The remaining six are retired police generals, academics, journalists and professionals.

With such a motley brief, the commission was always going to struggle to deliver public oversight. However, its first battle was simply to get started; the president delayed his approval of commissioners so long that it was only in 2007 that the commission became fully functional. Although the 2002 Police Law contained provisions to fund Kompolnas solely through the state budget, the commission's quarters were on police turf, and it used police infrastructure, administration and utilities. There is no evidence that Yudhoyono referred to Kompolnas for advice on police governance during his two terms in office. In interviews, commissioners complained that they were routinely sidelined by the cosy relationship between the president and the police. Unlike the Ministry of Defence, which, however nominally, at least 'coordinated' the TNI, Kompolnas had a deeply unbalanced relationship with Polri in which power rested largely with the police. For instance, in 2014, when Kompolnas commissioner Adrianus Meliala criticised police corruption, national police chief Sutarman repeatedly refused to meet with him, threatening defamation charges.

Yudhoyono's second term saw Kompolnas weakened considerably. For the second election of commissioners in 2013, the president overlooked a strong pool of police critics and policy specialists, and nominated a number of commissioners without experience in police governance. Logistical support declined noticeably. In early 2014, Kompolnas asked for the 2002 Police Law to be revised to strengthen its oversight capacities, but received no presidential response.

In sum, Indonesia's police and military are largely self-governing. Blame for this cannot be laid entirely at Yudhoyono's feet. First-generation reforms carried out under the Megawati and Wahid administrations established a legislative framework wherein legal, state and public oversight of Polri and the TNI was unclear and weak. Given the extensive political negotiations needed to erect that framework, it is perhaps understandable that Yudhoyono had little appetite for further legislative reform. However, when opportunities arose to correct flawed first-generation reforms or to deepen second-generation reforms—for example, by revising the 2002 Police Law or the military tribunal bill—Yudhoyono squandered them. Such failures suggest that the president held, at best, deeply ambivalent views about the principle of civil supremacy over the security institutions.

SECTORAL REFORM

As suggested previously, the literature on democratic security-sector reform rarely addresses the relationship between the police and the military. Bringing the two institutions into a single analytical frame draws attention to the division of authority between them and to their interrelationships. What emerges from such an analysis is that post-authoritarian police reform and military reform are not separate processes, but deeply intertwined. This is not problematic if institutions experience adequate state oversight and the reform agenda is determined by elected civilian representatives. However, for institutions like the TNI and Polri, which enjoy scope to determine their own reform agenda, what emerges is a reform stalemate, where the likelihood of internal reforms in one institution depends on the willingness of the other to undertake reforms.

As we have seen, since the transition to democracy in Indonesia, relations between the police and the military have been tense and competitive, largely due to enhanced police authority over the prized area of domestic security. First-generation reforms were unable to address these tensions because they involved a series of negotiated settlements with each institution, with little concern for how the outcomes might affect the overall working of the security sector. For instance, the absence of ministerial control of the police as per the 2002 Police Law antagonised the military and stymied wider debate about the necessity of deepening the military's subordination to the Ministry of Defence.

There are numerous examples of such reform failure, but the most severe and enduring was the failure to roll back the territorial command system (Komando Territorial, Koter) by which the military maintained a presence at every level of geographic administration. This system was the hallmark of New Order military authoritarianism. By 2000, as Mietzner (2009: 226) outlines, substantive discussion of reform of the territorial command system was dead in the water. While preserving the territorial apparatus was crucial to getting military buy-in to other reforms, this early first-generation decision preserved a vast military-run policing structure that mirrored Polri's own. This meant that, on the ground, police authority was systematically undercut by counterpart military units ostensibly engaged in domestic policing. For the police, the Koter system was a persistent reminder of the limits of democratic reform and of the need to jealously guard their turf from military incursion.

This was the fraught security landscape into which the Yudhoyono administration waded when, over the president's two terms, it attempted to pass several bills that pertained to the sector, including bills on state secrets, military assistance to the police, auxiliary defence components and national security. In this section, I concentrate on the bill on national security (*keamanan negara*), or what became known as the Kamnas bill. Given the fraught relations between Polri and the military, any legislative movement in this area was regarded as an attempt to recalibrate the balance of power between the military and the police, none more so than the Kamnas bill.

The need for sector-wide reform further regulating the police–military relationship was clear. Laws governing the security sector had many conflicting provisions, or raised questions. The 2002 Police Law ostensibly put the police in charge of 'security' (*keamanan*), which many, particularly Polri, interpreted as all domestic and national security issues. By contrast, article 7 of the 2004 TNI Law carved out a space for the TNI in 'activities other than war', including supporting governance in the regions, helping the police to protect citizens, protecting foreign dignitaries, assisting local government in cases of piracy, hijack or smuggling, assisting in natural disasters and fighting armed separatist movements. The TNI and Polri argued that they had signed numerous memorandums of understanding to plug the regulatory gap. In practice, however, the management of complex security issues—such as violence in Papua—was negotiated on an ad hoc basis at each level of the police and military commands.

The Kamnas bill was originally drafted to clarify the regulatory space between the police and the military. Yudhoyono's first defence minister, Juwono Sudarsono, drafted it in 2005–06, initially through a series of workshops involving a civil society group, Propatria, and police and military representatives. But Polri was suspicious from the beginning and police representatives consistently refused to turn up or, if they did, to endorse group decisions. Leaked elements of the draft bill suggested that the police would be placed under a ministry, souring relations. In the resultant media storm, police and military feuded by proxy over the Kamnas bill, deploying an army of experts, parliamentarians and previously unknown NGOs to accuse each other of betraying democracy and security sector reform. In 2007, Yudhoyono responded by calling the institutions into the palace and demanding they end the public debate.

The Kamnas bill was thus stalled until Yudhoyono's second term, when it was redrafted by the Ministry of Defence. The revised bill made no specifications about the position of the police, but Polri feared that the defence ministry's control would expand the role of the military in domestic security and reduce its own influence. In 2010, however, with the appointment of a weakened national police chief, Timur Pradopo, the TNI and the Ministry of Defence successfully strong-armed Polri into signing off on a new Kamnas draft, which it then sent to parliament. The bill was heavily criticised by the public, principally for expanding the role of the military in the management of communal conflict and expanding the role of the president in deploying the military. Although Polri said nothing in public, in private the police encouraged criticism of the bill through their civil society and parliamentary contacts. From 2010, the bill was drafted and redrafted numerous times and submitted to parliament at least twice. When it became evident in early 2013 that it would not pass, Yudhoyono drafted Presidential Instruction 2/2013 on the Management of Disturbances to Internal National Security. This deeply flawed executive regulation extended the president's powers to deploy the military in response to social conflict and terrorism without parliamentary approval, expanded the role of the TNI commander and authorised regional heads to deploy the TNI and Polri in cases of communal conflict.

This outcome should not be read as evidence of authoritarian or power-hoarding tendencies on the part of Yudhoyono. Rather, it showed his adherence to a set of conservative beliefs that have long characterised the Jakarta elite, including a belief in the sanctity of presidential office and a belief in the special status of the military in social and political life.

Throughout Yudhoyono's two terms in office, the president entrusted the Ministry of Defence and the TNI to draft numerous regulations that would govern the sector, an opportunity they used to expand the role of the military in public life, thus worsening relations with Polri. His reluctance to promote a strong democratic framework for governing security issues deepened the politicisation of the TNI and Polri. Both institutions were drawn into policy debate, and became adept at courting political parties and other social groups to wage their battles by proxy.

CONCLUSION

President Yudhoyono is generally praised for his record of democratic achievement, one part of which is his perceived reputation as a military reformer. However, this essay has demonstrated that, when viewed closely, the president's record of military and police reform is one of failure. The failures to rein in the security forces' economic privileges, to respond to calls for greater civilian oversight of these institutions and to stabilise the security sector by establishing a sound regulatory framework to govern it were not just the routine stumbles of a necessarily negotiated democratisation. Instead, they showed that Yudhoyono was prepared to squander—willingly and fully—unique opportunities to implement deeper second-generation reforms. Rather than using the possibilities opened up by first-generation reforms to push through greater oversight of the security institutions, the president avoided and in many cases sabotaged the chance to exact greater oversight.

Yudhoyono's brand of reform was characterised by a stress on professionalisation. The push for professionalisation was not itself unreasonable; indeed, professionalisation is a neglected final step in democratic security-sector reform. But in Indonesia, the premature focus on modernisation, increased procurement and budgetary inflation effectively rewarded Polri and the TNI, despite tenuous civilian supremacy and delayed second-generation reforms. Professionalisation was experienced as an entitlement of the TNI and Polri, rather than being levered as a bait to effect reform. The result was to entrench the status quo and further erode the prospects for reform. Succeeding Indonesian presidents are unlikely to be able to effect greater civilian control over the security forces.

As the coercive institutions of the state, the military and the police have the power to veto regime change, or at least to thwart and stall democratic consolidation. Consequently, democratic security-sector reform is by its nature negotiated and often incomplete. Is this why Yudhoyono made such heavy compromises in security sector reform?

But as Mietzner (2013) argues, the TNI never enjoyed full veto power over the political system and by the time of Yudhoyono's presidency, the first-generation reforms instituted by his predecessors had set the tone for future, if imperfect, democratisation. Meanwhile, as law-enforcers, the police enjoyed considerable bargaining power in a political system riddled with graft, but this leeway was balanced by the president's unparalleled control over Polri. Moreover, unlike his elected predecessors, Megawati and Wahid, the president was a former military man, with a decisive series of electoral wins under his belt, who should have possessed unique authority to push through security sector reform.

Yudhoyono's actions, and inaction, have frequently been chalked up to character flaws, notably a personal disposition to avoid conflict. But in the case of the security sector, Yudhoyono was also limited intellectually by his own soft-conservative leanings and his enduring belief in the special and sanctified nature of Indonesia's security sector, particularly the TNI. His behaviour in this area illustrates that he remained unconvinced by the idea of deep civilian supremacy and continued to see an important role for the security agencies in nation-building and national leadership. Far from offering the final step in a sequence leading to control and normalisation of the security institutions, Yudhoyono's presidency retarded security sector reform.

REFERENCES

Baker, J. (2012) 'The rise of Polri: the political economy of security in democratizing Indonesia', PhD thesis, Department of Government, London School of Economics, London.

Bandoro, B. (2014) 'Yudhoyono's Asian Tiger gaffe leaves the Indonesian military at sea' *Jakarta Globe*, 13 October. Available at http://thejakartaglobe.beritasatu.com/opinion/sbys-asian-tiger-gaffe-leaves-tni-sea/

Clark, M. (2014) *Police and Governance in Indonesia: The Police in the Era of Reformasi*, Routledge, New York.

Cottey, A., T. Edmunds and A. Forster (eds) (2002) *Democratic Control of the Military in Postcommunist Europe: Guarding the Guards*, Palgrave, London.

Dwiputriani, S. (2011) 'Effectiveness of public sector audit reports in Indonesia', PhD thesis, Crawford School of Economics and Government, Australian National University, Canberra.

Faridz, D. (2014) 'Indonesia's military marks 69 years of operation', *Channel News Asia*, 7 October. Available at http://www.channelnewsasia.com/news/asiapacific/indonesia-s-military/1402772.html

Firdaus, F. (2014) 'Pesan SBY ke Polri: sikat penjahat, lindungi masyarakat' [Message from SBY to Polri: bust the criminals, protect the community], *Okezone*, 1 July. Available at http://news.okezone.com/read/2014/07/01/339/1006799/pesan-sby-ke-polri-sikat-penjahat-lindungi-masyarakat

Harun, H. (2007) 'Obstacles to public sector accounting reform in Indonesia', *Bulletin of Indonesian Economic Studies*, 43(3): 365–75.

Haryanto, A. (2014) 'Polri terkena pemotongan anggaran Rp 5,78 triliun' [Polri subject to Rp 5.78 trillion budget cut], *detikNews*, 4 June. Available at http://news.detik.com/read/2014/06/04/005009/2599007/10/polri-terkena-pemotongan-anggaran-rp-578-triliun

Hills, A. (2007) 'Police commissioners, presidents and the governance of security', *Journal of Modern African Studies*, 45(3): 403–23.

Hinton, M.S. (2006) *The State on the Streets: Police and Politics in Brazil and Argentina*, Lynne Rienner, Boulder CO.

Honna, J. (2003) *Military Politics and Democratization in Indonesia*, Routledge, London and New York.

Howes, S. and R. Davies (2014) 'Survey of recent developments', *Bulletin of Indonesian Economic Studies*, 50(2): 157–83.

Ismanto, H. (2012) 'Gemuknya anggaran Polri hanya pada belanja personil saja' [Most of Polri budget spent only on personnel], *Indonesia Raya News*, 13 October. Available at http://indonesiarayanews.com/read/2012/10/13/25969/rss.xml

Mietzner, M. (2006) 'The politics of military reform in post-Suharto Indonesia: elite conflict, nationalism and institutional resistance', Policy Studies 23, East-West Center, Washington DC.

Mietzner, M. (2008) 'Soldiers, parties and bureaucrats: illicit fund raising in contemporary Indonesia', *Southeast Asia Research*, 39(3): 225–54.

Mietzner, M. (2009) *Military Politics, Islam and the State in Indonesia: From Turbulent Transition to Democratic Consolidation*, Institute of Southeast Asian Studies, Singapore.

Mietzner, M. (2013) 'Veto player no more? The declining political influence of the military in postauthoritarian Indonesia', in M. Künkler and A. Stepan (eds) *Democracy and Islam in Indonesia*, Columbia University Press, New York: 89–108.

Mietzner, M. and L. Misol (2013) 'Military businesses in post-Suharto Indonesia: decline, reform and persistence', in J. Rüland, M.-G. Manea and H. Born (eds) *The Politics of Military Reform: Experiences from Indonesia and Nigeria*, Springer-Heidelberg, New York: 101–22.

Ministry of Finance (2014) 'Nota keuangan dan anggaran pendapatan dan belanja negara perubahan: tahun anggaran 2014' [Financial notes and national revenue and expenditure budget amendments: budget year 2014], Jakarta. Available at http://www.anggaran.depkeu.go.id/dja/acontent/NKAPBNP2014.pdf

Peterson, A. (2014) 'The politics of audit', *Inside Indonesia*, 117(July–September). Available at www.insideindonesia.org/feature-editions/the-politics-of-audit

Pratomo, Y. (2012) 'SBY: pilpres 2014, sipil atau militer layak diperhitungkan' [SBY: presidential election 2014, civil or military candidates are a good option], *Merdeka.com*, 2 October. Available at http://www.merdeka.com/pemilu-2014/sby-pilpres-2014-sipil-atau-militer-layak-diperhitungkan.html

Rinakit, S. (2005) *The Indonesian Military after the New Order*, NIAS Press, Singapore.

Rizki, P. (2014) 'Pemerintah tetap prioritaskan profesionalisme dan modernisasi TNI' [Government still prioritises professionalism and modernisation of the TNI], *Voice of America*, 7 October. Available at http://www.voaindonesia.com/content/modernisme-tni-tetap-jadi-prioritas-pemerintah/2475503.html

Schreer, B. (2013) 'Moving beyond ambitions? Indonesia's military modernisation', Australian Strategic Policy Institute, Canberra, November.

Available at www.aspi.org.au/publications/moving-beyond-ambitions-indonesians-military-modernisation

Schreer, B. (2014) 'Military reform', lecture given at the Australian National University, Canberra, 29 April.

Sebastian, L.C. and Iisgindarsah (2013) 'Taking stock of military reform in Indonesia', in J. Rüland, M.-G. Manea and H. Born (eds) *The Politics of Military Reform: Experiences from Indonesia and Nigeria*, Springer-Heidelberg, New York: 29–56.

Witular, R. (2014) 'Red flag raised over arms deal', *Jakarta Post*, 10 December. Available at http://www.thejakartapost.com/news/2014/12/10/red-flag-raised-over-arms-deal.html

Yudhoyono, S.B. (1990) 'Profesionalisme perwira ABRI: masa kini dan masa depan' [Professionalism of ABRI officers: today and in the future], Seskoad, Bandung.

Yudhoyono, S.B. (1998) 'Kata pengantar' [Preface], in *ABRI Profesional dan Dedikatif* [A Professional and Dedicated Armed Forces], Pusaka Sinar Harapan and Yayasan Cadaka Dharma, Jakarta: vii-xi.

8 Yudhoyono's legacy on internal security: achievements and missed opportunities

Sidney Jones

Managing internal security affairs is one of the most vital policy portfolios for any president, especially in countries with a long history of communal, political and separatist violence. For Susilo Bambang Yudhoyono, this area should have been his primary area of expertise, given his military background and his many years as the key government minister in charge of security affairs. Nevertheless, his commitment to find solutions was not always accompanied by direct personal involvement or the necessary expenditure of political capital. Three of the biggest internal security problems confronting Yudhoyono when he took office in 2004 were the insurgency in Aceh, violence in Papua and terrorism. Generally, he has been given high marks on the first and the third, and credit for at least trying on the second (MacIntyre and Ramage 2008). On all three, however, he could have done much more. He was generally reactive rather than proactive, letting external events force policy changes rather than providing clear strategic direction. He liked setting intellectual guidelines, but rarely did any of the heavy lifting himself. The opposite of a micromanager, he was happy to leave implementation to subordinates. He was often more interested in form than in substance, using the creation of new institutions as proof of commitment without the necessary follow-up to ensure they actually worked. At no point during his two terms was there any attempt to step back and look at security policy in a way that assessed overall needs and developed capabilities accordingly.

Yudhoyono has received the most praise on Aceh, not only for the 2005 peace agreement but for also ensuring that the peace was maintained. Indeed, his first vice-president, Jusuf Kalla, had for some time been actively seeking contact with the leadership of the Free Aceh Movement (Gerakan Aceh Merdeka, GAM). Yudhoyono, as president, was open to pursuing international mediation, and it could be argued that he was proactive during his first few months in office. But without the 26 December 2004 tsunami to give peace-making a new impetus and urgency, Yudhoyono's habitual dithering would almost certainly have led to endless discussions without a clear resolution. Instead, with Kalla in charge of the government negotiating team, an agreement was signed in Helsinki in August 2005 after just five formal meetings. This peace accord, in turn, ended the conflict and eventually brought the old diaspora GAM leadership to power in the province. The Aceh agreement remains one of the most significant achievements of the Yudhoyono administration, but once it was achieved, the president seemed unwilling to press GAM leaders on a range of ongoing problems, including extortion, corruption and bad governance. Rather than demanding that GAM relinquish its old habits, he capitulated to their demands, apparently out of fear that to do otherwise would risk a return to conflict and place his reputation as peace-maker in jeopardy.

The various Papuan conflicts—separatist, interethnic, electoral and land- and resource-related—were largely an afterthought during Yudhoyono's first term, as Aceh dominated the agenda. A steady stream of violence and the recognition that special autonomy, granted in 2001, had led to very little change, motivated Yudhoyono to propose a 'New Deal' for Papua that would try to speed up economic development without addressing political issues. Even within its limited framework, he did little to make it work. When it failed, Yudhoyono still wanted to leave office with a lasting legacy on Papua, so in mid-2013 he suggested introducing 'enhanced' special autonomy. It proved to be more controversial than he expected, and he left office with Papua's problems as intractable as they were when he entered.

In the area of terrorism, Yudhoyono basked in the reflected glory of the police counterterrorism units, especially on trips abroad. However, he showed little inclination to risk political capital with conservative Muslims by actively encouraging the development of a counterradicalisation policy. It took the 2009 Jakarta hotel bombings to spur him to set up a national anti-terrorism agency—but this was largely because he himself had been targeted. Even then there was no urgency about drafting a national strategy. If terrorism casualties remained low, it was more because of effective law enforcement, cooperative neighbours and the lack of major local drivers than any successful preventive initiatives.

This chapter discusses Yudhoyono's legacy in the area of internal security. It evaluates, in turn, his achievements in Aceh, Papua and counterterrorism, weighing his lasting contributions against his reluctance to institutionalise and consolidate them. In all three areas, Yudhoyono was intellectually committed to reducing conflict, and he launched or supported initiatives that partially succeeded in doing so. But consistent with the evidence presented in other chapters in this volume (see Chapter 12 by Berger on Yudhoyono's human rights legacy, for example), he was not prepared to antagonise vested interests to achieve more meaningful reform. In the end, he often settled for whatever could be achieved without ruffling any feathers. Given his personal commitment to democracy and the rule of law, Yudhoyono should have been able to achieve much more—had he just been a little less risk-averse and a little more imaginative.

ACEH: THE CROWN JEWEL

The 2005 Helsinki agreement on Aceh was the jewel in the crown of the Yudhoyono administration. No achievement had such dramatic and lasting impact; no outcome received such international acclaim. The question is what role Yudhoyono played in generating that agreement and what interest he took in the follow-up. Yudhoyono's own version of events was that he was committed to finding an agreement with GAM even before he became president; that plans to have an international mediator, namely former Finnish president Martti Ahtisaari, involved as mediator were well under way when the tsunami struck; that, as president, he provided overall direction and helped secure a neutral stance from the military; and that he and Jusuf Kalla worked as a united team (Morfit 2007). All that is true, up to a point. Without a green light from the president, no agreement would have been possible. But it is also true that without Kalla's determination to take political risks and make quick and dramatic decisions, no agreement would have been achieved.

Yudhoyono's extreme caution made him an unlikely peace-broker. In general, he supported the peaceful resolution of conflicts as long as it did not conflict with vested interests or engender strong opposition within the political establishment. This was clear from his approach to Aceh when he was coordinating minister for political, social and security affairs, first under President Abdurrahman Wahid (2000–01), then under President Megawati Sukarnoputri (2001–04). He supported 'comprehensive measures' that would include both military operations and dialogue, and he became the most important champion within the Megawati administration of the peace process advocated by the Henri Dunant Centre (now known as the Centre for Humanitarian Dialogue) between 2000 and 2003 (Aspinall and Crouch 2003: 8–9). In this context, he and

Kalla—also a senior minister under Megawati—were in regular communication over Kalla's efforts to establish contact with different factions of GAM. But once it became clear that there was strong opposition, particularly from the military but also from important elements in the government, to talking to 'separatists', Yudhoyono was not prepared either to defend the position or to intervene to try to salvage a tenuous ceasefire. His main concern was 'to demonstrate to domestic and international audiences that [the government] had exhausted all attempts at negotiation' (Aspinall and Crouch 2003: 45).

After their election to the presidency and vice-presidency in October 2004, Yudhoyono and Kalla entered talks with Martti Ahtisaari's organisation, the Crisis Management Initiative, about facilitating negotiations. There was no indication, however, that Yudhoyono was willing to move far beyond established positions. Shortly after he was elected, he told *Time Magazine*:

> The current military operation under way in Aceh must be maintained; if there were to be a power vacuum, a new threat to security could arise. But there should also be a new approach to finding a peaceful solution. There is an opportunity for us to end the conflict in Aceh with a new policy. I appeal to the leaders of the separatists to reunite [with Indonesia], and to their soldiers to come out [from hiding] and disarm. That would be the end of the armed struggle, and would allow for special autonomy to be carried out. I will consult with parliament about granting amnesty to those who voluntarily surrender.[1]

He had no clear ideas to put on the table apart from an offer of an amnesty and he did not envision the government making any meaningful political concessions. It needed the December 2004 tsunami to focus the attention of both sides on peace, and the final arrangements for negotiations were quickly concluded. Yudhoyono gave his full support to the talks but was more than willing to let Kalla defend them against extensive political opposition (Aspinall 2005). As it turned out, the deal-maker for the Helsinki agreement was the issue of local political parties. GAM demanded to be given the right to form its own political party in Aceh, whereas Indonesian legislation decreed that all parties had to have a nationwide network. Yudhoyono's early statements suggested that any compromise here was out of the question because local parties were 'not known' in Indonesia (Aspinall and Crouch 2003: 35). Had it been up to Yudhoyono, the 'concession' would have been to get the established political parties to agree to nominate GAM-approved candidates. When GAM rejected this outright, it was Kalla, not Yudhoyono, who understood that Indonesia needed to allow for local parties in Aceh if it wanted to make peace.

---

1 'We need shock therapy', *Time Magazine*, 8 November 2004.

In the end Yudhoyono went along with this. Had he been in direct charge of the negotiating team, however, it is clear that there would have been no decisions, only endless consultations.

Yudhoyono was happy to take the credit and acclaim for reaching a peace deal, and bolstered by the international praise, he did play an important role in bringing the military — a major potential spoiler — on board. In this, he was enormously aided by the then commander of the armed forces, General Endriartono Sutarto, who, whatever his own misgivings about the peace agreement, was willing to tell senior officers in no uncertain terms that if they spoke out against government policy, they would have to leave the military (Morfit 2007: 15). When coming to office, Yudhoyono had insisted on keeping Endriartono Sutarto as commander, refusing to endorse Megawati's last-minute appointment of Ryamizard Ryacudu, the then army chief-of-staff, who had been a key opponent of the peace process with GAM (Mietzner 2006). It is unlikely that the military would have toed the line on the Helsinki peace accord had Ryamizard become commander in 2004.

But it was not enough just to discipline the military; the next major test was to sell the Helsinki agreement to a sceptical parliament that would have to enshrine its provisions in law. Yudhoyono appears to have set the guidelines — that is, to get a law adopted that incorporated as much of the agreement with GAM as possible — but did little of the actual work. There were two critical figures in this regard. One was Peter Feith, the head of the European Union-led Aceh Monitoring Mission responsible for ensuring the agreement's implementation. Feith had the trust of the GAM leadership and helped persuade them to accept, albeit temporarily, that not all stipulations of the Helsinki agreement had made it into the corresponding Indonesian law. The second was Ferry Mursyidan Baldan, head of the special parliamentary committee responsible for producing a final version. It was he who helped ensure that critical provisions, including on local parties and independent candidates, stayed in the law when early drafts from the Ministry of Home Affairs proposed dropping them (ICG 2006b).

By the time the law was passed, there were strong rumours that Yudhoyono and Kalla would win the Nobel Peace Prize, a factor that may have strengthened the presidential backbone.[2] In the end, the 2006 prize went to the founder of Bangladesh's Grameen Bank, Muhammad Yunus, but Yudhoyono's hope that the prize would be his stayed alive through 2007 and 2008. (It was only when Aceh mediator Martti Ahtisaari won the prize in 2008, without reference to Yudhoyono or Kalla, that those hopes were finally dashed.)

---

2 'SBY "deserves Nobel Peace Prize"', *Jakarta Post*, 28 September 2006.

When relatively fair and peaceful local elections were held in December 2006 and a GAM member, Irwandi Yusuf, was decisively elected governor, the peace process, as far as Yudhoyono was concerned, was basically complete. He welcomed the new governor at the palace in an important affirmation of the results and generally made himself available to senior GAM leaders for the rest of his presidency. But from late 2006 on, the Aceh success story, in Yudhoyono's view, had been written. From then on, Aceh intruded on presidential awareness only when it was necessary to ensure the success stayed untarnished.

One such occasion came in February 2009. As legislative elections approached in which the newly formed GAM political party, Partai Aceh, could compete for the first time, Aceh was wracked by a spasm of violence in which several GAM members were murdered. It seemed that some of the attacks had been encouraged by the regional military commander, who made no secret of his belief that the peace agreement had been a mistake (McBeth 2009). Yudhoyono, who was campaigning for a second term at this time, visited the capital and, standing beside Governor Irwandi, gave a classic Yudhoyono speech. On the one hand, he said that he hoped no one would disrupt the peace that the Acehnese people had chosen, which many interpreted as a warning to the commander. On the other, he expressed a platitudinous belief that Aceh was now a place where military operations and GAM no longer existed: 'We have moved beyond that, we are all Indonesians' (ICG 2009: 7).[3]

In fact, GAM did still exist; only its military wing had been disbanded, and even that had simply been disarmed and renamed the Aceh Transition Committee (Komite Peralihan Aceh, KPA). The structure was intact and continued to engage in extortion and other abuses. But Yudhoyono did not just believe that the peace agreement had dissolved GAM; he seemed to be convinced that Aceh had now become like all other Indonesian provinces. There is nothing to suggest that he recognised that the Helsinki agreement gave Aceh a fundamentally different level of political authority than other provinces enjoyed. He only recognised that he had a personal bond to the Acehnese negotiating team, whose members now constituted the leadership of Partai Aceh. That bond, which he was keen to cultivate for his own political purposes, only grew stronger in the 2009 presidential elections when the Partai Aceh machine used its muscle to produce a 92.3 per cent vote for Yudhoyono in the province.

---

3 He made the same assertion in 2006, when he wrote in an op-ed: 'We are holding GAM to its pledge to drop its demands for independence in exchange for its full participation in the political, economic, social and cultural life of the province. ... In the end, GAM will no longer exist and its members will no longer be armed' (Yudhoyono 2006).

Yudhoyono's unwillingness to challenge his political allies became apparent in late 2011 when he allowed Partai Aceh to blackmail his government into delaying the election for governor. The election pitted incumbent Irwandi Yusuf, standing as an independent with an obscure running mate, against the Partai Aceh pair of Zaini Abdullah, GAM's former 'foreign minister', and Muzakir Manaf, a former GAM military commander. Partai Aceh demanded first that no independent candidates be allowed to run,[4] then that the election be delayed until Irwandi was out of office and could no longer use government resources to advance his campaign. In late 2011, when it looked like it was not going to get its way, a rash of killings of Javanese workers began that fitted Partai Aceh's interest in creating security conditions that would force the postponement of the elections. Yudhoyono's team capitulated, apparently worried that if Partai Aceh's wishes were not accommodated, it would at best refuse to participate in the elections or, at worst, return to arms. With Yudhoyono's blessing, his palace aides pressured the Constitutional Court to delay the election.[5] The murderers of the workers, who also tried to bomb a convoy in which Irwandi was travelling, were eventually caught and identified as Partai Aceh supporters but, reportedly on instructions from Jakarta, the investigation did not probe who had given them their orders.

For a man who frequently pontificated about the importance of justice and the rule of law, Yudhoyono's caving-in to Partai Aceh seems curious. His behaviour may indicate the degree to which he was worried that his signature achievement could come undone. There may also have been a sense of loyalty to the men who had given him such resounding support in the 2009 elections. But while Yudhoyono was unwilling to hold his allies to account for murder, his deep-seated nationalism flared up in 2013 when the Partai Aceh-dominated provincial legislature passed a regulation making the old GAM flag the official banner of the province. Yudhoyono was upset enough to summon Aceh's newly elected governor, Zaini Abdullah, to the palace to urge that the regulation be revoked.

---

4   GAM argued that independent candidates had been allowed to stand in the 2006 elections only because Partai Aceh did not then exist. Now that the party had been formed and could nominate candidates, it was no longer necessary to maintain the mechanism through which independent candidates could participate in the race for the governorship—or so GAM insisted. But Indonesia's Constitutional Court had ruled in 2007 that independent candidates must be allowed across Indonesia, and the relevant national legislation had been changed accordingly.

5   Notes from a high-level meeting at the palace on 12 June 2012 made available to the author. One of the participants said that he and three other top officials had gone to the court to persuade it to delay the elections given the conditions in the field. The court obliged.

'I already gave an amnesty to all GAM members, so now anything that can be interpreted as a continuation of the separatist movement must cease', he said (ICG 2013: 5). The Partai Aceh leadership put the issue on hold, but the regulation stayed in force. The party's leaders were undoubtedly mindful of the fact that in all previous stare-downs with the Yudhoyono administration, it was the latter that had blinked.

PAPUA: GOOD INTENTIONS BUT NO FOLLOW-UP

In Aceh, Yudhoyono had Kalla and the tsunami to help get him over the hump of conservative, in-the-box approaches to conflict resolution. In Papua, he was on his own, and it showed. He wanted peace and the praise that came with peace-making, but without upsetting any important constituencies. He wanted law and justice upheld, but without confrontation. He saw himself as giving intellectual direction, but left the details to others. With no real understanding of Papua's complexities, he decided that the 'prosperity approach' — more money, without political change — was the way to solve its problems. He was inordinately sensitive to media criticism — the domestic press were insinuating that the ongoing violence was serving vested political interests, while international outlets were focusing on the fact that there was no accountability for human rights violations. In his second term, Yudhoyono's approach to Papua was inseparable from his close relationship with Papuan governor Lukas Enembe, the provincial chair of the president's own Democrat Party (Partai Demokrat, PD). His dependence on this one relationship ultimately thwarted his plan to leave a legacy in Papua in the form of expanded special autonomy.

As with Aceh, Yudhoyono wanted to exude magnanimity without expending much political capital. Throughout the 2004 presidential campaign, he promised to fully implement Papua's Special Autonomy Law (Law 21/2001), though he had to contend with the fact that as Megawati's coordinating minister for political and security affairs, he was seen as complicit in the 2003 division of Papua into two provinces (ICG 2003). Megawati had issued a presidential instruction in 2003 to revive a never-implemented 1999 law that created two new provinces in Papua: Central Irian Jaya and West Irian Jaya. The first failed to get off the ground. The second was eventually renamed West Papua (Papua Barat). The newly implemented law was challenged in the Constitutional Court, which, in a controversial ruling on 11 November 2004, ruled it unconstitutional but allowed it to stand.[6]

---

6 See Constitutional Court Decision 018/PUU-I/2003.

The division of Papua by fiat from Jakarta violated the 2001 Special Autonomy Law and alienated many in Papua's intellectual elite who had been willing to give autonomy a chance. A key provision of the autonomy law was that a Papuan People's Council (Majelis Rakyat Papua, MRP) would be set up to safeguard Papuan values. The Megawati government had deliberately delayed its establishment, fearing that it would turn into a pro-independence body. Yudhoyono fulfilled an early campaign promise shortly after he took office by issuing the necessary implementing regulation, briefly earning him praise from Papuan leaders — until he insisted that the MRP recognise the hated new province (ICG 2006a). Given the Constitutional Court decision, he probably had no choice, but he could have softened the blow by affirming that the MRP would remain a single institution representing all of Papua, as its creators had envisaged. Not only did he make no such statement but, in 2011, two years into his second term, he allowed West Papua to create its own MRP by fiat, without intervening in any way.[7]

Given developments in Aceh, Papua was not high on Yudhoyono's priority list through much of his first term. It was telling that the president's main advisor on Papua was a young Muslim Papuan, Velix Vernando Wanggai, who had little credibility in Papuan political elite or activist circles. Wanggai was an ardent proponent of economic development as the answer to all of Papua's problems. In 2006, when the arrival of Papuan asylum-seekers in Australia and riots in Timika and Jayapura made some presidential action on Papua unavoidable, it was Wanggai who articulated a policy called, American-style, 'New Deal for Papua'. The 'New Deal' was to focus on better social services, affirmative action for indigenous Papuans and accelerated development. At a typically glacial pace, the policy was announced in July 2006, a presidential instruction on the new policy (Presidential Instruction 5/2007) was issued in May 2007 and an agency to implement the policy, the Unit for the Acceleration of Development in Papua and West Papua (Unit Percepatan Pembangunan di Papua dan Papua Barat, UP4B), was finally set up in 2011.

Like other intractable problems that Yudhoyono preferred not to address directly — such as police reform, civil service reform and deradicalisation — Papua policy was placed in the office of Vice-President Boediono, who had succeeded Kalla in 2009. There, it was left to the vice-president's energetic political advisor, Dewi Fortuna Anwar, to handle. Yudhoyono showed mild interest in UP4B, and at the outset even seemed willing to entertain the possibility that its mandate be extended to

---

7 'Pelantikan MRP Papua Barat Bertentangan dengan UU Otsus' [The installation of the West Papua People's Council violates the Special Autonomy Law], *Suara Pembaruan*, 16 June 2011.

include some human rights and justice issues. But as violence continued, he backed away, returning Papua policy to his security team and rendering UP4B and its head, retired lieutenant-general Bambang Darmono, largely irrelevant from mid-2012 onward. Darmono's own shortcomings were part of the problem; among other things, he relied too heavily on his military network in an environment where a history of abuse and depredations by soldiers was a major source of local grievance. While UP4B had many programs, the one that attracted the most attention was a project to construct a road through central Papua using the military.

The fate of UP4B reflected Yudhoyono's lack of follow-through and his tendency to be diverted by issues in the news. This could be seen at a high-level meeting on Papua chaired by the president in June 2012, after a number of shootings in Jayapura, including of a German tourist.[8] The president started the meeting by noting that even if the violence in Papua was trivial compared to that in the Middle East, it had to be addressed. Why? Because newspapers, television and members of parliament were suggesting that the government was letting it happen. Beyond the violence, it was obvious from the meeting that UP4B had been marginalised. In the view of the president's senior advisors, the real issues were the tensions surrounding the long-delayed election for governor in Papua province; the growing power of highlanders relative to the coastal elite; the increasing number of conflicts surrounding district elections; and the activities of the pro-independence movement. The security forces and the State Intelligence Agency would have to handle these, but Yudhoyono warned them not to go overboard in doing so because any excesses would be exploited by the press and attract international attention. The concern, again, was image, not accountability. Meanwhile, UP4B was told to lie low, work behind the scenes and not touch anything outside its economic mandate. Evidently Yudhoyono had already lost interest in the agency he had created as his flagship for a new Papua policy.

He still wanted a legacy on Papua, however, and it was clearly not going to come from directly resolving conflict, as it had with Aceh. Instead, he put his hopes in initiatives by others. A civil society movement called the Papua Peace Network had made some headway in 2010 in trying to formulate a set of issues that it could then present to the government as an agenda for dialogue — on the understanding that the issue of independence or a referendum on Papua's political status was not on the table. Not wanting to be seen as making any political concessions, Yudhoyono had avoided using the word 'dialogue' because it implied two equal parties. In his August 2010 state of the nation address,

---

8 The following account is based on notes from a meeting at the palace on 12 June 2012 made available to the author.

he announced that he was ready for 'constructive communication' on Papuan development, but this was as far as he would go. After constant needling in the press, he finally used the word 'dialogue' in a meeting with Papuan church leaders in late 2011. Subsequently, a number of meetings took place between representatives of the Papua Peace Network and government officials, under the auspices of the vice-president's office. No political breakthrough occurred, however, and the network itself lost traction in Papua. A separate initiative by Farid Husein, a key member of the government's negotiating team on Aceh, to talk to the guerrillas of the Free Papua Organisation (Organisasi Papua Merdeka, OPM) got no support from the president at all.[9]

As his second term was drawing to a close with no legacy in sight, Yudhoyono decided to bestow enhanced special autonomy (*otonomi khusus plus*, or *otsus plus*) on Papua and West Papua. The idea emerged out of talks with newly elected Papuan governor Lukas Enembe in April 2013 and had all the elements that would appeal to Yudhoyono. It involved few risks and no political concessions. It responded to Papuan critiques that the lives of indigenous Papuans had not improved after more than a decade of special autonomy. It could help a political ally, since Enembe was also the chair of PD in Papua and could get out the votes for Yudhoyono's party, which was haemorrhaging support elsewhere in the country. And if all went according to plan, Yudhoyono could visit Papua before his last state of the union address and announce his final gift to the Papuan people. It did not work out as planned, however. Enembe quickly tried to turn the idea to his advantage, having his advisors produce a draft that effectively gave Enembe himself vastly enhanced powers and more access to resources. Activists led protests against *otsus plus* in the streets because no one had seen a draft and there had been no public consultation. Moreover, Papua and West Papua had very different visions of what enhanced autonomy should look like. By the time they finally agreed on a text, it was too late to be considered by the outgoing parliament, so Yudhoyono left office without a visit, a speech or any lasting legacy on Papua.

One way in which Yudhoyono could have made a significant difference to conflict in Papua was to put an end to the excessive splitting of districts, or *pemekaran*. In 2009, Yudhoyono had declared a general moratorium on further administrative fragmentation, but he failed to enforce it. Parliament was partly responsible, but Yudhoyono never tried seri-

---

9   In 2011, the president had reluctantly given Farid Husein a letter appointing him 'special envoy to certain groups', studiously avoiding the use of the term 'OPM'. Farid Husein then tried to meet with OPM leaders to discuss an Aceh-like formula for peace, but he had difficulty getting access to the top leadership and the president showed no interest in his efforts (ICG 2012: 25).

ously to stop *pemekaran*. Papua was particularly affected by this trend. On Yudhoyono's watch, the number of districts in Papua ballooned from 29 to 42 (29 in Papua and 13 in West Papua). Most of them clearly failed to meet the basic requirements for economic and political viability set out in the decentralisation law and other regulations. Many Papuans suspected that fragmentation along ethnic lines was in the interests not just of local Papuan elites, but also of the intelligence agencies, which wished to ensure that the independence movement stayed weak and divided. Whether this or simply inertia was a factor in Yudhyono's failure to halt administrative fragmentation, the proliferation of new districts encouraged more conflict and militated against the accelerated development that Yudhoyono wished to bring about (IPAC 2013).

COUNTERTERRORISM: EFFECTIVE ENFORCEMENT, WEAK PREVENTION

Many of the same qualities displayed by Yudhoyono in addressing the problems in Aceh and Papua emerged in his handling of counterterrorism. He delegated and stayed away from details. As with UP4B, he was happy to create an institution to respond to a felt need, in this case the National Counterterrorism Agency (Badan Nasional Penanggulangan Terorisme, BNPT). However, as in the case of Darmono's agency, Yudhoyono spent no effort actually trying to ensure the BNPT's effectiveness. He was sensitive to media coverage, playing the anti-terrorism card whenever he went abroad because this was what earned praise. But at the same time, he was unwilling to spend political capital at home to campaign against extremism and, in particular, its instigators. And he only became personally involved when terrorists directed their attention towards him.

When Yudhoyono took office, terrorism was only marginally on his radar screen. This was despite the fact that the district of Poso in Central Sulwesi was still wracked by extremist violence, three years after a peace agreement had ended communal fighting there between Christians and Muslims (ICG 2004). Similarly, the Australian embassy bombing had just taken place and its masterminds, Noordin Top and Azhari Husin, were still at large. But terrorism still barely rated a mention in Yudhoyono's first state of the union speech, and he seemed content to leave the follow-up work to the counterterrorism units of the police, Detachment 88 and the Anti-bomb Taskforce (Satgas Bom).[10] In May 2005, as the talks

---

10 Detachment 88 was created by Megawati after the 2002 Bali bombings. The less well-known but equally effective Satgas Bom was set up by the police in 2001 in the aftermath of the December 2000 Christmas Eve bombings.

in Aceh were reaching a critical stage, a bomb went off in a Christian market in Poso, killing 22 people. While the president made a point of visiting some of the injured and stated that the country was committed to ending terrorism, he nevertheless left the investigation in the hands of local police. This was the same local police force that had failed to discover the perpetrators of any of the dozens of bombings and other attacks that had taken place in Poso since the 2001 attacks.

Even the second Bali bombing on 1 October 2005 did not encourage Yudhoyono to take a stronger personal role in the management of counterterrorism efforts. To be sure, he flew to Bali immediately, again visiting the wounded. He said that Indonesia, as the world's largest Muslim country, would do everything in its power to prevent another attack.[11] It was important that the president was heard and seen as being committed to eradicating terrorism, but there was no push for a national strategy to achieve this goal, or any major new policy direction. When police discovered the videotaped statements of the bombers, it was not Yudhoyono but Jusuf Kalla who took action. The vice-president summoned leading Muslim clerics, including some well-known hardliners, to his house to watch the videos and told the clerics it was time to work on addressing the ideology involved. It was true that Kalla had the credentials with this community that Yudhoyono lacked, but if there was going to be sustained follow-up, the president's involvement was needed.

Within weeks, another horrific crime occurred in Poso, demonstrating that the terrorism problem was far from losing its urgency—in Central Sulawesi or in other parts of the country. This time, the beheading of three Christian schoolgirls stirred such public outrage that police assigned a special taskforce under Detachment 88 officer Tito Karnavian to find the killers and ensure their prosecution. Four months later, three of the masterminds were behind bars. From these key extremists, police got the information they needed to resolve all the thus far unsolved attacks that had occurred since 2001—almost all of which were linked to the local affiliate of Jemaah Islamiyah. The relatively easy and fast arrest of terrorism perpetrators in Poso after a high-profile incident suggested that had the government (including the Megawati administration) moved earlier to take the ongoing violence in Poso seriously, some of these attacks might have been prevented.

For the rest of Yudhoyono's first term, there were no major attacks. Thus, the issue of terrorism largely receded from view, although counterterrorism police continued to be effective, with the president's full support. For instance, police squads moved to clean up the radical network

---

11 'Diyakini bom bunuh diri' [It was definitely a suicide bomb], *Suara Merdeka*, 3 October 2005.

in Poso, ending with a major armed clash on the streets of Poso on 22 January 2007 that stopped violence there for the next four years (ICG 2007). In 2008, the police uncovered a plot to attack a cafe frequented by foreign tourists in Bukittinggi, West Sumatra, and arrested its members, some of whom seemed to have links back to the elusive Noordin Top. But in the absence of any spectacular incidents, the president saw no need for action. The sleepy Desk for Coordinating the Eradication of Terrorism, set up within the Coordinating Ministry for Political and Security Affairs in November 2002, remained without budget, executive authority or influence. Extremist clerics continued to radicalise young Indonesians without any government obstruction, sometimes even using government-funded schools and Islamic centres as venues to promote their violent vision of jihad.

It took the bombing of two luxury hotels in the heart of a Jakarta business district in July 2009, a little over a week after Yudhoyono was returned to power for a second term, to shake the president and the nation out of their complacency. Yudhoyono made an emotional speech condemning the 'handful of people who have no human feelings and who are not concerned about destroying our nation with this act of terrorism, which will have far-ranging impact on our economy, our business climate, our tourism and our image in the eyes of the world'.[12] He accused the perpetrators of being angry at the results of the election and then showed images of a terrorist training camp where trainees were shooting at blown-up photographs of Yudhoyono. The photos were real but they had no connection with the individuals who had bombed the hotels, and the target practice involved had taken place more than four years earlier. But as the investigation went on, police did discover that the hotel bombers had been planning to ambush the president's convoy near his home in a suburb south of Jakarta and kill him. Suddenly, terrorism was not just a serious crime aimed at foreigners or religious minorities; it was an urgent matter of state security. Counterterrorism measures went into high gear, with the president pressing for more involvement of the military. At the same time, however, he reaffirmed — to his credit — that terrorism was a law enforcement matter in which the police remained the lead agency.

The establishment of a new counterterrorism agency after the 2009 hotel bombings was a Yudhoyono initiative, but it also showed his traditional indecisiveness and hands-off approach. On 31 August 2009, Djoko Suyanto, the coordinating minister for political, legal and security affairs, met with the members of parliament's Commission I, responsible

---

12 'Siapa di balik bom JW Marriott dan Ritz Carlton?' [Who was behind the JW Marriott and Ritz Carlton bombings?], *Detik.com*, 18 July 2009.

for security, and secured a recommendation that the president set up a new agency to combat terrorism. Even with presidential backing, it took more than a year to bring the BNPT into being, as details of the division of labour between military and police were worked out. In the end, the new agency had three departments: prevention, operations and international cooperation. Police retained control of operations, with Detachment 88 serving as the new body's strike force, and a senior military intelligence officer with no experience in terrorism was put in charge of prevention and deradicalisation. This bifurcation—the military in charge of prevention and the police handling operations—weakened the body's effectiveness from the outset. The BNPT did not achieve anything that Detachment 88 and Satgas Bom could not have done on their own. It never succeeded in playing a genuine coordinating role between the police, military, intelligence agencies and prison authorities; the vested interests of each service were too strong. Yudhoyono could have made it better by insisting on a coherent strategy to tackle terrorism and demanding better interagency cooperation, but he never did so. When he left office, there was not even a system in place for informing Detachment 88 when a convicted terrorist would be released from prison.

In his final years in office, Yudhoyono was happy to play the role of counterterrorism champion overseas while largely staying silent at home, particularly as criticism grew of Detachment 88 tactics. In early 2010, a terrorist training camp had been discovered in Aceh, involving at least eight different groups (ICG 2010). In the course of operations against the camp, one of the fugitives shot and killed a Detachment 88 officer—the first fatality in the line of duty in the seven years of its existence. Several of the Aceh fugitives were subsequently killed by the police, and questions began to be raised about whether some could have been captured alive. The casualties included Dulmatin, one of the original Bali bombers who was thought to be still in the Philippines where he had fled in 2003. In fact he had returned to Indonesia in 2007 and had played a critical role in setting up the Aceh camp. In March 2010, Yudhoyono was on a state visit to Australia when police tracked Dulmatin down to an internet cafe on the outskirts of Jakarta and killed him. The president announced this event while addressing the Australian parliament, to enthusiastic applause. His critics at home took this as proof that Indonesia's policy on counterterrorism was being dictated by Australia and the United States. This mounting criticism goes some way to explaining why Yudhoyono shunned any high-profile defence of his administration's counterterrorism efforts.[13]

---

13 'Umumkan Dulmatin di Australia, upaya pencitraan SBY di mata internasional' [Announcing Dulmatin's death in Australia was an effort to burnish SBY's international image], *Detik.com*, 10 March 2010.

While no further attacks against Western targets took place after the 2009 hotel bombings, police became a steady target of individual drive-by shootings in Jakarta, Poso and Solo. The overall number of casualties stayed relatively low, however, ensuring that international praise for Yudhoyono's effective management of terrorism continued to flow. But there were many reasons for the low death toll. One was the pacification of several hot spots of communal violence. The single most important driver of recruitment to terrorism had been the conflicts in Ambon and Poso, where Muslims were dying on Indonesian soil and al-Qaeda's framework for global jihad could be translated into a local context. In this regard, it is worth noting that some 300 Indonesians trained on the Afghan–Pakistan border between 1985 and 1994, but none used violence until after the Ambon conflict erupted in January 1999, and almost all the bombings over the next three years had revenge for Muslim deaths in Ambon and Poso as at least a partial motivation. When peace agreements in late 2001 and early 2002 stopped those deaths, recruitment quickly tapered off. The Poso affiliate of Jemaah Islamiyah, the group responsible for the 2002 Bali bombings, continued its one-sided attacks until the January 2007 clash. Afterwards, the leaders of Jemaah Islamiyah decided that violence was counterproductive, taking one important player out of terrorism (at least temporarily).

The generally peaceful regional environment was another factor in the decline of large-scale attacks. Unlike the Middle East or South Asia, where regional rivalries stirred one country's support for terrorism in another, Indonesia had friendly and cooperative neighbours that were just as determined to combat the scourge of terrorism and very effective in doing so—Singapore and Malaysia being particularly active.

Finally, aided by state-of-the-art technology, particularly in cellphone monitoring, Detachment 88 and Satgas Bom were very effective in tracking down and arresting local jihadis. Once convicted, they were often ostracised by their former colleagues on suspicion that they had given too much information to the police. The arrests thus not only took individuals out of circulation but created divisions and splinters in the extremist communities. All of these factors played a role in keeping the death toll in Indonesia-based terrorism down; a good prevention program, however, was not one of them (IPAC 2014b).

Despite the decreasing number of incidents and casualties, it was clear that the recruitment of terrorists continued. This was especially visible in the number of Indonesians who decided to fight in Syria. In 2012, with the Syrian conflict attracting increasing attention in Indonesia, extremist groups began to raise funds and send humanitarian missions. But the conflict also had an apocalyptic dimension, as several traditions (*hadith*) of the Prophet Muhammad predicted that the final battle between good and evil, in which Islam would be victorious, would take place in Sham (Greater Syria) (IPAC 2014a: 1-2). Unnoticed by most in the Indonesian government, a trickle of Indonesians went to fight, some leaving from their places of study abroad, some directly from Indonesia. The formation of the group called the Islamic State of Iraq and Sham (ISIS) in October 2013 was welcomed on radical websites, and extremist preachers from outside Indonesia were featured speakers in public, pro-ISIS seminars that still caused no remark. When a pro-ISIS rally took place at Jakarta's main traffic circle on 16 March 2014, it was treated no differently from any other Islamist rally. It was only on 23 July, when an ISIS recruitment video was posted on YouTube, that the Yudhoyono government belatedly realised it had a problem. Bahrum Syah, the Indonesian who had organised the rally, appeared in the video alongside other Indonesians, urging Indonesians to join the ranks of those fighting for an Islamic state. Suddenly, ISIS was a threat to the Indonesian nation, a rival claimant for the loyalty of its citizens. Yudhoyono called a meeting of his closest security advisors, and within days ISIS was banned. Finally, just before handing over power to his successor, Joko Widodo, Yudhoyono announced a seven-point plan to curb ISIS teachings (IPAC 2014c). In the ten years of his presidency, it was the closest he had come to defining a counterradicalisation work plan.

CONCLUSION

Susilo Bambang Yudhoyono's reputation in internal security management may be somewhat higher than he deserves, especially in the international commentary, but his accomplishments should not be slighted. The Aceh agreement continues to stand as a huge achievement, particularly in the context of failed, protracted or violent resolutions of comparable problems in Indonesia's neighbourhood, from Sri Lanka to southern Thailand. It is clear that the Helsinki accord could not have happened without Yudhoyono's support, even if Kalla did most of the work. Where Yudhoyono stumbled was in the follow-through. He seemed to feel that the most important part of the peace agreement was the amnesty for GAM members, not the strengthened authority of the provincial government that should have made Aceh fundamentally different from other provinces. And he was reluctant to hold the elected GAM leadership to any democratic standards, refusing to call its bluff when it implicitly threatened a return to conflict if it did not get its political way. As a result, Aceh today may have seen the end of separatist violence, but GAM's rule has led to new forms of patronage, corruption, intimidation and generally bad governance.

As far as Papua is concerned, Yudhoyono genuinely intended to make a difference, but he wanted to achieve better relations without granting any political concessions. That was never going to work. Yudhoyono's approach to Papua revealed more fundamental patterns of his personality: he had noble goals and ideas, but was unwilling to go to the trouble of fighting for them. At the same time, the fault was not all Yudhoyono's — or Jakarta's, for that matter. The Papuans themselves were notoriously fractious, and even the Papua Peace Network lost a major chance to promote its own concept of dialogue when it veered too close to the independence movement. Had Yudhoyono had his own clear and realistic vision for Papua and what could be done to achieve it, his plan for enhanced special autonomy might have had a chance, even at the late stage that he launched it. Instead, he simply let his political ally Lukas Enembe come up with a plan that ended up alienating more Papuans than it brought on board.

In the area of terrorism, finally, Yudhoyono supported police efforts to track down suspects and was unstinting in his praise for the dangerous work they did, and that was crucial. Without his support, the military might have been more aggressive in demanding a role, which — given the armed forces' troubled history under the previous authoritarian regime — would have had significant implications for post-Suharto civil–military relations. Similarly, had Yudhoyono not stood behind the police, the post-2010 campaign against Detachment 88 might have gained more traction, with possibly negative consequences for the effectiveness of counterterrorism enforcement efforts. (To be sure, some of the criticisms of Detachment 88 were justified, but extremist elements used them to try to torpedo the entire counterterrorism work of the police and government.) Having said this, Yudhoyono could have demanded so much more from the BNPT, the agency he created to counter terrorism, especially on the prevention side. The agency suffered the same fate as most other bodies created under Yudhoyono's watch: its functions and powers remained unclear, and it operated without much overall guidance. In the same vein, Yudhoyono could have used his office far more effectively to condemn extremist teachings and those Muslim preachers responsible for them. This, however, would have required him to challenge a politically powerful constituency, which he was habitually reluctant to do. In short, Yudhoyono's performance in overseeing Indonesia's internal security was solid — but it would have been so much better had the president shown some willingness to confront the interests that continue to drive conflict in contemporary Indonesia.

REFERENCES

Aspinall, E. (2005) 'The Helsinki agreement: a more promising basis for peace in Aceh?', Policy Studies 20, East-West Center, Washington DC.
Aspinall, E. and H. Crouch (2003) 'The Aceh peace process: why it failed', Policy Studies 1, East-West Center, Washington DC.
ICG (International Crisis Group) (2003) 'Dividing Papua: how not to do it', Asia Briefing No. 24, Jakarta/Brussels, 9 April.
ICG (International Crisis Group) (2004) 'Indonesia backgrounder: jihad in Central Sulawesi', Asia Report No. 74, Jakarta/Brussels, 3 February.
ICG (International Crisis Group) (2006a) 'Papua: the dangers of shutting down dialogue', Asia Briefing No. 47, Jakarta/Brussels, 23 March.
ICG (International Crisis Group) (2006b) 'Aceh: now for the hard part', Asia Briefing No. 48, Jakarta/Brussels, 29 March.
ICG (International Crisis Group) (2007) 'Jihadism in Indonesia: Poso on the edge', Asia Report No. 127, Jakarta/Brussels, 24 January.
ICG (International Crisis Group) (2009) 'Deep distrust in Aceh as elections approach', Asia Briefing No. 90, Jakarta/Brussels, 23 March.
ICG (International Crisis Group) (2010) 'Indonesia: jihadi surprise in Aceh', Asia Report No. 189, Jakarta/Brussels, 20 April.
ICG (International Crisis Group) (2012) 'Indonesia: dynamics of violence in Papua', Asia Report No. 232, Jakarta/Brussels, 9 August.
ICG (International Crisis Group) (2013) 'Indonesia: tensions over Aceh's flag', Asia Briefing No. 139, Jakarta/Brussels, 7 May.
IPAC (Institute for Policy Analysis of Conflict) (2013) 'Carving up Papua: more districts, more trouble', IPAC Report No. 3, Jakarta, 9 October.
IPAC (Institute for Policy Analysis of Conflict) (2014a) 'Indonesians and the Syrian conflict', IPAC Report No. 6, Jakarta, 30 January.
IPAC (Institute for Policy Analysis of Conflict) (2014b) 'Countering violent extremism in Indonesia: need for a rethink', IPAC Report No. 11, Jakarta, 30 June.
IPAC (Institute for Policy Analysis of Conflict) (2014c) 'The evolution of ISIS in Indonesia', IPAC Report No. 13, Jakarta, 24 September.
MacIntyre, A. and D.E. Ramage (2008) 'Seeing Indonesia as a normal country', Australian Strategic Policy Institute, Canberra, May.
McBeth, J. (2009) 'Crimes, bombs and a shaky bureaucracy', *Straits Times*, 21 February.
Mietzner, M. (2006) 'The politics of military reform in post-Suharto Indonesia: elite conflict, nationalism and institutional resistance', Policy Studies 23, East-West Center, Washington DC.
Morfit, M. (2007) 'Beyond Helsinki: Aceh and Indonesia's democratic development', paper presented at the First International Conference on Aceh and Indian Ocean Studies, Jakarta.
Yudhoyono, S.B. (2006) 'Peace deal with Aceh is just a beginning', *International Herald Tribune*, 15 August.

9 Toning down the 'big bang': the politics of decentralisation during the Yudhoyono years

Dirk Tomsa*

When Susilo Bambang Yudhoyono became president in 2004, one of the biggest challenges he faced was the implementation of an ambitious regional autonomy program that had been initiated in 1999 by the first president of the post-Suharto era, B.J. Habibie. Famously described as 'big bang' decentralisation because of its sudden introduction and its comprehensive scope, regional autonomy commenced in practice in 2001 and was intended to be a key pillar of Indonesia's democratisation process. It encompassed a series of decentralisation measures that ranged from the devolution of political authority to the restructuring of fiscal relations between Jakarta and the lower administrative tiers in the regions (Aspinall and Fealy 2002; Hill 2014). In 2004, just before Yudhoyono took office, these initial steps were refined and complemented by additional measures, notably the introduction of direct elections for local executive positions such as governor, mayor and district head (Erb and Sulistiyanto 2009).

Throughout Yudhoyono's time as president, the implementation of regional autonomy received rather mixed reviews. On the one hand, scholars and activists, as well as many central government officials, were highly critical of decentralisation due to its failure to accelerate regional economic development or to broaden the range of actors represented

---

* The author would like to thank Michael Buehler, Gabe Ferrazzi, Blair Palmer and Erman Rachman for valuable feedback on an earlier draft. Research for this chapter was funded by the Australian Research Council through grant DP1096149.

in local politics (Buehler 2010, 2014a; Hadiz 2010). On the other hand, local elites and the Indonesian public at large enthusiastically embraced decentralisation. While the elites primarily relished the abundance of new patronage opportunities, many ordinary Indonesians regarded decentralisation as one of the defining features of their young democracy because it allowed them to realise their local aspirations through the creation of new administrative entities and, most importantly, the direct election of their local leaders.

By the end of Yudhoyono's presidency, however, direct elections for local leaders had come very close to being abolished and democracy in Indonesia was on the brink of suffering a major setback. In September 2014, less than a month before Yudhoyono was due to leave office, a new regional election law was passed, stipulating a return to indirect elections for governors, mayors and district heads. Only four months later, though, the law was overturned and direct elections were reinstated. Significantly, President Yudhoyono played a pivotal role in both the abolition and the prompt restoration of direct local elections. First, it was his failure to assert his authority over his cabinet and his Democrat Party (Partai Demokrat, PD) that allowed the contentious legislation to pass during a dramatic parliamentary session on 25 September 2014. Then, after a massive public outcry, it was his decision to overturn the law retrospectively through a government regulation in lieu of law (*peraturan pemerintah pengganti undang-undang, perppu*) that paved the way for the restoration of direct elections.[1]

Although ultimately short-lived, the abolition of direct local elections in September 2014 was a key political event of the Yudhoyono era because it signalled the culmination of a consistent, if highly contested, process of recentralisation and democratic stagnation that characterised particularly the latter years of the Yudhoyono presidency (Tomsa 2010; Kimura 2011; Mietzner 2012). Although Yudhoyono himself may not have openly supported this process, he did nothing to stop it until his own reputation, as well as that of Indonesia's democracy more generally, had been severely damaged. This dramatic end to Yudhoyono's term in office demonstrates that, despite persistent pressure from the central government, the process of redesigning regional autonomy has been fraught with contestation and dispute. As will be shown in this chapter, the government did not always get its way, and widespread resistance from local elites and the public at large exposed significant underlying tensions in what are often depicted as fairly stable centre–periphery relations.

---

1 Yudhoyono issued the *perppu* on 2 October 2014, but it needed parliamentary approval to take effect. Despite having passed a law abolishing direct elections only in September 2014, parliament endorsed the *perppu* on 20 January 2015. See 'Direct elections officially reinstated', *Jakarta Post*, 20 January 2015.

The argument is developed as follows. The chapter begins with a brief discussion of Yudhoyono's personal views on regional autonomy as expressed in his writings and public statements. It then provides a succinct evaluation of the main achievements and shortcomings of regional autonomy before highlighting that, despite the mixed balance sheet, the public has remained remarkably supportive of decentralisation. However, as demonstrated in the following sections, this public support was insufficient to prevent the central government from eroding decentralisation and returning more and more power to the centre. The discussion here pays special attention to the contested processes of administrative fragmentation (*pemekaran*) and local elections (*pemilihan kepala daerah, pilkada*), as well as the authority for local governments to raise taxes and issue permits for resource exploitation. The chapter concludes by revisiting the role of President Yudhoyono in decentralisation reform.

YUDHOYONO'S VIEWS ON DECENTRALISATION

When Susilo Bambang Yudhoyono took office in October 2004, Indonesia's decentralisation program had been under way for less than four years. The first signs of future problems with implementation were already visible at this early point. New administrative units were being created at a rapid and seemingly unsustainable pace (Kimura 2013), provinces and districts were bickering over the distribution of resources and responsibilities, and many cases of local-level corruption had already been exposed (Davidson 2007). These problems notwithstanding, Yudhoyono appeared to be committed to decentralisation. For example, in an early speech in 2004 that outlined the main priorities for his presidency, he included regional autonomy in a list of key issues his government was most determined to tackle in order to improve Indonesia's investment climate (Yudhoyono 2004). In another speech in May 2006, he expressed his belief that decentralisation was there to stay: 'I believe that the movement towards decentralisation and regional autonomy cannot be stopped and certainly cannot be reversed' (Yudhoyono 2006).

Shortly afterwards, however, his support became more qualified. Addressing the Regional Representative Council (Dewan Perwakilan Daerah, DPD) in August 2006, he bemoaned the inefficiency of many new regions that had been created as part of the *pemekaran* process. A year later, at the same forum, he reiterated those concerns, but this time 'his frustration was clearer and bolder'.[2] In addition to criticising *pemekaran*, he vented against local governments' propensity to issue local tax

---

2 'SBY slams self-interested new regions', *Jakarta Post*, 24 August 2007.

regulations that, in his view, inhibited local economic growth. Nevertheless, towards the end of his first term, Yudhoyono announced his overall satisfaction with decentralisation, highlighting in particular the socio-economic achievements.[3] Significantly, there were no indications that he was unhappy with the conduct of direct local elections. On the contrary, in mid-2010, shortly after his new home affairs minister, Gamawan Fauzi, had started attacking the *pilkada* system, Yudhoyono rebuffed his minister, stating that 'the best election [system] is a direct election'.[4]

Based on these early public statements, then, it is probably unfair to describe Yudhoyono as the driving force behind the gradual weakening of decentralisation. He himself certainly refutes this suggestion. In his book *Selalu Ada Pilihan* [There Is Always a Choice], published towards the end of his presidency, he puts the blame for the various problems associated with decentralisation on virtually everyone but himself. Claiming that neither the central government (presumably excluding himself), nor local governments, nor the public at large were ready for decentralisation, he states that centralistic and authoritarian thinking is still widespread within both the government and non-government organisations: 'They are not truly aware that we have to give more responsibility and authority to the regions to govern themselves' (Yudhoyono 2014: 25). Complementing his narrative with anecdotes from visits to the regions, he gives the narcissistic impression that he alone knows what decentralisation really means.

Despite—or perhaps precisely because of—this patronising view of other political stakeholders and the Indonesian people in general, Yudhoyono remained strangely detached from most of the divisive debates on reforming regional autonomy. Practically all the controversial initiatives aimed at weakening decentralisation originated in the Ministry of Home Affairs and other ministries, not in the presidential palace. And yet, this chapter will demonstrate that Yudhoyono was not simply an innocent bystander, indifferent to the polemics that unfolded around him. Rather, by virtue of his position as president, he actually played a crucial role in the recentralisation process, especially but not only in the *pilkada* debate. After all, it was he, as president, who was responsible for mandating the revisions to the main decentralisation laws in 2011, and it was he who let his minister put forward the original proposal to abolish direct local elections. Finally, when he later appeared to change his mind in favour of direct elections, it was also he as the president who failed to assert his authority over his own ministers, his party and the parliament.

---

3 'Yudhoyono declares regional autonomy a success', *Jakarta Post*, 19 August 2009.
4 'SBY: pilkada langsung pilihan terbaik' [SBY: direct local elections are the best option], *Viva News*, 28 July 2010.

EVALUATING DECENTRALISATION

The process of redesigning regional autonomy that occurred during the Yudhoyono years needs to be seen against the backdrop of the relatively mediocre governance and socio-economic results most of the key pillars of regional autonomy have produced. Public service delivery, for example, has improved, but as Schulze and Sjahrir (2014: 203) argue, 'the picture is not as clear-cut as might have been expected'. Poverty at the provincial level has declined consistently over the last decade (Ilmma and Wai-Poi 2014: 116), but there is little evidence that the devolution of financial authority to the local level has had a significant impact on regional development. In fact, most key features of Indonesian regional development have remained relatively stable when compared to the period before decentralisation, prompting Hill and Vidyattama (2014: 96) to conclude that 'decentralization has not markedly changed the country's regional growth patterns and social outcomes, or patterns of inter-regional inequality'. In particular, the large gap in economic productivity between Java and Bali on the one hand and Eastern Indonesia on the other remains nearly as pronounced as it was 30 years ago, though at least it has not worsened.

Of course, for many resource-rich regions decentralisation was a golden opportunity to exploit the commodity boom that coincided with the rollout of regional autonomy. But areas with poorly developed infrastructure and few natural resources reaped comparatively few benefits from decentralisation. Generally, though, a key problem has been that local governments from all regions, rich and poor, have largely failed to develop substantial revenue sources and continue to rely heavily on financial assistance from the central government (Patunru and Rahman 2014: 164). Large portions of these funds are either used for wages and administrative expenditures (Sjahrir, Kis-Katos and Schulze 2014) or disappear in fictitious projects, mark-ups and other forms of corruption and mismanagement. In short, central government assistance has not accelerated economic development in the way the architects of the regional autonomy framework had originally intended. A senior official in the Ministry of Home Affairs who was involved in the formulation of the decentralisation laws recalled that 'we thought that if we gave the regions money and the freedom to use it as they pleased they would use it to suit the needs of the local economy. But we were wrong'.[5]

It is partly because of these problems that the results of Indonesia's fiscal decentralisation are often described as disappointing. It is worth noting, however, that Indonesia's experience is by no means unique in

---

5 Interview with I Made Suwandi, 7 July 2014.

this regard. Examples from around the globe show that decentralisation rarely if ever produces even outcomes across different regions and sectors. Furthermore, issues such as administrative fragmentation and predatory capture of local state resources by newly empowered elites are well known in many developing countries (Bardhan and Mookherjee 2006; Lewis 2013). Nevertheless, some of the shortcomings in Indonesia are serious even by comparative measures. Local spending on administrative expenditures, for example, is, according to Schulze and Sjahrir (2014: 199), 'clearly excessive by any international standard', while the resulting low levels of investment in local infrastructure put Indonesia 'among the worst-performing countries in the world in terms of the quality of its infrastructure and, within the region, better only than the Philippines' (Lewis 2014: 144).

If improvement of service delivery and living standards was the primary socio-economic goal of the decentralisation project, then improvement of vertical accountability was the main political objective. The centrepiece of this political dimension of regional autonomy was the introduction in 2005 of direct elections for local executive leaders such as governors, mayors and district heads (*pilkada*). Ten years on, hundreds of *pilkada* have been held in Indonesia and modest improvements in accountability have indeed occurred. For example, in many of the elections contested by incumbent executives, voters have either eagerly rewarded those who were successful during their first terms or thrown out those who failed to deliver (Mietzner 2010). Significantly, these voting trends have resulted in the development of more specific policy programs in many areas, with many candidates now promising free access to primary education and basic health facilities for the poor (Aspinall 2014). In some regions, local leaders have taken proactive steps to attract investment and improve economic conditions, while others have sought to attract voters by focusing on cleansing local bureaucracies of entrenched practices of corruption and nepotism. In the process, a number of new reformist leaders have emerged at the local level and used their local executive positions as steppingstones for political careers at the national level (Mietzner 2014). Often decried as exceptions to the rule (Hadiz 2010), some of these locally trained leaders have reached exceptional prominence, none more so, of course, than the former mayor of Solo and Jakarta governor, Joko Widodo (Jokowi), who is now Indonesia's seventh president.

However, these positive aspects of direct elections were counterbalanced by a number of significant problems. First, vote-buying and other forms of money politics became omnipresent features in virtually all *pilkada*. Many voters simply expected candidates to distribute money and other material goods in the run-up to an election, while many candidates *believed* that this was what voters expected, and acted accordingly. But money politics also came in other guises, for example the widespread practice of political parties selling their nominations to the highest bidder. Second, *pilkada* were used by a growing number of influential families to establish political dynasties that could stifle competition and accountability. In some areas in Sulawesi, for example, wealthy families have entrenched themselves so deeply in the local state apparatus that it is difficult for political opponents to mobilise sufficient resources to challenge them (Buehler 2013). In Banten, the family of now disgraced former governor Ratu Atut Chosiyah dominated local politics for nearly a decade; only her arrest on corruption charges in December 2013 finally revealed the full extent of her family's empire to a national audience.[6] A third problem related, somewhat ironically, to the frequently praised institutional design of the elections, which made it mandatory for a candidate to run together with a deputy. Although this arrangement was credited with facilitating coalition-building between otherwise potentially hostile groups (Tomsa 2009; Aspinall 2010), the drawback was that many of the coalitions fell apart shortly after the election because deputies often felt excluded from the process of governing and, perhaps more importantly, from access to patronage resources. As a result, some local governments have been paralysed for extended periods by tensions between the top executives and their deputies (Tomsa 2015).

Finally, another consequence of decentralisation that has shaped local politics in the Yudhoyono years has been the growing fragmentation of the socio-political and administrative landscapes (Aspinall 2013a). The most obvious expression of this fragmentation is the explosion in the number of subnational administrative units, especially districts and municipalities, whose numbers rose from 294 at the end of the Suharto era to 510 by mid-2013 (Hill and Vidyattama 2014: 70).[7] Fragmentation could also be found in local parliaments, where the number of parties — both absolute and effective — increased significantly between 2004 and 2009, especially in the Outer Islands of Eastern Indonesia (Allen 2014; Tomsa 2014). This subnational party-system fragmentation was due in large part to overly permissive electoral rules that allowed small parties to flourish at the local level even though they were unable to meet the national parliamentary threshold.

---

6 'Dinasti politik Ratu Atut setelah delapan tahun berkuasa' [The political dynasty of Ratu Atut after eight years in power], *Kompas*, 18 December 2013.
7 The number of other subnational units, such as provinces, subdistricts and villages, also increased.

DIVERGING PERCEPTIONS OF REGIONAL AUTONOMY: JAKARTA, THE REGIONS AND THE GENERAL PUBLIC

Although the fragmentation of local political landscapes has posed challenges for governance, it must be seen as a genuine reflection of the political aspirations harboured by many Indonesians. Local politics is rarely dominated by well-oiled party machines, but rather by individualised clientelistic networks whose prime political objective is to capture state institutions such as parliaments and local governments. Given that decentralisation has given them the means to do this without much interference from Jakarta, it is hardly surprising that regional autonomy in general and *pemekaran* in particular is extremely popular with local elites (Aspinall 2013b). What is perhaps more surprising is that regional autonomy is also popular with the Indonesian public at large. Survey data cited by Lewis (2014: 150) and Mietzner (2014: 48) show that, despite frequent laments about local corruption in the Indonesian media, citizens are actually quite satisfied with their local political institutions and the quality of local service delivery.

These findings are supported by results from a public opinion survey conducted locally in two provinces in Eastern Indonesia in 2012 (LSI 2012). When asked about a broad range of issues, including corruption, law enforcement and trust in political institutions, respondents in North Sulawesi and Maluku overwhelmingly expressed higher levels of satisfaction with provincial and district institutions than with their national counterparts. For example, a huge majority of respondents (82 per cent) found corruption to be high or very high at the national level, but only 42 per cent found it to be high or very high at the provincial level. Similarly, provincial and district parliaments were regarded as cleaner and more trustworthy than the national legislature. Perhaps the most emphatic endorsement of decentralisation, however, was given when respondents were asked their opinion of *pemekaran*. Only 11 per cent agreed with the statement that *pemekaran* benefited only the elites, whereas a resounding 83 per cent expressed the view that it could actually improve development at the local level.

Despite the widespread public support, decentralisation is no longer so popular in Jakarta — if in fact it ever was. From the start, many ministries and government agencies, including the Ministry of Home Affairs, the Ministry of Forestry and the National Land Agency, resisted the implementation of regional autonomy (Thorburn 2004). Later, this passive refusal to implement certain policies turned into active opposition to key features of the decentralisation package. Led by senior members of the central government and top politicians from large political parties, calls for changes to the regional autonomy framework increased in both frequency and intensity. Some of these calls went relatively unchallenged and resulted in concrete steps to recentralise power in Jakarta, but others met with considerable resistance.

As in many other public debates, Yudhoyono remained largely silent during these discussions, but from the start of his presidency there were subtle indications that he would not stand in the way of efforts to revamp regional autonomy. For instance, when the Yudhoyono administration passed Government Regulation 38/2007 on the Division of Roles between National, Provincial and District/City Governments, some ministries used it as a welcome pretext to centralise their programs and budgets and to distribute only limited authorities to subnational governments. Significantly, Yudhoyono did nothing to stop these recentralisation tendencies. On the contrary, more concrete steps to rein in what many government officials liked to describe as 'excessive decentralisation'[8] were then taken during his second term. At the heart of these efforts to redesign regional autonomy were the requirements for *pemekaran* and the electoral system for *pilkada*. In addition, the government clamped down on district heads' fondness for mandating local taxes and levies and sought to restrict their rights to issue permits for lucrative resource exploitation.

CURBING THE DISTRICTS' TAXATION POWERS

Arguably the most obvious attempts to recentralise power were the Yudhoyono administration's efforts to revise legislation that structured the regulatory framework for taxation, levies and resource extraction permits at the local level. When decentralisation began, regional governments had gained significant new authorities in these areas, including the right to impose local taxes and levies and to issue lucrative permits for mining and logging concessions. Without proper oversight and accountability mechanisms, however, these reforms resulted in massive abuses of power. Using local regulations (*perda*) as their administrative weapon, district heads not only issued thousands of mining and logging licences without adhering to procedural requirements, but also created countless new taxes and user charges that were either in open breach of national legislation or simply 'unclear, unnecessary, misdirected, exploitative of citizens and investors, or even unconstitutional' (Butt 2010: 178). Between 2004 and 2009, the national government revoked 1,691 *perda* (Butt and Parsons 2012: 94), the vast majority of them tax regulations.

---

8 Interviews with senior bureaucrats in the Ministry of Home Affairs, 8 July 2014.

But many others are believed to have slipped through the Ministry of Home Affairs' review mechanisms due to a lack of capacity to keep on top of the many thousands being produced every year.

In 2009, the government responded by issuing Law 28/2009 on Regional Taxes and User Charges. It was intended to end the excessive use of taxes and levies at the local level by introducing a limited 'closed list' of specific taxes and user charges that could be imposed by provincial and local governments. Apart from setting stricter limits on what can and cannot be taxed, the law outlines sanctions that the central government can impose on regions that violate the closed list of taxes and levies. Yudhoyono justified the new restrictions by citing the need to improve the regional investment climate, but also warned, in typical Yudhoyono parlance, 'that the "principles of harmony and jurisdictional [limitations] in the provision of services and the running of local government" needed to be maintained' (Butt and Parsons 2012: 94).

At first sight, the law appeared to mark a dramatic shift in taxation powers from the local government level to the centre (Buehler 2009: 10). Indeed, the number of *perda* revoked by the government after the law was passed declined consistently from 407 in 2010 to 351 in 2011 and 173 in 2012.[9] This trend may be seen as vindication of the government's decision to set stricter guidelines, but it would be naive to conclude that the decline in revocations equalled a decline in the number of problematic *perda*. As Butt and Parsons (2012) point out, the 2009 law actually provides several loopholes and vague formulations that local governments can still exploit to impose questionable levies. Moreover, neither the review mechanisms nor the institutional capacity of the Ministry of Home Affairs have been strengthened significantly, so it is likely that many potentially problematic local regulations still go unreported or unchecked. In other words, it may well be that the shift in taxation powers from the regions to the centre was primarily a shift on paper rather than on the ground.

SHIFTING NATURAL RESOURCE MANAGEMENT TO THE PROVINCES

Potentially more far-reaching are the changes to the management of natural resources that were passed into law in September 2014. The revised Law on Regional Government (Law 23/2014) not only transfers responsibility for most natural resources (forestry, mining and energy, ocean

---

9 'Ada tren penurunan pembatalan perda' [Trend shows a decline in the number of revoked regional government regulations], *hukumonline.com*, 6 July 2013.

resources and fisheries) from the district to the provincial level,[10] it also strengthens the position of provincial governors as extended arms of the central government, reflecting the hope of many Jakarta-based officials that governors may be easier to control than district heads. These recentralisation measures constituted a direct reversal of earlier regional autonomy policies that had deliberately devolved authority for the management of natural resources to the districts.

Right from the start, however, many Jakarta elites had loathed this part of regional autonomy. In the forestry sector, for example, obstructive behaviour and efforts to recentralise power began even before the onset of the Yudhoyono era. Between 2000 and 2002, the Ministry of Forestry issued a number of regulations that were clearly intended to reinstate stronger central government controls over the sector (Barr et al. 2006). Throughout the Yudhoyono years, the ministry tried to use these regulations to reclaim some of the powers it had lost to new local actors, especially with regard to the classification of forest zones. Many district heads refused to accept this, however. In the ensuing turf war between the central and local governments, a number of legal ambiguities remained unresolved. This situation resulted in two diverging trends: some local governments saw opportunities for murky collaborations with officials from the central government,[11] while others decided to openly challenge the forestry minister by taking him to the Constitutional Court.[12] Significantly, the court ruled in favour of the district heads, illustrating the contested character of the drive towards recentralisation.

For a long time, President Yudhoyono showed only passing interest in these developments. Occasionally he weighed into the debate with some characteristically half-hearted appeals to governors and district heads 'not to hand out forest management permits easily',[13] but these appeals were largely ignored. Even when Yudhoyono upped the ante by launching a new initiative to tackle the widespread problem of

---

10 'RUU Pemda disahkan, ini implikasinya untuk gubernur' [Law on Regional Government passed, these are the implications for governors], *Republika*, 22 September 2014.
11 See, for example, the bribery case involving the district head of Bogor, Rachmat Yasin, who was detained by the Corruption Eradication Commission in May 2014 for allegedly accepting a Rp 1.5 billion ($127,050) bribe in return for issuing a recommendation to the central government endorsing the development of a housing estate on forest land. See 'Bogor's Black Forest', *Tempo*, 10 June 2014.
12 'Court decision in Indonesia may grant local authorities more power over forests', *Mongabay.com*, 14 June 2012.
13 'Presiden ingatkan bupati tak mudah berikan izin pengelolaan hutan' [President reminds district heads not to hand out forest management permits easily], *Tempo*, 8 June 2010.

overlapping concession areas through the development of a single, all-encompassing map of Indonesia (the so-called 'One Map' initiative) and by granting direct oversight functions for land-use permit review to his Presidential Working Unit for Development Monitoring and Oversight (Unit Kerja Presiden Bidang Pengawasan dan Pengendalian Pembangunan, UKP4), the impact on the ground was negligible. Frustrated by the recalcitrance of local leaders, the central government eventually resorted to the more drastic measures now found in the revised Law on Regional Government.[14] And while the initiative for these measures originated in the Ministry of Home Affairs, Yudhoyono was clearly in favour of the changes; when developments surrounding the passing of the new Law on Local Elections (Law 22/2014) prompted him to review both it and the Law on Regional Government (see below), he proposed significant changes to the former, but very few to the latter.

REINING IN 'EXCESSIVE DECENTRALISATION': REGULATING *PEMEKARAN*

Apart from restructuring the responsibilities and relationships of the different levels of government, the Law on Regional Government addressed the notorious proliferation of new districts (*pemekaran*). This was in fact one of the first elements of decentralisation to be publicly criticised by Yudhoyono. As early as August 2006, he had bemoaned the ineffectiveness of the process and the financial burden it imposed on the central government. Subsequently, he repeatedly expressed his concerns about *pemekaran* and in early 2009 he declared a moratorium on the creation of new districts and provinces.[15]

With the moratorium in place, the government began an evaluation of the performance of the new administrative structures, concluding that 80 per cent of all newly created districts and provinces had failed to achieve their targets.[16] In response, the government then drafted stricter

---

14 The government also sought the help of the Corruption Eradication Commission in this matter, signing a memorandum of understanding with the commission in order to put pressure on all stakeholders to improve the process of defining forest boundaries and access to land (Anderson 2014).
15 The exact start and end dates of the moratorium are unclear as it was never official policy. Yudhoyono declared his desire to postpone the formation of new districts in 2008, but it was not until North Sumatra legislator Abdul Aziz Angkat died during a rowdy demonstration to protest the rejection of a *pemekaran* proposal by the North Sumatra parliament that the national parliament agreed to a temporary halt on the formation of new districts.
16 'Presiden anggap pemekaran daerah gagal' [President deems creation of new administrative units a failure], *BBC*, 14 July 2010.

guidelines on the formation of new administrative structures that were announced in 2011 as part of the so-called 2010–2025 Grand Design for the Structuring of Regions. After protracted deliberations with the House of Representatives (Dewan Perwakilan Rakyat, DPR), the guidelines were eventually incorporated into the revised Law on Regional Government, imposing among other things the need for an aspiring new region to undergo a three- to five-year preparation period during which it will be evaluated by the central government. Significantly, the law gives the central government the option to reject a new region on the basis of this evaluation, shifting the final authority to endorse a new region from the national parliament to the president.[17]

That these new requirements were at last accepted by the DPR was a major victory for the Yudhoyono government. For more than a decade *pemekaran* had been lucrative business for the national parliament, as local elites keen to establish their own districts or provinces had to lobby national legislators to endorse their plans, often paying bribes as part of this process. Unsurprisingly, then, parliament was initially rather unsympathetic towards the president's concerns about the viability of new districts and provinces and the financial burden they imposed on the budget. In late 2012, the DPR declared the moratorium to be over and resumed approving the creation of new administrative entities, including the new province of North Kalimantan. But tensions with the government over *pemekaran* remained, as was evident in late 2013 when Home Affairs Minister Gamawan Fauzi refused to sign off on two new draft law packages that sought to create another 87 new provinces and districts. DPR members reacted angrily, but Fauzi succeeded in having the discussions shelved,[18] with the result that no new entities were created between then and the time Yudhoyono left office in October 2014.

Against this background, the agreement on the future requirements for *pemekaran* demonstrated that despite stubborn resistance from a variety of actors — in this case, the national parliament and local elites — the central government could actually impose its agenda on other political stakeholders, further intensifying the drive towards recentralisation. As with similar initiatives, the main impetus may have originated outside the presidential palace, but Yudhoyono's support for the measures was evident in many of his statements about *pemekaran*.

---

17 'RUU Pemda disahkan, pemekaran daerah diatur pusat' [Law on Regional Government passed, creation of new administrative units will be regulated by the centre], *Tempo*, 13 September 2014.
18 'RUU Pemekaran yang bermasalah bakal dikembalikan' [Problematic draft laws on the creation of new administrative units will be returned], *jpnn.com*, 2 September 2014.

ROLLING BACK LOCAL DEMOCRACY: THE *PILKADA* LAW CONTROVERSY

Apart from *pemekaran*, the other key concern of the central government was the format of local executive elections. Citing the high costs of electoral administration, the parties' corrupt candidate recruitment systems, the rise of dynasties and the frequent tensions between local executive leaders and their deputies, Home Affairs Minister Fauzi was one of the most vocal critics of the *pilkada* system during the second Yudhoyono term. In fact, it was only a few months after he had been appointed to cabinet in 2009 that Fauzi presented an early version of draft legislation that would have removed direct elections for governors (Buehler 2012). Although the main objective of the bill was not explicitly to recentralise power in Jakarta, the proposed changes still represented a major attack on regional autonomy in that they were aimed at undermining the popular support base of local executive leaders. The recentralising effect would thus be indirect; by abolishing direct local elections, power would be returned from the masses to the elites, who in turn would be easier to control, or at least influence, from Jakarta.

The proposal caused a massive public outcry (Mietzner 2012). Civil society organisations led the chorus of condemnation, but they were supported by a range of outspoken provincial governors—some with dubious democratic credentials—who were keen to maintain the system that had brought them to power (Buehler 2012). Ever fearful of such negative publicity, President Yudhoyono quickly rebuked his minister, saying that he preferred to maintain the popular system of direct elections. Some parties in parliament had also become wary, and so the draft legislation temporarily disappeared from public view. Behind the scenes, however, negotiations continued and the home affairs minister never abandoned his plan to abolish direct local elections. It is likely that Fauzi's defiance on this issue was based on the belief that the president's opposition was not a matter of conviction, but merely a short-term response to public pressure, and would therefore disappear once the public outcry had subsided.

Over the years the bill went through various incarnations, including a version that retained direct elections for governors but abolished them for mayors and district heads.[19] By late 2013, Yudhoyono seemed to have lost track of the arguments on both sides and claimed that he could no

---

19 'Mendagri: selama pilkada sudah 70 orang tewas' [Home affairs minister: since the introduction of direct local elections, 70 people have been killed], *okezone.com*, 24 April 2014.

longer decide which option was the best.[20] For a while it looked as if the bill might die a slow death in the parliament's committee system, but then the political polarisation after the 2014 elections provided a new impetus for the debate. As the party landscape divided into two coalition blocks, the Red and White Coalition led by Prabowo Subianto started promoting a version of the bill that envisaged the abolition of all direct elections at the subnational level. The coalition hoped this would enhance its chances of controlling local governments.

With public opinion still firmly in favour of direct elections, but parliament on track to vote for their abolition, Yudhoyono suddenly found himself at the centre of the debate. As president, he represented the government that had initially proposed ending direct elections, while as chair of PD he controlled the balance of power in parliament. Both positions would have allowed him to prevent the bill now being pushed by Prabowo from passing: as president he could have instructed his home affairs minister to oppose this latest version, and as leader of the largest party in parliament he could have instructed the PD legislators to side with those wanting to keep direct elections, led by the Indonesian Democratic Party of Struggle (Partai Demokrasi Indonesia–Perjuangan, PDIP). His last public statement on the issue before the vote indicated that his party might indeed join the PDIP-led coalition to retain direct elections. Speaking on his party's YouTube channel, *Suara Demokrat*, on 14 September 2014, Yudhoyono declared his support for direct local elections. But when voting day came on 25 September, all but six PD legislators walked out from the vote, enabling the Red and White Coalition to pass the bill abolishing direct elections by 226 to 135 votes.

Whether or not the decision to abstain from the vote had been approved by Yudhoyono initially remained unclear. While some PD legislators claimed that the president was in the loop, others said he was not. Yudhoyono, who was in the United States at the time, himself later said that he was not well informed about the course of the debate and vowed to repeal the legislation through a government regulation in lieu of law (*perppu*). By this point, however, he had lost a lot of credibility and many Indonesians greeted the issuance of the *perppu* with cynicism, well aware that it should never have come to this showdown in the first place. This attitude prevailed even when the *perppu* was eventually endorsed by parliament in early 2015. Many Indonesian media outlets refused to give Yudhoyono credit for his late intervention, instead reminding their readers that 'it was Yudhoyono's administration that originally proposed

---

20 'Presiden: terserah, pilkada langsung atau di DPRD' [President: I leave it to you whether local elections are conducted directly or through local parliaments], *Kompas*, 1 November 2013.

the legislation that eliminated regional elections; his dereliction as president—a tepid too-little, too-late flip-flop statement while on a final overseas grandstanding jaunt—allowed it to pass the House'.[21]

In fact, Yudhoyono had multiple opportunities to prevent the bill from becoming law, as the various drafts had been on the table for most of his second term. Indeed, it was Yudhoyono himself who had mandated the drafting of a new law on local elections back in 2011. Had he really been a firm supporter of direct elections, he could have made it clear back then that revising the law should not entail abolishing direct elections. He also had many subsequent opportunities to rein in his conservative home affairs minister, who kept insisting that direct elections had to go. But Yudhoyono chose to remain silent, paving the way for a dramatic and farcical showdown in parliament.

CONCLUSION AND OUTLOOK

Decided in parliament in the very last month of Yudhoyono's presidency, the abolition of direct local elections overshadowed many other developments related to decentralisation, not least because of the very high symbolic value many Indonesians attach to this particular feature of democracy. According to a *Jakarta Globe* editorial published a few days after the decisive parliamentary vote:

> For all their cons, direct elections are possibly what Indonesians are most proud of. For 10 years, we felt that elections single-handedly defined Indonesia's strong intention to become a good and democratic nation in the truest sense.[22]

This assessment expressed the widespread feeling that Indonesians had been robbed of one of the most significant political achievements of the reform period.

Though Yudhoyono's last-minute *perppu* paved the way for the eventual reinstatement of direct local elections, the fact that the *pilkada* law was actually passed during his presidency should not be seen as a surprise. Regional autonomy has long been a thorn in the side of the central government. Especially in Yudhoyono's second term, efforts to weaken the districts and cities intensified. And yet, for most of the Yudhoyono era, the president's vision of a 'grand design' for regional autonomy was hampered by his inability to set a clear agenda and then push it through against resistance from actors such as the DPR, local elites or, more

---

21 'Our democracy, like Jokowi, needs work', *Jakarta Globe*, 21 January 2015.
22 'Reasonable justice, irrationally denied', *Jakarta Globe*, 29 September 2014.

broadly, the general public. For years, the reform of regional autonomy looked more like a patchwork than a grand design as the government was effectively constrained by a multitude of political stakeholders. In particular, local elites demonstrated through their public protests that they were now an important element in the configuration of power. Indeed, their continuing resistance against a series of power grabs from Jakarta reveals that centre–periphery relations are not as smooth as they appear to be.

Ultimately, the pressure from local elites and the public at large was just enough to secure the eventual restoration of direct local elections. This demonstrates that the overall process of recentralisation, or what Buehler (2014b) calls the 'reassertion of the state', remains hotly contested. The forces behind this process, however, remain strong, especially in the central bureaucracy. During the Yudhoyono years, recentralisation was driven chiefly by senior cabinet ministers rather than the president himself. But Yudhoyono was at least complicit in pushing this agenda, as he decided not to intervene when Home Affairs Minister Gamawan Fauzi and his bureaucrats pushed forward steadily with their recentralisation efforts.

Yudhoyono's preferred approach of letting his minister and bureaucrats handle the more difficult aspects of policy-making was of course indicative of his general style of governing. Concerned with ceremony more than policy, and harmony more than conflict, he shied away from taking the lead in redesigning regional autonomy, just as he avoided leadership in many other policy fields. Ironically, however, in regard to decentralisation, large parts of Jakarta's elite actually supported the government's broader position that regional governments had too much power. Yudhoyono could have used that general consensus much more effectively to carefully recalibrate Indonesia's overall autonomy framework. Instead, he let some of the most conservative elements in his government dominate the debate, with the result that talk about decentralisation reform became entangled with a much broader agenda to roll back democracy.

Towards the end of the Yudhoyono era, the political dynamics surrounding the 2014 elections played into the hands of these conservative cabinet members led by Fauzi and they succeeded in pushing through most of their ambitious regional autonomy 'reforms'. But parliament's subsequent about-face and the reinstatement of direct local elections present a welcome opportunity for Yudhoyono's successor, Joko Widodo, to revitalise regional autonomy. It is worth remembering, however, that Gamawan Fauzi was also once regarded as a reformist advocate of decentralisation. Like Jokowi, he had risen to national prominence from small beginnings as a district head who had been empowered by regional autonomy. His transformation into one of the most ardent proponents of a democratic rollback—and the support he received for this position from large parts of the Jakarta elite—illustrates how immense the challenge of strengthening regional autonomy in Indonesia is going to be.

REFERENCES

Allen, N. (2014) 'From patronage machine to partisan melee: subnational corruption and the evolution of the Indonesian party system', *Pacific Affairs*, 87(2): 221–45.
Anderson, P. (2014) 'Indonesia promises to address forest destruction', *Asian Currents*, 3 December: 10–11.
Aspinall, E. (2010) 'The irony of success', *Journal of Democracy*, 21(2): 20–34.
Aspinall, E. (2013a) 'A nation in fragments', *Critical Asian Studies*, 45(1): 27–54.
Aspinall, E. (2013b) 'How Indonesia survived: comparative perspectives on state disintegration and endurance', in A. Stepan and M. Künkler (eds) *Indonesia, Islam, and Democracy*, Columbia University Press, New York: 126–46.
Aspinall, E. (2014) 'Health care and democratization in Indonesia', *Democratization*, 21(5): 803–23.
Aspinall, E. and G. Fealy (eds) (2002) *Local Power and Politics in Indonesia: Democratisation and Decentralisation*, Institute of Southeast Asian Studies, Singapore.
Bardhan, P. and D. Mookherjee (2006) 'Decentralization, corruption and government accountability', in S. Rose-Ackerman (ed.) *International Handbook on the Economics of Corruption*, Edward Elgar, Cheltenham: 161–88.
Barr, C., I.A.P. Resosudarmo, A. Dermawan and J. McCarthy with M. Moeliono and B. Setiono (eds) (2006) *Decentralization of Forest Administration in Indonesia: Implications for Forest Sustainability, Economic Development and Community Livelihoods*, Center for International Forestry Research (CIFOR), Bogor.
Buehler, M. (2009) 'The new regional taxation law: an end to predatory taxation?', *Van Zorge Report*, 11(8): 9–11.
Buehler, M. (2010) 'Decentralisation and local democracy in Indonesia: the marginalisation of the public sphere', in E. Aspinall and M. Mietzner (eds) *Problems of Democratisation in Indonesia: Elections, Institutions and Society*, Institute of Southeast Asian Studies, Singapore: 267–87.
Buehler, M. (2012) 'Angels and demons', *Inside Indonesia*, 108(April–June). Available at http://www.insideindonesia.org/feature-editions/angels-and-demons-4
Buehler, M. (2013) 'Married with children', *Inside Indonesia*, 112(April–June). Available at http://www.insideindonesia.org/feature-editions/married-with-children
Buehler, M. (2014a) 'Elite competition and changing state–society relations: shari'a policymaking in Indonesia', in M. Ford and T. Pepinsky (eds) *Beyond Oligarchy: Wealth, Power, and Contemporary Indonesian Politics*, Cornell Southeast Asia Program Publications, Ithaca NY: 157–75.
Buehler, M. (2014b) 'The reassertion of the state', *New Mandala*, 30 September. Available at http://asiapacific.anu.edu.au/newmandala/2014/09/30/the-reassertion-of-the-state/
Butt, S. (2010) 'Regional autonomy and legal disorder: the proliferation of local laws in Indonesia', *Sydney Law Review*, 32(2): 177–91. Available at http://sydney.edu.au/law/slr/slr_32/slr32_2/Butt.pdf

Butt, S. and N. Parsons (2012) 'Reining in regional governments? Local taxes and investment in decentralized Indonesia', *Sydney Law Review*, 34(1): 91–106.
Davidson, J.S. (2007) 'Politics-as-usual on trial: regional anti-corruption campaigns in Indonesia', *Pacific Review*, 20(1): 75–99.
Erb, M. and P. Sulistiyanto (eds) (2009) *Deepening Democracy in Indonesia? Direct Elections for Local Leaders (Pilkada)*, Institute of Southeast Asian Studies, Singapore.
Hadiz, V.R. (2010) *Localising Power in Post-authoritarian Indonesia*, Stanford University Press, Stanford CA.
Hill, H. (ed.) (2014) *Regional Dynamics in a Decentralized Indonesia*, Institute of Southeast Asian Studies, Singapore.
Hill, H. and Y. Vidyattama (2014) 'Hares and tortoises: regional development dynamics in Indonesia', in H. Hill (ed.) *Regional Dynamics in a Decentralized Indonesia*, Institute of Southeast Asian Studies, Singapore: 68–97.
Ilmma, A. and M. Wai-Poi (2014) 'Patterns of regional poverty in the new Indonesia', in H. Hill (ed.) *Regional Dynamics in a Decentralized Indonesia*, Institute of Southeast Asian Studies, Singapore: 98–131.
Kimura, E. (2011) 'Indonesia in 2010: a leading democracy disappoints on reform', *Asian Survey*, 51(1): 186–95.
Kimura, E. (2013) *Political Change and Territoriality in Indonesia: Provincial Proliferation*, Routledge, London and New York.
Lewis, B.D. (2014) 'Twelve years of fiscal decentralization: a balance sheet', in H. Hill (ed.) *Regional Dynamics in a Decentralized Indonesia*, Institute of Southeast Asian Studies, Singapore: 135–55.
Lewis, J.I. (2013) 'Local governance and the recentralization of political power in African states', *Centerpiece*, 27(2). Available at http://wcfia.harvard.edu/publications/centerpiece/spring2013/feature_lewis
LSI (Lembaga Survei Indonesia) (2012) 'Survei kerukunan umat beragama di Provinsi Sulawesi Utara dan Maluku' [Survey on harmony between religious groups in North Sulawesi and Maluku provinces], unpublished public opinion survey, Jakarta.
Mietzner, M. (2010) 'Indonesia's direct elections: empowering the electorate or entrenching the New Order oligarchy?', in E. Aspinall and G. Fealy (eds) *Soeharto's New Order and Its Legacy*, ANU E-Press, Canberra: 173–90.
Mietzner, M. (2012) 'Indonesia's democratic stagnation: anti-reformist elites and resilient civil society', *Democratization*, 19(2): 209–29.
Mietzner, M. (2014) 'Indonesia's decentralization: the rise of local identities and the survival of the nation-state', in H. Hill (ed.) *Regional Dynamics in a Decentralized Indonesia*, Institute of Southeast Asian Studies, Singapore: 45–67.
Patunru, A.A. and E.A. Rahman (2014) 'Local governance and development outcomes', in H. Hill (ed.) *Regional Dynamics in a Decentralized Indonesia*, Institute of Southeast Asian Studies, Singapore: 156–85.
Schulze, G.G. and B.S. Sjahrir (2014) 'Decentralization, governance and public service delivery', in H. Hill (ed.) *Regional Dynamics in a Decentralized Indonesia*, Institute of Southeast Asian Studies, Singapore: 186–207.
Sjahrir, B.S., K. Kis-Katos and G.G. Schulze (2014) 'Administrative overspending in Indonesian districts: the role of local politics', *World Development*, 59: 166–83.
Thorburn, C. (2004) 'The plot thickens: land administration and policy in post-New Order Indonesia', *Asia-Pacific Viewpoint*, 45(1): 33–49.
Tomsa, D. (2009) 'Electoral democracy in a divided society: the 2008 gubernatorial election in Maluku, Indonesia', *South East Asia Research*, 17(2): 229–59.

Tomsa, D. (2010) 'Indonesian politics in 2010: the perils of stagnation', *Bulletin of Indonesian Economic Studies*, 46(3): 309–28.

Tomsa, D. (2014) 'Party system fragmentation in Indonesia: the sub-national dimension', *Journal of East Asian Studies*, 14(2): 249–78.

Tomsa, D. (2015) 'Local politics and corruption in Indonesia's Outer Islands', *Bijdragen tot de Taal-, Land- en Volkenkund*, 171(2).

Yudhoyono, S.B. (2004) 'Mengenali masalah, menetapkan agenda dan arah' [Recognising problems, setting the agenda and direction], presidential speech, 17 November. Available at http://www.presidenri.go.id/index.php/pidato/2004/11/17/54.html

Yudhoyono, S.B. (2006) 'Gerakan desentralisasi dan otonomi daerah tidak bisa dihentikan' [Movement towards decentralisation and regional autonomy cannot be stopped], presidential speech, 23 May. Available at http://www.presidenri.go.id/index.php/fokus/2006/05/23/571.html

Yudhoyono, S.B. (2014) *Selalu Ada Pilihan* [There Is Always a Choice], Kompas Gramedia, Jakarta.

10 The rule of law and anti-corruption reforms under Yudhoyono: the rise of the KPK and the Constitutional Court

*Simon Butt**

President Susilo Bambang Yudhoyono came to office at a pivotal time for rule-of-law and anti-corruption reforms in Indonesia. The two institutions at the forefront of these reforms were already established by the time he was inaugurated on 20 October 2004, but they had not been operating long and were still finding their feet. The first, the Constitutional Court, was established just one year earlier, on 15 October 2003. The second, the Corruption Eradication Commission (Komisi Pemberantasan Korupsi, KPK), had been working since mid-December 2003. The Jakarta Anti-Corruption Court (Pengadilan Tindak Pidana Korupsi, Tipikor Court), which tried all of the KPK's defendants, handed down its first decision in March 2005, well after Yudhoyono took office.

During Yudhoyono's presidency, the Constitutional Court and the KPK firmly established themselves within a largely unaccommodating political environment, and then actively and professionally performed their functions, which have been critically important to overall post-Suharto reform. As we shall see, both institutions had a relatively slow start during Yudhoyono's first term, with the KPK choosing to target small fry and the Constitutional Court invalidating unconstitutional legislation. However, as Yudhoyono's second term commenced, both

---

* The author would like to thank Fritz Edward Siregar for excellent research assistance and the Australian Research Council for funding this research (project DPI095541).

institutions became perceptibly emboldened. The KPK began to target powerful politicians, while the Constitutional Court adopted more aggressive decision-making practices, such as amending constitutionally questionable legislation rather than simply invalidating it.

Although the KPK and the Constitutional Court became very popular with the public, they also faced significant obstacles, put in their path mainly by those whose interests were adversely affected by their work. For example, several KPK commissioners were arrested by police or prosecutors who either were themselves under KPK investigation or appeared to act at the behest of others being investigated. The paucity of evidence to support these arrests led to speculation that the commissioners had been framed. Sections of the national parliament—many members of which had been investigated or prosecuted by the KPK— threatened to cut the commission's budget and powers, and to reduce the potency of the anti-corruption courts. The Constitutional Court faced two efforts—one through a statute passed in 2011 and the other through a government regulation in lieu of law (*peraturan pemerintah pengganti undang-undang, perppu*) issued by the president himself in late 2013—to rein it in and to ensure that allegations of judicial misconduct could not be handled internally. The court defended itself from both interventions by invalidating Yudhoyono's regulation and most of the statute.

Even though Yudhoyono came to office and was re-elected on a reformist platform, there is little evidence that he contributed much to the success of either the Constitutional Court or the KPK. He rarely stepped in to defend them when they came into conflict with powerful and resentful political players. When he did act, he usually did so late and under significant public pressure, perhaps when these institutions had already averted the real dangers they faced. Yet, there is also little evidence to suggest that Yudhoyono sought actively to undermine or weaken them, even when the KPK successfully prosecuted senior members of his own Democrat Party (Partai Demokrat, PD) and a member of his extended family for corruption. Neither did Yudhoyono retaliate, at least publicly, when the Constitutional Court invalidated the *perppu* he issued in late 2013. There is also very little to suggest that Yudhoyono interfered in any Constitutional Court decision.

As with many other challenges facing his administration, particularly in its second term, Yudhoyono appeared to adopt a hands-off approach, allowing legal and anti-corruption reforms and controversies to be handled by others. While he faced significant criticism for doing so, as president, it was in fact his constitutional and statutory duty to refrain from interference, either to help or to hinder these institutions. Overall, his reticence created an environment in which both institutions could thrive, significantly enhancing rule-of-law and anti-corruption efforts in the country.

This chapter has six sections. I begin by describing the rise of the KPK as a major force in tackling corruption, and then the various setbacks it experienced as members of the political elite retaliated against its commissioners and tried to circumscribe its powers. The third section analyses Yudhoyono's relations with the commission. The fourth section describes the rise of the Constitutional Court as Indonesia's apex court for constitutional matters and, in particular, its posture of judicial activism. The fifth summarises Yudhoyono's attitude towards the Constitutional Court, noting his general readiness to accept court decisions and his reluctance to intervene in its affairs. In the concluding section, I return to the question of Yudhoyono's role. I argue that while we cannot point to much evidence of active or positive support for these two institutions by Yudhoyono, his reluctance to intervene against them at least gave them the space to develop independent authority and public support. Whether the president's reluctance to intervene was driven by a sense of constitutional propriety or by his well-known sensitivity to public opinion, however, remains an open question.

THE KPK AND ANTI-CORRUPTION REFORM

Indonesia is notorious for having high levels of corruption. Figure 10.1 illustrates Indonesia's progress over the course of Yudhoyono's presidency, at least from the perspective of Transparency International. It is commonly said that Yudhoyono was re-elected in 2009 on an anti-corruption platform, but that his second term was fairly disappointing from an anti-corruption perspective. The Transparency International figures do not support this view. During Yudhoyono's first term, Indonesia's ranking on the Corruption Perceptions Index improved from 133 to 111 among the 150 or so countries surveyed. During his second term, the country's ranking went slightly backwards to 118 in 2012 and 114 in 2013, but then improved to 107 in 2014, among roughly 180 countries surveyed. Despite the backsliding in 2012 and 2013, Indonesia's average ranking was 110 during the president's second term (2009–14), compared with 130 during his first term (2004–09).

As we shall see, Yudhoyono's second term witnessed the 'rise' of the KPK, as it began to target relatively senior and politically well-connected people suspected of corruption, and as the attempts of some of those suspects to retaliate against the commission were publicly exposed. During this period, Yudhoyono was inconsistent in his stance towards the KPK, on some occasions publicly chiding it but on others lending it his support.

Figure 10.1   Indonesia's ranking on the Corruption Perceptions Index, 2004–14

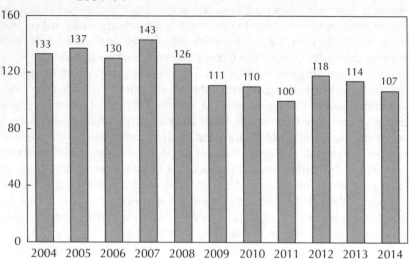

a   The lowest number of countries and territories surveyed during the period is 146 (in 2004); the highest is 183 (in 2011).
Source: Transparency International.

The KPK was established with jurisdiction to investigate and prosecute serious corruption cases and to take over corruption cases from police and prosecutors in some circumstances. It was also given special powers to wiretap, block accounts, impose travel bans and the like, usually without judicial approval. Importantly, the commission could not drop a case once it had formally named someone as a suspect. This was to prevent it from dropping cases in suspicious circumstances (Fenwick 2008). The KPK itself prosecuted all of its own cases before the sole Tipikor Court in Jakarta, established as a chamber of the Central Jakarta District Court in 2004.

The establishment of the KPK and the Tipikor Court outside the ordinary law enforcement apparatus reflected the fact that the general police, prosecutors and courts 'had not been effective or efficient in eradicating corruption'.[1] It was presumed that this was because those law enforcers were themselves corrupt (ICW 2001; World Bank 2003) or lacked the forensic skills to investigate complex financial crimes. Although the KPK and the Tipikor Court were formally independent of these law agencies, however, many KPK investigators and prosecutors were on secondment from them.

---

1   Law 30/2002 on the Corruption Eradication Commission, Preamble, part (b).

During its first few years the KPK chose easily winnable cases, targeting cases supported by clear evidence and focusing on relatively insignificant perpetrators, such as regional officials and civil servants. To the frustration of anti-corruption reformers, it avoided pursuing some of Indonesia's more notorious corruption cases, including those arising out of bank bailouts after the Asian economic crisis of 1997–98 and those involving Suharto and his inner circle. Nevertheless, this strategy allowed the KPK to establish and maintain a 100 per cent conviction rate in the cases it did prosecute.

Two factors are commonly cited to explain the KPK's high conviction rate. The first is that, unlike most Indonesian courts, the Tipikor Court had five rather than three judges presiding over each case, a majority of them ad hoc rather than permanent judges, mostly lawyers. The rationale for recruiting judges from outside the career judiciary was, as mentioned, that many career judges were considered corrupt. The second conventional explanation for the KPK's success was that it was better resourced, and its investigators better trained, than the ordinary police.

From 2009 the KPK began to pursue more powerful political figures, soon after Antasari Azhar became chair of the commission in December 2007. The KPK's more noteworthy scalps during this second period included a deputy governor of the central bank, several parliamentarians and businesspeople, and even a Constitutional Court chief justice.

- Miranda Gultom was sentenced to three years' imprisonment for bribing members of parliament's Finance Committee to support her candidacy for the position of deputy governor of Bank Indonesia. Nunun Nurbaeti, the businesswoman who distributed the bribes (in the form of traveller's cheques), also served time in jail, as did the 26 parliamentarians involved.
- The chair of the Prosperous Justice Party (Partai Keadilan Sejahtera, PKS), Luthfi Hasan Ishaaq, was given a 16-year sentence for attempting to manipulate Indonesia's beef import quota.
- The head of the energy regulator (SKK Migas), Rudi Rubiandini, was sentenced to seven years in jail for fixing tenders and manipulating the formula for determining the price of gas.
- Golkar parliamentarian Zulkarnaen Djabar was sentenced to 15 years' imprisonment for rigging two Ministry of Religion tenders for the procurement of Korans, on which he received kickbacks.
- Constitutional Court Chief Justice Akil Mochtar was given a sentence of life imprisonment for taking bribes to fix local election cases.

Famously, some of the KPK's targets were close to President Yudhoyono himself, including several members of his own party and a relative by marriage.

- Senior members of Yudhoyono's party, PD, were found guilty of corruption in connection with the construction of a sports complex at Hambalang, West Java. Sports minister Andi Mallarangeng was given a four-year sentence (appeal pending), party treasurer Muhammad Nazaruddin was given a jail term of almost five years (increased to seven years by the Supreme Court on appeal) and party chair Anas Urbaningrum was sentenced to eight years (appeal pending).
- Aulia Pohan, whose daughter is married to Yudhoyono's oldest son, was convicted for his role in disbursing around $10 million from the Indonesian Banking Development Foundation for improper purposes (Crouch 2010: 72–3). The former Bank Indonesia deputy governor was sentenced to four years and six months in jail for corruption, reduced on appeal to four years, then by the Supreme Court to three years; he was released on parole in 2010 after serving two years of his sentence (Sofyan 2010).

SETBACKS FOR THE KPK

The KPK's change in strategy in 2009 to target more prominent Indonesians with strong political connections invited stronger pushback. In particular, its decision to exercise its mandate to pursue law enforcement officials made it vulnerable to retaliation from police and prosecutors. Under article 32 of Law 30/2002 on the Corruption Eradication Commission (the KPK Law), apparently designed to protect the KPK's reputation, a KPK commissioner who is formally charged with a crime can be suspended immediately by the president, and can be dismissed once the case goes to trial—even without being found guilty of any crime. This gives police and prosecutors enormous power to affect the composition of the KPK, because they can charge and prosecute commissioners unilaterally.

In early March 2009, police and prosecutors used these powers to suspend KPK chair Antasari Azhar, who was suspected of ordering a murder, and then to remove him when the case went to trial. Later that year, two other KPK commissioners—Chandra Muhammad Hamzah and Bibit Samad Rianto—were arrested and charged on vague 'abuse of power' grounds. As it emerged that the police could not provide solid evidence of any wrongdoing by Bibit and Chandra, raising suspicions they had been framed, public support for the KPK—and public disdain for those who were trying to discredit it—grew. These suspicions were confirmed by wiretapped conversations between senior law enforcement officials and suspects the KPK was investigating at the time. The conversations were aired during Constitutional Court proceedings, broadcast live on television, to decide whether removing the commissioners from office before they had been convicted of a crime breached the presumption of innocence. The court found that Bibit and Chandra had been framed and ordered their release; it also found that their right to the presumption of innocence had been breached.

Antasari was not so fortunate, however. After a highly irregular trial at which prosecutors could provide no credible evidence of his guilt, he was convicted of ordering the murder of Nasruddin Zulkarnaen, a businessman. According to prosecutors, the victim had blackmailed Antasari after discovering that the commissioner and Nasruddin's wife had had a brief sexual encounter. Though the trial smacked of a set-up to remove Antasari, under whom the KPK was targeting bigger fish, his conviction was subsequently upheld. Unlike Bibit and Chandra, who enjoyed significant public support, Antasari had never been popular with reformists, because of the allegations of corruption surrounding both his appointment as KPK chair and some of the cases he had handled in previous prosecutorial posts (Handayani, Kustiani and Nilawaty 2009).

Around the same time, the KPK had begun to investigate another category of big fish: national parliamentarians. They had even more power to retaliate than the law-enforcers. Because the KPK and the Tipikor Court are creatures of statute, parliament can amend or revoke the statutory bases upon which both institutions exercise their powers. The main avenue of legislative push-back chosen by the parliamentarians was Law 46/2009 on the Anti-Corruption Court, which was being deliberated as the scandals surrounding the KPK commissioners were unfolding and as the KPK was investigating several serving and former parliamentarians. Law 46/2009 was drafted in response to a 2006 decision in which the Constitutional Court had held that having a dual-track system for handling corruption cases violated citizens' constitutional right to equal treatment before the law. The KPK had pursued its cases through the Tipikor Court. However, the bulk of corruption cases were pursued by ordinary (non-KPK) police and prosecutors through the general courts, under different procedures. This dual-track system resulted in very different conviction rates: 100 per cent in the case of the KPK and Tipikor Court but just 50 per cent in the case of the general courts (Diansyah 2009).

The new law required the Supreme Court to establish regional corruption courts—one in the district court of each provincial capital—by October 2011. Together with the original Tipikor Court in Jakarta, these courts now hear all corruption and money-laundering cases, thereby removing the dual-track system that had concerned the Constitutional Court. The new courts have been strongly criticised, however, for their high acquittal rates. Indonesia Corruption Watch claims, for example, that the regional Tipikor courts acquitted as many as 71 defendants between December 2010 and August 2012.[2] A handful of Tipikor court judges have themselves been convicted of taking bribes to fix bribery cases, and several more were being investigated at the time of writing.[3]

The perceived poor performance of the regional corruption courts has led to calls by some prominent figures for their disbandment (Aritonang 2012; Wijaya, Wijaya and Sunudyantoro 2012). In my view, however, such calls are misguided. Acquittal and conviction rates are, in themselves, poor measures of judicial performance and presume that anyone who is tried must be guilty. Also, although it would be highly desirable to have more professional and less corruption-prone Tipikor court judges, judicial integrity has long been a problem across the entire judiciary (Pompe 2005; Butt and Lindsey 2011), not just the Tipikor courts.

Law 46/2009 makes two critical changes to Indonesia's legal framework for handling corruption cases. First, it gives district court chairs the power to appoint a majority of career judges to each five-judge panel if the court lacks sufficient ad hoc judges. Given that the Supreme Court is having trouble finding qualified candidates to fill ad hoc judicial positions, career judges are now likely to constitute a majority on most panels. This change to the law has implications for conviction rates, because the ad hoc judges are generally considered more professional and less corruption-prone than the career judges. Recognising the scarcity of ad hoc judges, the new law also gives district court chairs the discretion to allocate three rather than five judges to cases in some circumstances. Despite this, many Tipikor courts still do not have enough ad hoc judges to handle cases. The Supreme Court estimates that it needs around 60 judges to fill all vacancies across Indonesia, but in 2013 it could find only one qualified candidate among the 289 candidates who had registered interest in becoming an ad hoc judge.[4]

The second change is that Law 46/2009 allows general public prosecutors to bring cases before the Tipikor courts. As Figure 10.2 shows, general prosecutors have always handled the vast majority of corruption prosecutions. This is because the KPK lacks both the jurisdiction and the resources to handle all corruption cases. Although it had around 200 investigators in 2013, it had fewer than 50 prosecutors (KPK 2013: 46). In

---

2 'Vonis bebas pengadilan Tipikor' [Corruption court acquittals], *Kompas*, 2 August 2012.
3 'KPK tahan eks hakim pengadilan tinggi Jawa Barat' [KPK detains former West Java high court judge], *hukumonline.com*, 8 August 2014; 'KPK tahan eks hakim Tipikor Bandung', [KPK detains former Bandung corruption court judge], *hukumonline.com*, 14 August 2014.
4 'MA krisis hakim ad hoc Tipikor' [Supreme Court crisis of ad hoc corruption court judges], *hukumonline.com*, 30 August 2013.

Figure 10.2 Corruption cases handled by general prosecutors and KPK prosecutors, 2004–14 (no.)

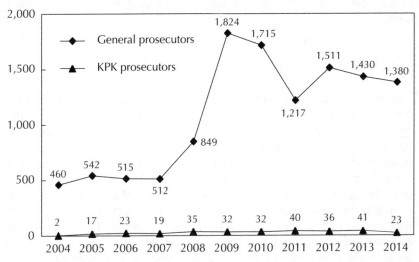

Source: Butt (2012a).

fact, the KPK does not even have regional offices, meaning that it largely restricts itself to Jakarta-based prosecutions.

Unless the KPK is radically expanded, there seems little alternative to allowing general prosecutors to appear in the Tipikor courts, even though the professionalism of KPK prosecutors is widely considered a key factor in the Jakarta Tipikor Court's high conviction rate. Unfortunately, when Yudhoyono's term in office ended in 2014, most corruption cases were still being handled in much the same way as they had been before he was elected in 2004. Though the KPK has been both bold and strong in pursuing corruption among the higher echelons, most cases continue to be pursued by general police, prosecutors and judges—the very people whose influence the KPK and the Tipikor Court were established to circumvent. The KPK prosecutes only a small proportion of cases, and ad hoc judges constitute a majority on some, but probably not most, Tipikor court panels.

Perhaps fearing or under KPK investigation, some legislators and government officials have continued to try to curb what they call the 'excessive' powers of the KPK. For example, proposals have long circulated to remove the commission's powers to investigate and prosecute, and to require it to obtain judicial permission to wiretap. Indeed, Law 46/2009 itself appears to anticipate this 'reform'; it does not mention the KPK at all, referring only to the powers of 'general' public prosecutors to prosecute before the Tipikor courts. This omission was not a drafting oversight (Dhyatmika et al. 2009; Wright 2009). These and other proposals to weaken the KPK's powers and lessen its impact continue to loom large.

YUDHOYONO AND THE KPK

Yudhoyono's popularity during his first term was partly due to his support for strong action against corruption, and partly a product of the spectacular prosecutions brought by the KPK. It is widely presumed that his resolve weakened during his second term, particularly after the KPK prosecuted, and the Tipikor Court convicted, his relative by marriage Aulia Pohan and members of PD. These scandals led to Yudhoyono's party being decimated as a political force at the 2014 legislative elections.

While this assessment is generally accurate, in fact Yudhoyono's support for the KPK during his first term was always qualified. For example, he publicly warned that the anti-corruption drive should 'respect the presumption of innocence' (Hotland and Taufiqurrahman 2006) and complained of the KPK's 'hyperactivity' in its investigations and prosecutions after it raided parliamentarians' offices.[5] In April 2008, in a speech to the National Law Convention, he said that the KPK should focus on preventing corruption rather than 'entrapping' citizens by 'taking advantage of their ignorance of laws and regulations on corruption' (van Klinken 2009). In early July 2009, as the Antasari, Bibit and Chandra sagas were unfolding, Yudhoyono said:

> Regarding the KPK, I must caution it. Power must not go unchecked. This KPK has become incredibly powerful. It seems to be accountable only to God. Be careful (Dhyatmika et al. 2009).

Yudhoyono did lend some support to the KPK, however, especially when the attacks on the commission rallied enormous public support behind it and made it the *cause célèbre* of 2009. By September 2009, with its chair removed and two commissioners suspended, the KPK's ongoing investigations and prosecutions had ground to a halt. Without Bibit and Chandra, its two chief investigators, the institution was struggling; the remaining two commissioners, Mochammad Jasin and Haryono Umar, were primarily responsible for corruption prevention and monitoring, and for information collection and distribution. On 21 September 2009, Yudhoyono issued a government regulation in lieu of law (*perppu*) giving

---

5 'Akhirnya, DPR persilahkan KPK menggeledah' [Finally, the DPR invites the KPK to conduct a search], *hukumonline.com*, 26 April 2008.

him the power to appoint KPK commissioners if three or more positions had become vacant.[6] A *perppu* is a regulation that can be enacted in times of emergency to serve as a statute until it has been confirmed or rejected by the DPR. On 6 October 2009, under his emergency regulation, Yudhoyono swore in three temporary KPK commissioners: Mas Achmad Santoso, Waluyo and Tumpak Hatorangan Panggabean.

Most media and legal commentators strongly criticised Yudhoyono for issuing the regulation,[7] accusing him of implicitly sanctioning the attacks on the KPK by filling Bibit and Chandra's positions, albeit temporarily (Azly 2009). Others pointed out that the KPK Law already provided a process for appointing KPK commissioners that helped avoid undue influence or interference. By contrast, under the new regulation, the president could unilaterally appoint commissioners who were loyal to him rather than dedicated to the eradication of corruption.[8]

While there was some truth to these criticisms, Yudhoyono ultimately chose well-regarded temporary commissioners, and the alternative would undoubtedly have been worse. Installing replacement commissioners using the procedures outlined in the KPK Law would have been a time-consuming process, requiring a selection committee to test and vet applicants and parliament to subject them to a fit-and-proper test. This would have stalled the KPK's work for many months, during which time further attacks on the institution could have been made. Also, given that some national parliamentarians were themselves under KPK investigation, the appointment process would probably have been highly fraught and susceptible to manipulation and rent-seeking.

Soon after issuing his emergency regulation, and with public and media condemnation of the handling of the Bibit and Chandra case reaching fever pitch, Yudhoyono established a 'Team of Eight' to investigate the case. It comprised eight highly esteemed lawyers and public figures, including noted lawyers Adnan Buyung Nasution and Todung Mulya Lubis. The team concluded that, although police and prosecutors had acted correctly in agreeing to investigate Bibit and Chandra, they should have dropped the case shortly afterwards when the lack of evidence against them became clear. That the case proceeded led to 'the impression that there had been engineering'. The team recommended that the cases against Bibit and Chandra be dropped, and that the police

---

6 Government Regulation in Lieu of Law 4/2009 amending Law 30/2002 on the Corruption Eradication Commission.
7 'LSM dan sejumlah tokoh tolak perpu plt pimpinan KPK' [NGOs and several figures reject government regulation in lieu of law on KPK leadership], *hukumonline.com*, 28 September 2009.
8 'KPK under siege', *hukumonline.com*, 4 October 2010.

investigator and deputy attorney general responsible for pursuing the charges resign.[9] Both recommendations were followed, though not at the request of the president (Haryadi 2009; KPK 2009).

In 2012, Yudhoyono sought to intervene in favour of the commission when the KPK and the police clashed over the KPK's decision to pursue allegations of high-level corruption within the police force. Both the KPK and the national police force claimed the authority to investigate Djoko Susilo, the chief of the traffic police, in connection with the awarding of contracts to procure driving simulators. When KPK investigators raided the headquarters of the National Police Traffic Corps in South Jakarta to obtain evidence for their investigations, police detained them and refused to release them until the following morning. After a stalemate lasting several months, Yudhoyono finally recommended that the police leave the case to the KPK and cooperate fully with the investigation (Pramudatama and Aritonang 2012). In September 2013, Djoko Susilo was found guilty in the Jakarta Tipikor Court and sentenced to ten years' imprisonment. His sentence was increased to 18 years on appeal (Rastika 2014).

Overall, we are left with a clear conclusion: while Yudhoyono never took the initiative in defending the KPK, his well-known sensitivity to public opinion (detailed by Fealy in Chapter 3 of this volume) did seem to have an effect. When public concern about the undermining of the KPK reached high levels, he tended to respond by acting in the commission's favour, even if he sometimes did so rather reluctantly.

THE CONSTITUTIONAL COURT

During its first decade (2004–14), particularly under the stewardships of founding chief justice Professor Jimly Asshiddiqie (2003–08) and his successor, Mahfud MD (2008–13), the Constitutional Court established itself as one of Indonesia's most successful post-Suharto institutions, widely respected by citizens, civil society and even government. Beyond the expectations of most, and with a few important exceptions, the Constitutional Court exercised its powers professionally — that is, impartially and with concern to justify its decisions by reference to the law.

The Constitution gives the Constitutional Court several functions, but two have taken up most of its time. The first is constitutional review, under which citizens and various legal entities can challenge the constitutionality of national legislation. If the court decides that a statute vio-

---

9 'Inilah dokumen lengkap rekomendasi Tim Delapan' [This is the complete recommendation of the Team of Eight], *Kompas*, 17 November 2009.

lates the Constitution, the court can invalidate it and declare it no longer binding. The court has exercised this power regularly to strike down legislation. The court's second main function is to resolve electoral disputes, a task it has carried out largely to the satisfaction of contesting parties. The court has handled thousands of disputes arising from polls for the presidency, for national, provincial, city and district legislatures, and for the Regional Representative Council (Dewan Perwakilan Daerah, DPD). In 2008 its jurisdiction was extended to disputes arising from elections for regional heads, although in May 2014, in a rather bizarre decision, the court decided that it no longer had jurisdiction to consider such cases.

Indonesia's Constitutional Court can be categorised as an 'activist' court by world standards (Dressel 2012). In Asia, the only other constitutional court that rivals it in terms of activism is the South Korean Constitutional Court (Ginsburg 2002, 2003) — the court the architects of Indonesia's Constitutional Court looked to for inspiration. At least three features of the court's decision-making processes justify its description as 'activist'.

First, the Constitutional Court is active in the sense that it actually performs its function and invalidates statutory provisions — or even entire statutes — deemed to be unconstitutional. It does not shy away from cases that are highly political or otherwise difficult, such as those involving significant vested interests. In contrast, many other Indonesian courts have traditionally avoided invalidating statutes. The Supreme Court, for example, was generally reluctant to exercise its powers of judicial review during the Suharto years (Pompe 2005; Huda 2010) and has begun to hear such cases only recently (Butt and Parsons 2014).

The Constitutional Court issued many landmark decisions during its first decade, some of which have been crucial for Indonesia's democratic development. For reasons of space, I mention only a few here. In one category of cases, the court was asked to uphold the right to freedom of speech. President Yudhoyono was well known for being willing to take legal action against journalists and others he perceived to be unduly critical of him. In one early case, the court invalidated criminal code provisions that prohibited citizens from insulting the president and government officials (the so-called *lèse-majesté* articles) and from 'sowing hate' (the so-called *hatzai artikelen*) (Royan 2008). In 2007, the court found that these provisions violated citizens' rights to freedom of expression (article 28E(2) of the Constitution), freedom to express an opinion (article 28D(3)) and freedom to communicate (article 28F).[10] However, in cases decided in 2008 and 2009, the court held that these 'free speech' rights

---

10 Constitutional Court Decision 013-022/PUU-IV/2006; Constitutional Court Decision 6/PUU-V/2007.

were overridden by article 28G of the Constitution, which gives citizens (including public figures) rights to protection of honour and reputation. In other words, the court decided that the reputational rights of government officials prevailed over the free speech rights of citizens.[11] As a result, most 'crimes' that prohibit citizens from insulting public officials, such as defamation, remain constitutional. Criticism of the government may therefore be a crime, even if that criticism is based on established fact.

The court has also helped shape Indonesia's electoral system (Dressel and Mietzner 2012). In one of its earliest cases, in 2003, it removed restrictions preventing former members of the Indonesian Communist Party and their families from standing for election, holding that those restrictions were discriminatory.[12] In 2009, the court held that citizens could vote even if they were not registered to do so, provided they presented a valid form of identification, such as an identity card or passport, to polling officials on election day.[13] In another case decided before the 2009 election, the court held that Indonesia's semi-open party-list system for electing legislative candidates was unconstitutional. Under this system, voters could cast their ballots for an individual candidate, a party or both. But candidates running as individuals had to achieve a quota of the total vote in the electoral district to be elected in their own right. If they failed to achieve that quota—and most did—then the seats would go to candidates in the order specified by the party list. In practice, this meant that candidates who had received fewer votes, but occupied higher positions on the party list, would be elected before candidates who had received a greater number of personal votes. The Constitutional Court's decision dramatically altered this system, requiring parties to allocate seats to candidates who had received the most personal votes, regardless of their position on the list or whether they had met the quota.[14]

The court has also issued momentous decisions upholding economic and socio-cultural rights. In 2012, for example, it decided that a child born out of wedlock had a civil legal relationship not only with its mother, as had previously been the case under Indonesia's Marriage Law, but also with its biological father. This *Wedlock* decision removed some legal roadblocks for such children to claim maintenance and receive inherit-

---

11 Constitutional Court Decision 14/PUU-VI/2008; Constitutional Court Decision 50/PUU-VI/2008; Constitutional Court Decision 2/PUU-VII/2009.
12 Constitutional Court Decision 011-017/PUU-I/2003. In the majority: Asshiddiqie, Marzuki, Natabaya, Harjono, Palguna, Fajar, Siahaan and Soedarso. In the minority: Roestandi. The provision in question was article 60(g) of Law 12/2003 on General Elections.
13 Constitutional Court Decision 102/PUU-VII/2009.
14 Constitutional Court Decision 22-24/PUU-VI/2008.

ances from their fathers. In 2013, in another landmark decision, the court upheld the traditional land rights of indigenous (*adat*) communities over coastal resources and forests, thus preventing the state from awarding concessions or rights over natural resources while ignoring the rights of recognised *adat* communities.[15]

The second reason for calling Indonesia's Constitutional Court 'activist' is that it has tested the boundaries of its jurisdiction. Many courts around the world do this, but usually more gradually and incrementally than Indonesia's Constitutional Court, which has exceeded its jurisdiction in many cases. For example, the statutes granting the court power to resolve electoral disputes authorise it only to decide disputes about vote-counting and, if errors are identified, to stipulate the correct count. The court has gone well beyond this, ordering recounts and even reruns of elections, and adjudicating on some types of breaches of the electoral laws that occur before counting even takes place (Butt 2013).

Perhaps the best examples of the court's expansion of its jurisdiction in constitutional review cases are those in which it decides that the statute being challenged is 'conditionally constitutional'. In such cases, the court declares that the statute it has reviewed appears to be constitutionally defective. However, rather than invalidating the statute as the court's governing law appears to require,[16] it decides that the statute under review can remain constitutional provided it is interpreted in such a way that its effect is not unconstitutional. The court issued several declarations of conditional constitutionality in its early decisions, and many more in its later decisions, particularly under Chief Justice Mahfud. Under the first chief justice, Jimly Asshiddiqie, around 35 per cent of successful challenges involved declarations of conditional constitutionality, but this increased to around 60 per cent under Mahfud. The court also consciously shifted towards declaring statutes 'conditionally unconstitutional' – that is, unconstitutional unless interpreted in a particular way or given a particular meaning. The court did this in response to perceptions that the government was not heeding its 'conditionally constitutional' decisions.[17] Perhaps most importantly, the court's decisions became more prescriptive and specific. If the conditions the court imposed early on were vague and aspirational, they later resembled legislative amendments. A clear example is provided by the *Wedlock* case

---

15 Constitutional Court Decision 35/PUU-X/2012, reviewing Law 41/1999 on Forestry; Constitutional Court Decision 3/PUU-VII/2010, reviewing Law 27/2007 on the Management of Coastal Areas and Small Islands. See also Constitutional Court Decision 55/PUU-VIII/2010, reviewing Law 18/2004 on Plantations.
16 See article 57 of Law 24/2003 on the Constitutional Court.
17 See, in particular, Constitutional Court Decision 54/PUU-VI/2008, para 3.22.

mentioned above. There, the court reviewed article 43(1) of the 1974 Marriage Law, which states that:

> A child born out of marriage has a civil legal relationship with its mother and her family.

The court's decision was to declare article 43(1) conditionally unconstitutional — that is, unconstitutional unless interpreted to read:

> A child born out of marriage has a civil legal relationship with its mother and her family, and its father and his family [provided that paternity] can be proven by science and technology and/or another form of legally recognised evidence that the father has a blood relationship with the child.[18]

Putting the obvious desirability of the decision to one side, the court, in essence, changed the wording of article 43(1) of the Marriage Law to grant additional rights to children, create obligations for biological fathers and establish how those rights and obligations arise.

The court's decisions in this and similar cases have the same effect as amending the legislation itself, and are arguably decisions better left to the legislature. On the other hand, declarations of conditional constitutionality are a pragmatic response to the highly realistic expectation that the legislature will respond to the court's decisions slowly, if at all. In this context, striking legislation down would probably result in a prolonged legal vacuum during which the invalidation might put the applicant in a worse position. Applied to the *Wedlock* case, for example, if the court had simply struck down article 43(1) of the Marriage Law, then children might have had no legal basis to claim from anyone, *including* their mothers.

The third way in which Indonesia's Constitutional Court can be called 'activist' is in rejecting interference from the legislature. Most dramatically, the court rejected attempts by the legislature to restrict the exercise of what it believed was its constitutionally mandated jurisdiction. Law 24/2003 on the Constitutional Court, for example, sought to restrict the court to reviewing statutes enacted after the first amendments to the 1945 Constitution in 1999, thereby preventing the court from reviewing Suharto-era legislation. The court invalidated this provision within its first year of operation. The Constitutional Court Law amendments passed in 2011 (Law 8/2011) sought to limit the types of decisions the court could issue, including prohibiting it from issuing declarations of conditional constitutionality. The court did not allow these amendments to hinder its decision-making practices, invalidating almost all of them within a few months of their enactment. The court has similarly rejected

---

18 Constitutional Court Decision 46/PUU-VIII/2010, para 3.13.

attempts by the legislature to empower the Judicial Commission (Komisi Yudisial) to monitor and supervise the court.

Nevertheless, the court has chosen to confine its own activism by giving its decisions limited effect. The court's decisions generally apply only prospectively; a statute is unconstitutional and no longer binding only once the court declares it to be. Any government action taken under a law before it is declared unconstitutional therefore remains valid. Unlike the decisions of other courts—the courts that resolve disputes between parties or determine whether a citizen has committed a crime—the decisions of the Constitutional Court are binding for *all* citizens. But the prospective nature of those decisions means that applicants who have suffered damage to their constitutional rights and had their cases upheld by the Constitutional Court are not entitled to redress. At best, they can claim only a moral victory, helping to prevent the constitutional rights of others who might have been affected by the statute from being diminished in the future. This limitation, it should be stressed, is self-imposed—the court itself has come up with this interpretation of its powers. It has not been a limitation imposed on it by the government or any other external body.

YUDHOYONO AND THE CONSTITUTIONAL COURT

Although the press occasionally reported that Yudhoyono had contacted members of the Constitutional Court to ask for advice, there is little evidence to suggest that he ever actively sought to influence a decision or that he refused to comply with one. Chief Justice Mahfud admitted that he knew Yudhoyono well, but said that the president never asked him about cases the Constitutional Court was hearing, let alone sought to interfere in them (Budiarti 2012: 171–5).

Only once did Yudhoyono actively seek to intervene in the processes of the court, through a *perppu* issued in late 2013.[19] The regulation was directed at remedying perceived defects in Law 24/2003 on the Constitutional Court brought to light by the arrest of Chief Justice Akil Mochtar on charges of corruption (discussed below). It sought to change the appointment process for Constitutional Court judges, presumably to prevent a repeat of this saga. The regulation required candidates to undergo a fit-and-proper test that would be administered by a Panel of Experts, to be appointed by the Judicial Commission. It also prohibited aspiring Constitutional Court judges from appointment if they had been a member of a political party in the past seven years, and sought to establish a

---

19 Government Regulation in Lieu of Law 1/2013 on the Constitutional Court.

permanent Constitutional Court Judge Honour Council (Majelis Kehormatan Hakim Konstitusi) to investigate allegations of misconduct.

Within only a few months, however, the Constitutional Court had invalidated these amendments.[20] One of the reasons it gave for its decision was that the participation of the Judicial Commission in both the appointment and dismissal of judges had the potential to affect the court's independence. The court also found that the requirement for a judicial candidate not to have been a member of a political party was discriminatory, following the *PKI case* (2003), while noting that, in any event, membership of a political party was not the sole indicator of political bias. In other words, Yudhoyono's one attempt to shape the Constitutional Court was unsuccessful.

Overall, the Constitutional Court faced few conspicuous failures or setbacks during the Yudhoyono years. Allegations of impropriety by judges or court staff were minimal, with one exception: the arrest and conviction, in 2014, of Chief Justice Akil Mochtar, who had served on the court since 2008. The court's reputation nosedived when Mochtar was arrested by the KPK for receiving bribes to fix electoral disputes. Mochtar was also investigated by police for narcotics offenses after illicit substances were found in his chambers. He was convicted of money-laundering and sentenced to life imprisonment. The court suffered significant reputational damage because of the scandal, with commentators concerned that it might not recover given that much of its public and political support was based on its perceived integrity and impartiality. In fact, however, the court regained much of the respect it had lost during this episode through its professional handling of the challenge lodged by losing candidate Prabowo Subianto to the 2014 presidential election result.

Despite this setback, the Constitutional Court has become an important institution in Indonesian democracy. From humble beginnings — initially it was run out of hotels and government offices — it is now housed in a grand court complex and is relatively well resourced. At first, it appeared that the court might have trouble convincing the government to comply with its decisions (Butt and Lindsey 2008), but this fear has largely dissipated, with compliance becoming the norm rather than the exception. While some of the legislative attacks on the court's decision-making mentioned above might be categorised as setbacks, I would cat-

---

20 Judicial commissioner Imam Anshori Saleh described the court's decision to invalidate the amendments as a 'tragedy for law enforcement', saying that 'a new Akil Mochtar' might emerge and little could now be done to prevent this. See 'Batalkan eks perppu, MK tetap tak mau diawasi' [Invalidating government regulation in lieu of law, the Supreme Court still does not want to be supervised], *hukumonline.com*, 13 February 2014.

egorise them as achievements. The court has had sufficient institutional legitimacy, buttressed by strong levels of public support, to defend itself from these attacks, so that the amendments to the Constitutional Court Law passed in 2011 hardly affected it. At the same time, the court experienced little attempted interference from the president.

CONCLUSION

During Yudhoyono's tenure, the KPK and the Constitutional Court developed into confident institutions willing to perform their functions in ways that disrupted high-level political interests. They managed to do this through careful strategy and prudent leadership. Critically, they built high levels of public support, born from their various and increasing successes. While Yudhoyono did not actively help them much, neither did he actively hinder them.

There are at least two plausible explanations for Yudhoyono's apparent reluctance to interfere with, or retaliate against, the KPK and the Constitutional Court. One is that he chose not to, deciding that it would be illegal or improper to intervene because both institutions are formally independent of the government. As mentioned at the outset of this chapter, the Constitution states that the Constitutional Court is to be independent of government. This independence is, of course, critical to the court performing its mandated role — of acting as a check on the exercise of government power. The independence of the KPK is also guaranteed by law. In short, it is possible that Yudhoyono was cognisant of the legal constraints within which he operated and was motivated above all by a sense of constitutional propriety.

An alternative explanation is that the KPK and the Constitutional Court (at least until the Mochtar scandal) had both become so popular with the public that any attempt to rein them in would have invited significant criticism and tarnished Yudhoyono's reformist credentials. Had he sought to resist or interfere — in response to the KPK's investigation into misconduct by members of his party, or in response to the Constitutional Court's decision to invalidate his government regulation in lieu of law — he may well have been unsuccessful, partly because the popularity of these institutions appeared to surpass his own, at least by the second half of his second term. Renowned for his sensitivity to public criticism, Yudhoyono presumably chose not to expose himself to public defeat and humiliation.

Despite the controversy that has occasionally surrounded them, both the Constitutional Court and the KPK are in better shape now than they were at the beginning of the Yudhoyono period. The Constitutional

Court is generally regarded as a good place for Indonesians to air their public law grievances. It usually gives applicants a fair hearing, regardless of the strength of their claims, and its proceedings are documented and often attract significant media coverage. In short, the court is a useful forum in which to push one's cause (Butt 2012b). The KPK, too, remains very popular with the public and still achieves convictions in all cases it prosecutes itself, despite its decision to target more powerful political players. Under a different president, both institutions might have notched up similar achievements, but under an obstructionist one, they could have fared much worse.

REFERENCES

Aritonang, M.S. (2012) 'Govt considers shutting down corruption courts in regions', *Jakarta Post*, 21 August.
Azly, E. (2009) 'News focus: president eventually issues perppu on KPK interim chief', *Antara*, 22 September.
Budiarti, R.T. (2012) *Kontroversi Mahfud M.D.* [The Mahfud MD Controversy], Konstitusi Press, Jakarta.
Butt, S. (2012a) 'Indonesia's regional anti-corruption courts: should they be abolished?', *Indonesia Law Review*, 2(2): 147–64.
Butt, S. (2012b) 'Indonesia's Constitutional Court: conservative activist or strategic operator?', in B. Dressel (ed.) *The Judicialization of Politics in Asia*, Routledge, Abingdon and New York: 98–116.
Butt, S. (2013) 'Indonesian Constitutional Court decisions in regional head electoral disputes', policy paper, Centre for Democratic Institutions, Australian National University, Canberra.
Butt, S. and T. Lindsey (2008) 'Economic reform when the Constitution matters: Indonesia's Constitutional Court and article 33', *Bulletin of Indonesian Economic Studies*, 44(2): 239–62.
Butt, S. and T. Lindsey (2011) 'Judicial mafia: the courts and state illegality in Indonesia', in G. van Klinken and E. Aspinall (eds) *The State and Illegality in Indonesia*, KITLV Press, Leiden: 189–213.
Butt, S. and N. Parsons (2014) 'Judicial review and the Supreme Court in Indonesia: a new space for law?', *Indonesia*, 97: 55–85.
Crouch, H. (2010) *Political Reform in Indonesia after Soeharto*, Institute of Southeast Asian Studies, Singapore.
Dhyatmika, W., A.L. Handayani, R. Kustiani and R. Munawaroh (2009) 'Ganging up on the KPK', *Tempo English Edition*, 7–13 July.
Diansyah, F. (2009) *Weakening of Corruption Eradication Commission (KPK) in Indonesia: Independent Report*, Indonesia Corruption Watch and National Coalition of Indonesia for Anticorruption, Doha, November.
Dressel, B. (ed.) (2012) *The Judicialization of Politics in Asia*, Routledge, Abingdon and New York.
Dressel, B. and M. Mietzner (2012) 'A tale of two courts: the judicialization of electoral politics in Asia', *Governance*, 25(3): 391–414.
Fenwick, S. (2008) 'Measuring up? Indonesia's Anti-Corruption Commission and the new corruption agenda', in T. Lindsey (ed.) *Indonesia: Law and Society*, second edition, Federation Press, Annandale: 406–29.

Ginsburg, T. (2002) 'Confucian constitutionalism? The emergence of constitutional review in Korea and Taiwan', *Law & Social Inquiry*, 27(4): 763–99.
Ginsburg, T. (2003) *Judicial Review in New Democracies: Constitutional Courts in Asian Cases*, Cambridge University Press, Cambridge MA.
Handayani, A.L., R. Kustiani and C. Nilawaty (2009) 'Tragedy of the dapper prosecutor', *Tempo English Edition*, 5 May.
Haryadi, R. (2009) *Chandra–Bibit; Membongkar Perseteruan KPK, Polri, dan Kejaksaan* [Chandra–Bibit: Breaking Open the KPK, Police and Prosecution Feud], Hikmah, Jakarta.
Hotland, T. and M. Taufiqurrahman (2006) 'SBY rallies anti-graft drive, but warns against excess', *Jakarta Post*, 12 December.
Huda, N. (2010) *Problematika Pembatalan Peraturan Daerah* [The Problems of Invalidating Regional Regulations], FH UII Press, Yogyakarta.
ICW (Indonesia Corruption Watch) (2001) *Menyingkap Tabir Mafia Peradilan (Hasil Monitoring Peradilan ICW)* [Pulling Back the Curtain of the Judicial Mafia (Results of ICW Court Monitoring)], Jakarta.
KPK (Komisi Pemberantasan Korupsi) (2009) *Laporan Tahunan KPK 2009: Perjuangan Melawan Korupsi Tak Pernah Berhenti* [KPK Annual Report 2009: the Struggle against Corruption Never Ends], Jakarta.
KPK (Komisi Pemberantasan Korupsi) (2013) *Laporan Tahunan KPK 2013* [KPK Annual Report 2013], Jakarta.
Pompe, S. (2005) *The Indonesian Supreme Court: A Study of Institutional Collapse*, Southeast Asia Program, Cornell University, Ithaca NY.
Pramudatama, R. and M.S. Aritonang (2012) 'Police ignore SBY and strike back at KPK', *Jakarta Post*, 6 December.
Rastika, I. (2014) 'Putusan berkekuatan hukum tetap, KPK eksekusi Djoko Susilo' [Decision becomes binding, KPK to enforce against Djoko Susilo], *Kompas*, 8 July.
Royan, N. (2008) 'Increasing press freedom in Indonesia: the abolition of the lese majeste and "hate-sowing" provisions', *Australian Journal of Asian Law*, 10(2): 290–311.
Sofyan, D. (2010) 'Corruption sentence cut reflects failed government', *Jakarta Post*, 3 September.
Van Klinken, G. (2009) 'Indonesia's politically driven anti-corruption agenda and the post-election future', *Asia-Pacific Journal*, 15(2). Available at: http://japanfocus.org/-gerry-van_klinken/3117.
Wijaya, A.S., I. Wijaya and Sunudyantoro (2012) 'Pengadilan Tipikor daerah diusulkan dibubarkan' [Regional corruption courts proposed to be disbanded], *Tempo*, 5 November.
World Bank (2003) *Combating Corruption in Indonesia: Enhancing Accountability for Development*, World Bank East Asia Poverty Reduction and Economic Management Unit, Jakarta.
Wright, T. (2009) 'Indonesia dilutes antigraft court', *Wall Street Journal*, 30 September.

PART 3

Gender, human rights and environment

11 Yudhoyono's politics and the harmful implications for gender equality in Indonesia

Melani Budianta, Kamala Chandrakirana and Andy Yentriyani

> Excuse me, Mr President ...
> I am impatiently waiting for your presidency to finish ...
> And I long for ... patriotic anthems ...
> not songs that you have composed yourself ...
> *(Open letter to Susilo Bambang Yudhoyono by senior journalist Linda Djalil, 18 November 2013)*

In 2004, Susilo Bambang Yudhoyono became the first Indonesian president to be elected directly by the people through free and peaceful democratic elections. In 2009, he was re-elected with impressive support of more than 61 per cent of the vote. Significantly, in both elections Yudhoyono enjoyed particularly high popularity among women voters. In 2009, for example, an exit poll conducted by the Indonesian Survey Institute (Lembaga Survei Indonesia, LSI) found that 66 per cent of women, but only 55 per cent of men, had supported Yudhoyono, prompting LSI researcher Saiful Mujani to conclude that the president had been 'saved by women voters'.[1] Maeswera (2009: 81) echoed this view, noting that Yudhoyono was particularly popular with mature women, including married women and mothers (*ibu-ibu*), due to his handsome appearance and his image as a guitar-playing songwriter. (Yudhoyono would produce four albums during his presidency.)

---

1 'SBY dibela perempuan, Mega disukai laki-laki' [SBY defended by women, Mega favoured by men], *Viva News*, 9 July 2009.

Recognising his standing with female voters, Yudhoyono made lofty promises to women's rights activists towards the end of his first term. Speaking at a national event in 2009 to commemorate the tenth anniversary of the founding of the National Commission on Violence against Women (Komisi Nasional Anti Kekerasan Terhadap Perempuan, Komnas Perempuan), Yudhoyono emphatically declared that the state should immediately implement its responsibilities to protect women from violence and injustice and empower women in all aspects of life, giving them greater choice and access to full participation in public life:

> I need to reiterate what I have said in various forums in the last five years. I have stated that all of us — especially the state — must give better protection to women; must promote them and give them opportunity and empowerment. I could not but underline these three important things, protection, promotion and empowerment of the women in our beloved country. We need not only policies and strategies, but more importantly operational and practical steps that can immediately be applied in our lives (Yudhoyono 2009: 2).

Towards the end of his second term, however, it was clear that these promises were nowhere near being realised. Political representation of women had dropped and the state was not reducing rates of violence against women or the maternal mortality rate. Indonesia's ranking on the World Economic Forum's Gender Gap Index fell during the last years of Yudhoyono's presidency, from 90 out of 135 countries in 2011 (with a score of 0.659) to 97 out of 142 countries in 2014 (with a score of 0.672) (WEF 2011, 2014). Unsurprisingly, therefore, many women activists were disappointed with Yudhoyono's presidency. Capturing this sense of disappointment, journalist Linda Djalil posted a lyrical open letter entitled 'Excuse me, Mr President ...' on the internet, which went viral in social media in late 2013 (Djalil 2013). In it, she described herself as a formerly ardent supporter of the president who now could not wait for his term in office to end, and who longingly remembered 'the time when the anniversary of independence on August 17 was filled with the patriotic anthems of Ismail Marzuki [a composer of nationalist songs], sung for decades by children choirs, not songs that you [the president] have composed yourself'. The letter went on to list a series of unfulfilled promises relating to Yudhoyono's handling of a number of controversial issues.

Djalil's letter reflected the general disappointment in Yudhoyono's performance towards the end of his presidency, particularly among women who had voted him into power (Manangka 2013). Against this background, this chapter seeks to explain the contradictions between Yudhoyono's apparently women-friendly declarations and the many setbacks for the status of women in public life during his presidency. We argue that it was the combination of the president's personal piety, his reluctance to tackle much-needed reforms and his personalised style in responding to the problems faced by women that was most harmful to the advancement of women's rights and gender equality in Indonesia. In developing this argument, we start by examining the state of women's affairs at the end of his presidency in 2014, with particular attention to women's political representation, the wellbeing of poor women and the framework for legal protection from discrimination. The second section of the chapter examines Yudhoyono's morality and religious politics, and his half-hearted social justice reforms. The conclusion summarises the main arguments and provides a brief outlook for the coming years.

THE STATE OF AFFAIRS IN 2014: BACKSLIDING ON GENDER EQUALITY

Women's political representation

Women activists have long struggled to increase women's political representation in Indonesia, especially at the national level, but also in local legislative bodies. One important strategy has been to advocate for the adoption of a quota system to increase women's representation at all levels of government (Siregar 2005). This was finally achieved when Law 12/2003 on General Elections included, for the first time, a quota of 30 per cent for women candidates on the party lists submitted for the 2004 elections. However, because the quota was non-mandatory, compliance was weak, and many of the female candidates who were nominated were placed at the bottom of the party lists, giving them very little chance of being elected (Bessell 2010: 230). As a result, the 2004 parliamentary elections led to only a small increase in the proportion of women in the national parliament, from 8 per cent in 1999 to 11.2 per cent in 2004.

To boost the numbers, women activists then campaigned for the introduction of a 'zipper' system for the 2009 elections, whereby male and female candidates would be placed alternately on the parties' lists of candidates. The revised Law 10/2008 on General Elections stipulated that at least one female candidate had to be included among every three male candidates on the party lists, although, as in 2004, there were no sanctions for political parties that failed to fulfil this requirement. The 2009 elections nevertheless resulted in a 7 per cent increase in the proportion of women in the national parliament, lifting it from 11.2 per cent to 18 per cent. The zipper system was further strengthened in 2014 when sanctions for non-compliance were introduced and rigorously applied by the independent General Elections Commission. According to Satriyo (2014), 77 candidates from five parties in seven electoral districts were disqualified because their parties failed to meet the quota.

Unfortunately, however, these affirmative action measures did not succeed in altering the dominant male-centric political culture in Indonesia. Not only did many parties struggle to fill their quotas, but their leaders made comments exposing barely hidden contempt for the quota system. Golkar politician Agun Gunandjar Sunarsa, for example, asked provocatively: 'So what should we do if women are not interested in entering the political arena? ... Do you think we need to recruit transsexuals just to meet the 30 per cent women's quota?'[2] While this may be an extreme and also homophobic reaction, virtually all parties' nomination processes were marred by strategies that clearly undermined the spirit of the quota system. Rather than seeking out ambitious and capable women, parties abused the quota system by recruiting a multitude of female celebrities and relatives of powerful party elites with questionable political competence. Moreover, they continued to give the least winnable spots—that is, the final positions in every group of three (positions 3, 6, 9 and 12)—to women (Kumoro 2014). It is therefore not surprising that the number of women in the national parliament fell from 103 (18 per cent) in 2009 to 97 (17.3 per cent) in 2014.[3]

The 2014 results show that Indonesia's political elites are not particularly concerned about or eager to address the structural roots of women's limited representation in formal politics. The issue of gender equality in political representation has had very little space to grow in the heteronormative and male-centric form of politics that prevails in Indonesia's democracy today. In an arena where money politics and sexism are rampant, it is hard for women politicians to survive. In fact, even high-performing women parliamentarians cannot be sure of re-election. For example, pro-democracy advocates and human rights defenders such as Eva Kusuma Sundari from the Indonesian Democratic Party of Struggle (Partai Demokrasi Indonesia-Perjuangan, PDIP), Nurul Arifin (Golkar) and Nova Riyanti Yusuf from the Democrat Party (Partai Demokrat, PD) all lost their seats in parliament in 2014, to the dismay of women activists. After the election, Sundari openly alleged that money politics and vote-buying by other candidates had been key reasons for her failure to win another term (Satriyo 2014).

One may argue that President Susilo Bambang Yudhoyono could hardly be blamed for the fall in women's representation in parliament. In fact, his own party, PD, performed reasonably well in recruiting female candidates, with more than 20 per cent of its elected candidates being female (Candraningrum 2014: 122). PD also appointed a woman,

---

2 'Kuota perempuan 30 persen tak bisa dipaksakan' [30 per cent women's quota cannot be forced], *Waspada Online*, 23 January 2014.
3 'Perempuan terpilih turun 1 persen' [1 per cent decline in women elected to parliament], *rumahpemilu.org*, 19 May 2014.

Nur Hayati Assegaf, to the position of chair of the party's faction in the national parliament. Moreover, Yudhoyono made at least some attempt to improve the gender balance in his cabinet by appointing four female ministers to both his 2004 and 2009 cabinets. Utomo et al. (2007) noted that this was the first time an Indonesian president had made such a conscious effort 'after 64 years of Indonesian independence'.[4]

At the same time, however, Yudhoyono contributed to the development of an inherently nepotistic political system, by giving his wife and son important positions in his party (Honna 2012). He also failed to prevent his party from being tainted by allegations of corruption and money politics. Significantly, several women in influential positions within PD were among those accused of corruption, thus revealing the complex roles played by women in the top echelons of political and financial institutions. Especially noteworthy in this regard were the large-scale corruption scandals involving Angelina Sondakh (deputy secretary-general of PD), Neneng Sri Wahyuni (wife of PD treasurer Muhammad Nazaruddin) and Haryati Moerdaya Poo (businesswoman and patron of PD). These scandals show very clearly that women are by no means immune to the temptations of power and that simply increasing the number of women in political institutions is insufficient to further the agenda of women's empowerment.[5]

The wellbeing of poor women

One outstanding achievement of Susilo Bambang Yudhoyono's government was the consistent economic growth of around 5–6 per cent per annum during his presidency (see Chapter 15 by Hill). From being the world's 27th-largest economy in 2000, Indonesia rose to 16th position in 2014, and it has joined the G20 major economies. This achievement was overshadowed, however, by increasing inequality. The World Bank (2014: 33) reported that inequality in Indonesia rose by 11 percentage points between 2000 and 2013, the largest rate of increase in the region after China. As a consequence, the richest 10 per cent of households accounted for nearly one-third of all household consumption and the richest 20 per cent for almost half (World Bank 2014: 34). The Bertelsmann Stiftung country report for 2014 notes that 'Indonesia's 40 richest citizens are far wealthier than those of Thailand, Malaysia or Singapore, collectively holding $71.3 billion in 2010' (BTI 2014: 13).

---

4 Note that Yudhoyono's successor, Joko Widodo, doubled that figure in 2014, appointing eight women to his cabinet.
5 'Ketika perempuan ikut korupsi' [When women participate in corruption], *Kompas*, 28 December 2012.

According to the World Bank (2014: 38), one-third of the inequality experienced by Indonesia today is 'due to circumstances that are beyond the control of an individual, such as gender, ethnicity, birthplace or family background'. It estimates that as much as 33 per cent of the total consumption inequality in 2012 is explained by just three factors: the gender of the household head, the level of education of the household head and the geographic location of the household. The Bertelsmann Stiftung report provides a more focused description of women's central position in this alarming picture of rising inequality in Indonesia:

> While equal opportunities to access education, public office or employment are generally available to citizens regardless of ethnicity or religion, there are significant hurdles for women, the poor and rural citizens. To begin with, women are underrepresented in the workforce, with 52% of women having some form of employment as opposed to 86% of men. Women are also less likely to have completed secondary school than are men (24% as compared to 31%) (BTI 2014: 18).

In this picture, women who are poor, who are the heads of their households and who are living in rural communities bear the brunt of inequality in Indonesia. In fact, these women often pay with their lives; according to data compiled by the United Nations Population Fund, the number of maternal deaths per 100,000 live births increased from 220 in 2010 to 359 in 2012, with young women aged 25–29 particularly badly affected.[6] Both numbers have standard errors that are so large that there is no statistical difference between the estimates. Nevertheless, it is clear that Indonesia's maternal mortality rates are relatively high and that they have been stubbornly unresponsive to health interventions over the last decade. This greatly inhibits the country's ability to achieve the Millennium Development Goal of reducing maternal mortality to 102 deaths per 100,000 live births by 2015.

For women's rights activists, the apparent rise in Indonesia's maternal mortality rate is cause for alarm. During the commemoration of International Women's Day on 8 March 2014, they made this policy failure the basis of their ten-point political agenda for the women's movement on the eve of the 2014 elections. Number one on their list was the fulfilment of women's sexual and reproductive rights, followed by the right to an education, an end to violence against women and an end to the feminisation of poverty (Indonesia Beragam 2014).

In the face of life-threatening poverty at home, many of Indonesia's poor rural women have opted to leave their families and communities to become migrant workers abroad. And yet, for many of these women, this

---

6 'Indonesia still haunted by high number of maternal and post-natal deaths', *Jakarta Globe*, 29 January 2014.

has turned out not to be a safe and viable option. In a report to the United Nations Committee on Economic, Social and Cultural Rights in 2014, Komnas Perempuan notes that 'Indonesian migrant workers are still predominantly women who work in the informal sector ... [where] many of them experience exploitation, sexual violence, trafficking and criminalisation' (Komnas Perempuan 2014). Large numbers are employed in the Gulf countries, particularly Saudi Arabia, but also in Malaysia and Hong Kong. Komnas Perempuan cites data from the National Agency for the Placement and Protection of Indonesian Migrant Workers (Badan Nasional Penempatan dan Perlindungan Tenaga Kerja Indonesia, BNP2TKI) showing that 2,209 migrant workers experienced sexual violence in 2011, 2,145 faced other forms of abuse and 1,730 were not paid (Komnas Perempuan 2013).

The Yudhoyono government placed a moratorium on sending migrant workers to Malaysia in 2009, and a moratorium on sending workers to Saudi Arabia in 2011. It also initiated memorandums of understanding (MOUs) with both of these countries to better protect migrant workers (see below). Even though these agreements fell short of the legally binding bilateral agreements advocated by women's rights activists, they nevertheless signalled that the government was prepared to act on this issue. In 2012, the national parliament went a step further, ratifying the International Convention on the Protection of the Rights of All Migrant Workers and Members of Their Families, with President Yudhoyono's endorsement. The situation on the ground, however, has not changed much, particularly in terms of victims' access to justice. A study conducted in 2012 by researchers from the University of New South Wales Law School concluded that, in Indonesia, the most frequently used redress mechanisms for migrant workers who faced harm 'often yield unsatisfactory or unfair outcomes for workers' and that the country's labour migration laws 'do not enable workers to access justice' (Farbenblum, Taylor-Nicholson and Paoletti 2013: 17–18).

Legal protection from discrimination

Another major issue affecting the status of women in Indonesian society during the Yudhoyono years was the inadequate legal protection for women from various forms of discrimination. This issue rose to prominence for the first time during the intense public debate surrounding the anti-pornography bill, which became law in October 2008 (Sherlock 2008). Law 44/2008 on Pornography took a draconian, protectionist approach to the prevention and reduction of pornography that threatened freedom of expression and legal certainty for women and people with diverse sexual orientations and gender identities (Allen 2009). The opponents of the law immediately initiated a judicial review by the Constitutional Court but failed to convince the judges that the law violated the Constitution's guarantee of human rights and non-discrimination for all. The law came into force in March 2010. In October 2011, Komnas Perempuan reported 20 cases of wrongful arrest, in which women had been detained on suspicion of being sex workers because of their attire, their gestures or simply their presence at certain places at certain times (Komnas Perempuan 2011).

Around the same time the Anti-pornography Law was passed, women activists were attempting to focus national attention on another issue: the rise of discriminatory local government regulations (*perda*) being produced in the wake of the introduction of regional autonomy. Based on monitoring of 17 districts in seven provinces in 2008–09, Komnas Perempuan (2010) identified 154 *perda* issued between 2000 and 2009 that were deemed discriminatory against women. As many as 63 of these regulations were directly discriminatory against women, while another 82 regulating religious life were not particularly focused on women, but had discriminatory effects nonetheless on women in religious-minority communities. These regulations restricted women's freedom of expression by prescribing how they should dress and undermined women's rights to legal protection and certainty by, among others things, making it a criminal offense for women to be in a public space at certain times of the day. The trend towards restricting women's freedoms not only continued but actually worsened during Yudhoyono's second term; the number of discriminatory *perda* rose from 154 in 2009 to 364 at the end of his second term in 2014, most of them following the same pattern as five years earlier.[7] This was the price paid by women for Indonesia's 'big bang' approach to decentralisation (Chandrakirana 2010).

The situation has been particularly dire for women in Aceh, the only province in Indonesia where sharia law is officially enforced. In September 2009, the Aceh provincial government produced a local regulation — known locally by the Arabic term *qanun* — on the Islamic criminal code (Qanun Jinayat). It was particularly alarming for women's rights activists because it not only adopted public caning as a form of punishment for crimes against Islamic values but also introduced stoning for the 'crime' of adultery. Komnas Perempuan (2009) publicly expressed its objection to the *qanun* and asked the president to 'take political action by producing a Presidential Instruction for government officials in ministries and local governments to carry out a comprehensive review of discriminatory and unconstitutional local regulations, and initiate processes of repeal'. The

---

7 'Jumlah perda diskriminatif bagi perempuan bertambah' [Rise of local regulations that discriminate against women], *Antara News*, 3 March 2011.

president took no action, but the *qanun* did not come into force because it was not approved by the governor of Aceh. Five years later, in September 2014, the Aceh provincial parliament passed a new version of the Qanun Jinayat, this time granting virtual impunity for rapists. It allows a person accused of rape to secure an acquittal if they are prepared to make an oath to God swearing that they are innocent. Although the provisions on adultery and rape in both versions of the Qanun Jinayat have not yet been implemented, they are now on the books, with the second version having been approved by the Aceh governor.

Throughout his ten years as president, Susilo Bambang Yudhoyono never broke the trend of increasing discrimination against women in Indonesia. None of the discriminatory regulations mentioned above was ever repealed despite frequent and specific requests by women activists to the president and his ministers. This is particularly noteworthy in view of the fact that the Ministry of Home Affairs did revoke many *perda* over the years, but almost exclusively those dealing with local taxes, not with discriminatory policies against women (Butt 2010; see also Chapter 9 of this volume by Tomsa). In 2012, at the completion of a review of Indonesia's compliance with the Convention on the Elimination of All Forms of Discrimination against Women, a United Nations committee concluded that Indonesian women still faced many forms of discrimination, but that they were 'unaware of their rights under this Convention and thus lack the capacity to claim them' (United Nations 2012: 3). To better understand why President Yudhoyono did so little to enhance the status of women in Indonesia, it is now necessary to examine more closely his personal attitudes towards morality, religion and tradition.

YUDHOYONO'S POLITICS

Morality and religious politics

To the outside world, Susilo Bambang Yudhoyono liked to portray himself as a cosmopolitan reformist who represented a modern and open Muslim democracy. But as Robin Bush demonstrates in Chapter 13 of this volume, under Yudhoyono Indonesia actually became increasingly conservative and intolerant towards deviance. Although the president himself was rarely an active driver of this trend, it was clearly a reflection of his personality. Significantly, Yudhoyono's conservatism had negative consequences not only for religious minorities; women's rights also suffered a major setback due to the president's conservative mind-set. The founder of feminist publication *Jurnal Perempuan* [Women's Journal], Gadis Arivia, probably saw the writing on the wall as early as 2004 when she watched some of Yudhoyono's recently appointed government ministers evaluating their first 50 days in office. What captured her attention were not the 'success stories' of the individual ministries, but rather a statement by the coordinating minister for social welfare, Alwi Shihab, that shed light on the president's television-viewing habits. In an opinion piece published by Indonesian national daily *Kompas*, Arivia (2005) recalled the day of the unexpected announcement:

> The government of President Susilo Bambang Yudhoyono has completed its first 100 days. When on its 50th day in office the cabinet announced an evaluation of its work, the explicit results were not articulated, but all the ministers seemed satisfied and optimistic about finishing 59 more programs. When the media announcement about this 'success' was about to finish, Coordinating Minister for Social Welfare Alwi Shihab suddenly added that there was one more important program (the 60th?) that he had to convey, at the special request of the president: the issue of women's navels. 'The president has asked me to warn the television media community not to show women's navels. It is very disturbing', said Alwi Shihab.

This statement provided perhaps the earliest indication that Yudhoyono would seek to regulate religious and sexual morals much more tightly than had his predecessors. Indeed, shortly after taking office, Yudhoyono, together with some of his ministers and his parliamentary vehicle, PD, ensured that the drafting of the anti-pornography bill was included in the parliament's national legislative program for 2005–09. The parliamentary committee assigned to draft and negotiate with the executive government on this bill was to be headed by Balkan Kaplale, a PD legislator. Once passed, the Anti-pornography Law became the ultimate national policy regulating public morality, in particular as it applied to women and sexual minorities. The stated objectives of the law included 'upholding belief in God' and 'providing guidance and education on the public's morality and behaviour'.

Much has been written about the Anti-pornography Law since it was initially deliberated, in both the media and academic circles (Allen 2007, 2009; Pausacker 2008; Sherlock 2008). However, President Yudhoyono's personal role in supporting this and other morality-oriented and religiously based legislation is often overlooked. This is somewhat surprising considering that, despite his much-noted silences during times of public controversy over cases related to freedom of religion, Yudhoyono actually had no qualms about speaking out publicly to defend the Anti-pornography Law. In mid-2010, when a performing artist by the name of Ariel was put in prison for making and distributing a sexually explicit video, Yudhoyono chimed in, revealing once more his own personal morality:

> Five years ago, in 2005, I was ridiculed by some when I prohibited a singer from entering the palace grounds for not being appropriately dressed. I

warned that, without our collective concern, starting from clothing and other things, we can all end up here.[8]

Yudhoyono's moral politics found fertile ground in a national climate where religion was actively politicised in the struggle for power. Religious politics had two disturbing faces: the emergence of laws and policies seeking to enforce public religiosity and morality based on religious beliefs, and the rise of religiously motivated violence and persecution. As Hwang (2013: 91) points out, such religiously based legislation was the work not merely of the religious political parties, but also of secular-nationalist parties that had shifted their positions on controversial bills and moral issues. Hwang (2013) contends that secular-nationalist parties, including Yudhoyono's PD, opportunistically used Islamic identity and moral issues to win votes.

Cases of religiously motivated discrimination and violence against women committed or tacitly condoned by the state apparatus occurred with alarming frequency during Yudhoyono's decade in office. The Islamic Defenders Front (Front Pembela Islam, FPI), for example, repeatedly threatened and harassed women and gender activists, especially those involved in lesbian, gay, bisexual and transgender (LGBT) conferences and film festivals, or other public forums that the FPI deemed morally reprehensible, without suffering any consequences. Discriminatory *perda* also had immediate consequences for women. One case that caused a stir in the media was that of Lilis Lindawati, a pregnant woman detained by the Tangerang police in March 2006 as she waited for a bus after working a late shift at a restaurant. She fell into a severe depression following her detention on suspicion of prostitution, and died in 2008 (Indraswari 2014). Another widely publicised case was that of a teenager called Putri Erlina who committed suicide after being detained by the sharia police in Aceh. In a heartbreaking letter to her father written in September 2012, she says:

> Father, please forgive me. I have shamed you and everybody. But I swear that I have never sold my body to anyone. That night I just wanted to watch a keyboard performance at Langsa and then I sat up through the night with my friends (Kholifah 2014).

Skin-deep, gender-blind social reforms

Despite owing a large part of his mandate to women, Yudhoyono did not consciously build a political constituency among advocates of women's rights and gender equality. Although he held almost annual meetings

---

8 'SBY angkat bicara soal video mesum mirip Ariel Luna Tari' [SBY raises voice over Ariel Luna Tari look-alike video], *Manycome.com*, 18 June 2010.

with representatives of Komnas Perempuan, which had been acting as a presidential commission on women's rights since its inception in 1999, there were no established mechanisms to follow up on these exchanges of views. That Komnas Perempuan initiated the annual meetings during Yudhoyono's presidency showed the high hopes held by women's organisations for the advancement of women during his presidency. Without follow-up mechanisms, however, their recommendations usually fell on deaf ears and the decade of exchanges did not lead to any cumulative outcomes that addressed not just the symptoms of gender-based discrimination and inequality, but also their root causes.

One such example where Yudhoyono initially appeared determined to defend women's rights but ultimately failed to go beyond rhetoric concerns the widely discussed issue of migrant workers. As mentioned earlier, thousands of Indonesian women go overseas each year in search of work as nannies and maids. Those who are successful remit billions of dollars each year to their relatives back home, but many others end up in workplaces where they face horrendous working conditions, receive extremely low pay or no pay at all, and may be abused sexually and physically by their employers. Judging by the media coverage, Yudhoyono was extremely sympathetic to the plight of Indonesia's female migrant workers. He was reportedly brought to tears when listening to the testimony of women who had been abused in their overseas workplaces, which in most cases were private homes. He even made a call to Erwiana Sulistyaningsih, a migrant worker in Hong Kong who had suffered terrible violence at the hands of her employer, and wept during the phone conversation. When Sumiati, an abused migrant worker charged with murder in Saudi Arabia, was executed in 2010, Yudhoyono suggested that every migrant worker should be given a cell phone so that they could call family members or authorities if they needed help. When Ruyati binti Satubi, another migrant worker charged with murder in Saudi Arabia, was beheaded in 2011, Yudhoyono dedicated one of his songs to her.

In fact, in late 2013, as many as 256 migrant workers were reported to be facing the death penalty, mostly in Malaysia and Saudi Arabia.[9] Well aware of the problem, non-government organisations and humanitarian groups had long pressed the Indonesian government to take more systematic and serious action to ensure the legal protection of migrant workers. In 2011, Yudhoyono established a special interdepartmental taskforce to deal with this alarming problem (Presidential Decree 71/2011). However, the mandate of the taskforce was so narrow that it could make only case-by-case interventions, and was not able to address

---

9 'Migrant Care: 256 TKI terancam hukuman mati di luar negeri' [256 migrant workers facing death penalty abroad], *liputan6.com*, 28 December.

deep-rooted underlying issues such as the lack of vocational training and training in cross-cultural communication for migrant workers before they left Indonesia.

Significantly, many of the problems faced by migrant workers have a specific gender dimension in that it is mainly women who are exploited and abused in a system dominated by men. Thus far, however, the government has not put in place standard legal aid mechanisms to protect migrant workers worldwide.

Yudhoyono's policy on migrant workers could be termed reactive and piecemeal and even, in some cases, counterproductive. For example, to make it easier for migrant worker agents to obtain business licences, the government through Presidential Instruction 3/2006 removed the requirement for agents to provide pre-departure training (Azmy 2011: 74). The intention was to reduce the costs and thus increase the foreign exchange earnings of migrant workers, but in fact the policy only deepened the problem of inadequate preparation of overseas workers.

The Yudhoyono government adopted a similar approach of putting financial considerations before human rights protection in the formulation of an MOU between Indonesia and Malaysia on migrant workers, signed by the president in Bali in 2006.[10] The MOU gave Malaysian employers of migrant workers the right to keep the passports of their Indonesian employees, putting those who wished to escape an abusive workplace in an invidious position.[11] In 2009 Indonesia froze Malaysian recruitment after a series of cases of severe abuse of Indonesian workers came to light, and in 2011 the MOU was revised in an effort to strengthen legal protections for Indonesian migrant workers in Malaysia. In the same year, Indonesia imposed a moratorium on sending migrant workers to Saudi Arabia after the execution of Ruyati, the aforementioned migrant worker accused of murdering her employer. While Yudhoyono was quick to issue both of these moratoriums, he did not push for the protection of Indonesian migrant workers during his meetings with the heads of government of the respective countries.

In an interview with Ricarda Gerlach, Yunianti Chuzaifah, the director of Komnas Perempuan from 2010 to 2014, expressed women's frustration with Yudhoyono's failure to undertake structural reform to protect migrant workers abroad:

---

10 Memorandum of Understanding between the Government of the Republic of Indonesia and the Government of Malaysia on the Recruitment and Placement of Indonesian Domestic Workers, dated 13 May 2006.

11 Appendix A(xii) of the MOU, on the responsibilities of the employer, specifies that 'The Employer shall be responsible for the safe keeping of the Domestic Worker's passport and to surrender such passport to the Indonesian Mission in the event of abscondment or death of the Domestic Workers'.

Our main demand is that the government provides shelter and defines what an appropriate shelter is. Furthermore the government should improve its relationships with embassy staff and government members of the receiving countries who have a good gender perspective. The embassy's staff should help the migrant workers to handle administrative issues and support them. SBY did not react to this demand (quoted in Gerlach 2010: 258).

One program that was considered to totally miss the point was People's Business Credit (Kredit Usaha Rakyat, KUR), a credit scheme for migrant workers launched by the president on 15 December 2010. The president claimed that since 'many migrant workers fall heavily into debt and suffer in the end', he wished 'to free them from all of that through this KUR credit scheme'. But as Migrant Care (2013: 89) has pointed out, the president merely 'transferred the migrant workers from the hands of the money lenders to those of the banks', instead of taking measures to reduce red tape and ease the cost of the payments migrant workers must make to their agencies.

Programs such as this were a temporary and reactionary response that revealed the government's poor understanding of the complex problem of unskilled migrant workers. Like the moratoriums with their lack of follow-up action, they failed to deal with the structural conditions that compelled uneducated, unskilled rural women to seek opportunities to earn foreign cash—the sort of money they could never hope to earn in their marginalised rural areas. Yudhoyono was content to respond in a symbolic, emotional and personal manner to these problems; a systematic evaluation of the underlying structural problems faced by migrant workers was never on the cards. Indeed, during the decade of Yudhoyono's presidency, no significant leaps were achieved in the protection of Indonesian migrant workers, despite the president's personal passion for this matter.

CONCLUSION

The last decade has shown that Susilo Bambang Yudhoyono's charm and his personal appreciation of women were not sufficient to generate a gender-friendly social and political transformation in Indonesia. On the contrary, in many ways life deteriorated rather than improved for women in Indonesia during the Yudhoyono years. This was evident in three main areas: stagnant levels of women's representation in key political institutions; declining indicators in health, maternal mortality and education; and worsening legal protection against gender-based discrimination. Significantly, the underlying reasons for these trends can be linked directly to President Yudhoyono and his policies, which were shaped by religious conservatism and symbolic gestures rather than affirmative action and genuine concern for women's issues.

This chapter has argued that a much more comprehensive and systematic approach to the structural causes of gender inequality was required to properly address women's issues in Indonesia. Advancing the role of women in politics cannot be done without cleansing political culture more generally of nepotism and corruption, which Yudhoyono and his party did not manage to do. Most importantly, Indonesian women's wellbeing and security depend on state protection against religious intolerance and a firm and consistent adherence to the Constitution. Yudhoyono's own moral beliefs and his political style of responding to symptoms rather than causes were clearly counterproductive in this regard, leaving women vulnerable to discrimination. This could be seen, for example, in the proliferation of discriminatory local regulations across the country and the Yudhoyono government's disinterest in repealing them. All in all, Yudhoyono's personalised approach and his piecemeal, trial-and-error interventions to serious problems, such as the difficulties faced by migrant women workers, showed the lack of a strategic and systematic plan to get to the root of Indonesia's major gender problems. In fact, even though he appointed four women to his cabinet and made personal promises to improve women's conditions, it is questionable whether Yudhoyono ever really took this matter seriously. A look at his hefty book, *Selalu Ada Pilihan* [There Is Always a Choice], which was published towards the end of his presidency, reveals that women's issues are mentioned on only two pages, and even then only in the context of a minor controversy over a Miss World contest (Yudhoyono 2014: 285–6). It is therefore not surprising that the data on the state of affairs for women in 2014 show some serious backsliding at the end of the Yudhoyono decade.

The letter by Linda Djalil quoted at the beginning of this chapter expresses the deep disappointment felt by many women about Yudhoyono's leadership. For Djalil, as for many other women, the Yudhoyono years were detrimental not only to gender equality and women's causes, but also to social cohesion more generally: 'I wish to experience religious tolerance in this country and firmness of leadership, admonishing quarrelling agitators who abuse people's beliefs here and there'. The letter also alludes to four weaknesses of Yudhoyono's that arguably had the most significant effect on the status of women: his ambivalence and indecision; his weak leadership in coordinating his subordinates; his habit of complaint and self-pity; and his inability to prioritise (Djalil 2014).

As the Yudhoyono decade ended in October 2014, women's hopes and expectations shifted to the newly elected president, Joko Widodo (Jokowi). Like Yudhoyono in 2004, Jokowi stood for reform and a new type of politics. His motto, 'Mental Revolution', captured a wish to break with the past. But the discussion in this chapter has pointed to the complex and challenging terrain of democratisation in Indonesia, and Jokowi lacks the overwhelming electoral mandate and political support of major parties enjoyed by Yudhoyono. This will make it very difficult indeed for him to tackle the many challenges that lie ahead.

Balancing economic growth with efforts to reduce inequality, including gender-based inequality, is perhaps the most important challenge for the new government. Another delicate matter is to tame morality and religious politics by adhering firmly to the Constitution and the rule of law, despite pressure from various societal and political groups seeking to impose a conservative moral agenda on all Indonesians. The new president will need to be more committed than his predecessor to values such as social cohesion and pluralism if he is to ensure women's lasting security and wellbeing.

REFERENCES

Allen, P. (2007) 'Challenging diversity? Indonesia's anti-pornography bill', *Asian Studies Review*, 31(2): 101–15.

Allen, P. (2009) 'Women, gendered activism and Indonesia's anti-pornography bill', *Intersections: Gender and Sexuality in Asia and the Pacific*, 19(February). Available at http://intersections.anu.edu.au/issue19/allen.htm

Arivia, G. (2005) 'SBY dan pusar perempuan' [SBY and women's navels], *Kompas*, 28 January. Available at http://permalink.gmane.org/gmane.culture.region.indonesia.ppi-india/808

Azmy, A.S. (2011) 'Negara dan buruh migran perempuan; kebijakan perlindungan buruh migran perempuan Indonesia pada masa pemerintahan Susilo Bambang Yudhoyono (2004–2010)' [The state and female migrant workers: policies to protect Indonesian female migrant workers during Susilo Bambang Yudhoyono's term (2004–2010)], MSc thesis, Faculty of Social and Political Science, University of Indonesia, Jakarta.

Bessell, S. (2010) 'Increasing the proportion of women in the national parliament: opportunities, barriers and challenges', in E. Aspinall and M. Mietzner (eds) *Problems of Democratisation in Indonesia: Elections, Institutions and Society*, Institute of Southeast Asian Studies, Singapore: 219–42.

BTI (Bertelsmann Stiftung Transformation Index) (2014) 'BTI 2014: Indonesia country report', Gütersloh. Available at http://www.bti-project.org/reports/country-reports/aso/idn/index.nc

Butt, S. (2010) 'Regional autonomy and legal disorder: the proliferation of local laws in Indonesia', *Sydney Law Review*, 32(2): 177–91. Available at http://sydney.edu.au/law/slr/slr_32/slr32_2/Butt.pdf

Candraningrum, D. (2014) 'Agama, pemilu 2014 dan status perempuan sebagai liyan' [Religion, the 2014 general elections and women's status as the other], *Jurnal Perempuan*, 19(3): 112–28.

Chandrakirana, K. (2010) 'Decentralization and discrimination in Indonesia: local democracy and the challenge of equal citizenship in a multicultural society',

unpublished paper, National Commission on Violence against Women (Komnas Perempuan), Jakarta.
Djalil, L. (2013) 'Mohon maaf, Pak Presiden ...' [Excuse me, Mr President ...]. Available at http://lindadjalil.com/2013/11/mohon-maaf-pak-presiden/
Farbenblum, B., E. Taylor-Nicholson and S. Paoletti (2013) *Migrant Workers' Access to Justice at Home: Indonesia*, Migrant Workers' Access to Justice Series, Open Society Foundations, New York.
Gerlach, R. (2010) 'Gender politics in Indonesia — recent developments: an interview with Yunianti Chuzaifah', *Austrian Journal of South-east Asian Studies*, 3(2): 254–64.
Honna, J. (2012) 'Inside the Democrat Party: power, politics and conflict in Indonesia's presidential party', *South East Asia Research*, 20(4): 473–89.
Hwang, J.C. (2013) 'Islamic identity yes, Islamic party, no', in M.H. Williams (ed.) *The Multicultural Dilemma: Migration, Ethnic Politics and State Intermediation*, Routledge, Oxon: 84–99.
Indonesia Beragam (2014) 'Deklarasi 10 agenda politik perempuan' [10-point political agenda for women], 11 July. Available at http://indonesia-beragam.blogspot.com/2014/07/deklarasi-10-agenda-politik-perempuan.html
Indraswari (2014) 'Prasangka budaya atas tubuh dalam perda-perda diskriminatif: politisasi agama atas perempuan' [Cultural prejudice towards the [female] body in discriminatory local regulations: the politicisation of religion against women], *Jurnal Perempuan*, 19(3): 88–99.
Kholifah, R. (2014) 'Draft kerta[s] posisi: penghapusan aturan hukum yang diskriminatif terhadap perempuan' [Draft position paper: the elimination of laws that discriminate against women], Asian Muslim Action Network (AMAN) Indonesia, 26 March. Available at http://womenandminority.blogspot.com/2014/03/draft-kerta-posisi1-penghapusan-aturan.html
Komnas Perempuan (Komisi Nasional Anti Kekerasan Terhadap Perempuan) (2009) 'Press release from the National Commission on Anti-Violence against Women Indonesia (Komnas Perempuan)', Jakarta, 15 September. Available at http://www.violenceisnotourculture.org/content/press-release-national-commission-anti-violence-against-women-indonesia-komnas-perempuan
Komnas Perempuan (Komisi Nasional Anti Kekerasan Terhadap Perempuan) (2010) 'In the name of regional autonomy: the institutionalization of discrimination in Indonesia. A monitoring report by the National Commission on Violence against Women on the status of women's constitutional rights in 16 districts/municipalities in 7 provinces', Jakarta. Available at www.komnasperempuan.or.id/en/wp-content/uploads/2011/11/otoda.pdf
Komnas Perempuan (Komisi Nasional Anti Kekerasan Terhadap Perempuan) (2011) 'National Human Rights Institution independent report regarding the implementation of the Convention on the Elimination of All Forms of Discrimination against Women in Indonesia, 2007–2011', Jakarta.
Komnas Perempuan (Komisi Nasional Anti Kekerasan Terhadap Perempuan) (2013) 'National Human Rights Institution independent report on the review of Indonesian report on the implementation of the International Covenant on Civil and Political Rights in Indonesia, 2005–2012', Jakarta.
Komnas Perempuan (Komisi Nasional Anti Kekerasan Terhadap Perempuan) (2014) 'National Human Rights Institution independent report on the review of Indonesian report on the implementation of the International Covenant on Economic, Social and Cultural Rights in Indonesia', Jakarta.

Kumoro, B. (2014) 'Keterwakilan politik perempuan' [Political representation of women], *Esquire Indonesia*, 19 March. Available at http://www.esquire.co.id/article/2014/3/368-Keterwakilan-Politik-Perempuan

Manangka, D. (2013) 'Pesona SBY di mata wanita meredub' [SBY's charm dims in women's eyes], *Inilah.com*, 18 November. Available at http://nasional.inilah.com/read/detail/2048064/pesona-sby-di-mata-wanita-indonesia-meredup#.VAEBd5VO4cA

Maeswera, G. (2009) *Biografi Politik Susilo Bambang Yudhoyono* [Political Biography of Susilo Bambang Yudhoyono], Penerbit Narasi, Jakarta.

Migrant Care (2013) *Selusur Kebijakan (Minus) Perlindungan Buruh Migran Indonesia* [Survey of policy for (not) protecting Indonesian migrant workers], Jakarta.

Pausacker, H. (2008) 'Hot debates', *Inside Indonesia*, 94(October–December). Available at http://www.insideindonesia.org/weekly-articles/hot-debates

Satriyo, H. (2014) 'The 30%', *New Mandala*, 28 April.

Sherlock, S. (2008) 'Indonesia's anti-pornography bill: a case study of decision-making in the Indonesian parliament', Hintergrundpapier No. 10/2008, Friedrich-Naumann-Stiftung für die Freiheit, Bangkok.

Siregar, W.Z. (2005) 'Parliamentary representation of women in Indonesia: the struggle for a quota', *Asian Journal of Women's Studies*, 11(3): 36–72.

United Nations (2012) 'Concluding observations of the Committee on the Elimination of Discrimination against Women: Indonesia', CEDAW/C/IDN/CO/6-7, New York, 27 July.

Utomo, I.D. et al. (2007) 'Gender depiction in Indonesian school text books: progress or deterioration', paper presented to the 26th IUSSP International Population Conference, Marrakech, 27 September – 2 October.

WEF (World Economic Forum) (2011) 'Global gender gap report 2011', Geneva. Available at http://reports.weforum.org/global-gender-gap-2011/#section=country-profiles-indonesia

WEF (World Economic Forum) (2014) 'Global gender gap report 2014', Geneva. Available at reports.weforum.org/global-gender-gap-report-2014/economies/#economy=IDN

World Bank (2014) 'Indonesia economic quarterly, July 2014: hard choices', Washington DC, July. Available at http://www.worldbank.org/en/news/feature/2014/07/21/indonesia-economic-quarterly-july-2014

Yudhoyono, S.B. (2009) 'Pidato Presiden RI Soesilo Bambang Yudhoyono' [Speech by the President of the Republic of Indonesia, Susilo Bambang Yudhoyono], speech commemorating the 10th anniversary of the National Commission on Violence against Women (Komnas Perempuan), 30 November.

Yudhoyono, S.B. (2014) *Selalu Ada Pilihan* [There Is Always a Choice], Kompas Gramedia, Jakarta.

12 Human rights and Yudhoyono's test of history

Dominic Berger

When Susilo Bambang Yudhoyono became Indonesia's first directly elected president in 2004, human rights were already a central element of the Indonesian state's political profile. After the fall of Suharto's authoritarian New Order regime, the People's Consultative Assembly (Majelis Permusyarawatan Rakyat, MPR) had enshrined the key tenets of human rights into Indonesia's Constitution through a series of amendments between 1999 and 2002 (Butt and Lindsey 2012: 22). In 1999, the People's Representative Council (Dewan Perwakilan Rakyat, DPR) had also passed Law 39/1999 on Human Rights, which continues to function as the key piece of legislation for the protection of human rights. Indonesia had also acceded to a number of important international human rights treaties, including the Convention against Torture and Cruel, Inhumane or Degrading Treatments or Punishments in 1998, and the Convention on the Elimination of All Forms of Racial Discrimination in 1999. Thus, with the basic framework for the protection of human rights largely in place at the time of Yudhoyono's inauguration, domestic and international observers expected the new president not only to consolidate these reforms, but also to push for the further deepening of human rights protections.

Opinion is divided on whether Yudhoyono fulfilled these expectations during his decade in power. In recent years, starkly differing assessments have emerged over whether human rights in Indonesia improved, stagnated or even worsened during his time in office. Some assessments, particularly those of foreign diplomats and media commentators, portrayed Yudhoyono's Indonesia as an increasingly open and plural society where human rights were largely protected.[1] Others, especially those of local human rights activists, frequently suggested that the protection of civil and political rights stagnated, and in some areas even declined, during the president's ten-year reign.[2] In light of such a lack of consensus on Yudhoyono's achievements and failures, this chapter aims to critically assess his legacy in the field of human rights, with a particular focus on his personal role and influence in this field.

A number of previous studies have attempted to locate the key factors driving human rights reform in post-New Order Indonesia. Hadiprayitno (2010: 397), for example, examined the international dimension of Indonesia's increasing adoption of human rights frameworks, concluding pessimistically that 'Indonesia's primary motivation throughout accepting international commitments has been merely to pre-empt international action'. Fitzpatrick (2008) examined how local culture and ideology have often undermined the application of universal human rights regimes in Indonesia, while others, such as Herbert (2008), have focused on the country's legal human rights framework. Rosser (2013), meanwhile, proposed that the underlying cause of Indonesia's continuing problem with human rights was the broader political economy. Drawing on the work of Robison and Hadiz (2004), he suggested that a 'powerful politico-business oligarchy' was to blame for most human rights abuses.

While not dismissing the legal, cultural and structural factors identified by these authors, this chapter argues that the role of the president is an underappreciated factor in explaining the quality and extent of human rights in Indonesia. I begin with a brief profile of Yudhoyono's personal views on human rights, contending that his lack of a principled belief in human rights, and his hesitant approach to politics, helps to explain his failure to use his presidential powers to resolve a number of key human rights issues. The discussion proceeds by mapping some of the highly divergent assessments by local and international human rights organisations of Indonesia's human rights record under Yudhoyono, which in large part reflect the weight placed on the role of the presidency. In the second half of the chapter, I examine the Yudhoyono government's approach to four critical cases in the field of human rights: truth and reconciliation efforts to deal with past human rights abuses, including the 1965 mass killings of suspected communists; the legal proceedings concerning the murder of human rights activist Munir Said Thalib; the political prisoners in Papua and Maluku; and freedom of expression

---

1 See, for example, President Obama's remarks to an audience at the University of Indonesia in Jakarta in 2010 (Obama 2010).
2 See, for example, the 2013 assessment by Indonesian human rights organisation Elsam (2013).

on the internet. These four case studies reveal that the actions taken by the president were of major consequence in the perseverance of human rights violations and the failure to resolve past abuses. In particular, they reveal that, at crucial moments, Yudhoyono consistently failed to exert his presidential authority to protect human rights. In short, the chapter shows that while other factors, such as the legal framework, culture or broader structural factors, have certainly contributed to Indonesia's continuing problem with human rights, Yudhoyono's personal motivations, views and actions (or lack of action) were also crucial factors in shaping the country's human rights record between 2004 and 2014.

YUDHOYONO: A HUMAN RIGHTS DEFENDER?

Dubbed 'the thinking general', Yudhoyono emerged from the New Order with no specific allegations of severe human rights violations levelled against him. Indeed, he was known as a leading figure in the reformist camp of Indonesia's armed forces (Honna 2003). Shortly after long-time strongman Suharto resigned in 1998, Yudhoyono successfully transformed himself from a career soldier into a budding politician. But while he stood out as a softliner during the dying days of the authoritarian New Order, in the context of the new democratic polity, his views on democracy and human rights were ambivalent, if not conservative. In fact, Yudhoyono frequently voiced his rejection of absolutist interpretations of human rights, stating at a seminar in 2004, months before his election, that 'democracy, human rights, concern for the environment and other concepts being promoted by Western countries are all good, but they cannot become absolute goals because pursuing them as such will not be good for the country'.[3] Hence, Yudhoyono adhered to a relativist interpretation of human rights, in which rights needed to be observed and defended only when not in conflict with other, supposedly superior, values. As president, then, Yudhoyono regarded human rights merely as one of many considerations to be taken into account in decision-making, leaving him prone to sacrifice human rights principles for other, more important interests.

One such interest was his family's reputation and socio-economic status. In this regard, Yudhoyono's marriage to Kristiani ('Ani') Herrawati had particularly debilitating ramifications for his willingness to address human rights issues related to the anti-communist killings of 1965 and to the political grievances of Papuans. In 1965, as commander of the Army

---

[3] 'Democracy, human rights must not become absolute goals: minister', *Antara*, 10 January 2004.

Para-commando Regiment, Ani's father, Sarwo Edhie Wibowo, had been instrumental in leading the purge of the Indonesian Communist Party (Partai Komunis Indonesia, PKI) and its supporters, personally mobilising civilian militias to execute thousands of suspected sympathisers of the party in Java and Bali (Jenkins and Kammen 2012). Indeed, Sarwo Edhie was a staunch backer of the New Order during its infancy, sponsoring the anti-communist student groups that hastened Sukarno's ouster by Suharto, and supporting greater restrictions on the party system. As regional commander in then West Irian, he repressed opposition to the so-called Act of Free Choice in 1969, which formalised Papua's integration into Indonesia. This stage-managed ballot, which Sarwo Edhie oversaw, remains at the heart of Papuan political grievances today. Clearly, Yudhoyono's intimate family connections to one of the main perpetrators of the killings of 1965 and the mastermind of Papua's political incorporation into Indonesia had a significant impact on his views on these two issues, and his preparedness to work towards their resolution. As Greg Fealy points out in Chapter 3 of this volume, Sarwo Edhie remained a saint-like figure for Yudhoyono throughout his presidency, inhibiting his willingness to make significant moves on 1965 or Papua's historical baggage.

International perceptions: excessive praise

Assessments of Yudhoyono's human rights record as president have often been either excessively glowing or overly damning. Visiting leaders of Western democracies and mainstream media commentaries, for instance, have generally cast Yudhoyono's Indonesia as a 'model' of tolerance and moderation (Wilson 2010). On a visit to Indonesia in 2009, US Secretary of State Hillary Clinton proclaimed that 'if you want to know if Islam, democracy, modernity and women's rights can coexist, go to Indonesia'.[4] In 2012, British Prime Minister David Cameron, speaking at Al-Azar University in Jakarta, declared that 'where once the government denied human rights to its people, today it promotes them, not just here, but right around your region' (Cameron 2012). In light of such praise, few other leaders in the region appeared as confident as Yudhoyono when addressing human rights issues in international forums. He was the first Indonesian president to actively leverage an apparent commitment to human rights in Indonesia's international diplomacy. Early on in his first term he began to promote human rights within ASEAN, and in 2008 he established the Bali Democracy Forum, an annual forum for the promotion of democratic values (Sukma 2011).

---

4 'Clinton praises Indonesian democracy', *New York Times*, 18 February 2009.

Undeniably, such efforts elevated Indonesia's diplomatic standing. In 2012, UN High Commissioner for Human Rights Navanethem Pillay stated that 'through its constructive role in the regional human rights mechanisms of the Association of Southeast Asian Nations (ASEAN) and at the Human Rights Council, Indonesia has made an important contribution to the advancement of human rights'.[5] Similarly, when US President Obama visited Indonesia in 2011, he praised 'Indonesia's leadership of the Bali Democracy Forum' and its 'commitment to making democracy and human rights platforms for ASEAN's development' (Obama 2011). In praising him, Western leaders and commentators often credited Yudhoyono for Indonesia's apparent embrace of the universality of human rights.

Of course, foreign leaders and commentators viewed Indonesia's progress on human rights in the context of a Southeast Asian region plagued by democratic stagnation and regression, or as an exception to the authoritarian and theocratic regimes dominating the Muslim world. Using such comparative perspectives, positive assessments of Yudhoyono's human rights record are methodologically and substantively plausible. Indeed, during the early years of his presidency, comparative democracy indexers published increasingly positive evaluations of Indonesia's protection of civil and political rights. For example, Freedom House rated Indonesia as 'free' for the first time in 2006, making it the only 'free' country in Southeast Asia in terms of its protection of civil and political rights (Figure 12.1). (Thailand experienced a coup in that year and the Philippines witnessed democratic backsliding under Gloria Macapagal-Arroyo.) Against this background, the increasing visibility of human rights in Indonesia's foreign policy cemented the country's image as a rights-respecting democracy, and allowed Yudhoyono to claim much of the credit for this achievement.[6]

One reason for the disproportionate credit allocated to Yudhoyono was the widespread misperception of the omnipotent role of the Indonesian presidency. While external observers found it easiest to single Yudhoyono out for praise based on Indonesia's overall improvement in rights indexes, the presidency was not the only institution responsible for the protection of human rights. For example, Indonesia's ratification of the International Covenant on Civil and Political Rights in 2005 enjoyed broad support in the Indonesian parliament and government,

---

5 'Indonesia increasingly contributing to human rights cause: UN', *Antara*, 13 November 2013.
6 In 2014, Freedom House recorded an eighth year of decline in global measures of civil and political rights (Freedom House 2014). On the broader decline of democracy in Southeast Asia in particular, see Kurlantzick (2014).

Figure 12.1 Freedom House: civil and political rights in Indonesia, 1998–2014

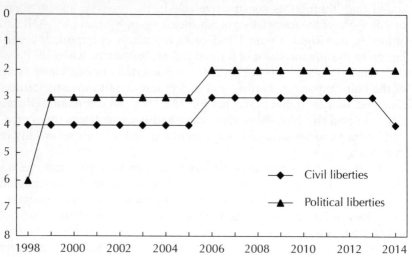

Source: Freedom House.

and had been in the proposal stage long before Yudhoyono became president (DPR 2005). Shortly after the covenant was ratified, in 2006, the Constitutional Court ruled that articles in the criminal code pertaining to insulting the president (articles 134, 136 and 137) were unconstitutional.[7] In 2007, the court ruled that articles 154 and 155 on 'sowing hate' were unconstitutional as well.[8] While greatly expanding human rights during the Yudhoyono years, these reforms could not be credited to the president himself. In fact, until the articles were ruled unconstitutional, Yudhoyono and his government had frequently used them to stifle peaceful criticism (Human Rights Watch 2010a).

Towards the end of Yudhoyono's second term, the dominant international narrative of Indonesia's democratic success began to be challenged somewhat. In 2012, for example the *New York Times* published an opinion piece by a Human Rights Watch researcher proclaiming that Indonesia was 'no model for Muslim democracy' (Harsono 2012). Similarly, John Sidel reacted to Prime Minister Cameron's Jakarta speech in the *Guardian*, cautioning that 'Indonesian democracy deserves closer scrutiny' (Sidel 2012). Despite such challenges, Yudhoyono left office with his global image of a rights-respecting president largely intact. The

---

7 Constitutional Court Decision 013-022/PUU-IV/2006.
8 Constitutional Court Decision 6/PUU-V/2007.

domestic commentary on his human rights policies, however, was vastly different.

Domestic commentary: excessive criticism

In contrast to the largely positive appraisals by international leaders and democracy indexers, domestic human rights defenders were highly critical of Yudhoyono's record. While international observers often credited the president personally for the positive aspects of Indonesia's human rights regime, domestic observers blamed him for its failures. Although Yudhoyono's domestic critics were far more aware of the multiple institutions affecting human rights, they nevertheless directed by far the greatest share of criticism at him. A 2013 survey by the Setara Institute of 200 Indonesian human rights activists found that over half (56 per cent) felt that the protection of human rights had remained 'stagnant' since 2004, while a further 36 per cent believed it had 'regressed' (Setara Institute 2013).[9] Only 3 per cent of respondents were convinced that the protection of human rights had improved during Yudhoyono's presidency. Activists overwhelmingly blamed Yudhoyono personally, rather than other institutions, for these developments. More than half (53 per cent) said that 'the commitment of the president' was the biggest challenge for the improvement of human rights, rather than cultural or legal factors (Figure 12.2).[10] In other words, most believed that the leadership of the president, or the lack of it, was the most important factor in upholding human rights. On Yudhoyono, the judgment was clear: only 5 per cent of the activists believed that he held a 'high commitment' to the protection of human rights, while more than half (52 per cent) found that he held a 'low commitment' and a further 38 per cent thought he had 'no commitment' (Figure 12.3).

As we will see below, there is indeed much evidence to suggest that Yudhoyono's leadership, or its absence, was responsible for some of the shortcomings in Indonesia's human rights record between 2004 and 2014. But just as international observers frequently overlooked the contributions of other institutions to the protection of human rights, Yudhoyono's

---

9 The respondents were drawn from 20 provinces, although a disproportionate number came from DKI Jakarta (17.5 per cent), West Java (12.3 per cent) and Banten (8.8 per cent). About 66 per cent of respondents were NGO activists, 20 per cent were academics, and the remainder consisted of journalists, researchers and civil society leaders.
10 Only 17 per cent of respondents cited 'lack of care amongst society [for human rights]' as the biggest problem, while 14 per cent believed that an 'unsuitable legal framework' was the biggest obstacle to deeper human rights protections.

Figure 12.2 Survey of human rights activists: what is the biggest challenge to the advancement and protection of human rights?

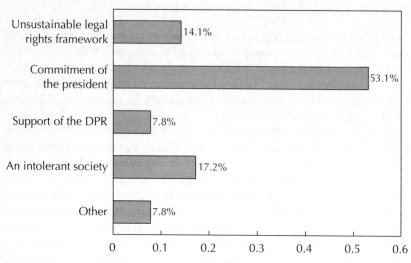

Source: Setara Institute (2013).

Figure 12.3 Survey of human rights activists: how do you rate Yudhoyono's commitment to human rights?

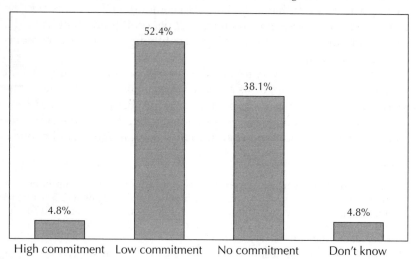

Source: Setara Institute (2013).

critics tended to downplay the role of other institutions and elites that pursued illiberal or anti-human rights agendas under his rule (Mietzner 2012). For example, at the national level, the DPR passed Law 44/2008 on Pornography in 2008 and Law 17/2013 on Societal Organisations in 2013. Local activists criticised these bills for reducing the freedom of expression and the freedom of association respectively, and they unsuccessfully lobbied law-makers to refuse to pass them into law. At the regional level as well, local executives and legislatures issued hundreds of regulations that contravened national and international human rights standards.[11] Many of these local by-laws (which regulated, among other things, obligatory dress codes for women or the right of religious minorities to exercise their faith) were the result of governors, district heads, mayors and local assemblies pandering to conservative societal interests. But despite these significant attacks on human rights at both the national and local levels by forces that enjoyed substantial institutional autonomy from the presidency, the local activists surveyed by the Setara Institute appear to have rated their impact on the overall quality of human rights as less significant than the (lack of) action taken by Yudhoyono (Figure 12.2).

This section has presented two contrasting narratives of Yudhoyono's human rights record. One narrative, frequently propagated by international leaders, observers and commentators, holds that Indonesia increasingly embraced human rights, both domestically and in its foreign policy, in large part as a consequence of Yudhoyono's leadership. The opposing narrative, almost unanimously advanced by local human rights activists, identifies Yudhoyono's failure to provide leadership as the primary reason for a supposed deterioration of human rights in Indonesia between 2004 and 2014. To further test the claims of these two narratives, the following section will examine the Yudhoyono government's approach to four crucial human rights issues.

FOUR CASE STUDIES

Case study 1: justice for past crimes

Before Yudhoyono's election in 2004, two major attempts were made to establish mechanisms to address the serious human rights abuses that had occurred during the New Order. First, Law 26/2000 on Human Rights Courts allowed the DPR to recommend the establishment of an ad

---

11 The United Nations (2012) found that by 2012 there were over 1,000 laws and regulations that violated national or international human rights standards, many of them pertaining to the rights of women and religious minorities.

hoc human rights court pertaining to a particular case of serious human rights violations, following which a court could be established through a presidential decree (Keputusan Presiden). In 2009, Yudhoyono refused to follow up on a recommendation by the DPR to set up such a court to investigate and prosecute the kidnappings and disappearances of student activists in 1997 and 1998 — a failure for which he was sharply criticised by the ombudsman (Dewi 2012). Second, in 2004 the DPR passed the Law on a Truth and Reconciliation Commission, which mandated the establishment of a commission to hear complaints of grave human rights violations. For nearly two years the process stalled as Yudhoyono failed to appoint commissioners. Without ever having been implemented, the law was declared invalid by the Constitutional Court in 2006, due to a clause that made reparations for victims conditional on amnesty for perpetrators.[12] Human rights groups, many of whom held hopes that an improved law would be passed, initially welcomed the decision. But hopes for a better law proved misplaced. In the eight years between the court's abolition of the law and the end of his term, Yudhoyono did not produce a replacement law. This failure did not come as a surprise to the chief justice of the Constitutional Court at the time of the verdict, Jimly Asshidiqie. Reflecting in 2009 on why the court had invalidated the law, Jimly stated that Yudhoyono's notorious hesitancy had played a major role. Clearly frustrated, he said that in light of 'the reality that the administration [had] not even set up the commission, we thought we should just scrap the whole law' (Hotland 2009).

With local avenues to justice for past abuses mostly unavailable, many victims and activists put their hope in Indonesia's possible accession to the International Criminal Court (ICC) through the ratification of the Rome Statute. This statute grants the ICC jurisdiction to prosecute crimes against humanity in instances where national institutions fail to do so. Indonesia included ratification of the statute in its 2011–14 National Plan of Action on Human Rights, a UN mechanism that aims to encourage member countries to develop a national roadmap to improve the protection of human rights. In 2011, Yudhoyono issued a presidential regulation that made it obligatory for the government to follow the plan, which in turn recommended ratification of the Rome Statute in 2013.[13] Yudhoyono subsequently reaffirmed Indonesia's commitment to accede to the statute in a letter to the ICC in 2012 (Sundari 2013). In early 2013 ratification appeared imminent when an official government delegation, led by deputy justice minister and Yudhoyono favourite Denny Indrayana, vis-

---

12 Constitutional Court Decision 006/PUU-IV/2006.
13 Presidential Regulation 23/2011 on the National Plan of Action on Human Rights for 2011–2014.

ited the ICC in The Hague with the apparent aim of clarifying whether the court possessed the power to investigate crimes committed before its establishment in July 2002. This was despite article 24(1) of the statute clearly stating that 'no person shall be criminally responsible under this Statute for conduct prior to the entry into force of the Statute'.[14]

The Yudhoyono government's publicly and repeatedly declared intent to ratify the Rome Statute notwithstanding, Defence Minister Purnomo Yusgiantoro announced in May 2013 — reportedly in response to lobbying from former generals and presidential hopefuls Prabowo Subianto and Wiranto — that more time was needed to study the consequences of ratification (Aritonang 2013a, 2013b). Evidently, then, widespread anxiety among conservative elites, many of whom had a personal interest in avoiding investigations into the past, was a powerful factor in eroding Indonesia's commitment to the Rome Statute. Yudhoyono, whose own family history tied him closely to the interests of these elites, still had not processed the ratification by the time he left office in October 2014. Thus, the president again prioritised key political interests (in this case, maintaining the allegiance of conservative political forces) over a principled commitment to upholding human rights. Importantly, this pattern also became visible in Yudhoyono's approach to public demands for a new government response to the killings of suspected communists during the political turmoil of 1965.

The killing of up to 1 million suspected members and sympathisers of the PKI in 1965, and the decades-long stigmatisation of the survivors and their family members, remains Indonesia's most intractable historical injustice. The old age of the surviving victims and perpetrators meant that Yudhoyono's presidency was perhaps the last window of opportunity for justice. In 2012, a number of events converged to generate public pressure on the Yudhoyono government to take substantive action for the sake of reconciliation. The most important development was the publication of an in-depth report by Indonesia's National Commission for Human Rights (Komisi Nasional Hak Asasi Manusia, Komnas HAM). The product of hundreds of interviews over three years, the report concluded that the persecution of the PKI, and the mass killings of its sympathisers, constituted a 'gross human rights violation' (Aritonang 2012a).

As the report was nearing completion in 2011, three Komnas HAM commissioners met Yudhoyono to brief him on its content. At the meeting, held on 13 May, the commissioners offered recommendations on how the president might respond to the report's findings. One was for

---

14 'Denny to leave for The Hague for study on Rome Statute', *Jakarta Post*, 4 March 2013.

Yudhoyono to issue a presidential apology that focused on acknowledging the state's role in the mass killings. The commissioners reminded the president that with only three years left in office, failure to respond appropriately to the report could become a stain on his legacy. According to one commissioner, Yudhoyono reacted with visible indignation, asking the commissioners: 'Why should I be the one to do something? I'm not one of the perpetrators!'[15] Despite Yudhoyono's apparent failure to grasp the symbolic power and responsibilities of the office of the president, the commissioners nevertheless convinced him to order a series of meetings between Komnas HAM, Attorney General Basrief Arief and Coordinating Minister for Political, Legal and Security Affairs Djoko Suyanto. While several meetings took place, as soon as Yudhoyono was no longer directly involved, officials from the attorney general's office became uncooperative, which effectively stalled the process.

In 2012, after Komnas HAM had compiled several reports on alleged serious human rights violations, the UN Committee against Torture expressed concern at the inability of Komnas HAM to force the attorney general to prosecute cases (United Nations 2012). Clearly, Yudhoyono's action or inaction in this regard was crucial. Almost apologetically, the attorney general pointed out that to follow up on the Komnas HAM report into the events of 1965, an ad hoc human rights court would be needed, which could only be established by the DPR and a presidential decree.[16] The failure of Yudhoyono to personally take responsibility for the process — instead effectively outsourcing it to his ministers — was at best a failure by omission, and at worst a dereliction of responsibility. Soon after the proposal for a presidential apology became public, groups of retired military officers and representatives of Islamic groups met with the president to voice their strong opposition to the idea.[17] Arguably, Yudhoyono's personal relationship with one of the main human rights offenders of 1965 and his inclination to appease powerful lobby groups led him, once more, to sacrifice progress on reconciliation. In late 2012, Djoko Suyanto, Yudhoyono's most senior minister, openly rejected the core finding of the Komnas HAM reports, suggesting that the killings were justified (Aritonang 2012b). Hopes for an apology quickly evaporated.

---

15 Interview with former Komnas HAM commissioner, Jakarta, 7 August 2014.
16 'Dibutuhkan pengadilan HAM "ad hoc"' ['Ad hoc' human rights court needed], *Kompas*, 25 July 2012.
17 Interview with Albert Hasibuan, head of Legal and Human Rights Affairs, Presidential Advisory Council (Dewan Pertimbangan Presiden, Wantimpres), Jakarta, 12 August 2014.

Case study 2: justice for Munir's murder

While violence towards human rights activists was not uncommon in the years immediately following the fall of Suharto, the murder of Munir Said Thalib on 7 September 2004 (around one month before Yudhoyono's inauguration) triggered unprecedented outrage. The implications for domestic and international perceptions of Indonesian human rights were enormous. Within weeks, there was a widespread belief that the murder had been planned and coordinated at the highest echelons of the State Intelligence Agency (Badan Intelijen Negara, BIN). Munir's prominence in Indonesia's human rights community, and the brazen circumstances of his murder — he had been poisoned on a flight to Amsterdam — suggested that the security apparatus continued to enjoy a shocking degree of impunity.

Soon after the murder, the parliament ordered the government to form an independent fact-finding team, Tim Pencari Fakta (TPF). On 24 November, Munir's widow, Suciwati, and other activists met Yudohyono at the presidential palace. During this encounter, the president famously stated that bringing the perpetrators to justice would be 'the test of Indonesia's history' (Harsono 2009). But by the end of Yudhoyono's presidency, Suciwati and other activists were deeply disillusioned with the outcome of numerous investigations and legal proceedings. Suciwati believed that beyond establishing the fact-finding team — the findings of which were, contrary to the president's own decree, never published — Yudhoyono had done little to bring Munir's assassins to justice.[18] While the murder had taken place before he took office, it was Yudhoyono's self-professed responsibility to prove that, under his presidency, the assassination of a human rights activist by a state institution would not go unpunished.

While an off-duty Garuda Indonesia pilot and suspected BIN agent travelling on Munir's flight, Pollycarpus Budihari Priyanto, was put on trial in 2005 and eventually convicted of Munir's murder, this failed to bring closure to the case. Instead, the trial revealed evidence highlighting BIN's deep involvement in the planning and execution of the murder. In a letter written in 2005, 68 members of the US Congress urged Yudhoyono to publicise the findings of the TPF, which reportedly pointed to the involvement of senior BIN personnel in the murder (United States Congress 2005). By 2008, prosecutors had charged BIN's deputy director, and former Special Forces commander, Muchdi PR, with Munir's murder. Never before had a senior figure from BIN or the Special Forces been charged with such a serious crime. As in many other cases, however,

---

18 Interview with Suciwati, Jakarta, 2 September 2014.

Yudhoyono's stance was ambivalent. On the one hand, he formally ordered BIN and other state agencies to cooperate with the investigation. Yet at the same time, he took care not to appear to 'intervene' in the actual legal process. This was despite the fact that officials assisting the attorney general, who reported to the head of state, prepared a strikingly weak indictment that many observers believed would lead to Muchdi's acquittal. When Muchdi was indeed acquitted, Yudhoyono complained:

> My staff tell me the journalists want a comment. I'm the president—it's not possible for me to comment on all matters in this country. I make policies, I can quickly comment if it's about a disaster or other emergency matters.[19]

But firm oversight of the legal proceedings was precisely what local and international activists demanded—especially when it became evident during Muchdi's trial that judges, prosecutors and witnesses were subject to enormous pressure and intimidation. In 2008, the European Parliament adopted a declaration expressing concern about the judicial process, reflecting the sustained international interest in the case (European Parliament 2008). Two years later, Komnas HAM noted serious flaws in the conduct of Muchdi's trial, and Human Rights Watch urged Yudhoyono to reopen the inquiry into the murder. The powerful evidence of significant BIN involvement, together with the continuing interest of the international and local human rights communities, offered Yudhoyono an opportunity to initiate broader reform of the still-opaque intelligence agency. At the very least he could have published the TPF's report, as mandated by his own decree. This could have assisted activists and investigators desperate for any leverage to bring new charges against senior BIN officials. Instead, Yudhoyono hid behind what he viewed as a presidential obligation not to intervene in the affairs of the judiciary, producing an outcome that was symptomatic of his overall approach to human rights: he condemned violations at a rhetorical level, but was not prepared to invest political capital in challenging their well-connected perpetrators.

Case study 3: political prisoners in Papua and Maluku

While Yudhoyono proudly (and rightly) lists the ending of the conflict in Aceh as one of his chief accomplishments, reducing political tensions and human rights abuses in Papua remained elusive throughout his tenure. In particular, the intensifying criminalisation of peaceful activism in Papua and Maluku under Yudhoyono stood in contrast to the increased

---

19 'Presiden SBY: saya tidak pernah intervensi kasus Munir' [President SBY: I never intervened in the Munir case], *detikNews*, 5 January 2009.

tolerance towards dissent in most other parts of Indonesia (Human Rights Watch 2010b). Despite the president's reputation as a softliner in the Aceh conflict, there is little evidence that he ever encouraged security forces to exercise restraint towards non-violent expressions of political positions, such as independence-flag raisings. While President Abdurrahman Wahid defined the Papuan Morning Star flag as a cultural symbol during his rule (1999–2001), granting it de facto legal status, Megawati Sukarnoputri's government oversaw a return to criminalisation—with the apparent approval of Yudhoyono, who was then serving as Megawati's coordinating minister for political and security affairs. In 2003, Yudhoyono warned that raising the Morning Star flag and discussions about Papuan independence would no longer be seen as 'cultural issues', stating that 'based on investigations throughout 2001 and 2002, these are the first signs leading to separatism'.[20] A few years later, as president, he would firmly institutionalise a zero-tolerance approach to expressions of separatism in Papua, whether peaceful or not.

Under Yudhoyono's presidency, the judiciary convicted hundreds of Papuan—as well as dozens of Malukan—activists who peacefully raised pro-independence flags, for the crime of 'rebellion' (*makar*) as defined in article 106 of the criminal code. To secure a conviction with a lengthy jail term for the crime of rebellion, a prosecutor typically required little more than evidence of a person's involvement in a flag-raising ceremony. In November 2014, Papuans Behind Bars documented the cases of over 200 Papuans who had been jailed for expressions of separatist sentiment between 2006 and 2014, many of them suffering torture and ill treatment during their arrest and imprisonment.[21] Amnesty International and Human Rights Watch have published detailed reports of Papua's and Maluku's 'political prisoners'—a term the Yudhoyono government consistently rejected (Primanita 2011). In 2011, the United Nation's Working Group on Arbitrary Detention found that the 15-year sentence handed to Papuan leader Filep Karma in 2005 was arbitrary and in breach of the International Covenant on Civil and Political Rights (United Nations 2011). But despite such clear breaches of international human rights standards, Yudhoyono's officials continued to justify the jailing of non-violent separatists as a necessity in accordance with national law. Officials routinely cited a government regulation issued by the Ministry of Home Affairs in December 2007 that banned the display of separatist flags. After the government issued this regulation, Amnesty International (2013) documented a notable increase in arrests.

---

20 'Minister says no room for separatist movements in Indonesia', *BBC Monitoring Asia Pacific*, 4 December 2003.
21 See www.papuansbehindbars.org.

In June 2007, shortly before the regulation was issued, Yudhoyono found himself unusually close to a case of separatist flag-raising. While the president was on a visit to Ambon, a group of about 20 protesters sneaked through layers of security, performed a traditional Malukan dance in full view of the president and other senior officials, and then unfurled the Benang Raja flag (of the Republic of South Maluku).[22] The members of the group were arrested, severely beaten and tortured, and sentenced to 7–20 years in jail for rebellion. The Ambon district court initially sentenced their leader, schoolteacher Johan Teterisa, to life imprisonment, but this was commuted to a 15-year sentence on appeal.[23] Yudhoyono was reportedly 'livid' at the blatant security breach, and it is highly plausible that the personal affront he took at the protest paved the way for prosecutors and judges to hand down the unusually long sentences. It is equally possible that the Ministry of Home Affairs' December 2007 regulation on separatist symbols was drafted to assuage the president's indignation, further justifying the arrest and imprisonment of pro-independence activists in Maluku and Papua.

Despite mounting pressure from local and international human rights organisations to take a more lenient approach to non-violent activists, Yudhoyono continued to view any political expressions in support of independence as acts of treason. In fact, he insisted that dealing with separatists, whether non-violent or otherwise, had nothing to do with human rights—a highly questionable contention, especially given the many human rights treaties Indonesia had now signed. In 2012, he told a class of graduating army officers at the military academy in Magelang that 'the attempts of those who want to secede from the Unitary State of the Republic of Indonesia are best described not as freedom of speech but as separatism. It must be stopped'.[24]

Case study 4: freedom of expression on the internet

Yudhoyono assumed the presidency at a time when the rapid growth of social media in Indonesia was beginning to provide increasing opportunities for citizens to express criticism and controversial views, and increasing opportunities for governments to restrict, monitor and criminalise them. Consequently, Indonesian and international human rights organisations started to view the internet as a critical site where fundamental human rights could be both realised and stifled. In its first

---

22 For details of this and other cases, see Amnesty International (2009).
23 'Life sentence for raising separatist flag', *Wikileaks*, 7 April 2008.
24 'SBY: stop separatism', *Republika*, 12 July 2012.

'Freedom on the net' report in 2011, Freedom House found that the internet in Indonesia was 'partly free', concluding that the government's practices of regulation had 'fallen short of international democratic standards' (Freedom House 2011). Yet, despite noting several attempts by the government to filter, monitor and block content, the report found that none were 'aimed at systematically targeting content critical of the government'. Similarly, a detailed 2014 report by the Indonesian human rights organisation Elsam found that 'so far, the ministry [of communications and information technology] has yet to fight against sites that contain security or conflict issues, as well as content on political criticism towards the government and the state ideology' (Djafar and Abidin 2014). Indeed, online sites containing material that would often have attracted repression from Yudhoyono's officials in the offline world, such as Marxist discussion forums or websites advocating Papuan independence, were flourishing, and there is little evidence that the Yudhoyono government attempted to implement systematic restrictions on such content.[25]

Rather than targeting overtly political material, Yudhoyono's internet censors took a hardline approach towards controversial moral or religious content. Such a pattern of internet censorship reflected the government's broader drift towards appeasement of conservative Islamic constituents. The public face of this approach was Yudhoyono's minister for communications and information technology, Tifatul Sembiring, a member of the conservative Islamic Prosperous Justice Party (Partai Keadilan Sejahtera, PKS). The major categories of blocked sites included those offering pornographic and other sexual content and those containing controversial religious content, including content deemed blasphemous (Djafar and Abidin 2014). During a 2012 speech to the UN General Assembly, Yudhoyono defended the banning of the Islam-critical film 'Innocence of Muslims', arguing that 'the Universal Declaration of Human Rights underlines that in exercising their freedom of expression, everyone must observe morality and public order. Freedom of expression is therefore not absolute' (Yudhoyono 2012).

However, while prepared to restrict the freedom of expression of liberals, non-Muslims and non-mainstream Islamic sects who challenged the moral code of the conservative religious establishment, Yudhoyono granted the latter the right to attack the former as immoral heretics, atheists and infidels. In consolidated democracies this type of language would be categorised as hate speech, but Yudhoyono proclaimed that the government could not intervene in such cases. Once again, he dem-

---

25 Interview with Wahyudi Djafar, Elsam, Jakarta, 20 August 2014.

onstrated his majoritarian view of human rights: while it was politically prudent to defend the rights of the demographic majority and powerful lobby groups, minority groups enjoyed no such privileges. Indeed, in Yudhoyono's view, it was within the government's democratic mandate to ensure that minorities did not disturb the overall harmony of society.

In addition to the censorship of moral and religious content, the Yudhoyono government oversaw the introduction of draconian online criminal defamation laws. While the criminal code already contained articles on defamation, providing for jail sentences of less than two years, in 2008 the DPR passed the Law on Information and Electronic Transactions. Drafted by the Ministry of Communications and Information Technology since 2003, it was introduced into parliament by Yudhoyono in 2005. It provided for a maximum sentence of six years for anyone who 'intentionally or without right distributes and/or transmits and/or makes accessible electronic information and/or electronic documents that contain insults and/or defamation'. The sudden prospect of a six-year sentence for online defamation was a sharp escalation in itself compared to the previous regulations. But perhaps more importantly, anyone suspected of a crime carrying a maximum sentence of more than five years could be subjected to pre-trial detention. Consequently, dozens of individuals merely accused of making defamatory statements on social media, in emails or even in text messages were jailed under Yudhoyono (Human Rights Watch 2010a).

In 2009, an alliance of civil society organisations, including the Alliance of Independent Journalists (Aliansi Jurnalis Independen) and the Press Legal Aid Institute (Lembaga Bantuan Hukum Pers), challenged the articles on defamation in the Constitutional Court, arguing that they stifled freedom of expression and threatened journalists. Indeed, Freedom House's 2013 'Freedom on the net' report found that the 2008 law had led to increasing self-censorship among social media users as well as journalists (Freedom House 2013). Nevertheless the Constitutional Court upheld the articles, apparently accepting the arguments proffered by the attorney general's representatives that the 'borderless' nature of the internet meant that insults and defamation perpetrated online had a higher impact, and hence required harsher penalties.[26]

The blame for a restrictive online environment does not lie exclusively with Yudhoyono, but as with the previous case studies, his lack of interest and leadership in the area indicated that human rights principles were of secondary importance to him.[27]

---

26 Constitutional Court Decision 2/PUU-VII/2009.
27 Interview with Indriaswati D. Saptaningrum, Elsam, Jakarta, 2014.

HUMAN RIGHTS AND PRESIDENTIAL AGENCY

This chapter has assessed two diametrically opposed narratives on Yudhoyono's human rights legacy. On the one hand, international leaders, diplomats and human rights indexers have proposed that Indonesians enjoyed relatively strong protection of human rights under Yudhoyono. And indeed, it is important to note that the protection of human rights overall did not deteriorate under Yudhoyono; it improved in some areas (through the resolution of the war in Aceh, for example) while eroding in others (especially the area of religious-minority rights, as Robin Bush demonstrates in Chapter 13 of this volume). Importantly, this balance and stability was established at a time when many of Indonesia's neighbours were experiencing serious deteriorations in human rights protection. Yet, at the same time, many Indonesians have been deeply disappointed with Yudhoyono's record on human rights, especially given the president's own promises, self-praise and long term in office. Time and again, the president missed opportunities to demonstrate progressive leadership on crucial human rights issues that could have deepened, rather than just maintained the existing levels of, Indonesia's democratic quality. Instead, he consistently prioritised other political and personal interests over human rights, leaving Indonesia with only slight changes to its human rights regime and practice.

In short, despite Yudhoyono's apparent embrace of human rights in Indonesia's international diplomacy, the available evidence suggests that he was not a principled supporter of human rights. The case studies presented in this chapter confirm that Yudhoyono subscribed to the concept of human rights only when it was politically expedient to do so. His overly cautious approach to politics, and his own entanglement with Indonesia's history of human rights abuses, repeatedly led him to conclude that a disappointed human rights community was preferable to antagonising powerful interests in the military, in the parliament or within his own family.

Ironically, what both defenders and critics of Yudhoyono could agree on was the importance of presidential agency for upholding human rights. But while his supporters believed that he used his presidential powers to promote a comprehensive human rights agenda and deserved praise for doing so, his detractors blamed him for not exercising his full authority to achieve a more solid defence of human rights. That the presidency has a significant impact on Indonesia's trajectory of democratisation in general, and on the protection of human rights in particular, was also implicitly acknowledged by scholars and activists who framed the election of Yudhoyono's successor as critical in this context (Mietzner 2014). Many of them believed that a Prabowo victory would be disastrous for human rights in Indonesia, while the prospect of a Joko Widodo (Jokowi) presidency raised cautious optimism for significant improvements. Of course, Jokowi will have to demonstrate first whether he can use the powers of the presidency more extensively than Yudhoyono did. But despite the continued relevance of cultural, legal and structural factors in determining the quality of human rights in Indonesia, this chapter has suggested that the nature of the individual occupying the office of the presidency is much more than a historical contingency—it has a critical effect on whether human rights are celebrated rhetorically or, in contrast, defended in practice.

REFERENCES

Amnesty International (2009) 'Indonesia: jailed for waving a flag: prisoners of conscience in Maluku', 26 March.
Amnesty International (2013) 'Indonesia: submission to the United Nations Human Rights Committee', 21 June.
Aritonang, M.S. (2012a) 'Komnas HAM declares 1965 purge a gross human rights violation', *Jakarta Post*, 23 July.
Aritonang, M.S. (2012b) '1965 mass killings justified: minister', *Jakarta Post*, 1 October.
Aritonang, M.S. (2013a) 'Politics stalls ratification', *Jakarta Post*, 16 May.
Aritonang, M.S. (2013b) 'Govt officially rejects Rome Statute', *Jakarta Post*, 21 May.
Butt, S. and T. Lindsey (2012) *The Constitution of Indonesia*, Hart Publishing, Oxford.
Cameron, D. (2012) 'PM's speech at Al Azhar University', Cabinet Office and the Rt Hon David Cameron MP, 12 April. Available at https://www.gov.uk/government/speeches/transcript-prime-ministers-speech-at-al-azhar-university
Dewi, S.W. (2012) 'SBY ignores missing persons case: ombudsman', *Jakarta Post*, 13 July.
Djafar, W. and Z. Abidin (2014) 'Repressing expression: case study of blocking and filtering internet content and criminalization of internet users in Indonesia', Institute for Policy Research and Advocacy (Elsam), Jakarta.
DPR (Dewan Perwakilan Rakyat) (2005) 'Risalah, RUU pengesahan Kovenant International Hak Sipil dan Politik' [Transcript, proposed bill on the ratification of the International Covenant on Civil and Political Rights], People's Representative Council (DPR), Jakarta.
Elsam (2013) 'Laporan situasi hak asasi manusia di Indonesia periode tahun 2013: ancaman berkelanjutan, penyelesaian stagnan' [Report on the human rights situation in Indonesia in 2013: continuing threats, stagnant settlement], Institute for Policy Research and Advocacy (Elsam), Jakarta.
European Parliament (2008) 'Declaration of the European Parliament on the murder of the human rights activist Munir Said Thalib', 10 April.
Fitzpatrick, D. (2008) 'Culture, ideology and human rights: the case of Indonesia's code of criminal procedure', in T. Lindsey (ed.) *Indonesia: Law and Society*, Federation Press, Annandale: 499–514.
Freedom House (2011) 'Freedom on the net 2011', Washington DC.

Freedom House (2013) 'Freedom on the net 2013', Washington DC.
Freedom House (2014) 'Freedom in the world 2014', Washington DC.
Hadiprayitno, I. (2010) 'Defensive enforcement: human rights in Indonesia', *Human Rights Review*, 11(3): 373–99.
Harsono, A. (2009) 'In failing to find Munir's murderers, SBY is failing his own test of history', *Jakarta Globe*, 23 January.
Harsono, A. (2012) 'No model for Muslim democracy', *New York Times*, 21 May.
Herbert, J. (2008) 'The legal framework of human rights in Indonesia', in T. Lindsey (ed.) *Indonesia: Law and Society*, Federation Press, Annandale: 456–82.
Honna, J. (2003) *Military Politics and Democratization in Indonesia*, Routledge, London and New York.
Hotland, T. (2009) 'Law annulment raises questions about Aceh', *Jakarta Post*, 9 December.
Human Rights Watch (2010a) 'Turning critics into criminals: the human rights consequences of criminal defamation law in Indonesia', New York.
Human Rights Watch (2010b) 'Prosecuting political aspiration: Indonesia's political prisoners', New York.
Jenkins, D. and D. Kammen (2012) 'The Army Para-commando Regiment and the reign of terror in Central Java and Bali', in D. Kammen and K. McGregor (eds) *The Contour of Mass Violence in Indonesia, 1965–68*, NUS Press, Singapore: 75–103.
Kurlantzick, J. (2014) 'Southeast Asia's regression from democracy and its implications', working paper, Council on Foreign Relations, New York.
Mietzner, M. (2012) 'Indonesia's democratic stagnation: anti-reformist elites and resilient civil society', *Democratization*, 19(2): 209–29.
Mietzner, M. (2014) 'Indonesia's 2014 elections: how Jokowi won and democracy survived', *Journal of Democracy*, 25(4): 111–25.
Obama, B. (2010) 'Remarks by the President at the University of Indonesia in Jakarta, Indonesia', Office of the Press Secretary, White House, 10 November. Available at http://www.whitehouse.gov/the-press-office/2010/11/10/remarks-president-university-indonesia-jakarta-indonesia
Obama, B. (2011) 'Joint statement by President Susilo Bambang Yudhoyono of the Republic of Indonesia and President Barack Obama of the United States of America', Office of the Press Secretary, White House, 18 November. Available at http://www.whitehouse.gov/the-press-office/2011/11/18/joint-statement-president-susiloi-bambang-yudhoyono-republic-indonesia-0
Primanita, A. (2011) 'Government: no political prisoners in Papua', *Jakarta Globe*, 12 December.
Robison, R. and V.R. Hadiz (2004) *Reorganising Power in Indonesia: The Politics of Oligarchy in an Age of Markets*, Routledge, London.
Rosser, A. (2013) 'Towards a political economy of human rights violations in post-New Order Indonesia', *Journal of Contemporary Asia*, 43(2): 243–54.
Setara Institute (2013) 'Ringkasan eksekutif, indeks kinerja hak asasi manusia (IKH) 2013' [Executive summary, index of human rights performance], Jakarta, 9 December.
Sidel, J. (2012) 'Indonesian democracy deserves closer scrutiny, David Cameron', *Guardian*, 13 April 2012.
Sukma, R. (2011) 'Indonesia finds a new voice', *Journal of Democracy*, 22(4): 110–23.
Sundari, E.K. (2013) 'Support the ratification of the Rome Statute, generals', 16 December.
United Nations (2011) 'Report of the Working Group on Arbitrary Detention', document 48/2011, 16 December.

United Nations (2012) 'Compilation prepared by the Office of the High Commissioner for Human Rights in accordance with paragraph 5 of the annex to Human Rights Council Resolution 16/21', document A/HRC/WG.6/13/IDN/2, 12 March.

United States Congress (2005) 'Letter from the Congress of the United States to President Susilo Bambang Yudhoyono dated 27 October 2005'. Available at http://www.kontras.org/data/Kongres%20AS%20to%20SBY,%20Oct%2005.pdf

Wilson, S. (2010) 'Obama praises Indonesia's "spirit of tolerance" as a model', *Washington Post*, 10 November.

Yudhoyono, S.B. (2012) 'Speech by H.E. Dr. Susilo Bambang Yudhoyono, President of the Republic of Indonesia, at the General Debate of the 67th Session of the United Nations General Assembly', New York, 25 September.

13 Religious politics and minority rights during the Yudhoyono presidency

Robin Bush

On most aspects of Susilo Bambang Yudhoyono's performance over his ten-year presidency, history will likely be kind—his cautious, indecisive, middle-of-the-road approach will earn more positive than negative accolades in areas of economic growth, foreign policy and even probably, at the end of the day, corruption. One area that is an unmitigated loss for him in terms of 'legacy points', however, is his administration's performance on religious freedom and minority rights. Especially during his second term, minority groups such as the Ahmadiyah, Shi'a and even Christian groups experienced sustained and repeated attacks—increasingly involving the use of violence. Indonesia's much-lauded international reputation for tolerance and pluralism has been tarnished significantly.

The score card on this issue is so straightforward that this chapter will not focus its analysis on arguing that minority rights and religious politics in Indonesia have regressed over the past decade; others have already effectively, and repeatedly, made that point. Human Rights Watch (2013: 6), for example, declared that

> President Susilo Bambang Yudhoyono has been inconsistent at best in defending the right to religious freedom. The absence of leadership has emboldened groups willing to use violence against religious minorities and the local and national officials who cater to them.

Similarly, the United States Commission on International Religious Freedom (2014: 125) concluded that

> Indonesia's transition to democracy and economic stability has been marred by sectarian violence, terrorist attacks, the growth of extremist groups, and rising intolerance toward religious minorities and 'heterodox' groups.

Numerous scholarly and media articles have also noted with concern that Indonesia's famed religious tolerance appears to be on the retreat (Fealy 2011; Jones 2013; Harsono 2014).[1]

Rather than reiterate these arguments, this chapter will focus on the role of the president himself in at best allowing, and at worst contributing to, the deterioration of minority rights and the politicisation of religion in Indonesia. Yudhoyono was elected in 2004 on a platform of anti-corruption and forward-looking progress for Indonesia. By the end of his first term, however, significant problems in Indonesia's religious relations were emerging. Nevertheless, he was re-elected in 2009 with a landslide victory and a huge mandate for reform (Timberman 2009). Observers felt that this would be the moment for Yudhoyono to take some bold action on minority rights. But as his second term began to pass by with no hint of such reform, observers, journalists and scholars began to question why the president was not taking action when he had been given such a large mandate for reform.[2] As the end of his time in office neared, it became clear that Yudhoyono was not going to do anything to turn the tides of regression, despite the potential damage to his legacy. Accordingly, a second question now began to present itself. Was this just a matter of benign neglect—did Yudhoyono simply have more pressing priorities, and prefer to leave religious conflict and minority issues to others? Or did he in fact, despite some public statements to the contrary (usually made abroad), share the view of those who were actively seeking to constrict space for minorities and religious pluralism in Indonesia?

Assessing the president's motivations and intentions is important not just to understand the reasons for Yudhoyono's inaction on this issue, but also to understand the nature of Islam and politics in Indonesia, and perhaps even the nature of Indonesian nationalism. When an incumbent president campaigns on a certain agenda, wins a landslide victory based on that campaign but then not only fails to implement but openly contradicts that agenda, there are important things to be learned. If he was simply focusing his energies elsewhere, that would tell us something about the role of religion at the highest levels of political office. If he was reacting to pressure from Islamist groups that had no public mandate and whose actions stood in stark contrast to public opinion, then that would tell us something about the power of these fringe groups. If, however, he was being true to his own internal belief system, then that may tell us something about both Indonesian Islam and Indonesian national-

---

1 Media coverage of the issue has been particularly extensive in Indonesia's English-language press. See, for example, 'Editorial: it's time for moderate Muslims to speak up', *Jakarta Globe*, 10 January 2014.
2 'Tolerating intolerance: Indonesia's president is accused of turning a blind eye to religious violence', *Economist*, 9 June 2012. See also Gorrindo (2011).

ism. My argument in this chapter is that the answer lies a bit in all three directions, but with more weight given to the latter two explanations. Susilo Bambang Yudhoyono, I argue, was not an innocent bystander to the deterioration of minority rights and religious pluralism during his presidency, but made conscious choices that contributed to it.

The next section will recap some of the primary evidence for a regression in minority rights and give some examples of violence against religious minorities. The chapter will then examine the role of Yudhoyono himself and his administration in responding to, alleviating or contributing to the problem. This will be examined through an exploration of Yudhoyono's own statements, his political appointments to key positions, and important legislation as well as executive regulations passed under and with the support of his administration. Finally, the chapter will examine how this empirical data can help us to understand not only the contours of political change in Indonesia, but also the relationship of Islam and politics, and the place of nationalism in this relationship.

RELIGIOUS MINORITIES UNDER ATTACK

Throughout Yudhoyono's presidency, organisations such as the Setara Institute and the Wahid Institute documented a disturbing trend of growing intolerance towards religious minorities in Indonesia. According to the Setara Institute (2013), for example, the number of incidents of religious violence increased from 90 in 2007, when it began monitoring, to 264 in 2012, with a slight subsequent dip to 220 in 2013. Cases of violation of religious freedom, meanwhile, rose from 93 in 2007 to 366 in 2012 before dipping to 288 in 2013.[3] Data from the Wahid Institute (2013: 3) show a similar pattern—the number of incidents of religious violence rose steadily from 2009 to 2012 and then dipped slightly in 2013. Most of the discrimination and violence was targeted at members of three religious-minority groups, namely the Ahmadiyah, the Shi'a community and Christian groups.

Ahmadiyah

The most egregious and oft-cited evidence for increasing violence towards religious minorities over the past decade involves the Islamic

---

3 When asked about the reasons for the dip in 2013, Budhy Munawar Rachman, who runs programs related to religious freedom at the Asia Foundation, expressed the opinion that it did not reflect a fall in the actual level of intolerance. Interview with Rachman, 3 September 2014.

minority group Ahmadiyah. Its presence in Indonesia dates from 1925. While originally embraced by other Muslim communities, the group was eventually declared heretical by mainstream organisations such as Muhammadiyah and Nahdlatul Ulama (NU). In 1980, the Indonesian Council of Ulama (Majelis Ulama Indonesia, MUI) issued a fatwa declaring Ahmadiyah to be heretical (Menchik 2014; Rogers 2014: 24). Subsequently, the group suffered discrimination and exclusion, but actual violence towards the Ahmadi began only in the early 2000s. This violence gained momentum after the minister for religious affairs, the attorney general and the minister for home affairs issued a joint decree in 2008 banning the propagation of Ahmadiyah teachings. Sporadic attacks on Ahmadiyah mosques and schools peaked in February 2011 when a mob of 1,500 people brutally attacked 21 Ahmadi in Cikeusik, West Java, killing three of them with striking savagery. Since then, many of the group's mosques have been either burnt or forcibly closed in various areas of West Java. There have also been scattered incidents of stone-throwing attacks on homes and mosques in West Java, attacks on Ahmadi living in displacement camps in Lombok and persistent workplace discrimination against Ahmadi (Rogers 2014: 71–9).

What was the role of the Yudhoyono administration in dealing with the Ahmadiyah issue? The three ministers responsible for issuing the 2008 joint decree were all appointed by Yudhoyono. Many observers saw this as a signal that attacks on Ahmadiyah would be tacitly condoned (ICG 2008; Platzdasch 2011). The minister for religious affairs, Suryadharma Ali, was particularly outspoken in his condemnation of Ahmadiyah, calling several times for the group to be banned.[4] But several other senior members of Yudhoyono's cabinet were also involved in anti-Ahmadiyah activity, including making statements that appeared to excuse or even condone the violence in Cikeusik (Fealy 2011). For example, the minister for justice and human rights, Patrialis Akbar, insisted that Ahmadi human rights had not been breached during the incident, while the minister for defence, Purnomo Yusgiantoro, approved a 'prayer mat' approach in which soldiers would 'occupy' Ahmadiyah mosques seeking to 'persuade' Ahmadi to return to the 'true path'. A week after the Cikeusik attack the minister for home affairs, Gamawan Fauzi, held what he said was a 'warm and friendly' meeting with Habib Rizieq, the chair of the Islamic Defenders Front (Front Pembela Islam, FPI), a hardline organisation suspected of involvement in the violence. Fauzi and Suryadharma also approved and upheld the attempts by several local governments (Pekanbaru, Garut, Tasikmalaya, South Sulawesi,

---

4 'Best to disband Ahmadiyah, religious minister says', *Jakarta Globe*, 28 February 2011. See also Rogers (2014: 31).

West Java, East Java) to ban or restrict Ahmadiyah activities, despite the ambiguous legality of these moves (Fealy 2011: 348).

As for President Yudhoyono himself, he took a safe, middle-of-the-road position. On the one hand, he condemned the violence and called for the rule of law to be upheld. He also did not issue the full ban on Ahmadiyah that was advocated by many hardline groups at the time. But on the other hand, he did not reprimand any of his ministers for their inflammatory statements, nor did he respond publicly to the threats of revolution issued by a number of Islamist groups should such a ban not be forthcoming. Fealy (2011: 350) has characterised his response as 'unwittingly' fanning intolerance by 'failing to respond resolutely to the Islamists' subversive threats and continuing intimidation of Ahmadiyah'. Arguably, though, this silence was not so much 'unwitting' as tacit approval expressed in safe, silent, Javanese style.

Shi'a

Indonesian Muslims are predominantly Sunni, but a Shi'a minority of more than 2 million has lived in Indonesia since pre-colonial days (Human Rights Watch 2013). Settling mostly in Aceh, but also in East and Central Java, Shi'a Muslims have largely lived in peace and integrated with the community. Since 2006, however, several outbursts of violence against Shi'a have been documented (Rogers 2014: 79). In 2010 and 2011, for instance, the Shi'a school Yayasan Pesantren Islam in Bangil, East Java, was attacked several times by militants, causing considerable damage and injuring nine students.

In Sampang, on the island of Madura in East Java, anti-Shi'a tension has a history dating back to the 1980s, when the son of a local religious teacher became a Shi'a and established a school in the district (Fealy 2013: 114). Violence broke out in 2011 when the school was set on fire. In December that year, a group attacked the Shi'a community in Sampang, destroying the home of the local Shi'a leader and the school, and forcing about 500 of the Shi'a community to flee (Rogers 2014: 79). In January 2012, the local MUI branch declared Shi'a teachings to be blasphemous, and in July Tajul Muluk, the Shi'a leader, was imprisoned for two (later increased to four) years under the blasphemy provisions of the criminal code. In August 2012, as members of the Shi'a community were preparing to send their children to school, they were attacked by a large mob. The attackers killed two of the Shi'a, injured several others and destroyed 45 houses, and the whole community of over 200 Shi'a was evacuated to a tennis stadium near the village (Fealy 2013; Rogers 2014). At several points over the ensuing year the local government cut off food supplies to the Shi'a, and increasingly large groups of Sunni protestors demanded their eviction. Finally, in June 2013, they were forcibly evicted to a refugee facility in Sidoarjo, East Java, where they remained in September 2014, despite promises from President Yudhoyono that they would be allowed to return to their homes.[5]

Yudhoyono's failure to fulfil this promise was hardly surprising, even though at the outset of the violence in Sampang he had criticised the police for not protecting the group. After the August 2012 incident, he had even summoned the heads of the police and military, as well as some key ministers, demanding stern measures to prevent further violence.[6] But as in other instances of religious violence, his statements were never backed up by action and he remained silent when his minister for religious affairs, Suryadharma Ali, repeatedly stated that Shi'a were not Muslims and should be forced to convert to Sunni Islam. Even though Suryadharma's statements were inflammatory and directly opposed to both Yudhoyono's own statements and those of the largest Muslim organisations in Indonesia, the president refrained from reprimanding his minister (Fealy 2013: 115).

Christians

For Indonesian Christians, the biggest issue during the Yudhoyono years was the recurring conflict around building houses of worship. This is not a new issue—the construction of churches has been regulated by the state since 1969—but over Yudhoyono's decade in office, and in particular after the 2006 Joint Regulation on Houses of Worship was issued, the Christian minority found it increasingly difficult to get permits to build churches, while existing churches were shut or attacked in increasing numbers. According to church-related sources, 430 churches have been attacked or have closed since 2004 (Rogers 2014: 54). The most often discussed cases are those of GKI Yasmin in Bogor and HKBP Filadelfia in Bekasi, both in West Java. In both cases, permits to build the churches were issued by state courts, following the procedures of the 2006 joint regulation. In the case of GKI Yasmin, even the Supreme Court ruled that the church was legal. But in both cases local officials refused to allow the churches to open and no higher authorities intervened to enforce the courts' decisions.

Yudhoyono's stance on the GKI Yasmin case is emblematic of his approach to minority rights more generally He issued a number of vaguely worded statements to the media calling for religious freedom

---

5 'Sampang Shiites tell SBY to resolve conflict', *Jakarta Post*, 12 April 2014.
6 'SBY summons cabinet members to explain deadly Sampang melee', *Jakarta Post*, 27 August 2012.

to be upheld, only to then immediately shift the responsibility to some other element of government. 'I have handed it over to the mayor and the governor of West Java, along with some ministers, to handle this case', he said, adding that while legal solutions were still being sought, extrajudicial issues were also involved.[7] Reacting to the president's hands-off approach, church communities expressed disappointment with Yudhoyono's handling of the GKI Yasmin case, calling on him to consider his legacy and the negative precedent the case was setting.[8] The Setara Institute called Yudhoyono's statements 'a mirage', saying they had no meaning if not accompanied by explicit instructions to lower levels of government to comply with the law (Setara Institute 2012a: 168).

Not only were explicit and concrete actions not forthcoming from Yudhoyono, but even symbolic gestures were not proffered. For example, GKI Yasmin and HKGB Filadelfia had invited the president to Christmas mass in 2012. When they were told that their churches were too far away for the president to visit (GKI Yasmin is 40 kilometres from Yudhoyono's official residence, and 20 kilometres from his private residence), they arranged for a mass to take place across the street from the palace itself, with a chair reserved for Yudhoyono in the front row. The chair remained empty.

HOW YUDHOYONO SHAPED RELIGIOUS POLITICS: APPOINTMENTS, ORGANISATIONS, REGULATIONS

The preceding section has provided a brief overview of the most contentious issues of minority rights and religious politics in Indonesia during Yudhoyono's decade in power, with particular attention given to the president's own position and actions on each issue. By and large, his response was to issue placatory statements while refraining from taking action to protect minority rights. It would be too simplistic just to say that Yudhoyono did not get involved. In fact, he did get involved, if only indirectly. This section will demonstrate that Yudhoyono did indeed shape religious politics in Indonesia, especially through his ministerial appointments and his support for certain institutions as well as legislation and other regulations. Of course, he had varying levels of direct influence across these areas. Nevertheless, it is often possible to identify

---

7 'SBY: pemerintah sedang mediasi kasus GKI Yasmin' [SBY: the government is mediating the GKI Yasmin case], *Suara Pembaruan*, 15 February 2012.
8 'Komitmen SBY dipertanyakan terkait kasus GKI Yasmin' [Questioning the commitment of SBY to the case of GKI Yasmin], *Sindonews.com*, 2 September 2013.

a fairly direct and intentional relationship between Yudhoyono and particular outcomes obtained during his presidency.

Key appointments

While one might argue that Yudhoyono cannot take the blame for societal shifts such as rising intolerance, or even for the many incidents of religious violence carried out by a wide range of non-state actors, he certainly can be held accountable for the actions and statements of his own appointees—at both the cabinet and non-cabinet levels. Here, the most obvious and directly relevant appointment is that of the minister for religious affairs, Suryadharma Ali. The minister's inflammatory, antiminority and often anti-state-policy remarks and actions with regard to Ahmadiyah, Shi'a and church closures have already been noted. In addition, he was a strong and vocal supporter of the FPI, the organisation named by the Setara Institute as one of the non-state actors most frequently responsible for acts of violence against religious minorities (Setara Institute 2011, 2012b). Suryadharma, who was also the chair of the United Development Party (Partai Persatuan Pembangunan, PPP) for most of the Yudhoyono years, even invited Munarman, the FPI's vitriolic spokesperson, to run as a legislative candidate for PPP (Wilson 2014a: 6).

Not far behind Suryadharma in terms of his ability to make astonishingly inflammatory remarks was Home Affairs Minister Gamawan Fauzi. In response to increasing calls for him to disband the FPI after multiple acts of violence attributed to the group, Fauzi said in October 2013 that it was a 'national asset', and that local and national leaders should work with the group (Wilson 2014a: 6). This statement came shortly after he publicly called on then Jakarta governor (and now president) Joko Widodo to replace the Christian subdistrict head of Lenteng Agung, Susan Zulkifli, following protests by locals who did not want a Christian to hold that position.[9] None of these statements had any repercussions for these ministers, with Yudhoyono either remaining silent or only half-heartedly reprimanding them.

Less well known, but perhaps far more influential in terms of access to Yudhoyono, was Ma'ruf Amin, appointed by the president in 2007 to the low-profile but at times influential Presidential Advisory Council (Dewan Pertimbangan Presiden, Wantimpres). Amin is a senior NU member and a former member of parliament. His most prominent public role, however, has been as a longstanding director (*ketua*) of the MUI, where he has chaired the Fatwa Commission since 2000. He was the pri-

---

9 'Gamawan describes FPI as an "asset to the nation"', *Jakarta Post*, 25 October 2013.

mary architect of some of the most conservative and controversial MUI fatwa, including one against secularism, pluralism and liberalism and the latest anti-Ahmadiyah fatwa, both issued in 2005. According to NU insiders, more than anyone else Amin had the ear, and confidence, of the president when it came to religious issues. Yudhoyono's trust in Amin further helps to explain why religious politics took such a conservative turn during his term in office.

Another presidential appointee/advisor with anti-pluralist and anti-minority views was retired Lieutenant-General Sudi Silalahi, who was secretary of state during Yudhoyono's second term. Silalahi's closeness to Yudhoyono pre-dated the presidency, and stemmed from their military days. During his time in the army, Silalahi's record already reflected his position on religious politics — he was reputed to have been one of the generals who allowed 'jihadists' into Ambon at the height of the Muslim-Christian conflict in Maluku in the early 2000s.[10] More recently, Silalahi was the designer and driving force behind Majelis Dzikir, a travelling religious study group credited with garnering a considerable number of Muslim votes for Yudhoyono's Democrat Party (Partai Demokrat, PD) during his 2009 campaign.[11]

The last direct appointment that must be noted here is that of the highly strategic position of chief of police. Throughout the Yudhoyono years, the police were utterly ineffectual in providing adequate protection for religious minorities, in some cases even assisting the perpetrators of religiously motivated violence (Setara Institute 2011, 2012a). Some of the pieces of this puzzle fall into place when one recalls that Yudhoyono appointed General Timur Pradopo to the position of national chief of police in 2010. Upon his appointment, Timur issued the controversial statement that 'the FPI should be embraced, and empowered, as they can contribute to national security'.[12] He had a history of close relations with the group, including working closely with FPI leader Salim Umar while head of the West Jakarta police between 1997 and 1999, when the FPI was invited to work with local police to provide security during Ramadan.

Organisations

Apart from appointing controversial anti-pluralists to influential positions, Yudhoyono shaped religious politics in Indonesia through his support for — or lack of action against — a range of organisations and

---

10 Interview with Ahmad Suaedy, Wahid Institute, 3 September 2014.
11 Interview with Ahmad Suaedy, Wahid Institute, 3 September 2014.
12 'Timur Pradopo: FPI bisa bantu keamanan' [Timur Pradopo: FPI can assist with providing security], *Tempo*, 7 October 2010.

institutions whose activities have clearly weakened minority rights in Indonesia. In this context, the FPI is arguably the foremost non-state actor involved in incidents of religious violence (Wilson 2014b). Its record of impunity indicates that it must have had support from key elements of the Yudhoyono administration, even though the president himself repeatedly criticised the organisation, indirectly threatening to shut it down. Each time this happened, however, the FPI responded with equal vigour, and ultimately Yudhoyono always backed down. In 2011, for example, immediately after the brutal attack on Ahmadiyah in Cikeusik, Yudhoyono reacted angrily, saying that 'the law enforcement apparatus must find all mechanisms that are legal (to prosecute the perpetrators of the violence) including if necessary banning or disbanding said organisations'.[13] While not named, the FPI clearly felt that it was the target of Yudhoyono's statement and responded with an ultimatum—if Ahmadiyah were not banned by 1 March 2011, it would lead a revolution to depose President Yudhoyono.[14] The response of the head of state to this clearly seditious statement was complete silence. This silence continued even when the court system shortly afterwards sentenced the perpetrators of the anti-Ahmadiyah violence to laughable sentences of less than six months in jail, and while local government officials issued decrees banning Ahmadiyah in contravention of state policy, but with the support of Home Affairs Minister Fauzi. Thus, while there is no evidence that Yudhoyono personally endorsed the FPI and its violence, members of his cabinet did, and as president Yudhoyono bore ultimate responsibility for their actions and statements.

A second institution notorious for weakening minority rights is the MUI. Established in 1975 by former president Suharto, the MUI has a standing line-item in the state budget, and in the past many of its central board members also occupied senior positions in the state apparatus. The Ministry of Religious Affairs' funding of the organisation increased during the Yudhoyono years, and under Ma'ruf Amin's tenure as head of the MUI's Fatwa Commission, a very close relationship existed between the Yudhoyono administration and the MUI (Hasyim 2013). During Yudhoyono's second term, four of his cabinet members sat on its board: Suryadharma Ali (minister for religious affairs), Hatta Rajasa (coordinating minister for economic affairs), Muhammad Nuh (minister of education) and Salim Segaf al-Jufri (minister for social affairs). The MUI has generally held conservative positions on issues of minority rights and religious tolerance. It issued several controversial fatwa during the Yudhoyono era, such as the 2005 fatwa against secularism, pluralism and liberalism

---

13 'Revolution rhetoric from Petamburan', *Tempo*, 21–27 February 2011.
14 'Revolution rhetoric from Petamburan', *Tempo*, 21–27 February 2011.

and the fatwa in the same year reiterating its stance that Ahmadiyah was a deviant sect. The MUI actively seeks to integrate its fatwa into national law and has been successful in doing so in several relevant cases. For example, the Blasphemy Law (discussed below) is very close in content to the MUI fatwa on deviant sects, and the joint ministerial decree on Ahmadiyah is very similar to sections of the MUI fatwa on Ahmadiyah (Hasyim 2013: 197).

A final institution worth mentioning here is the so-called Coordinating Board for Monitoring Mystical Beliefs in Society (Badan Koordinasi Pengawas Aliran Kepercayaan Masyarakat, Bakor Pakem). Bakor Pakem is housed within the attorney general's office, and follows Indonesian state structure and hierarchy, with branches in every province and district that are also housed within the local prosecutors' offices. During the Yudhoyono years, it was highly influential in pushing for the prohibition of Ahmadiyah propagation activities, the banning of the Shi'a faith and the prosecution of individuals such as Tajul Muluk (Shi'a leader), Hawan Suwandi (Ahmadiyah) and Alexander Aan, a civil servant from West Sumatra who was prosecuted for atheism after posting comments on a Facebook page (Suaedy 2010; Human Rights Watch 2013: 43).

Taken together, the FPI, the MUI and Bakor Pakem have been highly influential in pushing religious intolerance into the mainstream of Indonesian politics. However, it was only possible for them to become so influential because they had nurtured very intimate relationships with parts of the Yudhoyono administration. The president's tacit approval of these relationships further cemented their position as key driving forces behind Indonesia's deepening religious intolerance.

Legislation and executive regulations

One of the most visible products of a political administration is the legislation it enacts. It is interesting to note that during the ten years of Yudhoyono's presidency Indonesian voters' support for Islamist political parties decreased, yet during the same period party elites and ministers proposed, supported or passed a raft of laws and decrees deemed by both national and international observers to constrain religious freedom and restrict minority rights. Indeed, Rogers (2014: 32) quoted Andreas Harsono of Human Rights Watch as saying that Yudhoyono was 'the president who laid down the most sectarian regulatory infrastructure in Indonesia'. The most troublesome of these laws and regulations included the reaffirmation of the 1965 Blasphemy Law through the Constitutional Court, the 2006 decree on houses of worship and the 2008 decree on Ahmadiyah.

The Blasphemy Law (Law 1/PNPS/1965) was issued as a presidential decree by Sukarno in early 1965. It criminalises expressions of hostility or hatred against the religions officially recognised in Indonesia: Islam, Protestantism, Catholicism, Hinduism, Buddhism and, since 2006, Confucianism.[15] Between 2003 and 2014, over 150 Indonesians were arrested under this law, according to data from the United States Commission on International Religious Freedom cited by Rogers (2014: 35). For minority rights activists, the most problematic aspect of the law was the criminalising of 'deviation' from the 'basic tenets of a religion', which put state authorities in the role of establishing an orthodoxy of religious belief (Bagir 2011; Platzdasch 2011; Menchik 2014). In 2009, a group of human rights activists called the Religious Freedom Advocacy Team brought the Blasphemy Law to the Constitutional Court for judicial review on the grounds that it was often used to restrict religious minorities rather than protect minority rights, and that it violated the constitutionally guaranteed right to freedom of religion. In April 2010 the court ruled that the law was constitutional in its restriction of minority religious beliefs because it protected public order.[16] President Yudhoyono did not get involved in the debate surrounding the law, but two of his ministers, Suryadharma Ali and the minister for justice and human rights, Patrialis Akbar, strongly defended the law, insisting that it was necessary to maintain law and order (Human Rights Watch 2013: 31). Later in his administration, Yudhoyono made an appeal at the United Nations for an international anti-blasphemy protocol, in a move that was widely criticised by human rights activists (Crouch 2013a).[17] While this move was unrelated to the Indonesian Blasphemy Law decision, it reflected Yudhoyono's view that religious belief needed to be regulated by the state, or even supra-state bodies. Accordingly, it was hardly surprising that he did not stop his ministers from supporting the Blasphemy Law.

The 2006 Joint Decree on Houses of Worship updated the 1969 Joint Decree on Houses of Worship issued by the Ministry of Religious Affairs and the Ministry of Home Affairs. The original regulation in effect restricted non-Muslim religious practice, as it required approval of a majority of residents in the neighbourhood in which a house of worship

---

15 A Human Rights Watch report notes that while this law is frequently interpreted as providing official recognition for these six religions, a 2009 Constitutional Court ruling states that Indonesia recognises all religions, but protects only these six from blasphemy (Human Rights Watch 2013: 29).

16 For the complete decision of the Constitutional Court (No. 140/PUU-VII/2009 upholding Law 1/PNPS/1965), as well as many of the arguments made in favour of the judicial review by Bonar Tigor Naipospos (Setara Institute), Usman Hamid (KontraS), Zainal Abidin Bagir (Center for Religious and Cross-cultural Studies, Gadjah Mada University) and the human rights organisation ARTICLE 19, see Hasani (2010).

17 'Anti-blasphemy tool a diplomatic blunder', *Jakarta Post*, 10 October 2012.

was to be built, which was difficult to obtain in many Muslim-majority neighbourhoods. Shortly after taking office in 2004, Yudhoyono asked then Minister of Religion Maftuh Basyuni to review the 1969 decree, at the request of church leaders. Basyuni subsequently appointed Ma'ruf Amin to take the lead on drafting an updated decree (Human Rights Watch 2013: 34). Unsurprisingly, when the new Joint Decree on Houses of Worship was issued by the Ministries of Religion and Home Affairs in 2006, it was viewed by many as placing even more restrictions on minority religions. Among the various hurdles put in the way of building a house of worship were the need to obtain a permit from the regional government, support from 60 neighbours, written approval from the Ministry of Religious Affairs and written approval from the Religious Harmony Forum (Forum Kerukunan Umat Beragama, FKUB), a new body established by the decree comprising religious leaders and usually dominated by the majority religion (Crouch 2007, 2013b; Ropi 2007; Ali-Fauzi et al. 2011). Because of the difficulty of meeting these new requirements, many Christian congregations now meet in houses or in churches that were built prior to the 2006 decree without a licence. Militant Muslim groups have increasingly targeted these groups for violent action, in many cases with little censure by law enforcement, due to the technical 'illegality' of the churches.

The 2008 Joint Decree on Ahmadiyah issued by the attorney general, the minister for religious affairs and the minister for home affairs closely followed the 2005 MUI fatwa on Ahmadiyah. It stopped short of completely banning Ahmadiyah, but restricted its activities, including any teachings or activities that deviated from the principal teachings of Islam (Rogers 2014: 34). Following the issuance of this decree, as discussed earlier, several local governments issued local regulations banning all Ahmadiyah activity, in contravention of central government policy, and resulting in a spate of violence against Ahmadi communities (Ropi 2010; Platzdasch 2011; Crouch 2012). Even though these local regulations went beyond the wording of the joint decree, both Suryadharma Ali and Gamawan Fauzi supported them. Ma'ruf Amin was another strong proponent of the decree, and used his position on the Presidential Advisory Council (Wantimpres) to advocate for an even stronger version of it, calling for an outright ban on Ahmadiyah.

BENIGN NEGLECT OR DELIBERATE POLITICAL CALCULATION?

Having reviewed the main issues affecting religious minorities in Indonesia over the past decade, it is now imperative to look at President

Yudhoyono himself. Throughout his term in office he issued statements in support of religious tolerance and minority rights. 'Indonesia ... can project the virtue of moderate Islam throughout the Muslim world. We can be the bastion of freedom, tolerance, and harmony', he said at Harvard University in 2009, for example (Fealy 2013: 113). Despite these fine words, when examining his track record, many national and international observers find that the president's actions do not match his words. 'President Susilo Bambang Yudhoyono will be remembered for a lot of things, but being a bastion of pluralism is definitely not one of them', says Indonesian journalist Armando Siahaan (2011). Amnesty International (2014) maintains that Yudhoyono's decade in office was 'marked by only patchy progress on human rights, and even regression in some areas'. According to Andreas Harsono (2014), Yudhoyono's response to the growing intolerance in Indonesia was 'empty rhetoric and turning a blind eye to elements of his government passively or actively complicit in abuses of the rights of religious minorities'.

The mismatch between Yudhoyono's rhetoric, which enhanced his reputation in some circles of the international community (see Chapter 5 by Fitriani), and his verifiable track record on the ground was at no time more apparent than when the Appeal of Conscience Foundation, a US interfaith organisation, awarded him its so-called World Statesman Award in 2013 'in recognition of his work to support human rights and religious freedom in the country'. The announcement was met with an outpouring of rage and disbelief both within Indonesia and internationally. Petitions on Change.org and Facebook demanded that the award be revoked, while more serious statements by human rights organisations such as KontraS (2013) explained why Yudhoyono did not deserve the award. Outspoken Indonesian Jesuit priest and philosopher Franz Magnis-Suseno expressed his objections to the award in a passionate open letter sent to the foundation.[18]

How should we understand the apparent contradictions between some of Yudhoyono's public statements, especially those made abroad, and his track record of appointments and support for controversial legislation and organisations with questionable reputations? Is it a case of benign neglect, or intentional restricting of the space for religious minorities? This section will argue that Yudhoyono's actions were in fact consistent with his ideological worldview and with the rational political calculations of a cautious, conservative and sincerely pious Muslim nationalist. To understand this, I draw first on the work of Michael Buehler

---

18 'Surat protes Franz Magnis atas rencana penghargaan negarawan untuk SBY' [Letter from Franz Magnis protesting the plan to give SBY an award for statesmanship], *Kompas*, 17 May 2013.

(2014), who has argued that political change (and by extension political behaviour) in Indonesia can be explained by state elite competition. He says that 'state elites have only become more receptive to pressures from societal groups in places and situations where such players can provide them with resources they deem important to gain and maintain power' (Buehler 2014: 173). Using the lens of state elite competition to explain the spread of sharia legislation across the country—often instigated not by Islamist parties for ideological reasons, but by 'secular' political elites based on purely rational political calculations—he argues that sharia legislation gives state elites economic, cultural and social capital, and that as a political phenomenon it debunks the secular/religious binary that long dominated analyses of Indonesian politics (Buehler 2013). From this perspective, the pursuit of a conservative, anti-pluralist, pro-sharia agenda by a supposedly secular, non-Islamist state elite is completely rational and in no way contradictory. If applied to Yudhoyono, one can see how support for some of the most conservative ministers in his cabinet (Suryadharma Ali, Gamawan Fauzi) may be seen as a rational political calculation in line with perceptions of an increasingly conservative and even increasingly intolerant Muslim majority.

That said, Buehler's argument can be taken one step further. Rather than understanding Yudhoyono's actions as *purely* rational political calculation, I would posit that they also reflected a personal ideological worldview that was more religiously conservative than many observers assumed from his seemingly mainstream secular-nationalistic background. Jeremy Menchik (2014: 599) has argued that Indonesian nationalism is in fact 'assertively religious', constituting a 'godly nationalism' that is 'predicated on theological rather than geographic or ethnic exclusion'. Godly nationalism, according to Menchik (2014: 599–600), 'conceptualizes belief as a civic virtue that accrues both individual and social benefits ... The archetype of a good citizen is one who believes in God and uses that belief to motivate his or her behavior'. Menchik uses this framework to explain the increasing concern with blasphemy and deviance in Indonesia, and the high level of intolerance, especially towards Ahmadiyah. In his framework, the state is the 'conduit for religious belief, guiding its citizens toward proper faith and behavior ... and intolerance toward heterodoxy constitutes the nation' (Menchik 2014: 601). This framework not only effectively explains Indonesians' attitudes towards Ahmadiyah, but can also provide useful insights into Yudhoyono's positions on issues of religious tolerance.

Under this framework, there is no contradiction between a strong nationalism and a strong, conservative religious outlook. Religious belief is something that can and should be regulated and enforced by the state. Deviance is bad for the nation, and piety must be maintained, by the state apparatus if necessary. Thus, actions like Suryadharma Ali's endorsement of forced conversions of Ahmadi and Shi'a are to be supported, not reprimanded. The concern with deviance and blasphemy that Menchik argues is central to 'godly nationalism' could also explain why Yudhoyono called on the United Nations in September 2012 to adopt an international instrument to ban blasphemy. This move was criticised by many human rights activists globally, but for Yudhoyono it was probably a natural extension of his own personal godly nationalism to the global level. In short, the alleged mismatch between rhetoric and action may not be such a mismatch after all. Rather, flowery rhetoric and inaction are two sides of the same coin.

On the one hand, Yudhoyono seems to have felt the need to address at least rhetorically the concerns of religious minorities and civil society organisations. After all, the image of religious harmony that Indonesia had cultivated for so long was an asset for Yudhoyono in his efforts to portray the country as a model Muslim democracy. This was particularly important for him internationally, which may be why many of his most ringing public endorsements of religious tolerance came in speeches made overseas. But the direct benefits of this rhetoric were limited to international recognition and the occasional award from an obscure overseas organisation. More directly tangible benefits with immediate implications for domestic politics were to be reaped from *not* matching this rhetoric with action. After all, numerous opinion polls in recent years have shown that ordinary Indonesians are becoming increasingly intolerant towards religious minorities. As an avid consumer of opinion polls, Yudhoyono was certainly aware of these social trends, and since he was reluctant to go against what he perceived to be the majority view, inaction on incidents of religious violence was a logical, rational choice (Fealy, forthcoming). Significantly, though, this rational choice was made even easier because it also reflected Yudhoyono's personal worldview, a worldview so aptly described by Menchik as 'godly nationalism'.

CONCLUSION

The evidence is incontrovertible that during the period of Yudhoyono's presidency, Indonesia experienced rising levels of religious intolerance combined with increasing levels of religious violence and a contraction in the rights of religious minorities. Ahmadi, Shi'a and Christians have been the most seriously affected by these trends, but the growing religious intolerance has also been felt by liberal Sunni Muslims and atheists. Significantly, the central government has been a key driving force behind this trend and Yudhoyono, as the leader of this government between

2004 and 2014, bears ultimate responsibility for this. As this chapter has demonstrated, Susilo Bambang Yudhoyono was not just an innocent bystander, nor was his role simply one of benign neglect. Rather, I have argued that he directly shaped and influenced these trends through his appointment of and refusal to rein in key ministers such as Suryadharma Ali and Gamawan Fauzi, his appointment of and apparent attentiveness to advisors such as Ma'ruf Amin and Sudi Silalahi, and his unwillingness or inability to back up fulsome statements of support for tolerance and religious harmony with the decisive action necessary to make these statements anything more than flowery rhetoric.

Following the analysis of the broad trends, the chapter explored whether this inability/unwillingness was due purely to rational political calculation, or whether it was rooted in a more ideological adherence to a conservative position on issues of religious minorities and pluralism. Building on Menchik's description of a godly nationalism in Indonesia, I have argued that Yudhoyono's actions may very well have been something other than purely political expedience. In fact, it seems as if Yudhoyono may have been a more religiously conservative president than his cosmopolitan appearance on the international stage tended to portray. Domestically, he supported individuals, organisations and regulations that rolled back religious freedoms and minority rights to an extent that few if any observers would have predicted at the beginning of his presidency.

By allowing Indonesia to lose much of its reputation as a moderate and tolerant Muslim society, Yudhoyono has left a challenging legacy for his successor, Joko Widodo (Jokowi). Religious conservatism is now mainstream politics in Indonesia and many individuals and groups with anti-pluralist agendas are now entrenched in the state apparatus. It could be argued, however, that the election of Jokowi was, among many other things, a choice to return Indonesia to the tolerant reputation it once enjoyed, and a rejection of the alternative candidate who represented a continuation of many of the themes that had dominated the Yudhoyono years—embracing the FPI, fostering anti-minority sentiment through smear tactics, and seeking to deploy the state machinery to regulate and 'purify' religious diversity. As such, one might say that the election of Jokowi was in a small way a demand for change, on these as well as many other fronts.

REFERENCES

Ali-Fauzi, I. et al. (eds) (2011) *Kontroversi Gereja di Jakarta* [Controversy over churches in Jakarta], Centre for Religious and Cross-cultural Studies, Gajah Mada University, Yogyakarta.
Amnesty International (2014) 'Indonesia's next leader must prioritize human rights', 29 April.
Bagir, Z.A. (2011) 'Defamation of religion in post-*reformasi* Indonesia: new legal issues in the old politics of religion', paper presented at the Law and Religious Pluralism in Contemporary Asia conference, Asia Research Institute, National University of Singapore, Singapore, 17–18 December.
Buehler, M. (2013) 'Subnational Islamization through secular parties: comparing shari'a politics in two Indonesian provinces', *Comparative Politics*, 46(1): 63–82.
Buehler, M. (2014) 'Elite competition and changing state–society relations: shari'a policymaking in Indonesia', in M. Ford and T. Pepinsky (eds) *Beyond Oligarchy: Wealth, Power, and Contemporary Indonesian Politics*, Cornell Southeast Asia Program Publications, Ithaca NY: 157–75.
Crouch, M. (2007) 'Regulating places of worship in Indonesia: upholding freedom of religion for religious minorities?', *Singapore Journal of Legal Studies*, July: 96–116.
Crouch, M. (2012) 'Judicial review and religious freedom: the case of the Indonesian Ahmadis', *Sydney Law Review*, 34(3): 545–72.
Crouch, M. (2013a) 'The challenge of regulating religious freedom in Indonesia', *Right Now*, 18 February.
Crouch, M. (2013b) 'Shifting conceptions of state regulation of religion: the Indonesian draft law on inter-religious harmony', *Global Change, Peace & Security*, 25(3): 265–82.
Fealy, G. (2011) 'Indonesian politics in 2011: democratic regression and Yudhoyono's regal incumbency', *Bulletin of Indonesian Economic Studies*, 47(3): 333–53.
Fealy, G. (2013) 'Indonesian politics in 2012: graft, intolerance, and hope of change in the late Yudhoyono period', in D. Singh (ed.) *Southeast Asian Affairs 2013*, Institute of Southeast Asian Studies, Singapore: 103–20.
Fealy, G. (forthcoming) 'The politics of religious intolerance in Indonesia: mainstreamism trumps extremism?', in T. Lindsey and H. Pausacker (eds) *Pluralism, Intolerance and Democracy in Indonesia: Law, Religion and Conflict*.
Gorrindo, J. (2011) 'A worthy role model for the Arab world? Assessing democracy in today's Indonesia—part I', blog post, 28 March. Available at http://johngorrindo.wordpress.com/
Harsono, A. (2014) 'Undoing Yudhoyono's sectarian legacy', *New Mandala*, 13 May. Available at http://asiapacific.anu.edu.au/newmandala/2014/05/13
Hasani, I. (ed.) (2010) *Putusan Uji Materi Undang-undang No. 1/PNPS/1965 tentang Pencegahan Penyalahgunaan dan/atau Penodaan Agama terhadap Undang-undang Dasar 1945 di Mahkamah Konstitusi* [Decision on the Judicial Review of Law No. 1/PNPS/1965 on Prevention of the Misuse and/or Abuse of Religion in relation to the Constitution of 1945 in the Constitutional Court], Publikasi Setara Institute, Jakarta.
Hasyim, S. (2013) 'Council of Indonesian Ulama (Majelis Ulama Indonesia, MUI) and its role in the shariatisation of Indonesia', PhD thesis, Freie Universität Berlin, Berlin, December.
Human Rights Watch (2013) 'In religion's name: abuses against religious minorities in Indonesia', Report 1-56432-992-5, 28 February. Available at http://www.hrw.org/reports/2013/02/28/religion-s-name

ICG (International Crisis Group) (2008) 'Indonesia: implications of the Ahmadiyah decree', Asia Briefing No. 78, Jakarta/Brussels, 7 July.
Jones, S. (2013) 'Indonesian government responses to radical Islam since 1998', in M. Künkler and A. Stepan (eds) *Democracy and Islam in Indonesia*, Columbia University Press, New York: 109–25.
KontraS (2013) 'KontraS believes SBY not deserving of the Appeal of Conscience Foundation World Statesman Award because of ongoing, state-supported, religious intolerance in Indonesia', press release, 2 May. Available at http://www.kontras.org/eng/index.php?hal=siaran_pers&id=170
Menchik, J. (2014) 'Productive intolerance: godly nationalism in Indonesia', *Comparative Studies in Society and History*, 56(3): 591–621.
Platzdasch, B. (2011) 'Religious freedom in Indonesia: the case of the Ahmadiyah', ISEAS Working Paper: Politics and Security Series No. 2, Institute of Southeast Asian Studies, Singapore.
Rogers, B. (2014) 'Indonesia: pluralism in peril: the rise of religious intolerance across the archipelago', Christian Solidarity Worldwide (CWS). Available at http://dynamic.csw.org.uk/article.asp?t=report&id=179&search=
Ropi, I. (2007) 'Regulating worship', *Inside Indonesia*, 89(January–March).
Ropi, I. (2010) 'Islamism, government regulation, and the Ahmadiyah controversies in Indonesia', *Al-Jami'ah Journal of Islamic Studies*, 48(2): 281–320.
Setara Institute (2011) *Report on Freedom of Religion and Belief 2011*, Jakarta.
Setara Institute (2012a) *Leadership without Initiative: The Condition of Religious Freedom in Indonesia 2012*, Jakarta.
Setara Institute (2012b) *Report on Freedom of Religion and Belief 2012*, Jakarta.
Setara Institute (2013) 'Stagnasi kebebasan beragama: laporan kondisi kebebasan beragama/berkeyakinan tahun 2013' [The stagnation of religious freedom: report on the conditions of freedom of religion/belief 2013]. Available at http://setara-institute.org/wp-content/uploads/2014/11/Laporan-KBB-2013_Stagnasi-Kebebasan-Beragama_Setara-Institute.pdf
Siahaan, A. (2011) 'Jakarta journo: SBY's legacy soiled on freedom of faith', *Jakarta Globe*, 20 March.
Suaedy, A. (2010) 'Religious freedom and violence in Indonesia', in A. Ota, M. Okamoto and A. Suaedy (eds) *Islam in Contention: Rethinking Islam and State in Indonesia*, Center for Southeast Asian Studies, Kyoto University, Kyoto: 139–69.
Timberman, D. (2009) 'Yudhoyono's re-election: can SBY and Indonesia up their game?', *East Asia Forum*, 10 July.
United States Commission on International Religious Freedom (2014) '15th anniversary retrospective: renewing the commitment', annual report, Washington DC. Available at http://www.uscirf.gov/reports-briefs/annual-report/2014-annual-report
Wahid Institute (2013) 'Laporan tahunan kebebasan beragama/berkeyakinan dan intoleransi 2013' [Annual report on freedom of religion/belief and intolerance 2013], Jakarta.
Wilson, I. (2014a) 'Resisting democracy: Front Pembela Islam and Indonesia's 2014 elections', *ISEAS Perspective*, 24 February.
Wilson, I. (2014b) 'Morality racketeering: vigilantism and populist Islamic militancy in Indonesia', in K.B. Teik, V. Hadiz and Y. Nakanishi (eds) *The Transformation of Islamic Politics in the Middle East and Asia*, PalgraveMacmillan, Houndmills: 248–74.

14 Big commitments, small results: environmental governance and climate change mitigation under Yudhoyono

Patrick Anderson, Asep Firdaus and Avi Mahaningtyas

Under the Yudhoyono presidency, the environment featured in Indonesia's national and international politics with a prominence it had never previously achieved. It was not just the slew of new policies and initiatives; President Yudhoyono himself seemed to take the issue more seriously than any previous Indonesian president. This was most dramatically demonstrated at the G20 conference in Pittsburgh in 2009 when he announced to the world that, by itself, Indonesia would reduce its carbon emissions below business-as-usual projections by 26 per cent by 2020, and by 41 per cent if the country received international support. With some 80 per cent of Indonesia's emissions the result of forestry and land-use change, in 2010 Yudhoyono issued a two-year moratorium on the issuing of new permits to develop primary forests and peatlands, a proscription that covered 74 million hectares of forest land and that was subsequently extended until 2015. At a conference in 2011 he promised to 'dedicate the last three years of my term as President to deliver enduring results that will sustain and enhance the environment and forests of Indonesia' (Lang 2011). In 2013 he established a national agency for reducing emissions from deforestation and forest degradation. For these and other reasons, Yudhoyono has sometimes been lauded at home and abroad for his environmental commitments and achievements. Upon stepping down as Indonesian president, he goes on to become the chair and president of the Global Green Growth Institute, an international organisation with a mission to promote environmentally sustainable economic development.

This chapter assesses Yudhoyono's environmental record by considering two major initiatives that took place during his time in office: the passage and implementation of a new environmental law, and the introduction of plans for climate change mitigation. The new Environment Law, the aim of which was to provide environmental protection and management for the benefit of all citizens, resulted from the efforts of a broad coalition in parliament, including Yudhoyono's party, and created big opportunities to improve environmental management. Addressing climate change was very much Yudhoyono's own issue, which he promoted at home and especially abroad. The president and his government were able to bring in new environmental and climate policies and link them to public participation and anti-corruption efforts. Under the president's guidance, the government opened itself to public participation and much greater transparency in environmental and forest governance. The ambitious policy framework took Yudhoyono's government further than any previous administration in the environment sector.

Implementation of the new laws and policies required strong leadership to challenge established power bases in the sectoral ministries and undue influence from industry. Yudhoyono did not rise to that challenge, however, instead letting the Ministry of Environment and the new climate change agencies struggle to fulfil their mandates. Implementation of the Environment Law and climate commitments was hampered by Yudhoyono's failure to push through reform efforts against resistance from sectoral ministries and associated industries. Meanwhile, despite all the initiatives, the climate change policies had limited effect. After falling in the early 2000s, the rate of deforestation doubled during Yudhoyono's tenure and has yet to fall. During the same period Brazil halved its rate of forest loss, due in part to stronger leadership and more transparent and accountable government institutions. There was a yawning gap between President Yudhoyono's environmental commitments, and the results.

In the first section of this chapter, we assess the Environment Law of 2009. Although the law was a landmark in environmental protection and facilitated court action to prevent environmental destruction, its implementation was severely hampered by governmental paralysis when it came to introducing critical implementing regulations and law enforcement. In the second section we describe Indonesia's new policy framework for reducing greenhouse gas emissions. Next, we look at several policy steps the government took to reform the management of Indonesia's forests and so pursue the climate change agenda. Though the policy change was significant, in every area there were significant problems of implementation. In the fourth section we assess the results so far of Indonesia's attempts to reduce its greenhouse gas emissions, and summarise the problems of policy design and political economy that generated a record of failure. We conclude by contrasting the dramatic policy goals and frameworks introduced by the Yudhoyono administration with the disappointing results.

A NEW ENVIRONMENTAL LAW

Law 32/2009 on Environmental Protection and Management was issued in October 2009. The effort to create the new law came more from the parliament than the administration. Although legislators from Yudhoyono's party supported the law, the Ministry of Environment was active in its drafting, and the new law strengthened the role of the ministry in government. The Environment Law (which replaced Law 23/1997) was framed to address the significant increase in exploitation of natural resources, including mining and forest conversion for agriculture, and to increase public involvement and government accountability. It contained a number of new norms, including a mechanism for environmental permits, protection for environmental activists and punishment for officials who failed to fulfil their official duties.

A positive feature of the new law was how it linked protection and management of the environment to good governance; successfully preventing pollution and damage to the environment required the government to involve civil society through transparency, participation, accountability and fairness. Under the law, all new legislation at the national and regional levels affecting natural resources had to respect the principles of environmental protection and management, and all development plans had to undergo a strategic environmental assessment before they could be approved. The law treated corporations as subjects of environmental criminal law and mandated the establishment of regulations respecting indigenous peoples' local knowledge and rights in regard to protecting and managing the environment, a critical issue seeing that marginalisation of indigenous communities was so often linked to environmental destruction. The strength and ambition of the new law was recognised by civil society and academia (Santosa 2014).

The legal framework for good governance in environmental management produced by the law, however, did not lead to improved practices in the sector, due to the administration's failure to develop supporting regulations. The Environment Law mandated 19 government regulations to be issued within one year of its enactment. The most important of these was a regulation on strategic environmental assessments. In the year after the law was passed, the Ministry of Environment held extensive consultations with experts and civil society organisations and produced a draft regulation based on these efforts. Disappointed ministry staff noted, however, that the draft regulation was rejected by the other natural resource ministries, which saw it as threatening their current activities, which would have been limited by the strategic environmental assessments. In the end Yudhoyono failed to issue the regulation, and the Ministry of Environment was left without the means to implement the new law and rein in environmental damage being facilitated by other ministries.

By the end of the Yudhoyono presidency, five years after the Environment Law was passed, only one implementing regulation had been issued. This regulation created a system of environmental permits for managing and protecting the environment. Businesses whose activities would have an impact on the environment had to obtain an environmental permit before those activities could begin; any licences for plantations or mining would be null and void without the necessary permit. The system of environmental permits was not implemented consistently, however, because of conflicts of interest involving local authorities. District government heads (*bupati*) had been empowered in the years following the fall of Suharto to issue permits for the exploitation of natural resources and many of them accessed major patronage resources from doing so (KPK 2010). The district heads were also authorised to approve environmental and social impact assessments (Analisis Mengenai Dampak Lingkungan, AMDAL), a conflict of interest that inevitably saw destructive developments approved despite the environmental consequences. District environmental agencies (Badan Lingkungan Hidup Daerah, BLHD) were controlled by local governments, and the national Ministry of Environment remained unable to control AMDAL approvals. This situation was a major problem given the endemic corruption found in district governments. The Ministry of Home Affairs recently noted that 325 district heads—well over half of all the *bupati* in Indonesia—had been indicted for corruption in the past few years (Ministry of Home Affairs 2014).

A positive development resulting from the Environment Law was that it provided the legal basis for civil society organisations to bring cases against companies that damaged the environment. Between 2009 and 2014, the Indonesian Forum for the Environment (Wahana Lingkungan Hidup Indonesia, WALHI) brought 12 civil environmental cases to the courts and reported many other environmental crimes to the police, although none of them led to prosecutions. Of the 12 cases handled by WALHI, three led to court rulings against the defendant. In 2012, for example, WALHI won a lawsuit cancelling the business permit of PT

Kallista Alam for the development of an oil palm plantation covering 1,605 hectares in the Tripa peat swamp, part of the Leuser Ecosystem in southern Aceh, one of the most important habitats for orangutan in Sumatra.

Separately, the Ministry of Environment won a civil suit against PT Kallista Alam in the district court of Meulaboh, Aceh, in January 2014. After obtaining and verifying reports of fires in the company's concession in 2012, the ministry concluded that it had violated the law by using fire to clear 1,000 hectares of forest, or at least by letting the fires cause extensive damage. The court found that PT Kallista Alam had acted unlawfully and ordered it to pay roughly $1 million in damages and $2 million for remediation. The environment minister commented:

> The success in winning this lawsuit against the use of fire to clear forest is a good lesson for us in applying the polluter-pays principle. Payment for compensation and environmental recovery can be a deterrent to other environmentally destructive companies (Ministry of Environment 2014).

This was one of the first times that the government had used the courts to prosecute a company for burning peatland.

The case against PT Kallista Alam was brought as part of a much larger government effort. In 2009, Yudhoyono committed his administration to bringing 100 criminal and 100 civil environmental cases to the courts each year.[1] In practice, however, the government brought only 43 criminal cases involving violations of the Environment Law before the courts in the four years to mid-2013, and only 20 civil cases in the five years to mid-2014.

The Tripa case and a handful of other court victories showed that a legal framework more conducive to environmental protection was slowly coming into place, helped by the passage of the Environment Law. Overall, however, the deeply problematic implementation of the law was emblematic of the wider fate of environmental policy and protection under the Yudhoyono presidency. As a framework, the law was a clear improvement on previous legislation. But its implementation all but stalled as soon as the government encountered strong resistance from vested interests. In practice, policy paralysis was the result. In the end, much as in the past, citizens organised through the civil society sector (supported by some officials in the Ministry of Environment) were again thrown onto the frontline of environmental protection, where they confronted a mammoth task.

---

1 Presidential Regulation 5/2010 on the National Medium-term Development Plan 2010–2014. See also Ministry of Environment (n.d.).

REDUCING GREENHOUSE GAS EMISSIONS

Yudhoyono's leadership on climate change was especially clear in his commitments at the international level. As already noted, Yudhoyono's big climate change policy to reduce greenhouse gas emissions was made at the Pittsburgh G20 meeting in 2009. In pledging to reduce Indonesia's emissions by between 26 and 41 per cent below business-as-usual projections by 2020, Yudhoyono changed the game in the climate talks from one of cuts in emissions for developed countries only, to one of cuts for both developed and developing countries. His initiative set a high bar for other developing countries and generated new partnerships in addressing the impending climate crisis. At the international level, Yudhoyono's climate commitments received high praise and contributed to his global reputation as a visionary leader.

However, there was a wide gap between Yudhoyono's commitments and the development of his climate change program domestically. Neither national nor subnational governments were well informed about the president's promises and his office largely failed to coordinate follow-up actions to develop implementing policies. The progress that was made owed more to talented individuals than to wider efforts to integrate climate policy into the existing national government planning and bureaucracy. Fiefdoms in the natural resource ministries did not regard Yudhoyono's climate commitments as a priority, as they went against established development approaches.

Meanwhile, many at home saw Yudhoyono's policy commitment as being unrealistic. The methodology used to arrive at the 26–41 per cent target was never explained. Some officials said that the president wanted to challenge the G20 by offering to take on a reduction target that was 1 per cent higher than the commitment Japan had made two weeks before the Pittsburgh meeting.[2] Critically, although most of the policy debates in subsequent years have been based on achieving mitigation in line with Yudhoyono's commitment to reduce emissions by between 26 and 41 per cent, the government's plans to reduce deforestation, which is responsible for some 80 per cent of Indonesia's emissions, were not tied to a definitive rate of reduction within a specific timeframe.[3] At the end of Yudhoyono's presidency in October 2014, Indonesia had yet to announce

---

2   Avi Mahaningtyas's personal communication with Ministry of Forestry officials, 2011. See also 'Japan's new prime minister promises ambitious greenhouse gas cuts', *Guardian*, 7 September 2009.
3   Presidential Decree 61/2011 on the National Action Plan to Reduce Greenhouse Gas Emissions sets out the government's guidelines for achieving the 26–41 per cent emission reduction target.

Figure 14.1 Carbon dioxide emissions of the major emitters by sector (million tonnes)[a]

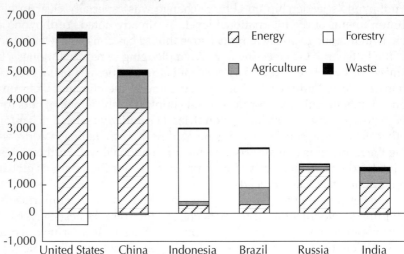

a The European Union is excluded from the comparison. If its 25 countries were included as a block, then the ranking would be United States, European Union, China and Indonesia. The data for energy emissions are from 2003; the data for agriculture and waste are from 2005; and the data for forestry are from 2000.
Source: World Bank (2007: 2).

the national emissions reference level from which emission reductions would be calculated.

Indonesia houses the third-largest area of tropical forests in the world, with about 122 million hectares (Satgas REDD+ 2012). These forests are home to rich biodiversity and the customary (*adat*) forests of tens of millions of indigenous people. Deforestation contributes most to Indonesia's emissions, and Indonesia is the third-largest greenhouse gas emitter after the United States and China (Figure 14.1). Deforestation in the 1990s was massive, with an annual rate of loss of 2 million hectares (Leitmann et al. 2009: 54). Forest fires in Borneo and Sumatra in the El Niño year 1997 released about 9 billion tonnes of carbon dioxide (CO^2), compared to an average annual rate of emissions from forest loss of 1.4 billion tonnes of CO^2. In comparison, Australia's annual emissions from all sources are roughly 500 million tonnes of CO^2. During the first term of Yudhoyono's presidency, the annual deforestation rate was around 1.5 million hectares (2005–09), compared to 1 million hectares annually from 2002 to 2004.

The problem for climate change mitigation policies that focus on deforestation is that they rapidly become entangled with Indonesia's complex political economy, and with powerful contrary interests. Timber, oil and mining have been key sources of revenue for Indonesia since the 1970s. Today, agriculture and plantations contribute more than 25 per cent to national revenue. Companies involved in these sectors have great lobbying power—and informal connections with political elites— at the central government level. Indonesia's framework for decentralised government is another complicating factor. In 1999, following the fall of the Suharto regime, many of the powers of the central government were devolved to district governments, including the right to issue permits for forestry and forest conversion. With district governments lacking spatial plans and transparent permitting procedures, decentralisation resulted in an even higher rate of deforestation, as well as conflicts with local communities and corruption in the licensing process. Bribes associated with licensing in the land-use sector remain a source of funding for politicians and their parties, with corruption driving misuse of land allocation procedures, deforestation and increased greenhouse gas emissions (KPK 2010; Burgess et al. 2012). While the period of Yudhoyono's administration saw anti-corruption efforts intensify, these efforts largely failed to tackle the informal system of election financing whereby illegal funds were raised through promises to provide licences in the forestry, mining and plantation sectors. As a result, a key driver of deforestation remained untouched.

The policy framework that Indonesia has been pursuing to reduce deforestation is known as Reducing Emissions from Deforestation and Degradation (REDD). REDD and its offshoot, REDD+, are financing programs to reward efforts to reduce greenhouse gas emissions caused by deforestation and degradation. REDD+ expands the REDD program to include support for sustainable forest management, afforestation and reforestation. In Indonesia the REDD+ program has developed a strong focus on reform of forest and land-use tenure and governance, and has been a catalyst for changes from business-as-usual development and top-down planning towards good governance practices that respect and support community rights (Larson, Brockhaus and Sunderlin 2012).

The REDD framework was proposed at the 2007 United Nations Framework Convention on Climate Change (UNFCCC) Conference of Parties, held in Bali. It was conceived as an international partnership that could reduce emissions and thus help to keep increases in global surface temperature to below 2 degrees Celsius. Indonesia was thrust into the international spotlight on climate change for the first time at the Bali conference, and that is when it began to develop national policy on the issue. The Bali conference inspired Yudhoyono to make his big announcement at Pittsburgh, to world acclaim. In subsequent UNFCCC meetings from Poznan (2008) to Warsaw (2013), Indonesia's approach in the climate talks was to make everyone a friend and no one an enemy.

While governments such as Brazil were concerned about the sovereignty implications of REDD+ because of its use of a market mechanism that could lead to the privatisation of forests, the Indonesian government said yes to every major proposal during the negotiations on REDD+, covering financing, safeguards, emission levels, deforestation, carbon stocks and technology transfer.

A major development six months after Yudhoyono's Pittsburgh speech was Norway's offer to give Indonesia $1 billion to reduce emissions from deforestation and the degradation of forests and peatland, involving a partnership based on measurable outputs and responsibilities. The letter of intent signed by Indonesia and Norway in May 2010 pushed forward the need for reform in forestry governance. Implementation of the partnership has encouraged the inclusion of diverse stakeholders and increased transparency in forestry planning, while its activities have focused on the implementation of the moratorium on licensing in primary forests and peatlands, the harmonisation of policies across government to achieve emission reductions and ways to increase respect for the rights of forest peoples.

The Indonesian government established a national REDD+ taskforce in late 2010. Known as Satgas REDD+, it was led by Kuntoro Mangkusubroto, an experienced and respected technocrat and the head of the Presidential Working Unit for Development Monitoring and Oversight (Unit Kerja Presiden Bidang Pengawasan dan Pengendalian Pembangunan, UKP4), established in 2009 to oversee the implementation of key government policies. The main tasks of Satgas REDD+ were to create a REDD+ national strategy; establish a REDD+ agency; set up financing mechanisms; establish independent monitoring, reporting and verification institutions; and select a pilot province for REDD+ implementation. The REDD+ agency was established in December 2013 and almost all the other objectives were achieved by early 2014 (Prasetyo 2014), although the financing mechanisms and standardised monitoring, reporting and verification methodologies were still under development in late 2014.

REFORMING FORESTRY AND PUTTING IN PLACE A REDD+ FRAMEWORK

Most studies and publications on REDD+ note that there can be no effective REDD+ implementation without transparency and accountability measures, and without addressing tenure conflicts and insecurity for forest peoples (Larson, Brockhaus and Sunderlin 2012; Anderson and Colchester 2013). As already noted, corruption in the forestry and land-use sectors stands out as the major factor driving deforestation and limiting reform efforts in Indonesia (KPK 2010, 2013; Sjafrina, Widoyoko and Abid 2013). The government did address these issues, but in ways that fell far short of achieving the ambitious goals set by Yudhoyono. The following points cover the range of activities undertaken by the government to address Indonesia's high emissions, as well as its major governance challenges in forestry and land use.

Promoting community forests

Seventy per cent of the land area of Indonesia is classified as forest zone, and some 33,000 villages, home to tens of millions of people, are located within this area. Villages within the forest zone, however, are denied the right to own, use and manage their forests, with the government instead issuing industrial forestry licences over the same areas. For decades, Indonesian communities and non-government organisations have been protesting this state control of forests and consequent criminalisation of forest communities, and calling for government recognition of community rights within the forests. In response, early in Yudhoyono's administration — even before the climate change agenda became a major driver of policy change — the Ministry of Forestry created regulations for community forestry licences. While still a long way from recognising customary forest rights, these licensing schemes offered communities forestry management rights and paths out of poverty. Research around the world has shown that where communities have secure rights in forests, there are major environmental, social and economic benefits compared to when the same forests are under government or industry management (Colchester et al. 2005; Porter-Bolland et al. 2011: 9).

In 2009, Yudhoyono's administration stated that by the end of 2014 it would establish 2 million hectares of community forests, 500,000 hectares of village forests and 250,000 hectares of community plantations — different forms of leasehold tenure newly available to communities. If established, community licences over this area would represent about 3 per cent of the forest estate — tiny in comparison to industrial forestry licences, which cover more than 30 per cent, but an important step nevertheless towards recognising community rights in forests. However, by the end of 2014 only 85,000 hectares of community forests, less than 70,000 hectares of village forests and less than 200,000 hectares of community plantations had been licensed. After five years, the government had reached only 10 per cent of its target for community forestry, covering less than 0.3 per cent of the forest estate. The Ministry of Forestry is known as one of the most corrupt agencies in Indonesia, a captured bureaucracy serving the forestry industry, and an entity that fiercely defends itself from outside pressures for reform. Yudhoyono was not willing to take on the challenge of insisting that small areas of forests be licensed for communities and proved unable to hold the ministry to its promises to reform itself.

Forest tenure reform and recognition of indigenous peoples' role in forest management

In July 2011, in connection with a proposal to develop a single map delineating forest usage rights (see below), Kuntoro Mangkusubroto, the head of both UKP4 and the REDD+ taskforce, called for greater efforts to resolve conflicts in forest use and ownership and undertake forest tenure reform. In his speech, he called for recognition of local communities and indigenous peoples in forest management and conflict resolution (Mangkusubroto 2011). He also supported calls from civil society groups for the establishment of a multi-stakeholder working group on tenure in Jakarta to work closely with the Ministry of Forestry to create a roadmap for forest tenure reform.

In a related development, the Constitutional Court ruled in 2012 that, contrary to the provisions of the Forestry Law, the forests of customary communities were not state forests. After decades of being treated as illegal squatters in the forest zone, indigenous peoples hoped that their rights would now be respected, and that the government would stop issuing industrial logging and plantation licences over their forest areas. In response to the decision, Yudhoyono instructed the Ministry of Forestry to accelerate the implementation of the court's decision.

In 2014, the Ministry of Home Affairs issued a regulation setting out the procedure for district governments to recognise and endorse customary communities—a prerequisite for halting further encroachment on indigenous lands and resolving conflicts among rival claimants.[4] In September 2014, Vice-President Boediono launched a national program to recognise and protect indigenous peoples through the implementation of REDD+. Supported by nine ministries and government agencies, the program aimed to give indigenous peoples the legal standing and capacity to make them an integral part of the country's REDD+ activities.

The above steps increased the likelihood that Indonesia's programs to reduce emissions from deforestation would be successful. The implementation of these important policies, however, will be up to the next government.

---

4 Ministry of Home Affairs Regulation 52/2014 on Guidelines for the Recognition and Protection of Customary Communities.

The One Map Movement

In the same speech in which he called for increased recognition of indigenous communities in forest management, Kuntoro Mangkusubroto instructed government agencies to construct a single map from the numerous maps, spatial datasets and licensing information held by various ministries (Mangkusubroto 2011). This initiative was called the One Map Movement, to demonstrate the government's aspiration to involve both state and non-state actors—including the thousands of local communities and indigenous peoples living in Indonesia's forests—in the compilation of a single, comprehensive map.[5]

At the time, the maps held by different ministries showing licences, concessions, conservation areas and the like were almost impossible to obtain. Even when those maps were made available, they often conflicted with each other, indicating that different entities had rights over the same land. The absence of a credible, comprehensive map created uncertainty for investors and communities alike. In the business licensing process, this uncertainty aided corruption. A map of forestry concessions overlaid on a map of forest cover showed that most of Indonesia's remaining areas of forest were available to be exploited for logging, mining and pulpwood plantations or for conversion to agriculture. This had important implications for climate change policy; the planned payments for performance in reducing emissions could only be made if land was not subject to overlapping licences. Measuring, reporting and verification procedures to reward efforts to reduce emissions from deforestation also required a comprehensive map and baseline.

Forest communities asked for their rights to their customary forests to be recognised as part of the process of synchronising Indonesia's conflicting maps and land-use plans. In response to a request from UKP4's One Map working group, in 2012 the Alliance of Indigenous Peoples of the Archipelago (Aliansi Masyarakat Adat Nusantara, AMAN) submitted the latest versions of its maps of customary (*adat*) community lands, identifying some 3 million hectares of perhaps 50 million hectares of community forests. To help indigenous groups present their maps in a standardised format, the government's REDD+ and geospatial agencies have launched a computer application for participatory mapping.[6]

---

5 For more on the origins of and thinking behind the One Map Movement, see the interview with Kasmita Widodo, director of the Participatory Mapping Network and head of the Ancestral Domain Registration Agency, in Down to Earth (2012).
6 An online version of this mapping tool can be accessed at http://petakita.ina-sdi.or.id.

UKP4's One Map working group, consisting of both government and non-government representatives, has also developed a claim and verification procedure that the Ministry of Forestry will be able to use to address third-party claims in the forest delineation process. With many parties expected to submit claims over the same areas of forest, this procedure will be important in guiding conflict resolution efforts to settle conflicting claims.

Memorandum of understanding on the acceleration of forest gazettement

In May 2013, President Yudhoyono, Kuntoro Mangkusubroto and leaders of the Corruption Eradication Commission (Komisi Pemberantasan Korupsi, KPK) witnessed the signing of a memorandum of understanding (MOU) between 12 ministries and state agencies to accelerate forest gazettement as part of forest governance reform.[7] Gazettement involves delineating the boundaries of the forest zone and establishing which forest areas are burdened with rights, including those of licence holders and local communities. Like the One Map Movement, it is a critical preparatory step in reform, involving clarifying exactly who has rights over what land, but it has in the past been stalled by corruption associated with licensing and land allocation. If done properly and justly, this process should involve the national government, local governments, landowners and land users, including local communities.

The MOU was a breakthrough in getting ministries and the National Commission for Human Rights (Komisi Nasional Hak Asasi Manusia, Komnas HAM) to cooperate in reforming forest and natural resources governance. The KPK with its legal enforcement authority and UKP4 with its supervisory mandate drove implementation of the MOU. All 12 institutions involved submitted action plans and indicators for the achievement of forest gazettement based on a self-assessment framework. In mid-2014, the team working to implement the MOU produced a list of 400 actions to speed up gazettement. In late 2014 it compiled a list of actions that had been taken to address licensing violations, including corruption cases against 250 district heads involved in the illegal issuance of mining licences and the associated revocation of 600 mining permits in forest areas. Other actions included the investigation and prosecution of governors, ministers, bureaucrats and corporations suspected of licensing violations.[8] In a related move, in 2014 Komnas

---

7 Memorandum of Understanding (Nota Kesepakatan Bersama) 12 K/L.
8 This information comes from an unpublished internal report based on feedback from the 12 ministries involved. See also Ministry of Forestry (2014a).

HAM launched a national inquiry into violations of indigenous peoples' rights in contested forests, with 140 cases registered within a few months (Satriastanti 2014).

In mid-2014, the Ministry of Forestry claimed to have gazetted more than half the forest zone, in stark contrast to its efforts over the previous 40 years in which it had managed to gazette only about 10 per cent, even while it handed out exploitation licences over half the forest area. However, the ministry's process in 2013 and 2014 did not involve forest communities, and non-government organisations are challenging the ministry's flawed process and claims.[9]

Moratorium on new licences in primary and peat forests

In 2011, President Yudhoyono instructed his ministers and staff to enforce a two-year moratorium on the issuance of new licences in primary forests and peatlands, which was subsequently extended until mid-2015 (Presidential Instructions 10/2011 and 6/2013). The instructions received a mixed response from the public, because they did not include sanctions for violations or cover secondary forests. Nevertheless, the moratorium had some positive effects. The team set up to implement the moratorium took the action that led to the court decision to revoke the permit of the plantation company draining the Tripa swamp in Aceh, discussed above. Communities and civil society groups were also able to contribute to the effectiveness of the moratorium by reporting violations to the government (Rompas and Waluyo 2013; Mangkusubroto 2012).

However, the Ministry of Forestry found a simple way to subvert the licensing moratorium, by changing the area to which it applied; a 2014 map shows the moratorium area of primary and peat forests as being 5 million hectares smaller than the moratorium area agreed in 2011. The definitions of forest, primary forest and peat forest are still subject to debate and are based on administrative boundaries; they are therefore dependent on political and business interests as much as science. The government's response to breaches of the moratorium was confused, highlighting the need for clear instructions (Mangkusubroto 2012; Eyes on the Forest 2013; Rompas and Waluyo 2013). As a result of such factors, the licensing moratorium has not led to a reduction in the deforestation rate (Butler 2013, 2014a).

---

9 'Kemenhut dituntut buka informasi tata batas hutan' [Ministry of Forestry told to provide access to information on forest boundaries], *hukumonline.com*, 19 May 2014. See also Saturi (2014).

ASSESSING THE OUTCOMES OF CLIMATE CHANGE POLICY

It is important to acknowledge that climate change policy was placed firmly on the nation's development agenda during Yudhoyono's tenure, and that this would not have happened if the president had not made a personal commitment to the issue. To be sure, Yudhoyono may have been driven by a desire to burnish the international image of himself and his government. Even so, by making climate change a government priority, he set in train a chain of events that may end up significantly transforming Indonesia's approach to environmental management and economic development.

The political and empirical debates that have accompanied the development of climate change policies have begun to change the paradigm of development employed in Indonesia. In particular, they have promoted calls for greater transparency, accountability and public participation in development, and for greater respect for the rights of marginalised groups. A large number of much-needed reforms are now embodied in government decrees, new laws and regulations. By creating visibility for the struggles of rural communities and indigenous peoples, the REDD+ debate has helped make government more transparent and responsive to rights violations and more accessible to society using modern means of communication. Implementation of government promises concerning forest management can now be monitored almost in real time. Remote communities can send complaints about impacts on their customary lands to government officials by text message or web-based applications. Lapor, a web-based application developed and run by UKP4, enables users to report directly to the president's office on problems such as violations of the moratorium on new forestry permits.

Despite these positive developments, however, a lack of capacity, weak leadership and conflicts of interest in the sectoral institutions managing forestry and agricultural policy have slowed the pace and depth of reform. Political leaders and parties rely on revenue collected by their cadres and supporters, including by plundering the resources of the state, with natural resource income being one lucrative revenue stream (Sjafrina, Widoyoko and Abid 2013). Companies with forestry and mining concessions tell stories of the unofficial fees they must pay to obtain licences and the payments they must make to elected officials when elections are approaching. Over the last decade, dozens of politicians, many high-level bureaucrats and a plantation CEO have been convicted of corruption associated with the issuance of forest permits (Pramudatama 2012). However, such cases have not yet changed the underlying forces driving corruption in land-use allocation.

There have also been problems with policy design in the climate change area, and limits on the extent to which climate change policy has been able to influence other government priorities. Despite Yudhoyono's promise to reduce greenhouse gas emissions by 2020 and the subsequent action plans, the government failed to produce a clear roadmap to achieve its targets. At the end of his term in office, Indonesia still lacked a deforestation reduction target, accurate maps, greenhouse gas accounting methodologies and even clear definitions of forests, deforestation and its drivers. Economic development strategies pursued at the national and district levels continued to promote deforestation. Oil palm plantations were expanding at 1 million hectares annually, often replacing forests and draining peatlands.[10] With the blessing of the Ministry of Trade, the Indonesian Palm Oil Association (Gabungan Pengusaha Kelapa Sawit Indonesia, GAPKI) set a goal of doubling crude palm oil production from 30 million tonnes in 2012 to 60 million tonnes in 2030.[11] National, provincial and district budgets still funded deforestation, and the Master Plan for the Acceleration and Expansion of Economic Development in Indonesia (Masterplan Percepatan dan Perluasan Pembangunan Ekonomi Indonesia, MP3EI) released in 2011 was based on a model of high carbon-emission development. The six corridors of infrastructure development across Indonesia in the master plan caused fragmentation of ecosystems, migration, conflicts and more deforestation (Rachman 2014). Meanwhile, foreign assistance in support of climate change amelioration was rarely channelled to district-level activities, let alone to communities wanting to protect and manage their forests. Of the $1 billion promised by Norway in May 2010, less than 2 per cent had been disbursed by mid-2014 (Norad 2014).

The ultimate test of the effectiveness of the new policies was of course their impact on the ground, especially in slowing forest loss. Here the picture was very bleak. Estimates of deforestation rates in Indonesia differed by orders of magnitude. The Ministry of Forestry claimed in mid-2014 that the deforestation rate for primary forest in 2011–12 was only 24,000 hectares per year as a result of the licensing moratorium, but it did not reveal its methodology for arriving at this figure (Ministry of Forestry 2014b). More credible estimates put Indonesia's annual loss of primary forests in 2011–12 at between 450,000 hectares (Saturi 2013) and 840,000 hectares (Margono et al. 2014). At the end of 2013, the president reported a decline in deforestation from 3.5 million hectares per year in 1998–2003 to 450,000 hectares per year in 2011–12 (Yudhoyono 2013). Yet other assessments have found that the rate of deforestation in Indonesia

---

10 'Luas kebun sawit mencapai 13.5 juta hektare' [Oil palm plantations expand by 13.5 million hectares], *Tempo*, 5 December 2013.
11 'GAPKI: pasar minyak sawit makin besar' [GAPKI: market for palm oil expands], *Business News*, 23 September 2014.

has doubled in the last decade from 1 million to 2 million hectares annually (Hansen et al. 2012; Margono et al. 2014).

It is informative to compare climate change policy development in Indonesia with the situation in Brazil. In 2007, the Brazilian federal government announced that it would reduce deforestation by 80 per cent below 2000 levels by 2020. A clear methodology for measuring deforestation and the implementation of real-time mapping were announced as part of its National Plan on Climate Change (Government of Brazil 2008). The provision of a reward-and-punishment mechanism in 2008 led to improved governance and business practices in the beef and soya industries, which were the main drivers of deforestation. A national system of publicly accessible, real-time monitoring of deforestation attracted civil society to take part in the monitoring program to combat deforestation. Improved security of tenure for indigenous peoples and local communities led to very low levels of deforestation in the areas they managed (Nepstad et al. 2009; Arima et al. 2014). NGO campaigns encouraged companies to source commodities from cattle ranches and soya farms that pledged, and demonstrated, that they were not contributing to deforestation. Disincentives for municipalities included being added to a 'Ring of Fire' list (a red list of municipalities with high rates of forest fire and deforestation), which meant that they could not easily access government credit facilities (Viana et al. 2012).

Yet, reducing deforestation in Brazil did not hamper commodity production or slow economic development. Brazil's economy grew about 40 per cent during the period of declining deforestation (Butler 2014b). The comparison with Indonesia is dramatic: Brazil succeeded in introducing effective mechanisms in many areas while Indonesia still struggled even to define its targets. It is not surprising that Indonesia surpassed Brazil as the country with the highest annual deforestation rate, despite Indonesia's forest area being only one-quarter the size of the Brazilian Amazon (Margono et al. 2014).

CONCLUSION

Our discussion of policy challenges in this chapter hardly exhausts the list of critical areas of environmental and land policy where the Yudhoyono government proclaimed grand goals but achieved, at best, mixed results. We might have devoted space, for example, to the issue of forest fires, lit each year to clear forest for pulpwood and oil palm plantations in Sumatra and Kalimantan, and spreading haze across much of Southeast Asia. Yudhoyono's 2009 environmental targets included a commitment to reduce the number of forest fires by 20 per cent each year in

Kalimantan, Sumatra and Sulawesi. Addressing this issue required prosecuting plantation companies that used fire to clear forests—an illegal activity. However, many plantation companies are owned by Indonesia's wealthiest businessmen, some of whom are major political donors. As a result, despite growing pressure from Malaysia and Singapore, which continue to be blanketed in haze each year, there has been no significant reduction in the number or area of fires. The few companies that have been prosecuted have received insignificant fines.

The passage of the 2009 Environment Law was a significant development that offered big opportunities for improved environmental protection and management. However, Yudhoyono failed to furnish the law with the required implementing regulations, and the environmental targets he set for his administration in his 2009 five-year plan were not realised. In the climate change area, his administration was able to turn bold promises into policies, regulations and new agencies. But the next critical step of actually using those initiatives to reduce deforestation failed, and associated emissions did not fall. The failings reflected the president's unwillingness to take on the tough fight against the powerful sectoral ministries that were resisting reform, and the vested interests behind them.

Susilo Bambang Yudhoyono has often been accused of being interested above all in image-building and personal reputation. In the case of environmental policy, it is hard to judge the depth of his motivations to protect Indonesia's environment and reduce the country's rate of greenhouse gas emissions. Certainly, before his dramatic Pittsburgh speech in 2009, Yudhoyono was not known for taking a major personal interest in environmental issues. But his 2009 promises captured world attention and moved environmental issues to the centre of policy-making in ways that had not previously been seen in Indonesia. With his new role in the Global Green Growth Institute, Yudhoyono now has an international platform that will extend beyond his presidency. Yet the failures of follow-up in critical areas of environmental policy can only provide additional ammunition for those who accuse Yudhoyono of being concerned with image above substance.

REFERENCES

Anderson, P. and M. Colchester (2013) 'Local forest governance, free, prior, and informed consent and REDD+ in Indonesia: a case study from Aceh, Sumatra', in H. Jonas, H. Jonas and S.M. Subramanian (eds) *The Right to Responsibility: Resisting and Engaging Development, Conservation, and the Law in Asia*, Natural Justice and United Nations University–Institute of Advanced Studies, Malaysia: 176–87.
Arima, E.Y., P. Barreto, E. Araujo and B. Soares-Filho (2014) 'Public policies can reduce tropical deforestation: lessons and challenges from Brazil', *Land Use Policy*, 41: 465–73.
Burgess, R., M. Hansen, B.A. Olken, P. Potapov and S. Sieber (2012) 'The political economy of deforestation in the tropics', *Quarterly Journal of Economics*, 127(4): 1,707–54.
Butler, R.A. (2013) 'Deforestation accelerates in Indonesia, finds Google forest map', *Mongabay.com*, 14 November.
Butler, R.A. (2014a) 'Despite moratorium, Indonesia now has the world's highest deforestation rate', *Mongabay.com*, 29 June.
Butler, R.A. (2014b) 'Deforestation in the Amazon', *Mongabay.com*, 9 July.
Colchester, M. et al. (2005) 'Facilitating agroforestry development through land and tree tenure reforms in Indonesia', ICRAF Southeast Asia Working Paper No. 2005_2, World Agroforestry Centre (ICRAF), Bogor.
Down to Earth (2012) 'Indonesia's "one map policy"', DTE 93-94, December. Available at http://www.downtoearth-indonesia.org/story/indonesia-s-one-map-policy
Eyes on the Forest (2013) 'Kalimantan forest monitoring consortium: APP supplier continues forest clearance after moratorium', Pontianak, 17 December. Available at http://www.eyesontheforest.or.id/?page=news&action=view&id=683
Government of Brazil (2008) 'Executive summary: National Plan on Climate Change, Brazil', Interministerial Committee on Climate Change, Brasilia, December.
Hansen, M.C. et al. (2013) 'High-resolution global maps of 21st-century forest cover change', *Science*, 342(6,160): 850–53.
KPK (Komisi Pemberantasan Korupsi) (2010) 'Corruption impact assessment: titik korupsi dalam lemahnya kepastian hukum pada kawasan hutan' [Corruption impact assessment: corruption points to the legal uncertainty over forest areas], Directorate of Research and Development, KPK, Jakarta.
KPK (Komisi Pemberantasan Korupsi) (2013) 'Kajian sistem perizinan di sektor sumber daya alam (SDA): studi kasus sektor kehutanan' [Review of the licensing system in the natural resources sector: case study in the forestry sector], progress report, Directorate of Research and Development, KPK, Jakarta, 6 February.
Lang, C. (2011) 'President Yudhoyono promises to dedicate the next three years to protecting Indonesia's forests', *redd-monitor.org*, 28 September. Available at http://www.redd-monitor.org/2011/09/28/president-yudhoyono-promises-to-dedicate-the-next-three-years-to-protecting-indonesias-forests/
Larson, A.M., M. Brockhaus and W.D. Sunderlin (2012) 'Tenure matters in REDD+: lessons from the field', in A. Angelsen, M. Brockhaus, W.D. Sunderlin and L.V. Verschot (eds) *Analysing REDD+: Challenges and Choices*, Center for International Forestry Research (CIFOR), Bogor: 153–75. Available at http://www.cifor.org/publications/pdf_files/Books/BAngelsen1201.pdf

Leitmann, J. et al. (2009) *Investing in a More Sustainable Indonesia: Country Environmental Analysis*, CEA Series, East Asia and Pacific Region, World Bank, Washington DC.

Mangkusubroto, K. (2011) 'Importance of land and forest tenure reforms in implementing a climate change sensitive development agenda', keynote address to the International Conference on Forest Tenure, Governance and Enterprise, Lombok, 12 July. Available at http://www.rightsandresources.org/documents/files/doc_2483.pdf

Mangkusubroto, K. (2012) '1 tahun pelaksanaan Inpres X/2011: penundaan pemberian izin dan penyempurnaan tata kelola pada hutan alam primer dan lahan gambut' [One-year implementation of Presidential Instruction 10/2011: suspension of new permits and improvement of good governance over primary forest and peatland], Powerpoint presentation, Unit Kerja Presiden Bidang Pengawasan dan Pengendalian Pembangunan (UKP4), Jakarta, 21 May.

Margono, B.A., P.V. Potapov, S. Turubanova, F. Stolle and M.C. Hansen (2014) 'Primary forest cover loss in Indonesia over 2000–2012', *Nature Climate Change*, 4: 730–35.

Ministry of Environment (2014) 'MenLH menangkan gugatan kasus kebakaran lahan di rawa Tripa-Aceh' [Ministry of Environment wins case on peat fire in Tripa-Aceh], Jakarta, 13 January. Available at http://www.menlh.go.id/menlh-menangkan-gugatan-kasus-kebakaran-lahan-di-rawa-tripa-aceh/

Ministry of Environment (n.d.) 'Fact sheet', Jakarta. Available at http://www.menlh.go.id/DATA/kebakaran_hutan.PDF

Ministry of Forestry (2014a) 'Kemajuan penetapan kawasan hutan: menuju kawasan Indonesia yang mantap' [Progress on forest rezoning: towards definitive forest gazettement in Indonesia], presentation of Directorate General of Forestry Planning, Ministry of Forestry, Jakarta, 15 August.

Ministry of Forestry (2014b) 'Deforestasi Indonesia pada tahun 2011–2012 hanya sebesar 24 ribu hektaa' [Deforestation in Indonesia in 2011–2012 is only 24,000 hectares], Press Release No. S. 409/PHM-1/2014, Jakarta, July. Available at http://www.dephut.go.id/uploads/files/ce7d69be1e3df78967e11864d92d34e1.pdf

Ministry of Home Affairs (2014) 'Saat ini, 325 kepala daerah tersangkut korupsi' [Today, 325 heads of districts and provinces are involved in corruption], Jakarta, 9 May. Available at http://keuda.kemendagri.go.id/berita/detail/1516-saat-ini--325-kepala-daerah-tersangkut-korupsi

Nepstad, D. et al. (2009) 'The end of deforestation in the Brazilian Amazon', *Science*, 326(5,958): 1,350–51.

Norad (Norwegian Agency for Development Cooperation) (2014) 'Real-time evaluation of Norway's International Climate and Forest Initiative: synthesising report 2007–2013', Oslo.

Porter-Bolland, L., E.A. Ellis, M.R. Guariguata, I. Ruiz-Mallén, S. Negrete-Yankelevich and V. Reyes-García (2011) 'Community managed forests and forest protected areas: an assessment of their conservation effectiveness across the tropics', *Forest Ecology and Management*, 268: 6–17.

Pramudatama, R. (2012) 'Prosecutors want to jail tycoon Hartati Murdaya for five years', *Jakarta Post*, 29 November.

Prasetyo, H. (2014) 'REDD+ in Indonesia: challenges and progress', presentation to a stakeholders meeting, Jakarta, 23 April.

Rachman, N.F. (2014) 'MP3EI: master plan percepatan dan perluasan krisis sosial-ekologis Indonesia' [MP3EI: master plan for the acceleration and expansion of socio-ecological crisis in Indonesia], in Sajogyo Institute (ed.) *Proses-proses Kebijakan dan Konsekuensi dari MP3EI* [Processes and Consequences of the MP3EI], Bogor.

Rompas, A. and A.N. Waluyo (2013) 'Laporan pemantauan kejahatan sektor kehutanan di wilayah moratorium Kalimantan Tengah' [Report on monitoring forest crimes in moratorium areas in Central Kalimantan], WALHI Kalteng, Palangkaraya.

Santosa, M.A. (2014) 'Kata pengantar' [Preface], in R. Sembiring (ed.) *Anotasi Undang-undang No. 32 Tahun 2009 tentang Perlindungan dan Pengelolaan Lingkungan Hidup* [Annotation of Law 32/2009 on Environmental Protection and Management], Indonesian Center for Environmental Law (ICEL), Jakarta: iv-xiv.

Satgas REDD+ (2012) 'REDD+ national strategy', REDD+ Taskforce (Satgas REDD+), Jakarta, September.

Satriastanti, F.E. (2014) 'Indonesia probes violations of indigenous rights in contested forests', Thomas Reuters Foundation, 29 May. Available at http://www.trust.org/item/20140529110927-5sw62/?source=fiOtherNews3

Saturi, S. (2013) 'Data deforestasi RI meragukan, metodologi dipertanyakan' [Indonesia's deforestation data are dubious, methodology is questionable], *Mongabay.com*, 13 February.

Saturi, S. (2014) 'Dinilai tertutup, rame-rame desak Kemenhut buka informasi tata batas hutan' [Too tight, public demands that Ministry of Forestry provides information on forest boundaries], *Mongabay.com*, 18 May.

Sjafrina, A., J.D. Widoyoko and L. Abid (2013) 'Menguras bumi, merebut kursi: patronase politik-bisnis alih fungsi lahan. Studi kasus dan rekomendasi' [Extracting earth, grabbing positions in government: patrons in the political business of land conversion. Case study and recommendations], policy paper, Indonesia Corruption Watch, Jakarta, 23 December. Available at http://www.antikorupsi.info/id/doc/menguras-bumi-merebut-kursi

Viana, C., E. Coudel, J. Barlow, J. Nunes Ferreira, T. Gardner and L. Parry (2012) 'From red to green: achieving an environmental pact at the municipal level in Paragominas (Pará, Brazilian Amazon)', paper presented to the 12th Biennial Conference of the International Society for Ecological Economics, Rio de Janeiro, 16-19 June.

World Bank (2007) 'Executive summary: Indonesia and climate change', Working Paper on Current Status and Policies, Department for International Development (World Bank) and PT. Pelangi Energi Abadi Citra Enviro (PEACE), Jakarta, March.

Yudhoyono, S.B. (2013) 'Speech by H.E. Dr. Susilo Bambang Yudhoyono, President of the Republic of Indonesia, at the opening of international workshop on "Tropical Forest Alliance 2020: Promoting Sustainability and Productivity in the Palm Oil and Pulp and Paper Sectors"', Jakarta, 27 June. Available at http://www.forestpeoples.org/sites/fpp/files/news/2013/06/27%20Juni%202013%20-%20Opening%20Speech%20President%20RI%20-%20TFA%202020%20Workshop%20%28Rev%202%20SBY%29%20check%20against%20delivery.pdf

PART 4

The economy and social policies

15 The Indonesian economy during the Yudhoyono decade

*Hal Hill**

After a decade in power, President Susilo Bambang Yudhoyono left Indonesia a more prosperous country than any of his five predecessors. He pledged to be a president who would be 'pro-growth, pro-jobs, pro-poor and pro-green'. That is, he staked his leadership credentials on rapid socio-economic development. At one level, one could argue that he achieved this goal, as the Indonesian economy enjoyed moderately strong growth during his tenure. If one digs deeper, however, it becomes clear that there are contrasting narratives on his economic record. According to one viewpoint, he inherited a fragile economy and political system, and he consolidated both, to the point where Indonesia is now the world's tenth-largest economy (as measured by purchasing power parity) and a robust democracy. An alternative narrative recognises these achievements but also laments Yudhoyono's timidity on key economic reform issues, notably fuel subsidies, the infrastructure deficit, economic nationalism and inequality. These narratives need to be assessed in the light of a range of contextual factors that take into consideration the weight of public expectations in Indonesia, the regional and global economic environments and comparative assessments of the economies of neighbouring states or of the BRIC states (Brazil, Russia, India and China).

---

* I am grateful to the editors for detailed comments on earlier drafts, and to Update participants for useful exchanges. I wish to thank Dr Haryo Aswicahyono, on whose joint work I have drawn. I have also drawn extensively on the detailed analytical commentaries in the 'Survey of recent developments' published regularly in the *Bulletin of Indonesian Economic Studies*.

In this chapter I examine the performance of the Indonesian economy during Yudhoyono's decade in power (2004–14), asking four main questions. First, how did the economy perform according to conventional economic yardsticks? Second, how does this record compare with earlier periods of Indonesian economic development, and with those of comparable countries? Third, how have contextual factors affected Indonesia's economic track record? Fourth, to what extent can one draw a direct causal connection between the economic outcomes and the Yudhoyono presidency, in the sense that the outcomes were a result of initiatives and decisions of the president himself?

Drawing tight causal connections between an administration and a country's economic outcomes is a hazardous exercise given that many factors are not directly amenable to presidential control. This is obviously so in the case of global economic conditions, but domestically too there are many 'veto players' who can frustrate economic policy-making and reform. With this caveat, two broad themes inform this analysis. First, President Yudhoyono presided over a decade of moderately strong economic growth. Coming in the wake of the deepest economic crisis in Indonesian history, and in the context of unprecedented global economic volatility, this must be counted as a major achievement. I explore the factors underpinning this growth and the contribution of the Yudhoyono administration in achieving this outcome. Second, although Yudhoyono presided over the system, he did not, or perhaps could not, attempt any significant economic reform. His economic management was reactive more than proactive. With the key macroeconomic policy settings established, he appointed competent ministers to oversee them—to emphasise, a significant achievement—but as I will argue below, it is difficult to discern any major policy reforms elsewhere. The result has been an economy that is most likely 'crisis-proof', but one that will be unable to achieve the economic dynamism required to lift Indonesia into the ranks of upper middle-income economies as quickly as the Indonesian public expects or some of the official rhetoric projects.

The chapter is organised as follows. The first section establishes some key markers—criteria by which to evaluate the economic record—and considers some contextual factors that affected Indonesia's economic performance over Yudhoyono's decade in office. The second provides an overview of the economy during the Yudhoyono years. The third investigates macroeconomic management, a policy area characterised by both notable successes and a failure to tackle the subsidies issue. The fourth section examines the commercial policy environment, and the fifth provides a case study of one key area of underperformance, infrastructure. The concluding section sums up the main arguments. Yudhoyono inherited a somewhat fragile economy, but one in which the economic policy framework and parameters were clearly established and operational. His major economic legacy was to consolidate this framework and to guide the economy through the 2008–09 global financial crisis. But he was clearly not a reformist president, and he had difficulty tackling a range of admittedly complex policy issues, most notably fuel subsidies and the deepening infrastructure deficit.

SOME PRELIMINARY CONSIDERATIONS

The holder of a PhD in economics from a leading Indonesian university, Bogor Agricultural University (Institut Pertanian Bogor), President Yudhoyono declared that he would be a 'pro-growth, pro-poor, pro-jobs and pro-green' leader.[1] Thus, he clearly articulated the goal of rapid socio-economic development, and he had the intellectual training to develop an analytical framework in pursuit of this objective. It is therefore appropriate to evaluate his administration at least in part according to its economic achievements.

Economic development is about both means and ends. The former refers to the factors that are generally understood to be the key explanators of the large intercountry variations in economic performance. These include prudent macroeconomic management, a stable and outward-looking commercial environment, a trusted and independent legal system that includes protection for property rights, inclusive and broad-based socio-economic development, and politically neutral institutions that underpin these objectives.

What are the major ends? The first rule of government is arguably to 'do no harm', by preserving the socio-economic achievements and legacies of previous governments, ensuring that living standards are protected through economic stability and, importantly, avoiding economic crises. Beyond this conservative agenda, achieving rapid economic growth is the most important criterion, and I will therefore examine the growth record in some detail. Additional core objectives include raising living standards in general and protecting the poor and the vulnerable in particular, enhancing institutional and governance quality and ensuring environmental sustainability. I do not address these additional issues as they are examined elsewhere in this volume.

One could also evaluate the Yudhoyono presidency according to the quality of key ministerial appointments, on the assumption that he had a major, though by no means exclusive, say in his cabinet selection. The

---

1 See, for example, his speech at the 2011 Business for Environment Global Summit, transcribed in Kovacevic (2011).

two most important economic policy-making positions in the Indonesian government are the minister of finance and the governor of the central bank, Bank Indonesia. Here President Yudhoyono's record is exemplary. After an initial transition period, he appointed three finance ministers who were all highly regarded: Sri Mulyani Indrawati (2005–10), Agus Martowardojo (2010–13) and Chatib Basri (2013–14). The Bank Indonesia governors were also regarded as highly competent: Burhanuddin Abdullah (2003–08), Boediono (2008–09), Darmin Nasution (2009–13) and Martowardojo (2013–14).[2] The quality of coordinating economics ministers was more variable, reflecting the fact that this position tends to be as much a political as a technical appointment: Aburizal Bakrie (2004–05), Boediono (2005–08), Sri Mulyani Indrawati (2008–09), Hatta Rajasa (2009–14) and Chairul Tanjung (2014). The standouts among this group were Boediono, vice-president in the second Yudhoyono administration and the country's most important and highly regarded technocrat since the fall of Suharto, and Sri Mulyani during her brief tenure.

As technical, non-party appointments, the effectiveness of ministers holding economics portfolios depends not only on their technical competence and political acumen, but also on the presidential support and protection they receive, especially in difficult times. (The position of the Bank Indonesia governor is institutionally protected.) Here the record is mixed. The one major test case concerned the dispute between Finance Minister Sri Mulyani and Coordinating Minister for Social Welfare Bakrie over the former's refusal to support the latter's business interests during the global financial crisis of late 2008. This case involved a protracted and highly personal public campaign against Sri Mulyani, who was a reforming and highly regarded minister. Eventually her position became untenable and she was forced to resign. The president remained oddly silent throughout this episode and did not publicly support Sri Mulyani.[3] This sent a strong message to the rest of the cabinet, with the clear implication being that reforming ministers who became embroiled in political disputes could not expect presidential support. This was arguably a key reason for the much slower reform momentum during the second Yudhoyono administration.

---

2 Bank Indonesia is an independent agency and presidential appointments require the approval of the parliament. Governors are appointed for five-year terms, and thus Abdullah was inherited from the Megawati administration. Boediono stepped down to become Yudhoyono's vice-presidential running mate in 2009, and Nasution completed his term.

3 See the 'Survey of recent developments' in various editions of the *Bulletin of Indonesian Economic Studies* over this period.

Three contextual factors are relevant in thinking about the economy during the Yudhoyono decade. First, Indonesia has experienced decades of quite rapid economic growth since the mid-1960s. Although it has never grown as fast as China since the late 1970s or the newly industrialising economies (NIEs) in earlier years, among developing countries since the late 1960s it is in the top decile of performers.[4] This emerges clearly from detailed comparative assessments such as the World Bank's 1993 'East Asian miracle' study and its 2008 Commission on Growth and Development report (World Bank 1993, 2008). In other words, growth has been the norm for Indonesia for most of the last half-century, and the record of the past decade should be judged accordingly.

Second, Yudhoyono came to power when Indonesia was still fragile economically and of course politically and institutionally.[5] The country was just five years out from the deepest economic crisis it had ever experienced. Not only had the economy contracted by 13 per cent in 1998, but the banking system and the value of the currency had also collapsed. As in the early years of the Suharto regime, economic growth was by no means assured. Indonesia's economic and political crisis of 1997–98 was comparable to that in the Philippines in the mid-1980s, Argentina in 2001 and the former Soviet Union in the early 1990s. It needs to be remembered that in the Philippines, the closest comparator to Indonesia, it took 20 years (1983–2003) for the country to return to pre-crisis levels of per capita income, compared to just seven years (1997–2004) for Indonesia. The Philippine comparison is particularly apposite because the countries had economic contractions of similar magnitude, 14 per cent in the Philippines in 1985–86, and 13 per cent in Indonesia in 1998. In both countries, a long-lived authoritarian leader was removed from power, after 20 years in the case of the Philippines and 32 years in the case of Indonesia, but without well-defined democratic and constitutional procedures for succession. Both countries had acrimonious relationships with the International Monetary Fund during and after the crises. Both instituted major decentralisation programs within a few years. Both resorted to populist labour market policies that resulted in very weak growth in formal sector employment subsequently.[6]

---

4 Since 1960, per capita income in Indonesia has risen about six times, compared to at least 12 times in China and the four Asian NIEs (Perkins 2013).
5 Technically, per capita income had already returned to pre-crisis levels by 2004, the year in which President Yudhoyono assumed power, so the recovery had been completed. But this is a judgment with the benefit of hindsight. The economy was still fragile in many respects, and growth was not assured.
6 See Pritchett (2011) for a more general examination (and positive comparative assessment) of Indonesia's post-crisis economic performance.

Third, for any assessment of the Indonesian economy over the Yudhoyono decade, the state of the regional and global economies does matter. The decade can be divided into three distinct subperiods in which regional and global economic conditions ranged from highly supportive to very hostile: 2004–08, 2008–09 and 2009–14. From 2004 to mid-2008, the global economy was extremely supportive for Indonesia: there were record commodity prices and easy money, while the global economy was growing strongly.[7] Following the collapse of Lehmann Brothers in September 2008, however, the global economy experienced the most serious economic recession since the 1930s. Growth in the advanced OECD economies declined sharply, triggering serious economic declines in Indonesia's outward-looking neighbours.[8] Commodity prices fell sharply, there was large-scale capital flight from emerging economies such as Indonesia, and for several months international capital markets were frozen. Crucially, however, China continued to grow strongly, thanks to a massive fiscal stimulus. Although the global economy avoided the depression that had been widely forecast, the period since 2009 has also been difficult for Indonesia, characterised by an anaemic global economy, periodic Eurozone near-crises, declining commodity prices and international capital volatility, the latter illustrated by the response of financial markets to the Bernanke 'shock' of May 2013.[9]

THE ECONOMIC RECORD: AN OVERVIEW

Indonesia's growth dynamics since the 1960s are summarised in Figure 15.1. Average per capita income has risen about six-fold, while economic growth (real GDP growth) has been positive in every year since 1965, except during the Asian financial crisis. Over the Yudhoyono decade, growth was positive in every year, generally in the range 5–6 per cent, compared to the 5–8 per cent growth (6.5 per cent average) that was more the norm during the Suharto era. For the decade as a whole, average per capita income rose by a little over 50 per cent.[10] Thus, average annual growth for the decade was respectable, albeit about one percentage point

---

7   Indonesia did, however, experience one challenging subperiod of food price spikes and supply uncertainty in 2007.
8   Singapore, Malaysia and Thailand all experienced negative growth in 2009. For Singapore, it was the most serious economic recession in the nation's history.
9   The Bernanke shock and its implications for Indonesia are discussed in detail in Aswicahyono and Hill (2014).
10 Rather than the claimed trebling reported in some official statistics, based on nominal rupiah amounts.

Figure 15.1 Growth in GDP and GDP per capita, Indonesia, 1960–2013

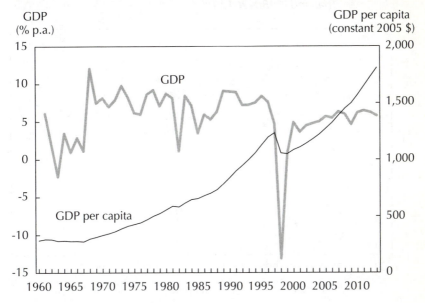

Source: World Development Indicators.

below the official GDP targets (and also the Suharto-era average). Given the initial vulnerabilities and the difficult external environment since 2009, this should be judged a positive achievement.

How did Indonesia fare compared with its middle-income ASEAN neighbours? In 2004–12, its per capita growth rate was comparable to that of the Philippines and Thailand at around 3.5 per cent (Figure 15.2). Its average for the decade was marginally higher owing to the fact that the other two countries experienced sharper contractions during the global financial crisis. The three countries faced the same external environment, with Indonesia benefiting more from the commodity boom and enjoying greater political stability. So this too reflects positively on the Yudhoyono record.

It also needs to be observed that the drivers of growth in the Yudhoyono decade differed from those in the Suharto period. In particular, Indonesia became an increasingly services-driven economy, while manufacturing growth slowed, averaging about half the growth rate of the Suharto period (Figure 15.3). The slower manufacturing growth, misleadingly referred to in some Indonesian commentary as 'deindustrialisation', was partly due to factors beyond the government's control, driven by the commodity boom, which rendered non-commodity tradable sectors such as manufacturing less competitive (through exchange rate and

Figure 15.2   Growth in GDP per capita, Indonesia, the Philippines and Thailand, 1980–2012 (%)

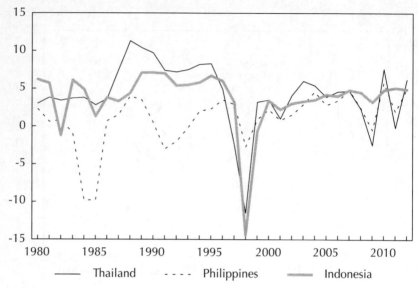

Source: World Development Indicators.

Figure 15.3   Growth in GDP by sector, Indonesia, 1960–2013 (%)

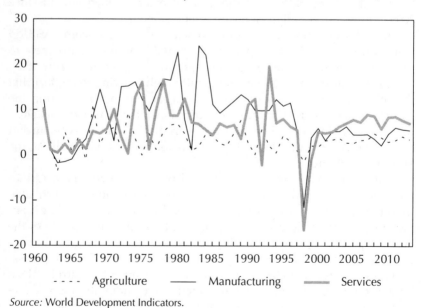

Source: World Development Indicators.

domestic cost effects), and by the global lowering of the prices of lower-end manufactures as China came to dominate these export markets.[11] But it was also a result of the domestic policy environment, characterised by high logistics costs, a less welcoming environment for foreign investors and uncompetitive labour costs. I return to these issues below.

Ineffective industry policy was also a feature of most of the Suharto era. But whereas agriculture was consistently accorded high priority by Suharto, with generally competent ministers and senior officials in the Ministry of Agriculture, during the Yudhoyono period the portfolio was run by officials from the Prosperous Justice Party (Partai Keadilan Sejahtera, PKS), and food policy was both ineffective and corruption-prone. In the latter period, the policy focus was on rents and import-licensing, including costly periodic rice import bans, rather than on productivity and growth. The overall agricultural growth rate held up mainly because of the strong performance of cash crops, driven by buoyant commodity prices.

MACROECONOMIC MANAGEMENT: SUCCESSES AND MISSED OPPORTUNITIES

Macroeconomic stability is crucial to economic progress. Economic crises invariably have their origins in macroeconomic mismanagement, while macroeconomic instability results in slower economic growth. This is therefore a major criterion by which to judge the Yudhoyono administration. With one major exception (the failure to cut subsidies), macroeconomic management was one of the administration's strengths, explaining much of Indonesia's economic growth and resilience over the decade. The administration can take credit for these outcomes, given the high-quality appointments to senior economic policy-making positions.

The Yudhoyono administration inherited a macroeconomic policy framework that had been established in the wake of the Asian financial crisis. The fiscal policy parameters were guided by Law 17/2003 on State Finances, which essentially adopted the EU Maastricht principles that fiscal deficits and the stock of public debt were not to exceed 3 per cent and 60 per cent of GDP respectively. The monetary policy framework, under a then newly independent Bank Indonesia, involved inflation-targeting and a flexible exchange rate. These new arrangements constituted both continuity and change for Indonesia. The continuities were, first, fiscal prudence, enshrined in the Suharto era in the so-called 'balanced budget rule'; second, a mild aversion to inflation; and third, the

---

11 See Aswicahyono, Hill and Narjoko (2013) for a discussion of these factors.

Figure 15.4   Public debt as a share of GDP, Indonesia, 1991–2013 (%)

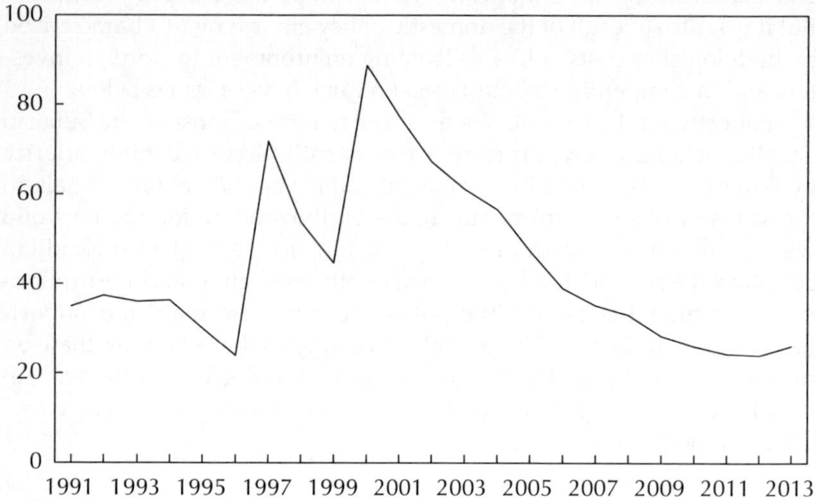

Source: 1991–99: World Development Indicators; 2000–13: Ministry of Finance.

maintenance of an open capital account. But the two major changes in the wake of the Asian financial crisis were significant and desirable. The first was central bank independence, meaning, importantly, that the government could no longer require Bank Indonesia to finance its deficits. The second was a floating exchange rate. A floating rate greatly facilitates management of the boom-and-bust commodity cycle, which has been an ever-present challenge for Indonesia's policy-makers. In effect, it partially insulates the economy from large fluctuations in the terms of trade. Importantly, too, a floating rate imposes a certain discipline on domestic policy excesses, since financial or political uncertainty often triggers capital flight and hence rupiah depreciation.

Unlike the European Union, Indonesia adhered to its fiscal policy framework, with deficits of 1–3 per cent of GDP. Combined with moderate economic growth, some exchange rate appreciations and asset sales, the result was a dramatic fiscal consolidation (Figure 15.4). Before the crisis, Indonesia's public debt was equivalent to about one-quarter of GDP. It then peaked at 90 per cent in 2000 — the danger level according to the highly influential and much-cited Reinhart–Rogoff analysis (Reinhart and Rogoff 2009) — but by 2011 it had returned to the pre-crisis ratio. As a result, Indonesia improved its fiscal policy space and greatly reduced its vulnerability to crises. The consolidation was well under way by the start of the first Yudhoyono term, but it was maintained throughout the decade.

Figure 15.5 Inflation, Indonesia, the Philippines and Thailand, 2000–13 (% p.a.)

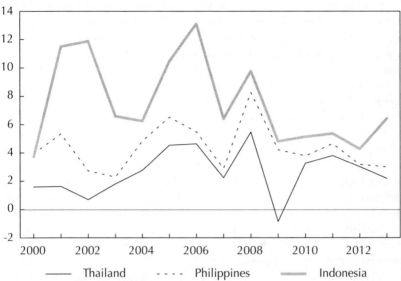

Source: World Development Indicators.

The administration also kept inflation well under control. Indonesia has a history of occasional very high inflation; it experienced hyperinflation in the mid-1960s, for example, and again in 1998 as Bank Indonesia lost control of the money supply. Inflation has been contained since 2000, however, and in most years has been in single digits (Figure 15.5). Nevertheless, Bank Indonesia has struggled to keep inflation at levels comparable to those in neighbouring countries. Inflation has consistently been higher in Indonesia than in the Philippines and Thailand, for example. Once again, this represents continuity with Suharto-era economic management.

The Yudhoyono administration navigated the 2008–09 global financial crisis effectively, in marked contrast to the country's shambolic response to the crisis of 1997–98. As noted, growth dipped only slightly in Indonesia during this period, whereas neighbouring Malaysia, Singapore and Thailand all experienced negative growth in 2009. This achievement was due to a combination of good management and good luck (Basri and Hill 2011). In the latter category were China's continuing strong growth in 2009 and Indonesia's limited participation in East Asia's global production networks in electronics and automobiles, which imploded temporarily during the crisis. In the former category were the government's fiscal prudence in the years preceding the crisis, the floating exchange rate regime, which allowed the rupiah to depreciate and therefore act as a 'shock absorber', and a better-regulated financial sector.

The major weakness in macroeconomic policy was of course the failure to reform fuel subsidies. At the end of the Yudhoyono decade, they were equivalent to 4 per cent of GDP and absorbed about 20 per cent of the government's budget. They were threatening to cripple the government's capacity to supply crucial goods and services, from infrastructure to health and social security. They were also undermining the president's claim to be a pro-poor and pro-green leader, since the subsidies were enjoyed overwhelmingly by the rich, while the artificially low fuel prices were obviously encouraging excessive consumption of fossil fuels. Each attempt at minor reform was overtaken by subsequent budget blowouts, resulting either from reduced domestic production relative to demand or from increased international prices. Thus, in relative terms the subsidies cost the nation about as much at the beginning of the Yudhoyono decade as at the end (Howes and Davies 2014). At several points during Yudhoyono's presidency, most notably in 2011, a deal with the parliament (Dewan Perwakilan Rakyat, DPR) over the accompanying compensation package seemed to be within reach, only to vanish at the last minute, reportedly owing to the president's prevarication. It was only under his last finance minister, Chatib Basri, that at least a cap was put on the amount of subsidy, with a link established between domestic and international prices. But no progress was made towards creating a mechanism for systematic subsidy reduction through a scheduled reduction in the gap between domestic and international fuel prices.[12]

Overall, therefore, the Yudhoyono administration's record of macroeconomic management is a positive one. The government appointed competent people of integrity to run the economy, maintained the macro policy framework it had inherited and continued the process of fiscal consolidation commenced in 2000. Yudhoyono failed to support a very able finance minister during a major internal disagreement, but at least her successors were competent. The failure to reform subsidies was a major weakness, as was the absence of any significant tax reform, resulting in a continued weak tax effort.[13] The chance to implement a broader

---

12 Yudhoyono's inability to reduce the subsidies in the latter years of his administration is in sharp contrast to the decisive action of his successor, Joko Widodo, who cut them significantly in one of his first major policy pronouncements. Time will tell whether this decision portends a major break with the past. Yudhoyono took similar steps early in his first administration, only to be overcome with reform fatigue as his presidency progressed.

13 In a country of 250 million people, Indonesia has approximately 20 million registered taxpayers, 10 million of whom file a return, and a minuscule 1.5 million of whom actually pay income tax.

reform program during the global financial crisis, working from the premise that crises are frequently an opportunity to push through otherwise unpopular measures, was also missed.

As an aside, Indonesia enjoyed one of its largest commodity booms during the Yudhoyono presidency, centred mainly on coal and palm oil, on a scale similar to the oil boom in the 1970s. In both cases, the macroeconomic and political economy consequences were similar: the real exchange rate appreciated (that is, Indonesia experienced the familiar, and inevitable, 'Dutch disease' effects), and economic nationalism resulted in more restrictive trade and investment policies. Commodity booms are always temporary, so a more important question for longer-run development is whether Indonesia invested the proceeds more wisely, and saved more for future generations, in the earlier or later episodes. The answer is almost certainly the 1970s boom. Despite the spectacular international debt accumulated by the state oil company, Pertamina, in the mid-1970s, and associated corruption on a grand scale, Indonesia recycled much of the proceeds of the boom into infrastructure and rural development (Hill 2000). One result was to transform the rice economy. Once the world's largest importer of rice, Indonesia achieved rice self-sufficiency in the mid-1980s, with an attendant acceleration of poverty reduction. During the 2000s boom, the infrastructure deficit became more serious, the government continued to run fiscal deficits and inequality rose. Perhaps the only lasting investment legacy from the period was the decision, rather late in the boom, to commit 20 per cent of government expenditure to education.

In fairness to the Yudhoyono administration, the two booms differed in important respects. The 1970s boom was in a single product—oil—that was directly under the control of the state. In the 2000s, the two main commodities were coal and palm oil, the ownership of which was diffused. In the former period, there was a strong, centralised administration, in effect a single tax collector, in contrast to the 2000s when regional autonomy had been implemented and there were many more tax collection points.

STILL (PRECARIOUSLY) OPEN

For much of its history since independence, Indonesia has remained 'precariously open'—a term that Chatib Basri and I have found to be a convenient characterisation of the fact that Indonesia has remained a fairly open economy for most of the period since 1966, despite a dominant intellectual narrative that has been at best sceptical of (and more frequently hostile to) the merits of a liberal, internationally oriented economic policy (see, for example, Basri and Hill 2008). This openness has been driven by the inevitable embrace of East Asian economic integration; the demonstrated success of the region's outward-looking economies; the occasional ascendancy of reformers in government; and the sheer impracticability of turning inward, which would also constitute a rejection of the country's membership of ASEAN and would in any case invite large-scale illegal trade.

The tensions between economic nationalism and liberalism were evident throughout the Suharto era and they continued into the Yudhoyono decade, with both structural and political factors combining to increase protectionist pressures. The main structural factor was the strong terms of trade from around 2005. A recurring empirical regularity in Indonesian political economy has been the inverse correlation between the country's terms of trade (that is, the ratio of export prices to import prices) and open trade policies.[14] During the 1970s commodity boom, the liberal reforms of the late 1960s were overturned, only to be reinstated in the 1980s. A similar trend has been evident during the most recent boom. Although circumstances differed in each period, a common driver of increased protectionism was the real appreciation of the rupiah, which increased competitive pressure on the tradable goods industries from the now cheaper imports. The increased resource flows from high commodity prices in turn weakened the voices of caution and restraint coming from the technocrats in cabinet, and emboldened both those who believed in grand theories of technological advance and the blatant rent-seekers. The latter frequently presented their arguments in the guise of the former, as 'nation-building' projects.

We know little about Yudhoyono's views on international economic policy, other than that he generally embraced globalisation while recognising the importance of developing the national economy. With regard to his appointments, Yudhoyono started on a very high note. His minister of trade from 2004 to 2011 was Mari Pangestu, one of Indonesia's leading economists and an internationally acknowledged authority on trade policy. She was able to resist much, but by no means all, of the pressure for protectionism. How effective that resistance was can be seen from the direction of trade policy after her departure, with her successors, Gita Wirjawan and Muhammad Lutfi, signalling a U-turn on trade policy. Both were much more ideologically sympathetic to protectionism, and were amenable to lobbying by vested interests. The highly protectionist 2014 trade law, Law 7/2014 (and the industry law of the same year, Law

---

14 The first systematic analysis of these political economy forces was undertaken by Chatib Basri (later to become finance minister) in his PhD dissertation. See Basri (2001).

3/2014), which Pangestu had blocked, as well as the vociferous opposition to the ASEAN–China Free Trade Agreement in 2009 (even though the agreement had been signed five years earlier), are further manifestations of the drift in trade policy during the second Yudhoyono term.

Marks and Rahardja (2012) provide the most comprehensive recent study of Indonesia's trade regime. On the basis of their estimates of nominal and effective rates of protection in 2008, they concluded that protection had fallen considerably since 1987 and 1995, the years of earlier estimates using similar methodologies. However, some exceptions to this trend were evident, in sectors such as rice, sugar and, more recently, a range of horticultural products. Importantly, Marks and Rahardja concluded that more than half the effective support provided to tradable sectors now came in the form of subsidies to energy use rather than from trade policies. It is probable that protection is now a good deal higher, because these estimates pre-date the rise of economic nationalism and the departure of Trade Minister Pangestu, and because much of the increase has taken the form of non-tariff barriers that are difficult to quantify.

A puzzling feature of the globalisation debate in Indonesia is how little public discussion there has been of the fact that the country is missing out on opportunities in the fastest-growing and largest segment of East Asian trade. These are the global production networks centred on the electronics and automotive industries, which now account for about half of intra-East Asian (and intra-ASEAN) trade. Indonesia's share of this trade is well below that of the traditionally open Southeast Asian economies, Singapore, Malaysia and Thailand. The country is also overshadowed by the Philippines, and on present trends will be overtaken by Vietnam. It is therefore missing out on hundreds of thousands of relatively well-paid jobs, and the opportunity to move up the ladder in technological sophistication. These globally integrated, multi-country operations require liberal policies towards foreign investment, since most of the trade occurs under the auspices of multinational enterprises. They also require highly efficient logistics and export–import procedures so that parts and components can move quickly between multi-country production points. Removing both obstacles would have required relatively modest reforms, but the Yudhoyono administration was unable to implement them (Soejachmoen 2012). There was much public discussion of the need for stronger employment growth and technological upgrading, but oddly, this discourse failed to connect with a major opportunity to address these problems.

Meanwhile, and related to this outcome, there has been no significant reform of the domestic business environment. On comparative assessments, such as the World Bank's widely used 'Ease of doing business' surveys, Indonesia ranks well below its higher-income neighbours, and

Figure 15.6   Ranking on 'Ease of doing business' surveys, selected Southeast Asian countries, 2013–14

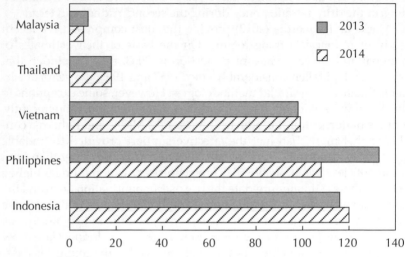

Source: World Bank.

also below those with a similar per capita income (Figure 15.6). In an era of probable lower commodity prices, these are the countries with which Indonesia is competing for mobile capital and skilled labour. This low ranking has persisted in spite of several initiatives, most notably a major new investment law, several revisions to the Investment Coordinating Board's 'Negative List' and the consolidation of regional government autonomy.[15]

THE INFRASTRUCTURE DEFICIT

In this section I examine the record on infrastructure provision during the Yudhoyono decade. In any country, let alone the world's largest archipelagic state, the efficient provision of infrastructure is important

---

15   It might have been hoped that the implementation of the 1999 regional autonomy laws would have improved the regulatory environment in at least some localities, to the extent that the better-governed regions wishing to attract footloose capital and labour would be motivated to offer a more attractive business climate. In well-functioning federal systems, this inter-regional competition can also trigger a 'race to the top' and therefore have national repercussions. There is no evidence to date that this is occurring in Indonesia, however (Lewis 2014).

Figure 15.7 Ranking on Logistics Performance Index, selected Southeast Asian countries, 2007–14

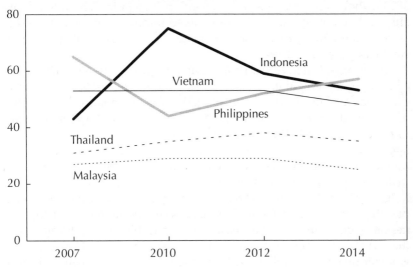

Source: World Bank.

for economic growth, and as a means of creating economic opportunities for the poor. It was also a high priority for the Yudhoyono government, which held several infrastructure summits and released an ambitious Master Plan for the Acceleration and Expansion of Economic Development in Indonesia (Masterplan Percepatan dan Perluasan Pembangunan Ekonomi Indonesia, MP3EI). Launched in 2011, the master plan was designed to enable Indonesia to achieve advanced country status by 2025, through enhanced domestic and international connectivity involving 22 economic activities and six economic corridors.

Despite the flurry of official activity, here too progress was disappointing. By the end of the Yudhoyono decade, Indonesia still lagged behind most of its East Asian neighbours on most infrastructure and logistics indicators. The high-profile infrastructure summits had produced few tangible results, and it seems likely that the MP3EI will be confined to the dustbin. As a result, Indonesia continues to have considerably higher logistics costs than its competitors, sometimes by a very large margin. Figure 15.7 shows the results for one of the most widely used indicators, the World Bank's Logistics Performance Index, a composite of several infrastructure indicators.

These comparative indicators are consistent with the detailed microlevel research on Indonesian infrastructure. For example, Sandee, Nurridzki and Dipo (2014) noted Indonesia's very high interisland transport costs and consequent large inter-regional price differences. In the country's major port, Tanjung Priok, throughput doubled between 2007 and 2013 without any commensurate expansion in facilities. The authors concluded that 'no substantial investments to improve productivity and to start planning for an extension were made for many years' (Sandee, Nurridzki and Dipo 2014: 394).

The problems derive from both limited infrastructure investment and continuing high regulatory barriers. The underinvestment in infrastructure since the late 1990s has contributed to the low quality and quantity of new roads, ports and railways. As a percentage of GDP, Indonesia's infrastructure expenditure is about half that in the Suharto era. Regulated constraints on competition and efficient service provision compound these problems. The contrast between the successful deregulation in air transport and the lack of reform in shipping is striking. Indeed, in a step backward, Law 17/2008 on Shipping introduced cabotage principles that limit the movement of cargo between Indonesian ports to Indonesian flagged vessels. The master plans and blueprints developed in the early 2010s lay out a strategy to improve connectivity. The question is whether they will be able to address crucial bottlenecks, such as the lack of coordination between local and central governments and the uncertain commercial environment for potential private sector providers.

Why are the problems so serious, and to what extent is the Yudhoyono administration responsible? President Yudhoyono's views on the matter are on record: 'I don't enjoy being asked for a solution [to traffic] in Jakarta, Bandung, Surabaya and other places', he said in 2013. 'It is the governors and mayors that are in charge of providing an explanation for this' (Sihite 2013). Under the 1999 regional autonomy laws, he maintained, local governments had the prime responsibility for such problems. This argument certainly has some validity, because subnational governments are now receiving large, discretionary resource flows without delivering much in the way of improved local service quality (Lewis 2014).[16] The president could also have added that after the economic crisis of 1997–98 Indonesia's number one priority was to restore macroeconomic stability, and so for several years the government was focused primarily on reducing the public sector debt burden.

---

16 The fact that responsibility for infrastructure and other services has been delegated to local governments does not of course mean that the central government has no further responsibilities. In fact, well-functioning federal systems require an activist national government overseeing effective inter-jurisdictional coordination, in the case, for example, of infrastructure projects straddling local administrative boundaries. Central governments also need to provide appropriate incentives, and penalties in the case of local government underperformance.

But other factors under the influence of the president did contribute to the infrastructure deficit. First, and most obviously, fuel subsidies diverted resources away from infrastructure and other expenditure priorities. Even if only one-quarter of the revenue released from subsidy reduction had been channelled into infrastructure, spending on infrastructure would have risen by about one percentage point of GDP, which would have covered about one-third of the estimated infrastructure spending gap. Moreover, together with the country's grossly inadequate mass public transport system, cheap fuel provided an incentive for private automobile use, thus compounding the chronic urban congestion and pollution evident in Indonesia's major cities.

Second, the administration did not undertake the major reforms needed to fix the competition policy framework. The most successful deregulation in Indonesia since the Asian financial crisis, that of domestic civil aviation, actually pre-dated the Yudhoyono administration, while the regulatory agency established after the crisis, the Business Competition Supervisory Commission (Komisi Pengawas Persaingan Usaha, KPPU), has had a mixed record in promoting a more competitive environment. Similarly, the four state corporations with responsibility for the country's ports and harbours, known collectively as Pelindo, and the state electricity company, PLN, have effectively maintained their monopoly regulatory powers, for both provision and supervision, resulting in high charges and poor service quality. These agencies are all answerable to the national government. Reforming them would require the support of the parliament, as would measures to remove the unrealistic price ceilings on some infrastructure pricing in order to encourage the entry of private providers. With a large block of votes in the parliament under the control of Yudhoyono's Democrat Party (Partai Demokrat, PD) and a very large coalition majority, the president should have been able to tackle these admittedly difficult policy areas. Late in its term, the outgoing parliament did at least ratify the revised land law, Law 2/2012 on Land Acquisition. It came into force on 1 January 2015, paving the way for streamlined land acquisition for major infrastructure projects.

CONCLUSION

President Yudhoyono inherited an economy that had recovered from the deepest of crises, and one in which the building blocks for macroeconomic stability had been established. The economy was fragile when he took office, and growth was by no means assured. His administration was, moreover, an institutionally weakened one, with a rainbow cabinet of highly variable quality, an occasionally obstructive parliament where economic literacy was in short supply, increasingly powerful and assertive local governments with guaranteed revenue flows, an active anti-corruption commission and an increasingly independent judiciary.

Yudhoyono has left two principal economic legacies. The first is that he presided over an economy that achieved moderately strong economic growth, and avoided a recurrence of economic crisis, during a period in which a strong commodity boom was followed by several years of global economic stress and volatility. The key to this achievement was the restoration and maintenance of macroeconomic stability. Yudhoyono can take considerable credit for this, in that he maintained the recently established macroeconomic policy framework and he appointed competent officials to run the two major agencies responsible for macroeconomic management.

But second, reflecting his highly cautious nature and a reluctance to confront powerful vested interests, Yudhoyono either deferred or left unaddressed practically every difficult economic policy challenge that arose during his tenure. He was no reformist. The failure to make any progress in subsidy reform must be counted as the number one shortcoming. There are numerous other areas where little if any progress was made; summits and grand plans were no substitute for action to address the country's mounting infrastructure deficit, for example. The rising tide of economic nationalism threatened Indonesia's participation in the East Asian economic mainstream just as its commitments to a 'seamless ASEAN economy' under the ASEAN Economic Community were taking effect. The government's populist labour market policies choked growth in formal sector employment and exacerbated wage inequality. More generally, there was little progress in the areas of tax policy, regulatory simplification, civil service reform, institutional development and much else. Moreover, notwithstanding the administration's commendable anti-poverty rhetoric, the Yudhoyono decade witnessed the sharpest increase in interpersonal inequality in Indonesian history (see Chapter 16 by Manning and Miranti).

In some respects, Yudhoyono's presidency resembles that of former Indian prime minister Manmohan Singh, another leader with a technocratic disposition (and a PhD in economics), who was contemporaneously in power for a decade. Both leaders assumed office amidst high expectations, but both disappointed their supporters with a timid record of economic reform, and departed with their administrations engulfed in scandal. An assessment of the Singh decade that could arguably be applied to the Yudhoyono presidency was that 'India's departing prime minister makes an easy punchbag, but critics are too harsh'.[17] Perhaps

---

17 'Manmohan Singh: man out of time', *Economist*, 3 May 2014.

this assessment simply reflects the difficulty of governing the two most populous Asian democracies, where power is diffused and decentralised, institutional checks on abuse of office are limited and populist economic rhetoric is in the ascendancy.

One puzzle remains. Yudhoyono arguably achieved more in his first term than in his second. Yet, one might have expected the reverse. The second term was his last opportunity to leave a durable legacy. Yudhoyono had a much stronger personal and party mandate in 2009–14, and therefore diminished political opposition. He had five years of presidential experience under his belt and he had adroitly managed the global financial crisis. He could have used the fear of a threatening global economy to push through reforms, and he had the country's most able and experienced technocrat as his vice-president. Instead, the president became more cautious and risk-averse, seemingly preferring to stride the international stage rather than get on with reform at home (see Chapter 5 by Fitriani). Perhaps that should not be a surprise. Economic reform is difficult, and globetrotting is more pleasurable. But as a result, Yudhoyono left an extensive agenda of unfinished business to the Joko Widodo administration. Time will tell whether Joko Widodo's government is able to tackle this agenda, or whether Indonesia's political structures and processes, together with the dominant ideological narrative, make reform extremely difficult.

REFERENCES

Aswicahyono, H. and H. Hill (2014) 'Survey of recent developments', *Bulletin of Indonesian Economic Studies*, 50(3): 319–46.

Aswicahyono, H., H. Hill and D. Narjoko (2013) 'Indonesian industrialization: a latecomer adjusting to crises', in A. Szirmai, W. Naude and L. Alcorta (eds) *Pathways to Industrialization in the Twenty-first Century: New Challenges and Emerging Paradigms*, Oxford University Press, Oxford: 193–222.

Basri, M.C. (2001) 'The political economy of manufacturing protection in Indonesia, 1975–1995', PhD thesis, Australian National University, Canberra.

Basri, M.C. and H. Hill (2008) 'Indonesia: trade policy review 2007', *World Economy*, 31(11): 1,393–408.

Basri, M.C. and H. Hill (2011) 'Indonesian growth dynamics', *Asian Economic Policy Review*, 6(1): 90–107.

Hill, H. (2000) *The Indonesian Economy*, Cambridge University Press, Cambridge.

Howes, S. and R. Davies (2014) 'Survey of recent developments', *Bulletin of Indonesian Economic Studies*, 50(2): 157–83.

Kovacevic, M. (2011) 'Transcript of President Yudhoyono's speech at B4E Global Summit', Forests News: a blog by the Center for International Forestry Research (CIFOR), Jakarta, 28 April. Available at http://blog.cifor.org/2713/indonesian-president-announces-plans-to-utilise-degraded-land#.VJPXvs-AA

Lewis, B.D. (2014) 'Twelve years of fiscal decentralization: a balance sheet', in H. Hill (ed.) *Regional Dynamics in a Decentralized Indonesia*, Institute of Southeast Asian Studies, Singapore: 135–55.

Marks, S.V. and S. Rahardja (2012) 'Effective rates of protection revisited for Indonesia', *Bulletin of Indonesian Economic Studies*, 48(1): 57–84.

Perkins, D.H. (2013) *East Asian Development: Foundations and Strategies*, Harvard University Press, Cambridge MA.

Pritchett, L. (2011) 'How good are good transitions for growth and poverty? Indonesia since Suharto, for instance?', in C. Manning and S. Sumarto (eds) *Employment, Living Standards and Poverty in Contemporary Indonesia*, Institute of Southeast Asian Studies, Singapore: 23–46.

Reinhart, C.M. and K.S. Rogoff (2009) *This Time Is Different: Eight Centuries of Financial Folly*, Princeton University Press, Princeton NJ.

Sandee, H., N. Nurridzki and M.A.P. Dipo (2014) 'Challenges of implementing logistics reform in Indonesia', in H. Hill (ed.) *Regional Dynamics in a Decentralized Indonesia*, Institute of Southeast Asian Studies, Singapore: 386–405.

Sihite, E. (2013) 'President denies role in Jakarta's bad traffic', *Jakarta Globe*, 6 November. Available at http://thejakartaglobe.beritasatu.com/news/jakarta/president-denies-role-in-jakartas-bad-traffic/

Soejachmoen, M. (2012) 'Why is Indonesia left behind in global production networks?', PhD thesis, Australian National University, Canberra.

World Bank (1993) *The East Asian Miracle: Economic Growth and Public Policy*, Oxford University Press, Washington DC.

World Bank (2008) *The Growth Report: Strategies for Sustained Growth and Inclusive Development*, Commission on Growth and Development, Washington DC.

16 The Yudhoyono legacy on jobs, poverty and income distribution: a mixed record

*Chris Manning and Riyana Miranti**

Outcomes in the general area of job creation, poverty and income distribution were ambiguous during the Yudhoyono years. Jobs growth flip-flopped between rapid expansion of informal jobs in President Yudhoyono's first term, and then of formal employment during the resources boom in his second term. On the positive side, rates of poverty declined almost continuously throughout his period in office, and policy in this area was one of the big achievements of his presidency. But these improvements for the poor were not reflected in a better distribution of income. In fact, inequality worsened strikingly during Yudhoyono's second term of government.

Although strong and sustainable jobs growth can be associated with both declining poverty and improvements in income distribution, in Southeast Asia rapid economic growth has quite often been associated with rising inequality (Booth 1999). Indonesia appeared to be the exception during the Suharto period but there are good reasons to expect that this may not be the case now. While poverty alleviation is widely accepted as a legitimate focus of government policy, middle-class interests have more influence in a democratic polity, and these will not always

---

* The authors would like to thank Vivi Alatas, Emma Allen, Rahma Irjanti, Suahasil Nazara, Sudarno Sumarto, Asep Suryahadi and Mathew Wai-Poi for giving up their time to discuss some of the issues raised in this paper. We are also grateful to Raden Muhammad Purnagunawan, who assisted us with some of the national labour force data. The normal disclaimers apply; the authors are entirely responsible for any errors and omissions in the manuscript.

favour rapid employment growth or more equitable fiscal arrangements. Moreover, organised labour did not support policies that could have achieved a more rapid expansion of blue-collar jobs in Indonesia in the early *reformasi* period, and subsidised energy and other fiscal arrangements have mainly benefited the better-off, facilitating growing inequality (Manning 2010; Dartanto 2013).

President Susilo Bambang Yudhoyono projected a greater concern for and a deeper knowledge of policy alternatives in areas affecting the welfare of the poor than any of Indonesia's first three *reformasi* presidents, B.J. Habibie, Abdurrahman Wahid and Megawati Sukarnoputri.[1] This chapter will show that he oversaw considerable progress in social programs oriented towards overcoming poverty, and that he personally supported some major innovations in this field. At the same time, the president's extreme caution in policy-making in areas affecting the poor, his aversion to conflict and his need to take political calculations into account all meant that his government avoided making some difficult decisions that could have benefited lower-income groups much more. More progressive fiscal policies could also have prevented a sharp rise in the share of income accruing to the top 10 per cent of households in the country. But short-term political considerations often dominated, and these held more sway towards the end of the Yudhoyono presidency when his popularity was at its lowest and his party was in some disarray.

The next section discusses some of the broad contextual relationships that bear on the Yudhoyono record in the areas of employment and social welfare. This is followed by a discussion of developments in three main areas: jobs, poverty and inequality. The treatment is necessarily selective given the broad scope of the subject matter. In the section on jobs, the focus is on labour policy, which was a difficult issue for both Yudhoyono administrations. The discussion of poverty deals with some of the main government strategies and the role of the president and vice-president in guiding policy. On the third topic, we seek to evaluate the effects of policy on inequality, to discuss the likely causes of rising inequality and to outline what the government might have done to ameliorate these trends.

THE ECONOMIC AND SOCIAL CONTEXTS

When Yudhoyono came to power in 2004, Indonesia had more or less recovered economically from the major disruptions of the Asian financial

---

[1] Indeed, the parallels with Suharto are much more striking in this regard. Both presidents came from poor rural backgrounds and both paid close attention to rural policies, food production and prices, and the poor.

crisis and regime change in 1998 (Aswicahyono and Hill 2004; Sen and Steer 2005). Total poverty as measured by the national poverty line was just under 17 per cent, which was close to the level in 1996 on the eve of the crisis. It was widely understood, however, that better economic performance was necessary if living standards were to rise significantly, after some lacklustre years of 3–5 per cent growth under Presidents Wahid and Megawati. Job creation in particular had been a problem since the crisis. Unemployment was just on 10 per cent, and more than double that rate among young people (Manning 2012). Indonesia had lost almost a decade in the fight to create better jobs and lift living standards. On the policy front, it had developed a range of new welfare policies as a result of the crisis to deal with poverty and shocks to living standards (Miranti et al. 2013), but consolidation of these gains was still in its early stages when Yudhoyono was elected in 2004.

On inequality, official figures suggest that incomes were relatively evenly distributed when Yudhoyono came to power in Indonesia.[2] Moreover, the distribution was much the same as in the early 1990s, although there had been some improvements during the crisis, attributable to the difficulties faced by the urban middle class at that time. Most economists believe, however, that expenditure data (on which measures of income distribution are based) are not a true reflection of the huge gap in wealth and incomes between the upper 1 per cent and 10 per cent of the Indonesian population and the rest, a gap that almost certainly widened during the Suharto era (Leigh and van der Eng 2009).

Yudhoyono's election in 2004 created high expectations. Coming to office after several years of mediocre economic performance and inchoate presidential authority, the new president promised not only a return to higher levels of growth but also a better investment climate for business. Also on offer were social policies that would protect the poor and create jobs. Yudhoyono's team aimed to halve both the poverty and unemployment rates. The president placed special emphasis on reviving agriculture. In this he drew heavily on advice from his former professors at Bogor Agricultural University (Institut Pertanian Bogor), and especially the advice of the Brighton Institute, which was particularly concerned with the protection of farmers (Aswicahyono and Hill 2004: 279, 303).

When Yudhoyono ran for re-election in 2009, the government's agenda continued to give priority to employment and poverty alleviation as two of the four key objectives of the administration. Although

---

2 According to one measure, the Gini ratio, inequality was not high. In 2004, official data put it at 0.32, compared with higher and less equitable ratios of 0.38 in Malaysia, 0.42 in Thailand and 0.45 in the Philippines around this time. See below for a more detailed discussion of measures of income distribution.

his government had not achieved its goals for either poverty reduction or unemployment in 2004–09, enough progress had been made for this not to be a major obstacle to re-election.[3] After the 2009 elections, Yudhoyono's own party, the Democrat Party (Partai Demokrat, PD), held 26 per cent of the seats in the national parliament, up from 10 per cent, giving the president and his party a much clearer mandate to initiate reform.

The broader political and economic changes during the Yudhoyono years might be expected to have influenced social indicators such as employment and poverty rates in various ways. Drawing on data presented in Hill's chapter in this book, we find that three points seem relevant. First, improved rates of economic growth under Yudhoyono should have been positive for jobs and poverty alleviation compared with the early post-crisis years. Second, while agriculture and services performed reasonably well, the manufacturing sector's share of GDP actually fell in the Yudhoyono years, and the share of manufacturing exports plummeted, in contrast to the experience of almost all other successful East Asian countries at similar stages of development.[4] The sad state of manufacturing was likely to affect growth in employment and incomes, due to the range of linkages that this sector has to other industries in the economy. Third, economic policy became more nationalistic and protectionist under Yudhoyono—a development that was also likely to have an adverse effect on jobs and productivity, at least in the medium to longer term. Five new laws (*undang-undang*) affecting competitiveness were passed in the later years of the administration: Law 13/2010 on Horticulture, Law 18/2012 on Food, Law 19/2013 on the Protection and Empowerment of Farmers, Law 3/2014 on Industry and Law 7/2014 on Trade (Davies and Howes 2014: 160–61). All were heavily oriented towards protecting domestic firms and industries, and eschewed international competition in key sectors (especially agriculture). While these laws were designed to protect vulnerable farmers and businesses from stiff competition in Asia, they were also likely to lead to higher prices for consumers and producers. This part of Yudhoyono's legacy raises questions about the prospects for longer-term improvements in real incomes, employment growth and associated poverty alleviation in the years to come.

---

3 During his second term, Yudhoyono was more careful and strategic in managing the unemployment and poverty goals, by expressing them in the form of a range ($x - y$ per cent) rather than as finite targets (x per cent).

4 The decline in the share of manufacturing exports was partly a consequence of the commodity export boom but it was also related to stagnation in exports from labour-intensive industries (see below).

EMPLOYMENT AND LABOUR POLICIES

The first Yudhoyono government's stated commitment to high rates of economic growth, support for rural investment and backing for agricultural production was consistent with its goal of creating more jobs after the disappointing post-crisis years. However, aiding a recovery of the export-oriented industries that had driven employment growth and contributed to poverty decline in the decade before the crisis was not a high priority (Athukorala 2006).

In designing its labour policy, the Yudhoyono government faced a dilemma also encountered by some neighbouring countries—such as the Philippines—that were at a similar stage of transition towards becoming a middle-income country. As the economy grew, aspirations for better living standards spread among an increasingly politically active and vocal urban-based working class, which had now started to rub shoulders with a much more prosperous urban middle class. Other East Asian countries, such as China, Thailand and Malaysia (and much earlier South Korea and Taiwan), had dealt with the potentially negative effect of above-market wages on employment by resisting demands for higher wages and promoting exports in the labour-intensive sectors during the early stages of industrialisation (Felipe and Hasan 2006). Wage rates and wage incomes increased gradually at first, and later steeply, as the low-wage informal sector began to contract. By this time, those countries had reached what many have referred to as the 'turning point' at which labour moves out of low-wage industries and into higher-wage and higher-value-added industries.[5]

Indonesia had been well on the way to this turning point in the 1990s, until jobs and wages suffered a major setback during the Asian financial crisis in 1997–98. Almost a decade later, employment had grown very little in the export-oriented industries (Aswicahyono and Manning 2011). Thus, Yudhoyono's democratic Indonesia faced a major challenge in following this 'East Asian' model of economic development. The government would have to tough it out and sell a 'jobs-first' agenda in the political arena. Added to this, just a year before Yudhoyono's election to the presidency in 2004, Indonesia had passed a labour law (Law 13/2003) that promised an unusually wide range of protections for wage workers. From the outset, it threatened to discourage investment and

---

5 In Korea and Taiwan this turning point occurred in the mid to late 1970s, whereas in China, which has a huge labour market, it occurred much later, around the mid-2000s, after some two decades of very rapid rates of economic growth (Garnaut 2010).

employment growth in labour-intensive industries, and to open up a large gap between earnings and labour conditions in the formal sector and those in the informal sector.

Revision of the Labour Law during Yudhoyono's first term

One of the early challenges for the Yudhoyono government was to soften some of the provisions of the 2003 Labour Law, especially the high rates of severance pay,[6] to help create jobs and encourage investment in Indonesia's faltering export-oriented industries. The government did take steps in 2006 to revise the Labour Law, but the effort was half-hearted at best and it quickly backed down when it met with political opposition.[7] Even though the union-led demonstrations against the changes were mild by international standards, in May 2006 Yudhoyono announced that the proposed revisions to the law would be withdrawn from the national economic reform package, just months after they had begun to be debated in the public domain. The president then appointed a 'Five University' team of experts (comprising economists, lawyers and sociologists) to examine options for labour reform. The experts recommended several changes to regulations to help promote employment. But despite being moderate in tone, their report was subsequently shelved because it, too, was regarded as too hot politically for the administration. Reform of the Labour Law was not revisited by the government during Yudhoyono's first term and only fleetingly in his second term. The president was not prepared to enter into a serious public dialogue on the issue, even though there was a widespread belief that the law was adversely affecting jobs.

The failure to deal with controversial articles in the Labour Law was reflected in the employment record in Yudhoyono's first term. Formal sector employment was flat in 2004–09 and most employment was in the informal sector (Figure 16.1). Wages, too, hardly grew during this period. Even though Indonesia continued to be a major exporter of labour-intensive goods, growth in this area was far below pre-crisis levels (Aswicahyono, Hill and Narjoko 2011). Unemployment had begun to come down from the double-digit figures recorded in 2005–06, and had reached 7.9 per cent by 2009. However, Indonesia's youth unemployment rates were among the highest in Southeast Asia—only the Philippines registered comparable rates.

---

6 Severance pay is the compensation (usually in months of wages) that workers are entitled to if they are laid off.
7 The discussion of this issue draws heavily on Manning (2010).

Figure 16.1   Distribution of agricultural and non-agricultural jobs in the formal and informal sectors, 2004–13 (%)

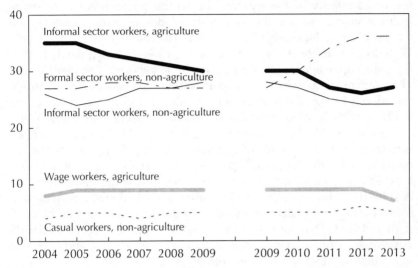

Source: BPS, National Labour Force Survey (Sakernas), August round, 2004–13.

An end to the low-wage era

During Yudhoyono's second term, the government's approach to labour costs and international competitiveness changed. There was a growing sense in Jakarta that wages were too low by regional standards. The administration's policy orientation shifted from seeking to promote jobs in labour-intensive industries and minimise labour costs to promoting more technologically advanced industries and wage justice. The shift in focus to justice is captured in Yudhoyono's address to the historic 100th annual session of the International Labour Organization (ILO) in 2011 (his presence at the meeting was in itself a signal):

> It is not enough that we provide jobs that ensure the workers' daily subsistence. They and their children should be guaranteed a future. Decent jobs entail dignity, equality and a sense of prosperity (Yudhoyono 2011).[8]

In 2012, unions seized the opportunity afforded by this subtle shift in attitude to initiate a well-planned and very effective campaign run

---

8   It should be noted that non-government organisations such as Migrant Care voiced scepticism of the president's newfound commitment to labour reform, especially in light of the government's weak efforts to improve the treatment of Indonesian migrant workers abroad and to pass legislation to protect household helpers at home.

over six months asking for substantially higher minimum wages and an end to outsourcing. While the adjustment of minimum wages was the responsibility of the regions, the central government gave strong indirect support to the unions with its pledge to bring an end to low wages. When in November 2012 Jakarta's recently elected governor, Joko Widodo (now Indonesia's seventh president), issued a decree that raised the minimum wage for Jakarta workers by 44 per cent,[9] President Yudhoyono was quick to throw his support behind the measure. In an influential speech to regional leaders, senior military and police in November 2012, he publicly announced that the era of low-wage policy was over.[10]

At least in part, this change in policy can probably be attributed to the turnabout in formal sector employment during the government's second term (Figure 16.1), and especially Indonesia's success in avoiding a major economic downturn and job losses during the global recession of 2008–09.[11] However, the administration's newly discovered sympathy for workers should not be divorced from the increased need of the president and PD to look for new areas of public support, especially after the government came under heavy attack from the opposition and the media in a number of high-profile corruption cases.[12]

Nevertheless, given the potential for a conflict between significant increases in wages and the creation of industrial jobs, the government's decision was surprising, especially if one bears in mind that the Yudhoyono government had targeted rapid increases in jobs as a key aspect of its development strategy. The implication was that Indonesia no longer needed to seek to compete in the internationally competitive labour-intensive sectors that had been so effective in creating jobs and lifting wages and living standards in other East Asian countries.

The steep rise in minimum wages in the Greater Jakarta region in 2013 appears to have adversely affected employment in labour-intensive industries in Java in particular. For example, one study of 66 firms in two of the most vulnerable industries, garments and footwear, in East Java

---

9   Wage increases in some districts near Jakarta were even higher, for example 71 per cent in Bogor city and around 60 per cent in Tangerang city and Tangerang district.

10 'SBY: era buruh murah sudah usai' [SBY: the era of cheap workers is over], *Detik Finance*, 30 November 2012.

11 Yudhoyono proudly referred to this achievement in his speech to the 100th annual session of the ILO. See ILO (2013) on recent employment trends in Indonesia.

12 In particular, it was put on the back foot by the exposure of losses from the Bank Century bailout in 2008 and by the Hambalang sports complex corruption case that broke in 2011, in which PD treasurer Nazaruddin was deeply implicated.

and the Greater Jakarta region found that a majority of firms experienced a fall in production and profits, and significant lay-offs or a decrease in hours worked, as a result of an average 20–30 per cent increase in labour costs during 2013 (Prasetyantoko et al. 2013).[13] Overall, employment in manufacturing fell in 2013 for the first time in several years. It seems likely that the sharp increase in minimum wages contributed to that fall.

POVERTY ALLEVIATION

A commitment to poverty alleviation ranked high among Yudhoyono's policy goals. He is reported to have taken a personal interest in programs such as the National Program for Community Empowerment (Program Nasional Pemberdayaan Masyarakat, PNPM), which has become one of the largest schemes of its kind in the world. When running for a second term, the president campaigned strongly on poverty alleviation, citing both his past record and his plans for an expansion of government efforts. In contrast to his opponents, Yudhoyono showed that he had an unusually well-informed grasp of detail and of the general strategy required (Perdana and Maxwell 2011: 283). In this he was supported by his vice-presidential candidate, Boediono, who worked closely with a team of experts on economic policy and social programs leading up to the election.

Yudhoyono's pride in his record on fighting poverty is clear in his last Independence Day speech to the national parliament in 2014:

> The government has continuously undertaken pro-people [pro-*rakyat*] policies on a massive scale, including giving social assistance and protection and community empowerment, as well as systematically galvanising small and micro enterprises.[14]

One might query the adjective used in this description of government programs ('massive') and the president's claim to have 'galvanised' small and micro enterprises. Nonetheless, Yudhoyono's poverty alleviation programs were widely supported by political parties and the general public, in contrast to the lack of support for more contentious areas of reform such as labour policy. Yudhoyono not only modified several of the poverty alleviation programs introduced after the Asian financial

---

13 Several of the firms were very large, employing over 5,000 workers, and most of these firms produced mainly for international markets. The effects on employment were more intense in the garments industry, where labour costs were a higher share of total costs, than in footwear.
14 Excerpt from the president's 17th of August speech, delivered to the national parliament in Jakarta on 16 August 2014.

Figure 16.2 Poverty rates for urban and rural areas, 2000–14 (%)

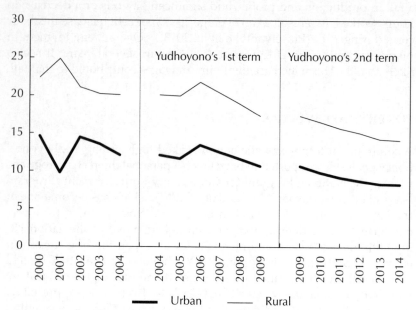

Source: BPS, National Socio-economic Survey (Susenas), 2000–14.

crisis in 1998,[15] he also initiated a number of new activities. Although varying in their effects, most made some contribution to the subsequent declines in poverty rates, which were sustained and large (Sumarto, Suryahadi and Bazzi 2008; Syukri et al. 2010; Yulaswati and Sumadi 2011).[16] When Yudhoyono was elected in 2004, the national poverty rate was 16.7 per cent, but by 2014 it had declined by almost a third to 11.3 per cent. Close to eight million people were lifted out of poverty during the Yudhoyono period as poverty rates declined in both urban and rural areas (Figure 16.2). At the same time, the share of the population below the international poverty line (that is, living on less than $1.25 per day) also fell steeply, comparable to similar declines in China and India during the first decade of the 2000s.[17]

---

15 For surveys of the various programs, see especially Alatas, Purnamasari and Wai-Poi (2011), Yulaswati and Sumadi (2011) and Miranti et al. (2013).
16 This was despite a hiccup in 2005–06 associated with the rise in oil prices, coinciding with poor management of Indonesia's rice import bans, which pushed domestic rice prices up sharply compared with international prices (Basri and Patunru 2006; Warr 2011).
17 Based on data from the World Development Indicators database.

Government programs

Of course, not all of the decline in poverty was due to special government programs. But it is reasonable to conclude that Yudhoyono's innovative poverty alleviation policies played a major role in lowering poverty. In his second term, the president set up a new institution, the National Team for Acceleration of Poverty Reduction (Tim Nasional Percepatan Penanggulangan Kemiskinan, TNP2K), to manage all poverty alleviation efforts. In collaboration with the National Development Planning Agency (Badan Perencanaan Pembangunan Nasional, Bappenas), TNP2K developed a number of programs that were trialled through careful research. Three of the most prominent were an unconditional cash transfer program (Bantuan Langsung Tunai, BLT), a conditional cash transfer program (Program Keluarga Harapan, PKH) and the previously mentioned National Program for Community Empowerment (PNPM). The unconditional cash transfers were significant because they were introduced to help poor households deal with price shocks, the most important of which were due to oil price rises. The conditional cash transfers were dependent on households taking action that would help lift them out of poverty. The community-based PNPM program was designed to be much broader in scope than either of these two, more narrowly targeted, programs.

Unconditional cash transfers (BLT)

The BLT program had no conditions attached; once judged to be poor, a household qualified to receive the payments. The first unconditional cash transfers, from October 2005 to September 2006, were targeted to the poorest 30 per cent of households and were intended to compensate them for a rise in fuel prices. The program was re-introduced in 2008 and again in 2013 when the international fuel price rose and the subsidy for imported fuel threatened to crowd out other development expenditures.

Each time this situation arose, Yudhoyono showed extreme caution in approving fuel price increases. In 2005, the rise in fuel prices was delayed for several months, partly because the program of compensation was not ready. These episodes indicate two things: first, a genuine concern on the president's part to lessen the burden of the price increases on the poor; and second, a high level of apprehension about a potential political backlash against the president as a result of the price increases.

When the BLT program was first implemented on a national scale in 2005–06, leakages and mis-targeting of payments received widespread media attention. Nevertheless, it was an improvement on the system of social safety net payments adopted during the 1998 crisis and was generally judged a success by international standards (Perdana and Maxwell

2011). The main criticisms were not so much about corruption or malpractice as about the failure to accurately identify which households were and were not 'poor households' deserving of assistance—a major challenge given the size of the program.[18] By 2013, a national register of poor households and a social protection card issued to poor households had substantially reduced problems of identification, although some observers still believed that cash hand-outs were wasteful.

Conditional cash transfers (PKH)

The conditional cash transfer program (PKH) targeted the extreme poor, that is, those having a monthly income of less than 80 per cent of the amount that constitutes the official poverty line. Its expansion during the Yudhoyono years indicated the government's concern for marginalised people and signalled a more professional approach to poverty alleviation programs. In line with other programs of its type around the world, the PKH program aimed not only to reduce current levels of poverty, but also to increase the quality of human capital among poor households in the longer term so as to break the cycle of poverty.[19] The coverage of the program was small, with only 1.5 million households accessing the payments up to 2012 (TNP2K 2013). But it was considered increasingly effective by international standards. In particular, the program raised performance on health indicators, as shown by an increase in the number of immunised children and a rise in the number of women's pre- and post-natal visits (Yulaswati and Sumadi 2011). The PKH program was also considered much more efficient than several other household-targeted programs, such as subsidised rice for the poor, due to its limited 'leakages'.

Community empowerment (PNPM)

The PNPM program began in 2007 and had reached all subdistricts in Indonesia by 2012 (World Bank 2012a). It was formally wound up at the end of 2014. The program aimed to help communities rather than households, and involved a suite of activities covering village infrastruc-

---

18   In 2005, for example, payments of Rp 100,000 ($10.30) per month were made directly to over 15 million poor households over a 12-month period through the national post office network.
19   For details, see World Bank (2011, 2012b) and TNP2K (2013). The program delivered quarterly cash benefits to households with school-aged children up to 18 years and households with pregnant or lactating women. Eligibility of households was verified regularly by checking school enrolment and a variety of health performance indicators.

ture, revolving credit schemes among women, and greater community engagement in health and education services, in both urban and rural areas. PNPM Generasi, for example, was involved in the provision of physical infrastructure for basic education and maternal and child health services (Febriany et al. 2011). PNPM Peduli, meanwhile, concentrated on strengthening the capacity of civil society organisations to improve the socio-economic conditions of the poorest households, through programs, for instance, that encouraged the establishment of businesses run by marginalised groups (World Bank 2013).

While the PNPM program was considered more effective than several other anti-poverty programs, it was also the target of criticism, related especially to the capture of programs by local elites and the lack of support from local governments (Miranti et al. 2013; McCarthy et al. 2014). From most accounts, many of these criticisms were well founded, as one might expect for such a huge program of social assistance. McCarthy et al.'s searching case studies of PNPM activities in nine Outer Island provinces questioned the program's longer-term contribution to poverty alleviation when dealing with established hierarchies, in the absence of other major reform efforts (McCarthy et al. 2014: 256–7). At the same time, the study found that PNPM was an improvement on the top-down approaches of the Suharto years, although the success of individual activities depended very much on the quality of the existing local government.

Other poverty alleviation initiatives

The Yudhoyono government took several other policy initiatives to address poverty during its second term. These included the development of an integrated and unified database (Pendataan Program Perlindungan Sosial, PPLS) containing information on the economic characteristics of those people who were likely to be the most appropriate beneficiaries of poverty alleviation programs. Initially developed to assist with the distribution of cash transfers, the database now covers the poorest 40 per cent of the population. Through the careful construction of a unified database, the government was able to include many more people omitted in early programs (that is, lessen exclusion errors) and refrain from providing benefits to families who were not eligible for support (reduce inclusion errors). The database was used to establish eligibility for the social protection card launched in 2013, which allows poor households to access benefits across a range of programs. Other new initiatives included the opening in 2013 of the Southeast Asia office of the Massachusetts Institute of Technology's Abdul Latif Jameel Poverty Action Lab (J-PAL), which aims to ensure that policy reduction strategies are informed by hard scientific evidence; and the launch in January 2012 of the government's Master Plan for the Acceleration and Expansion of Poverty Reduction (Masterplan Percepatan dan Perluasan Pengurangan Kemiskinan Indonesia, MP3KI), which provides a set of targets to reduce poverty to a level of 3–4 per cent by 2025.

A final, albeit delayed, achievement of the Yudhoyono administration was the launch of an integrated social security package providing health and accident cover, death compensation and pensions. Beginning with a program of universal basic health insurance in 2014, this package marks an important transition point as the country begins to move away from safety nets and targeted interventions, towards a broader system of social protection for all households.

INCOME DISTRIBUTION[20]

At the same time as the incidence of poverty fell, the income distribution—or relative poverty—worsened in the Yudhoyono years. Higher-income groups gained much more than those at the bottom. How serious is this, and how much can this development be attributed to actions taken, or not taken, by the Yudhoyono government? In this section, we argue that structural factors related to the drivers of economic change played an important role in the deterioration of the income distribution. Nonetheless, the government could have done more to prevent this. In particular, it could have targeted its expenditures better to help lower-income groups, and designed and implemented a tax regime favouring these groups.

A note of warning: the data on which the following discussion of patterns and trends in income distribution is based have some serious deficiencies, especially in relation to the incomes and expenditures of the rich. These are problems in all countries, but especially in countries like Indonesia where corruption, tax evasion and informal sources of income are widespread.[21]

In Indonesia, growing inequality emerged as an important policy issue mainly during Yudhoyono's second term. Under Suharto, the Gini

---

20 In this section, the terms 'income' and 'expenditure' are used interchangeably. While the general topic is income distribution, in the Indonesian case, expenditure data from the National Socio-Economic Survey (Susenas) are used as a proxy for income.

21 We can be certain that the data understate the level of inequality, especially between the highest 0.1 per cent and 1 per cent of the population and the rest. But how these factors affected *trends* in inequality during the Yudhoyono period is unknown.

Figure 16.3 Gini index for urban and rural areas, 2000–13

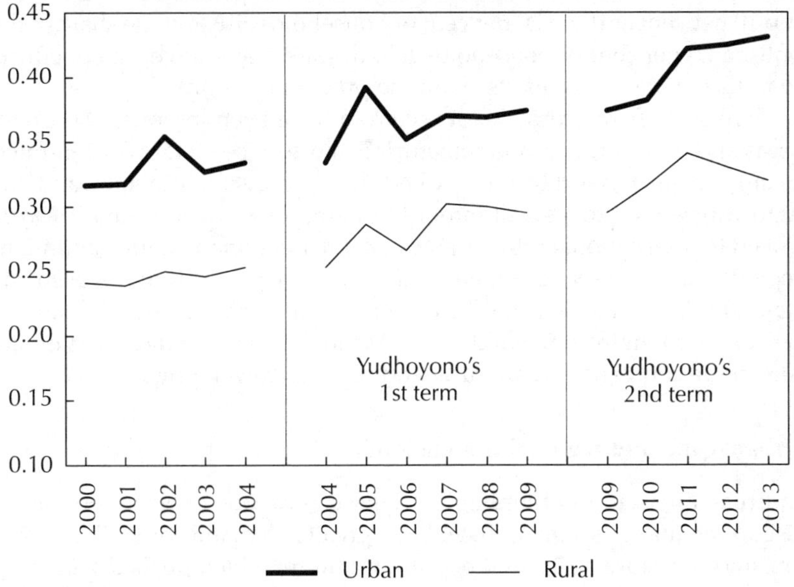

[Figure: Line chart showing Gini index for urban and rural areas from 2000 to 2013, divided into three periods: pre-Yudhoyono (2000–2004), Yudhoyono's 1st term (2004–2009), and Yudhoyono's 2nd term (2009–2013). Urban line rises from around 0.32 to 0.43; rural line rises from around 0.25 to 0.32.]

Source: Yusuf, Sumner and Rum (2014).

ratio – the most commonly used measure of inequality – was surprisingly stable, fluctuating between 0.30 and 0.36 (where zero is perfect equality and one is perfect inequality).[22] Thus, the starting point in 2004 was a relatively even distribution of income by developing country standards. A comparison of countries with comparable datasets suggests that the magnitude of the subsequent increases in the Gini ratio in Indonesia was second only to China, and was higher than in other Asian countries such as India and Bangladesh during a similar timeframe (the 1990s and the latest available figures in the first decade of the 2000s) (Kanbur, Rhee and Zhuang 2014: 3).

During the Yudhoyono years, the Gini ratio worsened substantially. According to the official figures, it rose from the mid 0.30s to an unprecedented 0.41 and has remained there since 2011. Significantly, the increases in inequality occurred in both urban and rural areas (Figure 16.3). Also,

---

22 It should be noted that Indonesia's Gini ratio is based on consumption data, which tend to understate the level of inequality compared with a ratio based on income data. If based on income data, the Gini ratio could be expected to have been around ten points higher before the crisis, and would probably be around 0.5 today. However, the expenditure data and income data should still be broadly comparable if one is dealing with *changes* in Gini ratios.

data from the National Socio-Economic Survey Survei Sosio-Ekonomi Nasional, Susenas) show that not only did the expenditure shares of the top 10 per cent and top 20 per cent of households rise, but the share of the bottom 20 per cent of households fell, despite major government efforts to reduce poverty (as discussed in the previous section).

Two sets of structural factors seem to have been important in urban areas and in the modern manufacturing and service sectors concentrated mainly in Java: shortages of skilled and professional labour, and the high wages paid to a small minority of employees whose salaries were linked to international rates of pay. In rural areas and resource-abundant regions outside Java, the main factors would probably have been the rents (both official and unofficial), profits and wages earned from the resources boom from the mid-2000s. We look at each of these sets of factors in the context of urban–rural and regional developments.

Urban–rural and regional dimensions

In urban areas and in more industrialised Java, one explanation for the rise in inequality seems to have been greater demand for skilled workers, and therefore a rise in the 'skill' premium, which pushed wages up at the top end of the income distribution. Lee and Wie (2013) found that a rising skill premium and widening wage inequality were associated with technological change, imported materials and foreign investment in manufacturing in Indonesia in the first decade of the 2000s. Meanwhile, slow growth in demand for blue-collar workers was not conducive to rising relative wages at the lower end of the wage distribution (see the section above on employment and labour policies).

The data presented in Figure 16.4 show some of these trends. The share of the total wage bill accruing to the top decile of employees rose from 25 per cent to 32 per cent over the period 2004–12, while that of the bottom quintile fell from 8 per cent to 5 per cent. In other words, the gap between the share of wages at the top and the share at the bottom increased by more than 50 per cent over eight years.[23]

The data suggest that Indonesia is following the international trend towards increased inequality among wage earners. The French economist Thomas Picketty in particular has shown not only that capital has become concentrated in fewer hands globally, but also that wage incomes have risen spectacularly among the top percentile and the top decile of

---

23 According to the National Labour Force Survey (Survei Angkatan Kerja Nasional, Sakernas), the top decile of wage earners earned an average of Rp 5.1 million ($522) per month in 2011, compared with Rp 360,000 ($36.85) per month for workers in the bottom quintile.

Figure 16.4   Share of the highest wage decile and lower wage quintiles in the total wage bill, 2004 and 2012 (%)

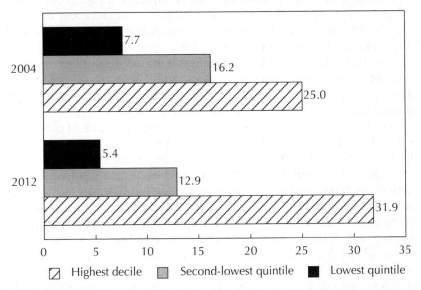

Source: BPS, National Labour Force Survey (Sakernas), August round, 2004 and 2012.

the income distribution range (Picketty 2014). While Picketty's work is based mainly on historical data from Europe and America, a similar pattern seems to be emerging in the developing world, including in Indonesia (Aizenman, Lee and Park 2014; Zhuang, Kanbur and Rhee 2014).

Regional disparities are another potential economic driver of inequality for emerging economies such as Indonesia (OECD 2011; Miranti et al. 2013; Yusuf, Sumner and Rum 2014). The west–east divide between the resource-rich provinces of Sumatra and Kalimantan and the poorer eastern regions appears to have deepened over the past decade, although booms in commodities such as palm oil and coal did benefit some regions in the east of Indonesia as well (Burke and Resosudarmo 2012). The Yudhoyono government sought to address these problems by launching a Master Plan for the Acceleration and Expansion of Indonesian Economic Development (Masterplan Percepatan dan Perluasan Pembangunan Ekonomi Indonesia, MP3EI) in 2011. One of its goals was to pursue more balanced regional development. However, it will take a long time to make this a reality given the slow rates of expenditure on infrastructure across the country. Sumatra's and Kalimantan's natural resources are likely to remain the main magnet for investment, as will Java's industrial agglomerations.

Fiscal policy

Government can hope to have its greatest impact on equity through fiscal policy in general—the level of expenditures and taxes and the pricing of public goods—as distinct from subsidies that are directly allocated to poverty alleviation, which account for a very small share of the total budget. Given that economic growth inevitably contributes to inequalities between sectors, between regions and between socio-economic groups, a major task of government is to counteract these effects through fiscal policy to ensure a more just and equitable society.

During the two terms of the Yudhoyono government, fiscal policy targeting the expenditure side had only a weak effect on equity, and during his second term, the failure to initiate reforms in this area undoubtedly contributed to a worsening of the income distribution. Comparisons of Gini ratios at the levels of both market income (gross wages and salaries and other income) and final income (which takes taxes, subsidies and transfers into account) show that the impact of fiscal policy has been less equalising in Indonesia than in countries such as Brazil, Mexico and Sri Lanka (Afkar, Jellema and Wai-Poi, forthcoming). Previous research has also found that Indonesia's fuel subsidies are regressive in nature and that they impede key expenditures on infrastructure required to create better jobs and raise incomes at the bottom end of the distribution (Yusuf and Resosudarmo 2008; Dartanto 2013; Yusuf, Sumner and Rum 2014).

Tackling the issue of inequality should also involve policies on the revenue side targeted towards higher-income groups. But income tax collection among higher-income groups remained problematic and ineffective during the Yudhoyono era. As Miranti et al. (2013) have shown, the tax-to-GDP ratio was low (12 per cent) during 2002–10 and collection rates were even lower. Although the ratio of tax revenue to GDP was higher in Indonesia than in China (11 per cent), it was lower than in neighbouring countries such as Malaysia and Thailand (16 per cent). All in all, there was limited tax reform during the Yudhoyono years.

CONCLUSION

The Yudhoyono decade produced mixed outcomes in the areas of job creation, poverty alleviation and income distribution. Employment and unemployment were major challenges when Yudhoyono came to office in 2004 and remained so throughout his first term. The job situation only began to turn around somewhat during his second term. The decline of poverty in Indonesia was impressive by international standards after some hiccups early in the president's first term. But inequality turned out to be the unexpected bogey. It began to rise gradually during Yudhoyono's first term, then more steeply early to midway in his second term, before levelling off in the last couple of years.

The two quotations from Yudhoyono's speeches in this chapter leave no doubt as to his personal commitment to assist the mass of poor households in Indonesia, although many have argued that he should have done more. His administrations had some notable successes, and certainly achieved more in the field of poverty alleviation policy than any preceding government (even if the *rate* of poverty decline was faster under Suharto). It may not be drawing too long a bow to suggest that Yudhoyono's simple, small-town family background and upbringing (discussed in detail by Greg Fealy in Chapter 3 of this book) may have given him a greater sense of empathy with the circumstances of the poor than the other post-Suharto presidents who spent their formative years in urban, upper-middle-class environments. But empathy is not always enough for good policy. Political considerations and the president's inability to make timely decisions meant that some reforms did not go far enough, especially when confronted with strong opposing interests.

Our conclusion is equivocal in attempting to answer the main question raised in this chapter: how much the successes and failures in the three main areas dealt with here—job creation, poverty and income distribution—can be attributed to policies adopted by the government, or the president, and how much to structural effects and changes set in motion before President Yudhoyono came to power? The answer seems to be 'a bit of both'. The government was active in promoting poverty alleviation programs throughout the Yudhoyono years, and these initiatives were closely watched by the president himself. Job creation involved a much broader mix of strategies and sometimes played second fiddle to several other concerns of the president, such as wages and working conditions for those who already had jobs. Given a large backlog of low-productivity workers, tight regulation of labour standards was not always consistent with transferring large numbers of workers into better jobs.

The emergence of new issues, such as a rapidly expanding middle class and rising inequality, surprised many during the president's second term. Apart from efforts to deal with corruption, the administration did not mount a specific array of policies to deal with inequality, especially the rising shares of income among the better-off. One could argue that rising inequality was inevitable in a country that depended so much on the exploitation of natural resources, and at a stage where new investment combined with the deployment of unskilled workers was still the main driver of longer-term improvements in living standards. However, poor targeting of fiscal policy compounded the effects of the resource boom. The removal of inequitable subsidies, such as those for fuel, had become a pressing need by the end of the Yudhoyono presidency, and an issue on which the administration had failed to act decisively. On the eve of the inauguration of the new president in October 2014, it appeared that reforms in this area were likely to be critical for the success of the new government.

REFERENCES

Afkar, R., J. Jellema and M. Wai-Poi (forthcoming) *Taxes, Transfers and inequality in Indonesia*, World Bank, Jakarta.

Aizenman, J., M. Lee and D. Park (2014) 'Structural change and inequality: a conceptual overview', in R. Kanbur, C. Rhee and J. Zhuang (eds) *Inequality in Asia and the Pacific*, Asian Development Bank and Routledge, London and New York: 134–55.

Alatas, V., R. Purnamasari and M. Wai-Poi (2011) 'Targeting of the poor and the vulnerable', in C. Manning and S. Sumarto (eds) *Employment, Living Standards and Poverty in Contemporary Indonesia*, Institute of Southeast Asian Studies, Singapore: 313–32.

Aswicahyono, H. and H. Hill (2004) 'Survey of recent developments', *Bulletin of Indonesian Economic Studies*, 40(3): 277–305.

Aswicahyono, H. and C. Manning (2011) 'Exports and job creation in Indonesia before and after the Asian financial crisis', Working Papers in Trade and Development, Arndt-Corden Department of Economics, Australian National University, Canberra.

Aswicahyono, H., H. Hill and D. Narjoko (2011) 'Indonesian industrialization: jobless growth?', in C. Manning and S. Sumarto (eds) *Employment, Living Standards and Poverty in Contemporary Indonesia*, Institute of Southeast Asian Studies, Singapore: 113–33.

Athukorala, P.C. (2006) 'Product fragmentation and trade patterns in East Asia', *Asian Economic Papers*, 4(3): 1–27.

Basri, C. and A. Patunru (2006) 'Survey of recent developments', *Bulletin of Indonesian Economic Studies*, 44(2): 295–319.

Booth, A. (1999) 'Initial conditions and miraculous growth: why is South East Asia different from Taiwan and South Korea?', *World Development*, 27(2): 301–21.

Burke, P.J. and B.P. Resosudarmo (2012) 'Survey of recent developments', *Bulletin of Indonesian Economic Studies*, 48(3): 299–324.

Dartanto, T. (2013) 'Reducing fuel subsidies and the implication on fiscal balance and poverty in Indonesia: a simulation analysis', *Energy Policy*, 58(C): 117–34.

Davies, R. and S. Howes (2014) 'Survey of recent developments', *Bulletin of Indonesian Economic Studies*, 50(2): 157–83.

Febriany, V., N. Toyamah, J. Sodo and S. Budiyati (2011) 'Qualitative impact study for PNPM-Generasi and PKH on the provision and the utilization of the maternal and child health services and basic education services in the provinces of West Java and East Nusa Tenggara', research report, SMERU Research Institute, Jakarta, January.

Felipe, J. and R. Hasan (eds) (2006) *Labor Markets in Asia: Issues and Perspectives*, Palgrave Macmillan for the Asian Development Bank, London.

Garnaut, R.G. (2010) 'The turning point in Chinese economic development: conceptual issues and new empirical evidence', in R. Garnaut, J. Gollay and L. Song (eds) *China: The Next Twenty Years of Reform and Development*, ANU E-Press, Australian National University, Canberra: 19–37.

ILO (International Labour Organization) (2013) *Labour and Social Trends in Indonesia 2013: Reinforcing the Role of Decent Work in Equitable Growth*, Jakarta.

Kanbur, R., C. Rhee, and J. Zhuang (2014) 'Introduction', in R. Kanbur, C. Rhee and J. Zhuang (eds) *Inequality in Asia and the Pacific*, Asian Development Bank and Routledge, London and New York: 1–18.

Lee, J.-W. and D. Wie (2013) 'Technological change, skill demand, and wage inequality in Indonesia', Asian Development Bank Economics Working Paper No. 340, Manila, March.

Leigh, A. and P. van der Eng (2009) 'Inequality in Indonesia: what can we learn from top incomes?', *Journal of Public Economics*, 93: 209–12.

Manning, C. (2010) 'The political economy of reform: labour after Soeharto', in E. Aspinall and G. Fealy (eds) *Soeharto's New Order and Its Legacy: Essays in Honour of Harold Crouch*, ANU E-Press, Australian National University, Canberra.

Manning, C. (2012) 'Indonesia's turnabout in employment and unemployment in the 2000s: progress or not?', in A. Booth, C. Manning and T.K. Wie (eds) *Land, Livelihood, the Economy and the Environment in Indonesia: Essays in Honour of Joan Hardjono*, Obor Foundation, Jakarta: 217–43.

McCarthy, J., D. Steenbergen, G. Acciaioli, G. Baker, A. Lucas, V. Rambe and C. Warren (2014) 'Dilemmas of participation: the National Community Empowerment Program,' in H. Hill (ed.) *Regional Dynamics in a Decentralized Indonesia*, Institute of Southeast Asian Studies, Singapore: 233–59.

Miranti, R., Y. Vidyattama, E. Hansnata, R. Cassells and A. Duncan (2013) 'Trends in poverty and inequality in decentralising Indonesia', OECD Social, Employment and Migration Working Paper No. 148, OECD Publishing, Paris.

OECD (Organisation for Economic Co-operation and Development) (2011) *Divided We Stand: Why Inequality Keeps Rising*, Paris.

Perdana, A. and J. Maxwell (2011) 'The evolution of poverty alleviation policies: ideas, issues and actors', in C. Manning and S. Sumarto (eds) *Employment, Living Standards and Poverty in Contemporary Indonesia*, Institute of Southeast Asian Studies, Singapore: 273–90.

Picketty, T. (2014) *Capital in the Twenty-first Century*, Belknap Press, Cambridge MA.

Prasetyantoko, A., H. Aswicahyono, N. Poerwana and T.A. Hervino (2013) 'Dampak dan respon dunia usaha terhadap kebijakan upah minimum provinsi (UMP) 2013: industri alas kaki dan garmen' [The impact of and private sector response to provincial minimum wage policies in 2013: footwear and garments], unpublished report, Atmajaya University, Jakarta.

Sen, K. and L. Steer (2005) 'Survey of recent developments', *Bulletin of Indonesian Economic Studies*, 43(3): 279–309.

Sumarto, S., A. Suryahadi and S. Bazzi (2008) 'Indonesia's social protection during and after the crisis', in A. Barrientos and D. Hulme (eds) *Social Protection for the Poor and Poorest: Concepts, Policies and Politics*, Palgrave Studies in Development, Palgrave Macmillan, London.

Syukri, M., S. Arif, M. Rosfadhila and W. Isdijoso (2010) 'Making the best of all resources: how Indonesian household recipients use the CCT allowance', *IDS Bulletin*, 41(4): 84–94.

TNP2K (Tim Nasional Percepatan Penanggulangan Kemiskinan) (2013) 'Program Keluarga Harapan (PKH): Indonesian conditional cash transfer programme', TNP2K Research Brief No. 42, International Policy Centre for Inclusive Growth, Jakarta.

Warr, P. (2011) 'Poverty, food prices and economic growth in Southeast Asian perspective', in C. Manning and S. Sumarto (eds) *Employment, Living Standards and Poverty in Contemporary Indonesia*, Institute of Southeast Asian Studies, Singapore: 47–66.

World Bank (2011) 'Program Keluarga Harapan: main findings from the impact evaluation of Indonesia's pilot household conditional cash transfer program', Jakarta.

World Bank (2012a) 'After five years, PNPM Mandiri becomes an integral part for the development of communities across Indonesia', 7 August. Available at http://www.worldbank.org/en/news/feature/2012/08/07/after-five-years-PNPM-Mandiri-becomes-an-integral-part-for-the-development-of-communities-across-indonesia0.

World Bank (2012b) 'Protecting poor and vulnerable households in Indonesia', World Bank Office, Jakarta. Available at http://documents.worldbank.org/curated/en/2012/02/15879721/protecting-poor-vulnerable-households-indonesia.

World Bank (2013) 'Indonesia: a Nationwide Community Program (PNPM) Peduli: caring for the invisible', April. Available at http://www.worldbank.org/en/results/2013/04/04/indonesia-a-nationwide-community-program-pnpm-peduli-caring-for-the-invisible.

Yudhoyono, S.B. (2011) 'Statement by H.E. Dr. Susilo Bambang Yudhoyono, President of the Republic of Indonesia, at the 100th International Labour Conference', Geneva, 14 June. Available at http://ilo.org/ilc/ILCSessions/100thSession/media-centre/speeches/WCMS_157638/lang--en/index.htm.

Yulaswati, V. and P. Sumadi (2011) 'Reducing poverty by increasing community and female participation', in C. Manning and S. Sumarto (eds) *Employment, Living Standards and Poverty in Contemporary Indonesia*, Institute of Southeast Asian Studies, Singapore: 291–312.

Yusuf, A.A. and B. Resosudarmo (2008) 'Mitigating distributional impact of fuel pricing reform: the Indonesian experience', *ASEAN Economic Bulletin*, 25(1): 32–47.

Yusuf, A.A., A. Sumner and I.A. Rum (2014) 'Twenty years of expenditure inequality in Indonesia, 1993–2013', *Bulletin of Indonesian Economic Studies*, 50(2): 243–54.

Zhuang, J., R. Kanbur and C. Rhee (2014) 'What drives Asia's rising inequality?', in R. Kanbur, C. Rhee and J. Zhuang (eds) *Inequality in Asia and the Pacific*, Asian Development Bank and Routledge, London and New York: 37–57.

17 Ambitious but inadequate: social welfare policies under Yudhoyono

Dinna Wisnu, Faisal Basri and Gatot Arya Putra*

During his ten years in office, President Susilo Bambang Yudhoyono spoke on many occasions about his commitment to improving the social welfare of Indonesian citizens. In a speech delivered in Bali in December 2012, he described four key priorities: eradicating poverty; providing access to decent jobs and economic opportunities (which he called 'inclusive growth ... through financial inclusion'); making basic needs available to and affordable for the poor; and providing a social safety net for people living below the poverty line (Yudhoyono 2012). These goals echoed the three pillars of socio-economic development that Yudhoyono had announced at the start of his tenure in 2005: economic growth, jobs growth and poverty reduction, to which he added environmental protection in 2007.

This chapter analyses the approaches and programs that Yudhoyono initiated during his ten years in power to advance these goals. We focus on education, health and social assistance, looking at the targets Yudhoyono set for his government, the strategies he implemented to achieve his goals and whether he met his targets. We conclude that the outcomes fell far short of expectations because the president's approach became ensnared in three sets of challenges that he never managed to resolve satisfactorily.

---

* Dinna Wisnu would like to thank the Indonesia Project, Australian National University, Canberra, for hosting her as a visiting researcher in January–February 2014, during which time part of this article was developed.

The first challenge was to reconcile the competing demands on the budget of massive subsidies and an expanding number of poverty alleviation programs. The president maintained numerous subsidies, notably fuel subsidies, that ate away at the fiscal space for other agendas, including social welfare. At the same time, he initiated various poverty alleviation and social protection programs for individuals, households and communities. Unfortunately, these programs were rolled out unevenly across Indonesia, and the ad hoc nature of many of them limited their long-term impact. In the end, Yudhoyono's strategy to alleviate poverty was mainly limited to disbursing social assistance, neglecting long-term strategies to free poor people from poverty and strengthen the competitiveness of the economy.

The second challenge was to lay down a coherent, strategic plan for social welfare and implement it across Indonesia's many competing ministries and government agencies. Under Yudhoyono the government produced ambitious plans for national development, economic growth and poverty reduction. However, these grand frameworks rarely overcame a basic lack of coordination between the many separate social welfare policies initiated by ministries and agencies. The government did not set clear targets to achieve its plans and rarely used benchmarking; there were serious failures even to coordinate basic data on the poor.

The third major challenge was to manage social welfare policy within the framework of decentralisation. Over the course of Yudhoyono's tenure, there was obvious and repeated confusion about the policy-making, budgeting, implementation and monitoring responsibilities of the different levels of government and how to coordinate the programs offered by them. For example, the new national health insurance system introduced in 2014 continued to operate alongside, rather than replacing, the numerous regional health-care programs introduced by provincial and district governments in earlier years. Although district and provincial governments were required to allocate funds to support the national scheme, and national social welfare programs in general, the regions continually expressed concerns about aspects of national policy, the lack of good national data on local-level poverty and interference by national agencies. Similar problems were evident in the delineation of budget responsibilities and implementation of national programs in the education sector.

We begin our assessment by reviewing the policy context when Yudhoyono took office in October 2004. As we shall see, he inherited a legislative framework that mandated significant action on social welfare, particularly education and health. We then provide a short overview of Yudhoyono's approach to social welfare, which we believe was characterised above all by a tension between his desire to maintain expenditure on fuel subsidies on the one hand and, on the other, to provide social assistance programs for underprivileged groups. This approach placed considerable strains on the budget and stalled efforts to develop a robust and sustainable social security system. To illustrate the argument, we evaluate the design, intent and outcomes of social welfare policies in three areas — health, education and social assistance — in each case comparing policy design and intent with results. We conclude that the Yudhoyono presidency was in many respects a decade of lost opportunity for social welfare policy in Indonesia.

POLICY CONTEXT

When Yudhoyono came to office in October 2004, democracy was already in full bloom in Indonesia. President B.J. Habibie (1998–99) had initiated the transition to democracy and the presidencies of Abdurrahman Wahid (1999–2001) and Megawati Sukarnoputri (2001–04) had cemented it. Yudhoyono benefited from improving macroeconomic conditions and a legacy of prudent fiscal policy. His predecessors had tackled the worst of the challenges arising from the financial crisis that had shaken the Indonesian economy in 1997–98. When he became president the growth rate was 4.3 per cent, the global economy was strong and international donors were keen to support Indonesia's economic reform efforts. These were propitious circumstances for bold reforms aimed at improving the social welfare of the Indonesian people.

Of course, the new government also faced challenges: fuel subsidies were eating up the central government's budget and limiting options for social welfare spending; the competitiveness of a number of labour-intensive industries was declining; and the industrial relations environment was testing. Yudhoyono inherited a legacy of weak coordination across different tiers and agencies of government (Aswicahyono and Hill 2004) but he was also equipped with a strong mandate to improve social welfare. The amended 1945 Constitution passed under his predecessor stipulated that all Indonesian citizens had 'the right to live in physical and spiritual prosperity [and] obtain medical care' and 'the right to social security' (article 28H). It required the state to 'develop a system of social security for all of the people', 'empower the weak and underprivileged in society in accordance with human dignity' and 'provide sufficient medical and public service facilities' (article 34). It also gave all citizens the right to receive an education (article 31).

Yudhoyono inherited a significant social welfare agenda in the form of laws passed during the Megawati presidency. In particular, Law 40/2004 on the National Social Security System aimed to achieve universal health insurance coverage, with salaried workers and other income earners to gain protection by paying regular financial contributions, and the government paying contributions on behalf of the poor. The spirit of the law was that no citizen would be denied access to quality health care simply because he or she was poor. In the education sphere, Yudhoyono was required to implement Law 20/2003 on the National Education System. It aimed to make education freely available and to increase school autonomy and community participation in education. It also stipulated that 20 per cent of central and local government budgets should be allocated to education, as required by the Constitution (article 31). As we will argue below, Yudhoyono's record in implementing this inherited legislative agenda was mixed, with relatively quick action on teacher and school reform, but foot-dragging on establishing a national health insurance system that lasted almost until the end of his presidency.

In his first term, Yudhoyono wanted to make better progress towards achieving the Millennium Development Goals for Indonesia set in 2000, including the goal of halving poverty by 2015. His approach was to protect the poor against economic shocks by providing direct and unconditional cash transfers to the poor following cuts in fuel subsidies, distributing subsidised rice to poor families, dispensing conditional community development grants, establishing conditional cash transfer programs to give pregnant women, mothers and infants access to health care and so on. We examine these social assistance programs in more detail below. At this point it is important to note that although Yudhoyono inherited a number of such programs from preceding governments, he also expanded them.

In his second term, Yudhoyono focused on tackling problems of lack of coordination of the many social programs that had grown up over the preceding decade. This task was delegated to the president's newly established National Team for the Acceleration of Poverty Reduction (Tim Nasional Percepatan Penanggulangan Kemiskinan, TNP2K), chaired by Vice-President Boediono, with implementing bodies at the provincial and district levels. TNP2K set guidelines for the relevant technical ministries and developed a national database of poor households, listing them by name and address. During his two terms in office, the president also produced ambitious plans to guide national policy-making, including two National Medium-term Development Plans, the Master Plan for the Acceleration and Expansion of Economic Development in Indonesia (Masterplan Percepatan dan Perluasan Pembangunan Ekonomi Indonesia, MP3EI) and the Master Plan for the Acceleration and Expansion of Poverty Reduction in Indonesia (Masterplan Percepatan dan Perluasan Pengurangan Kemiskinan Indonesia, MP3KI).

Table 17.1 Share of national government expenditure by sector, 2005–13 (% of GDP)

	Civil service	Economy	Health	Law & order	Social protection	Education	Energy subsidies
2005	9.23	0.86	0.22	0.58	0.07	1.04	3.75
2006	8.48	1.17	0.36	0.72	0.06	1.35	2.84
2007	8.00	1.11	0.40	0.71	0.08	1.29	2.96
2008	10.79	1.05	0.28	0.14	0.06	1.11	4.50
2009	7.46	1.07	0.28	0.14	0.05	1.52	1.68
2010	7.32	0.81	0.29	0.22	0.05	1.41	2.17
2011	7.70	1.23	0.19	0.30	0.05	1.32	3.45
2012	7.87	1.31	0.18	0.35	0.06	1.28	3.72
2013	7.77	1.21	0.20	0.40	0.19[a]	1.26	3.41

a Expenditure on social protection increased significantly from Rp 5 trillion in 2012 to Rp 17 trillion in 2013. It then declined sharply in 2014 to Rp 8 trillion, and is projected to stay at this level in 2015.

Source: Authors' calculations based on data from the Ministry of Finance and BPS.

Despite this proliferation of policies and guidelines, budgetary allocations for social welfare were always inadequate. Over Yudhoyono's two terms in office, spending on social protection, health and even education barely changed as a proportion of GDP (Table 17.1). During his second term, however, spending on energy subsidies ballooned from 1.7 per cent to 3.4 per cent of GDP. This points to a major failure to reform budget policy, one that greatly limited the president's room to expand government expenditure on social welfare or related areas such as infrastructure.

In fact, Yudhoyono did cut energy subsidies three times: in 2005, 2009 and 2013. But he also increased subsidies three times: once at the end of 2008 and twice in 2009. Moreover, he generally compensated poorer Indonesians for the subsidy cuts by expanding social assistance programs, including unconditional cash transfers. The overall effect of these contradictory policies was to significantly delay the creation of a more sustainable instrument of social welfare that could transcend the Yudhoyono presidency. It also led to accusations that the president was using both the fuel subsidies and the compensation packages to boost his popularity for electoral purposes.

Yudhoyono's choice of budget policy had two main implications, both of them negative. First, it put pressure on the state budget given the certainty of the rupiah depreciation cycle. The energy subsidies exposed the rupiah and reduced the government's ability to counter the negative impacts of global shocks. The World Bank (2013: iv–v) cited the fuel subsidy as the main source of fiscal and foreign exchange risk in Indonesia. Bank Indonesia (2013: 258) argued that rupiah depreciation was triggered by rising fuel imports, stoked by the subsidies. Expenditure on fuel subsidies, meanwhile, crowded out spending in other areas, including social welfare. The most dramatic example was the Rp 100 trillion cut to the state budget in 2014, which included cuts of 30 per cent to the budget of the Ministry of Social Affairs, 12 per cent to the budget of the Ministry of Health and 30 per cent to the budget of the Coordinating Ministry for Social Welfare.

Second, Yudhoyono's approach to social welfare entailed costly dependence on subsidies and cash transfers as a means of providing social protection, even though both have been proven to be ineffective in alleviating poverty (World Bank 2012: 6, 10, 29). In countries where data on citizens are poorly organised and unreliable, and where the state budget is limited, programs targeting the poor are typically less effective than planned because cash is dispensed thinly and unevenly, the targeting misses large numbers of poor households and the monitoring of implementation and results is weak. In Indonesia, the reliance on social assistance schemes transformed social welfare into another form of subsidy to be sustained by the central government, rather than being a means to empower the poor. Yet everybody knew that the central government lacked the fiscal space to disburse enough money to make significant improvements in the lives of all persons who qualified as recipients of the various schemes.

Having provided this brief overview, we are now in a position to review the design, implementation and results of policies in three key areas: health, education and social assistance.

HEALTH

As noted above, when Yudhoyono came to the presidency he inherited a law that set out a framework for universal health insurance. Rather than implementing Law 40/2004 on the National Social Security System to improve access for all citizens, however, he opted to expand the existing, free health-care programs. The government-financed programs for the poor and near-poor—Community Health Insurance (Jaminan Kesehatan Masyarakat, Jamkesmas), financed by the central government, and Regional Health Insurance (Jaminan Kesehatan Daerah, Jamkesda), financed by provincial and district governments—were developed out of the social safety net programs that Yudhoyono had inherited from the Megawati period (Wisnu 2012). By 2011 the government had added Maternity Insurance (Jaminan Persalinan, Jampersal), a maternal and neonatal health-care program. The Ministry of Health announced proudly that in June 2012, over 60 per cent of Indonesians had healthcare cover (Mikail 2012). After prompting from parliamentarians and civil society groups, Yudhoyono eventually approved a new law (Law 24/ 2011 on Social Security Providers) establishing a national health insurance system. Called simply National Health Insurance (Jaminan Kesehatan Nasional, JKN), this program was being rolled out as Yudhoyono left office. The president boasted shortly before he stepped down that 'This public policy is not only innovative but also revolutionary'.[1]

Although government spending on health increased under Yudhoyono, OECD data indicate that in 2011 total health expenditure was still only 2.7 per cent of GDP, much lower than the 5 per cent recommended by the World Health Organization (OECD 2014). Among ASEAN countries, only Brunei Darussalam spent less on health as a proportion of GDP, while Thailand, the ASEAN country with which Indonesia is most often compared, spent 4.1 per cent. The average for all East Asian and Pacific developing countries, meanwhile, was 4.8 per cent. In terms of health expenditure per capita based on purchasing power parity, among the developing countries in East Asia and the Pacific, only Timor-Leste spent less than Indonesia in 2011. The average per capita expenditure for the region was $355, but Indonesia spent only $127 (OECD 2014).

This underfunding of health led to serious shortcomings in health facilities and the health workforce, especially in remote and rural areas outside Java. For example, in 2009 the National Development Planning Agency (Badan Perencanaan Pembangunan Nasional, Bappenas) found that over 80 per cent of villages had no access to a physician (Sarjunani 2009: 18). A review of policies enacted between 2004 and 2011 confirmed that there was serious inequality of access to specialist physicians across Indonesia, with Eastern Indonesia particularly poorly served (Meliala, Hort and Trisnantoro 2013: 32). Problems of recruitment and retention of midwives in rural and remote areas also persisted, despite programs to improve the distribution of midwives.[2]

Such problems translated to poor health outcomes for the Indonesian population, despite the expansion of free health-care schemes. Indonesia's maternal mortality rate is still higher than the rate for Asia as a whole. Though there has been a downward trend in the rate, if one

---

1 'Education meaningless without healthcare system: SBY', *Jakarta Post*, 15 August 2014.
2 Interview with Emi Taufik, chair of the Indonesian Midwives Association (Ikatan Bidan Indonesia), 25 August 2014.

deconstructs the data one can see that Indonesia's maternal mortality rate has in fact been stagnating (World Bank 2009). Stunting is also a very serious problem, with 37.2 per cent of children aged 0-4 having a height more than two standard deviations below the average in 2013 (Ministry of Health 2013: 4). To the extent that there was progress on health indicators under Yudhoyono, this was mainly because of a continuation of long-run trends, not because of the interventions taken by his government. We conducted tests on health indicators for which perfect time-series data were available, such as immunisation rates for diphtheria, pertussis and tetanus (DPT) and measles. Immunisation rates improved both over the long run (1980-2012) and in the Yudhoyono era (2003-12), but the rate of improvement was about 50 per cent lower under Yudhoyono. In the case of health expenditure per capita (in purchasing power parity terms), our statistical tests again showed that there were no significant differences between the two periods.

Another major shortcoming of the Yudhoyono government was its failure to implement Law 40/2004 on the National Social Security System for almost ten years. Although a new national health insurance system was being rolled out by the time Yudhoyono left office, this had come after much foot-dragging. The first years of his presidency passed without any progress at all in this area, despite numerous reports and drafts from experts and stakeholders (Wisnu 2012: 129-32, 134-6). Yudhoyono issued a presidential regulation setting up a national social security council in June 2008, but then failed to take any further action, prompting a civil society coalition to file and win a lawsuit in 2010. Still the government did not budge, but the action had drawn the attention of the public and some legislators to the need to act on Law 40/2004 (Wisnu 2012: 136-40).

The efforts of civil society and the parliament were rewarded in 2011 with the passage of Law 24/2011 on Social Security Providers authorising the establishment of a new national health insurance system. But the birth of this law was not easy. The government did not want the law to include specific details on how the relevant agencies and their programs would be run, while the parliament wanted to bind the government to clear commitments. Some ministers and senior government officials argued that the country could not afford a universal health insurance system, while the president remained silent on this issue (Wisnu 2012: 140-63). Overall, it was obvious that the government saw the new system more as a fiscal burden than as an investment in the health of Indonesian citizens.[3]

---

3 For accounts of the politics leading to this outcome, see Aspinall (2014) and especially Wisnu (2012).

During all the delays in the implementation of Law 40/2004 on Social Security Providers and the uncertainty over the establishment of a national health insurance system, President Yudhoyono allowed a proliferation of regional health insurance (Jamkesda) schemes. In effect, he allowed local governments to create their own social assistance schemes in the health-care area in lieu of a national health insurance system. (The legal basis for them to do so was a 2008 regulation issued by the minister of health.) By 2010, 33 provinces and 349 districts were operating such schemes, most of them covering primary health-care services (both inpatient and out-patient). The lure of free health care became an attractive bargaining chip for politicians to dangle before the electorate when seeking election, especially when the beneficiaries were not confined to the poor and near-poor. These schemes created a perception among some citizens that they should not have to contribute towards the cost of their health care, even if they could afford to do so. As a result, many citizens who had not been required to pay a single rupiah under their local Jamkesda schemes were disappointed to learn that they would have to contribute under the National Health Insurance (JKN) system launched in 2014. At the same time, both the Jamkesda and Jamkesmas schemes were not organised on the basis of proper actuarial calculations. Demand was high but funding was insufficient, leaving many local governments owing large debts to local hospitals and clinics. No systematic studies on this aspect of the schemes have yet been conducted, but media sources have reported numerous failures of the Jamkesda and Jamkesmas programs.

Law 24/2011 on Social Security Providers stated that Jamkesda and Jamkesmas were to be integrated into the national health insurance system, and established a centralised 'super-agency', the Agency for Social Security Providers (Badan Penyelenggara Jaminan Sosial Kesehatan, BPJS Health), to oversee this process. Few regions were willing to give up their programs, however. Local governments obtained political benefits for providing free health care directly to their people, and they questioned the ability of BPJS Health to provide coverage for all poor persons in their regions, distrusting the data held by national bodies. In mid-2014, for example, a health official from the mayor's office in Semarang claimed that the national agency's data missed 20 per cent of the poor in that city.[4] Many hospitals were also reluctant to join BPJS Health because they feared they would experience delayed payments, as

---

4 This comment was made at a workshop on decentralisation and social protection organised by Paramadina Graduate School, Bappenas, GRM International and the Australian Department of Foreign Affairs and Trade, 4 July 2014.

under Jamkesmas and Jamkesda.[5] When Yudhoyono left office in 2014, the mess surrounding the implementation of Law 40/2004 had not yet been resolved.

Overall, the slow and ponderous establishment of a national health insurance system shows that Yudhoyono was very reluctant to implement the original goal of Law 40/2004 of securing affordable access to health care for all citizens. Concerned about creating a new system that would bring about drastic change, he called on his ministries to study the details of any proposed changes carefully before moving forward. Although one could argue that he was simply being prudent, Yudhoyono was also clearly reluctant to do what the law ordered him to do. The main reason was that he was worried about the impact on the budget. The president was deeply concerned about introducing a health insurance system that would place pressure on the state budget at a time when he was maintaining costly energy subsidies; perhaps he feared that increasing health expenditures would force him to reduce subsidies at a politically inopportune time.

Yudhoyono's fiscal conservatism also explains why his administration shifted much of the burden for health-care financing to local governments, by encouraging them to run their own health insurance systems. Despite all three of his health ministers being called before parliament to explain why Law 40/2004 had not been implemented, he refused to budge on this issue for many years. And in the end, when he did finally establish a national scheme, Yudhoyono allowed his minister of finance to set the government's contribution towards the health insurance premiums of the poor at a miserly Rp 19,225 per head, again presumably to save government revenue. Once again, the burden was being thrown onto hospitals and people on low incomes. Though his ministers took much of the heat for these decisions, ultimately Yudhoyono must bear the responsibility.

EDUCATION

President Yudhoyono frequently declared that education was a major priority for his government. Yet the results of his policies were generally disappointing, especially when measured in terms of educational outcomes for students.

---

5 Dinna Wisnu's interview with representatives of the Regional Hospitals Association (Asosiasi Rumah Sakit Daerah, ARSADA) and the Indonesian Hospitals Association (Perhimpunan Rumah Sakit Seluruh Indonesia, PERSI), 29 August 2014.

Law 20/2003 on the National Education System, passed one year before Yudhoyono took office, set four major objectives: basic education should be free of all charges; schools should be given the authority to manage their own programs; community participation in education should be encouraged; and the financing of education should be based on the number of students, rather than number of schools, in a particular region. If well implemented, this strategy could be expected to achieve good results. In South Korea, for example, where schools have autonomy to establish their own curricular and assessment policies, educational performance is outstanding. A year into Yudhoyono's first term, in 2005, his administration passed a new law on teachers (Law 14/2005). It set minimum levels of competency for teachers, introduced a new teacher certification program and prohibited teachers from having more than one job. Also in 2005, the government introduced a program to increase enrolment rates, called Schools Operational Assistance (Bantuan Operasi Sekolah, BOS). Under BOS, the government provided cash directly to schools based on the number of students enrolled. In addition to the specific goals in the Education Law, the ultimate goals of Yudhoyono's government were clear: increasing enrolment rates and providing higher-quality education to all students.

One way to assess the results is to look at the educational attainment of Indonesian students as measured by the tests conducted since 2003 as part of the Programme for International Student Assessment (PISA). Indonesia does not perform well on this indicator. The scores of 15-year-old Indonesian students in mathematics, science and reading have consistently been below those of students in Thailand, a relevant regional comparator. In addition, our calculations indicate that the trajectory of Indonesian students' performance decelerated during the Yudhoyono period—that is, that the rate of improvement in the scores of Indonesian students has been declining.

As shown in Table 17.2, between 2003 and 2012 Indonesian students' performance in mathematics decelerated at a rate of –0.7, a worse result than any country except Qatar. Mathematics is an important subject because performance is closely correlated with GDP per capita. But despite the introduction of standardised national examinations under the Education Law, Indonesia's PISA scores in mathematics barely improved, from 360 in 2003 to 391 in 2006, 371 in 2009 and 375 in 2012. Indonesia also performed poorly in reading, with a deceleration rate of –0.4 in 2003–12. This was much worse than Thailand, where the rate of improvement accelerated by 0.7. Thailand also outperformed Indonesia in science. In 2006, 2009 and 2012, the mean science scores for Indonesian students were 393, 383 and 382 respectively, compared with 421, 425 and 444 for Thai students.

Table 17.2 Rate of acceleration or deceleration in mean mathematics performance (quadratic term) in the PISA tests, selected countries, 2003–12[a]

	Coefficient	Standard error
Hong Kong	0.3	(0.21)
Indonesia	–0.7	(0.26)
Jordan	–0.2	(0.51)
Latvia	0.1	(0.20)
Liechtenstein	0.3	(0.25)
Lithuania	0.7	(0.37)
Macao	0.4	(0.14)
Montenegro	0.2	(0.31)
Qatar	–2.3	(0.21)
Romania	0.3	(0.54)
Russian Federation	0.1	(0.23)
Serbia	0.0	(0.45)
Taiwan	1.3	(0.52)
Thailand	0.2	(0.17)
Tunisia	0.3	(0.20)
Uruguay	–0.6	(0.18)

a Rates for Singapore and Malaysia are not included in the table because they did not participate in the 2003 PISA tests. Singapore scores highly in subsequent tests; Malaysia performs less well, but nevertheless better than Indonesia.
Source: Authors calculations based on OECD (2013).

When investigating the returns to investments in human capital, it is important to note that past educational performance is a proxy for the current productive potential of individuals. The negative consequences of Indonesia's poor educational outcomes, both for the livelihoods of millions of individual Indonesians and for the prosperity of the nation as a whole, should be obvious.

On some other measures, Indonesia's performance looks better. For example, as part of its drive to achieve education for all, Indonesia made significant progress in improving enrolment figures, particularly at the lower levels of education. According to data from the National Socio-economic Survey (Survei Sosio-Ekonomi Nasional, Susenas), between 2003 and 2012 school enrolment rates increased from 96.4 to 97.9 per cent for children aged 7–12 years, 81 to 89.5 per cent for those aged 13–15 years, 51 to 60.9 per cent for those aged 16–18 years, and 11.7 to 15.7 per cent for those aged 19–24 years. But again, statistical tests suggest that the quadratic growth rates in the Yudhoyono era (2003–12) did not differ from those under preceding governments (1980–2002). In other words, the improvements experienced under Yudhoyono were not a particular achievement of his presidency, but rather a continuation of a long-term trend. Even without any of the new programs, enrolment rates would still have been higher in the Yudhoyono era than previously. Similarly, the improvements in pupil-to-teacher ratios that had begun in the preceding period continued in the Yudhoyono period, without any marked acceleration attributable specifically to the policies of his administration.

What accounts for the failure of the Education Law to bring about measurable improvements in performance? For one thing, under Yudhoyono the principle of school autonomy enshrined in the Education Law did not work well. The priority of schools was to ensure that their students passed the national examinations, but the two ministries in charge of the country's schools did not provide feedback or support to help them improve their performance. The Ministry of National Education and the Ministry of Religious Affairs continued to dictate national curricular and assessment policies, and to set standards for the *output* of education in terms of national examinations for primary and secondary school students, but they did not provide pathways to help schools achieve those standards. They did not reward schools or teachers whose students excelled in the national examinations, for example, or implement strategies to lift the performance of those that performed poorly. Moreover, both ministries were so politically powerful that they could easily ride roughshod over the principles of community participation and school autonomy enshrined in the Education Law. As a result, those principles were never fully implemented, despite their importance for producing high-quality outcomes (Schleicher 2011). The education system also suffered from inadequate funding. The BOS program rarely provided sufficient funds to fully cover schools' operational costs, with some local governments having to provide additional funds to help the schools in their areas.

Another major problem was that the Yudhoyono administration failed to establish a comprehensive system to select, train, compensate and develop teachers and school principals in a way that would systematically ensure teacher quality. Law 14/2005 on Teachers set minimum competency standards for teachers but did not establish a realistic method for improving that competency. The teacher certification process established under the law has been assessed as providing 'no evidence as yet that it has improved the performance of Indonesian students or reduced rates of teacher absenteeism' (Suryahadi and Sambodho 2013: 157).

In short, while there was significant policy change in the education sector under Yudhoyono, the results were far from impressive.

SOCIAL ASSISTANCE PROGRAMS

Social assistance programs are programs that target the poor with funding allocated from the government budget. President Yudhoyono was a great believer in this style of social welfare, and the national government ran a great number of such programs during his tenure. Some were continued or adapted from earlier periods; in particular, a large number of social assistance programs introduced as short-term responses to the financial crisis of 1997–98 were continued by subsequent governments (World Bank 2004). Among the chief social assistance programs offered during Yudhoyono's tenure were unconditional cash transfers paid to very poor households to compensate them for cuts to the fuel subsidy. These were known as Direct Cash Assistance (Bantuan Langsung Tunai, BLT) and later as Direct Temporary Cash Assistance (Bantuan Langsung Sementara Masyarakat, BLSM). There were also numerous other schemes providing conditional cash transfers or other forms of social assistance to individuals, households or communities, including the National Program for Community Empowerment (Program Nasional Pemberdayaan Masyarakat, PNPM), Raskin (a subsidised rice program) and the Hopeful Families Program (Program Keluarga Harapan, PKH). Yudhoyono saw such programs as helping to strengthen the country's poverty reduction efforts, and thus helping to achieve key Millennium Development Goals.

Rather than attempting to review all these programs, we will focus briefly on one that became especially closely identified with Yudhoyono's approach to social welfare: PNPM. Building on an earlier program introduced by the World Bank in 1998, it provided block grants to subdistricts and villages based on competitive proposals prepared by local communities. Launched in 2007, the scheme was based on the idea that stakeholders—in particular, local communities—should get a say in determining their own development priorities and managing their own projects. As part of the same participatory development idea, Yudhoyono encouraged community members to participate in grassroots development planning meetings (*musyawarah perencanaan pembangunan, musrenbang*), designed to allow ideas from the bottom (villages and subdistricts) to influence national policy-making and budgeting. Overall, PNPM and the model of participatory development that underpinned it have been subject to much positive evaluation, including from actors such as the World Bank (2011).

Despite the government's good intentions, however, the *musrenbang* process did not run smoothly. The bureaucrats running the meetings tended to be captured by a rigid administrative mindset that was unresponsive to community input and driven by a desire to maintain uniformity across provinces. One of the few systematic studies on this topic concludes that, in practice, the *musrenbang* procedure was of questionable effectiveness in bringing local priorities to national attention (Ma'rif, Nugroho and Wijayanti 2010). This is backed up by testimony from participants posted on websites and blogs. The process of synchronising the plans submitted by villages and subdistricts before sending them to the provincial level would typically take just a single day, making it impossible for national planning to reflect all of the ideas submitted by communities. Moreover, the meetings that took place at the provincial and national levels tended to focus on how programs could be inserted into the national agenda, rather than how the national budget could be adjusted to respond to the priorities identified by local communities. In effect, this meant that grassroots planning was often futile. On top of that, there were no mechanisms for citizens to monitor whether or how their ideas were implemented by the central government.

The PNPM program itself has been criticised for being ineffective (Wisnu 2013). One problem was that the main program spawned about a dozen derivative programs run by dozens of ministries and agencies. Thus, PNPM Generasi Sehat Cerdas, an education and health program for mothers and children, was managed by the Directorate General of Rural Development Programs in the Ministry of Home Affairs and funded by the Australian aid agency, AusAID; PNPM Peduli, targeting vulnerable groups such as trafficking victims, sex workers and people with disabilities, was managed by selected non-government organisations and funded from grants provided by the PNPM multi-donor support facility; and PNPM Pariwisata, a program to identify opportunities in the tourism sector, was managed by the Ministry of Culture and Tourism. There were wide variations across regions in terms of how easy it was to gain access to grants, with communities in remote areas finding it particularly difficult to obtain funding. At the same time, because PNPM was reliant not only on Indonesian government funds but also on assistance from multiple international donors, many programs reflected donor rather than community priorities, and some areas (such as Aceh, West Java and Jakarta) attracted multiple donors while other areas did not attract any (Wisnu 2013: 24–6).

Overall, the various PNPM programs were rolled out unevenly, often leaving out isolated areas, islands and border areas that actually needed them the most (Wisnu 2013; Yulaswati 2013: 13; Coordinating Ministry for Social Welfare 2014). Implementing agencies tended to defend themselves against charges that they were neglecting needy areas by saying that their programs were pilots that would be rolled out to poorer areas in the future as funding became available. But if that was the case, there should have been attempts to measure the multiplier effects of those pilot programs, and subsequent programs should have built on the lessons learned from earlier iterations. For instance, the failure of very poor Indonesians to participate in the *musrenbang* process should certainly have been noted and remedied. Soul-searching of that type rarely happened, however (Wisnu 2013: 26–7).

The absence of performance measurement was a major problem for a program that was supposed be based on a bottom-up policy-planning process. Yudhoyono failed to appreciate that, in Indonesia, stakeholders have always interpreted the term 'social assistance' (*bantuan sosial*) very loosely — as being more akin to a donation (*amal*) than to a planned process. Many providers understood social assistance simply to mean handing out cash, or creating programs that provided interest-free loans or free training, without any obligation on the part of the beneficiary. Accordingly, many agencies focused on distribution, without clear performance measures or benchmarking. Those performance indicators that were used tended to focus on whether a program had actually been executed and how many agencies had been involved, rather than the more critical questions of how it had performed and whether it had reached a growing number of beneficiaries over time. Moreover, the lessons learned from pilot projects were hardly ever used as inputs for subsequent planning.

In the face of the proliferation of programs, in his second term Yudhoyono attempted to reorganise social assistance under the banner of pro-poor policy. He tried to introduce uniform policies across the various ministries and levels of government responsible for implementation. For instance, in December 2006 he instructed his ministries to stop conducting their own separate poverty surveys, and instituted a single method for measuring poverty across the country. One goal was to increase the accuracy of targeting of social assistance programs; it had long been recognised as a major problem that much of the assistance was benefiting wealthier groups rather than the poor (see, for example, Suryahadi et al. 2010). The National Team for the Acceleration of Poverty Reduction (TNP2K) cooperated with the national statistics agency (Badan Pusat Statistik, BPS) to develop a single, nationwide, household-based database that listed poor households by name and address. Ministries and both national and local government agencies, including Jamkesmas, Jamkesda and BPJS Health, could use the database to identify the households most in need of social assistance. The data remained problematic, however, because they did not include poor people who were not living in households, such as street children, orphans and prisoners. The data also quickly became outdated, and the national agencies failed to engage with local governments to keep the database up-to-date.[6]

Yudhoyono was a strong believer in grand, strategic planning as a means to improve social welfare. Therefore, in addition to grassroots planning processes such as *musrenbang*, he developed a master plan for economic development (MP3EI), a master plan for poverty reduction (MP3KI) and two ambitious national medium-term development plans. But although he believed that good planning was essential to achieve satisfactory outcomes, he seems to have forgotten that good planning works best in sound institutions where people share the same basic understanding of the issues and are competent at implementing plans and assessing their effects (Hanney et al. 2003). Where multiple agencies are involved, one must be aware of the possibility that priorities and approaches will differ. In the context of Indonesia, the grand planning model that Yudhoyono promoted created yet another level of complexity in policy implementation, giving rise to serious coordination problems among government agencies, to say nothing of civil society and the private sector. Every ministry was allowed to develop its own sectoral vision, creating multiple layers for the interpretation and integration of policies. Moreover, given the limited budgets available for the various social assistance programs, the government's grand plans were not matched by a commensurate capacity to deliver. Agencies under the president's direct control could implement only a fraction of what was planned, especially given that decentralisation handed much of the power for delivering programs to the districts. Although social assistance programming looked impressive on paper, delivery on the ground was much more limited.

CONCLUSION

In this chapter, we have identified the key programs and approaches to social welfare that President Yudhoyono adopted during his ten years in office. Overall, it is our view that the president chose to play safe in this policy area. He generally avoided clear targets, performance indicators, benchmarking and visionary efforts to anticipate future challenges. Rather than committing himself personally to particular programs, he put a safe distance between himself and his policies by encouraging a plethora of complex bureaucratic procedures, establishing new agencies

---

6 Interviews with West Java and Central Java local government heads, 4 July 2014.

and giving ministries free reign to pursue their own grand plans and regulations. While social welfare programs proliferated, they suffered from poor design and short-term thinking, as was demonstrated clearly by Yudhoyono's decade-long reluctance to establish a new national health insurance scheme, despite being mandated to do so by a law he had inherited from his predecessor. Instead, the president's paradigm of social welfare stressed piecemeal social assistance programs funded from the central budget. At the same time, Yudhoyono hampered his government's ability to deliver such programs, or to develop more ambitious plans, by persisting with a budget policy of providing costly energy subsidies.

The consequences of Yudhoyono's policy choices were dire. The cost of subsidies meant that when Indonesia experienced external shocks—such as a rise in the price of fuel, as happened in 2014—social welfare programs were slashed. Progress in health and education stagnated. Short-term social assistance programs were given precedence over comprehensive, long-term plans to lift poor Indonesians permanently out of poverty. The negative effects of these policy failures will be felt for the next 20–30 years. Circumstances were very favourable for Indonesia when Yudhoyono came to office: the country had recovered from a terrible financial crisis, it was reaping a demographic dividend, China's economic development was surging, and Indonesia was seen as one of the most promising and attractive economies in Southeast Asia. President Yudhoyono failed to take full advantage of these circumstances to improve the basic welfare of the Indonesian people.

REFERENCES

Aspinall, E. (2014) 'Health care and democratization in Indonesia', *Democratization*, 21(5): 803–23.
Aswicahyono, H. and H. Hill (2004) 'Survey of recent developments', *Bulletin of Indonesian Economic Studies*, 40(3): 277–305.
Bank Indonesia (2013) *Laporan Tahunan Perekonomian Tahun 2013* [Annual Economic Report 2013], Jakarta.
Coordinating Ministry for Social Welfare (2014) 'Siaran pers nomor: 13/Humas Kesra/IV/2014' [Press release no. 13/Humas Kesra/IV/2014], Jakarta, 21 April.
Hanney, S.R., M.A. Gonzales-Block, M.J. Buxton and M. Kogan (2003) 'The utilisation of health research in policy-making: concepts, examples and methods of assessment', *Health Research Policy and Systems*, 1(2): 1–28.
Ma'rif, S., Nugroho and Wijayanti (2010) 'Evaluasi efektivitas pelaksanaan musyawarah perencanaan pembangunan (musrenbang) Kota Semarang' [Evaluation of the effectiveness of *musrenbang* implementation in Semarang city], *Riptek*, 4(2): 53–62.

Meliala, A., K. Hort and L. Trisnantoro (2013) 'Addressing the unequal geographic distribution of specialist doctors in Indonesia', *Social Science and Medicine*, 82: 30–34.
Mikail, B. (2012) 'Tahun 2014, 70 persen masyarakat punya asuransi kesehatan' [By 2014, 70 per cent of the population will have health insurance], *Kompas*, 29 June. Available at http://health.kompas.com/read/2012/06/29/16340953/Tahun.2014.70.Persen.Masyarakat.Punya.Asuransi.Kesehatan
Ministry of Health (2013) 'Riset kesehatan dasar: Riskesdas 2013' [National report on basic health research 2013], National Institute of Health Research and Development, Ministry of Health, Jakarta.
OECD (Organisation for Economic Co-operation and Development) (2013) *PISA 2012 Results: What Students Know and Can Do. Student Performance in Reading, Mathematics and Science (Volume I)*, Paris.
OECD (Organisation for Economic Co-operation and Development) (2014) 'OECD health statistics 2014', online database. Available at http://www.oecd.org/els/health-systems/health-data.htm
Sarjunani, N. (2009) 'Kebijakan pembangunan SDM kesehatan dalam draft rancangan RPJMN 2010–2014 dan pendekatan kewilayahan' [Policy on developing a health workforce in the draft National Medium-term Development Plan 2010–2014 and the regional approach], presentation to a cross-sector, cross-program meeting at PPSDM Kesehatan, Ministry of Health, Palembang, 5–7 October.
Schleicher, A. (2011) *Building a High-quality Teaching Profession: Lessons from around the World*, Organisation for Economic Co-operation and Development, Paris.
Suryahadi, A. and P. Sambodho (2013) 'An assessment of policies to improve teacher quality and reduce teacher absenteeism', in D. Suryadarma and G.W. Jones (eds) *Education in Indonesia*, Institute of Southeast Asian Studies, Singapore: 139–59.
Suryahadi, A., W. Widyanti, D. Suryadarma and S. Sumarto (2010) 'Targeting in social protection programmes: the experience of Indonesia', in S. Cook (ed.) *Social Protection as Development Policy: Asian Perspectives*, Routledge, New Delhi.
Wisnu, D. (2012) *Politik Sistem Jaminan Sosial* [Politics of the Social Security System], PT Gramedia Pustaka Utama, Jakarta.
Wisnu, D. (2013) 'Indonesia's experience with targeting schemes: is it heading towards universal coverage? Case of PNPM and PKH', unpublished report for UNESCAP, Jakarta, 25 July.
World Bank (2004) 'Protecting the vulnerable: the design and implementation of effective safety nets', Washington DC.
World Bank (2009) '"… and then she died": Indonesia maternal health policy assessment', Report No. 53327, Washington DC, February.
World Bank (2011) 'Indonesia: 60,000 rural villages to benefit from new World Bank support for PNPM Mandiri', press release, Jakarta, 14 July. Available at http://www.worldbank.org/en/news/press-release/2011/07/14/indonesia-60000-rural-villages-benefit-new-world-bank-support-pnpm-mandiri
World Bank (2012) 'BLT temporary unconditional cash transfer: social assistance program and public expenditure review 2', Report No. 67324, Jakarta and Washington DC. Available at http://documents.worldbank.org/curated/en/2012/02/15893823/bantuan-langsung-tunai-blt-temporary-unconditional-cash-transfer

World Bank (2013) 'Pertumbuhan melambat; resiko tinggi' [Slowing growth; high risk], *Indonesia Economic Quarterly*, Jakarta, December. Available at http://www.worldbank.org/in/news/feature/2013/12/16/indonesia-economic-quarterly-december-2013

Yudhoyono, S.B. (2012) 'Leaving poverty behind, promoting sustainable growth with equity through enhanced global partnership: towards a new development agenda post-2015', speech at the opening of the Regional Meeting and Stakeholder Consultation on the Post-2015 Development Agenda, Bali, 13 December.

Yulaswati, V. (2013) 'Targeting dalam program-program perlindungan sosial' [Targeting of social protection programs], Powerpoint presentation at the National Consultation seminar organised by Paramadina University and UNESCAP, 4 June.

Index

A
ABRI
    see Indonesian Armed Forces
Aceh, 138–43
    Aceh Transition Committee, 141
    conflict, 30, 78, 136, 139, 231
    Crisis Management Initiative, 139
    Free Aceh Movement (Gerakan Aceh Merdeka, GAM), 36, 137, 138, 139–43, 152
    flag, 142
    governor election, 141, 142
    local regulation on Islamic criminal code (Qanun Jinayat), 206–7
    military support for peace agreement, 140
    Partai Aceh, 141, 142, 143
    peace agreement, 1, 11, 27, 30, 35, 36, 45, 46, 102, 136–7, 138, 139, 140, 142, 230
    sharia law, 206, 209
    terrorist training camp, 150
    Tripa peat swamp case, 262, 271
    tsunami, 27, 137, 138, 139
    women, 206, 209
    2009 violence, 141
actor-specific theory, 74, 84
AEC
    see ASEAN Economic Community
Agency for Social Security Providers (Badan Penyelenggara Jaminan Sosial Kesehatan, BPJS Health), 333, 340
agriculture, 260, 264–5, 288, 289, 305–6
    employment, 309

Ahmadiyah, 8, 12, 100, 241–3, 248, 251, 253
    decree banning teachings of, 242, 249, 251
Ahtisaari, Martti, 138, 139, 140
Ali, Suryadharma, 8, 29, 100, 242, 244, 246, 250, 251, 254, 255
Alliance of Indigenous Peoples of the Archipelago (Aliansi Masyarakat Adat Nusantara, AMAN), 269
AMAN
    see Alliance of Indigenous Peoples of the Archipelago
Ambon, 151, 232
Anti-bomb Taskforce (Satgas Bom), 147, 147n, 150, 151
Aquino, Corazon, 60, 62
ASEAN, 28, 73, 76, 77, 79–80, 81, 220, 221, 294, 331
    +3, 79
    border conflicts, 76
    economic growth, 287
    global production networks, 295
    Indonesia as chair, 79, 80
    Intergovernmental Commission on Human Rights, 81
    –United Nations partnership, 80
ASEAN Economic Community (AEC), 78–9, 300
Asian financial crisis 1997–98, 1, 27, 78, 286, 289, 290, 298–9, 304–5, 307, 311–12, 313, 327, 338, 342
    see also global financial crisis
Australia, 144, 150
    AusAID, 339
    carbon dioxide emissions, 264

Australian embassy bombing, 147 A
authoritarianism, 16, 17, 29, 59, 60–1,
  62, 98, 118, 131, 158, 219, 221, 285
  Subianto, Prabowo, 18, 56
  Suharto era, 1, 15, 25, 95, 130, 217
  transition to democracy, 1, 57, 58,
  59, 60–2, 65, 78, 94, 115, 116, 129

B
Bakor Pakem
  see Coordinating Board for
  Monitoring Mystical Beliefs in
  Society
Bakrie, Aburizal, 8, 45, 47, 101, 284
Bali Democracy Forum, 28, 80–1, 220
Bangladesh, 140, 317
Bank Century, 101, 104–5, 310n
Bank Indonesia, 104, 179, 284, 284n,
  289, 290, 291, 330
Bappenas
  see National Development
  Planning Agency
Basri, Chatib, 123, 284, 292, 293, 294n
BIN
  see State Intelligence Agency
BKPM
  see Investment Coordinating
  Board
BLT
  see poverty, unconditional cash
  transfer program
BNP2TKI
  see National Agency for the
  Placement and Protection of
  Indonesian Migrant Workers
BNPT
  see National Counterterrorism
  Agency
Boediono, Vice-President, 24, 30, 47,
  48, 102, 106–7, 144, 268, 284, 311,
  328
BOS
  see education, Schools
  Operational Assistance
BPJS Health
  see Agency for Social Security
  Providers
BPK |
  see Supreme Audit Agency
BPS
  see national statistics agency

Brazil, 259, 264, 266, 274
  National Plan on Climate Change,
  274
Brunei Darussalam, 331
Business Competition Supervisory
  Commission (Komisi Pengawas
  Persaingan Usaha, KPPU), 299

C
Cameron, David, 220, 222
Cebongan jail, 126
Centre for Humanitarian Dialogue,
  138
China, 79, 203, 285, 289, 291, 307, 312,
  317, 320, 342
  carbon dioxide emissions, 264
  –US relations, 77
Christian groups, 147, 148, 239, 241,
  244–5
civil service, 94, 96–7, 100, 106–8
  economic reform influence, 108
  influence drafting legislation,
  106–8
  Law 17/2011 (State Intelligence
  Agencies), 107
  Law 5/2014 (Civil Service Law),
  106–7
  obstructionist, 108, 109
Civil Servants Corps (Korps Pegawai
  Negeri, Korpri), 106
civil society, 25, 28, 53, 116, 126, 127,
  131, 145, 234, 260, 261, 262, 268,
  271, 315, 331, 332
climate change policy, 272–4
  see also environment; forests
  and forestry; greenhouse gas
  emissions
Clinton, Hillary, 220
coal, 293, 319
communists, mass killing, 218, 228
  presidential apology proposal,
  227, 228
  see also Indonesian Communist
  Party
Community Health Insurance
  (Jaminan Kesehatan Masyarakat,
  Jamkesmas), 330, 333–4, 340
Constitution (1945), 12, 24, 94, 95, 186,
  188, 214, 328
  amendments, 93–7, 102, 105, 106,
  110, 190, 217, 327

Constitutional Court, 25, 142, 142n, 143, 165, 175–6, 179, 186–91, 206, 222, 249, 250n, 268
  activist court, 187, 189–90, 191
  corruption of chief justice, 179, 191
  declarations of conditional constitutionality, 189, 190
  economic and socio-cultural rights decisions, 188–9
  electoral system decisions, 188
  establishment, 175
  freedom-of-speech decisions, 187–8
  functions, 186–6
  judicial appointment process, 191–2
  KPK commissioners case proceedings, 180–1
  land rights decisions, 189
  rejection of interference from legislature, 190–1
  Wedlock case, 188, 189–90
  Yudhoyono view, 191–3
Convention against Torture and Cruel, Inhumane or Degrading Treatments or Punishments, 217
Convention on the Elimination of All Forms of Discrimination against Women, 207
Convention on the Elimination of All Forms of Racial Discrimination, 217
Coordinating Board for Monitoring Mystical Beliefs in Society (Badan Koordinasi Pengawas Aliran Kepercayaan Masyarakat, Bakor Pakem), 249
corruption, 1, 8, 17, 23, 29, 137, 152, 162, 167, 175–94, 203, 310, 314
  cases handled by general prosecutors and KPK prosecutors, 183
  Corruption Perceptions Index ranking, 178
  Democrat Party (PD), 180, 184, 310, 310n
  district heads (*bupati*), 261, 270
  food policy, 289
  judiciary, 179
  land-use sector, 265, 266, 267–8, 269, 272
  local level, 157, 160, 162, 165n, 261, 270, 272
  money politics, 25, 160–1, 202, 203
  security sector, 120, 128, 129, 186
  Transparency International UK's Government Defence Anti-Corruption Index, 121
Corruption Eradication Commission (Komisi Pemberantasan Korupsi, KPK), 1, 8, 11, 16, 17, 28, 29, 48, 126, 165n, 166, 175–6, 177–84, 270
  arrest of and case against commissioners, 48, 176, 180–1, 184, 185–6
  conviction rate, 179
  dual-track system of prosecutions, 181
  establishment, 175
  judicial appointments, 179, 182
  prosecutions of powerful figures, 179–80
  public support for, 176, 180
  regional corruption courts, 181–2
  role, 178
  weakening powers of, 183–4
  wiretapping, 178, 180, 183
  Yudhoyono support for, 184–6, 193–4
counterterrorism, 27, 35, 137, 147–52

D

decentralisation, 26, 147, 155–72, 265, 296n
  outcomes, 159–61
  public satisfaction with, 162
  recentralisation, 63, 156, 158, 163, 165, 167
  social welfare, 326, 341
  taxation powers, 163–4
  2010–2025 Grand Design for the Structuring of Regions, 167
defence
  see military
democracy, 15–18, 25–6
  commencement in Indonesia, 327
  effect of presidentialism and multi-party systems, 7–8
  stagnation, 2, 17, 18
Democrat Party (Partai Demokrat, PD), 5, 29, 43, 49, 51, 53, 98, 104, 122, 126, 143, 146, 156, 176, 202, 208, 299, 310

corruption, 180, 184, 310, 310n
female representation, 202–3
democratic elections, 26
   heads of provinces, districts and cities (*pilkada*), 11, 16, 17, 25, 155, 156, 157–8, 160–1, 163, 168–70
   presidential, 4, 5, 15, 16, 18, 23, 24, 25, 28, 44, 46, 48, 56, 63, 141, 142, 171, 199, 305
   protection of system of, 11, 25, 28, 53, 83, 104, 156, 169
   women's political representation, 201–3
   'zipper' system of listing candidates, 201
   see also women, political participation
deregulation, 298–9
Detachment 88, 27, 29, 147, 147n, 148, 150, 151, 153
DPD
   see Regional Representative Council
DPR
   see People's Representative Council

E

East Asia Summit, 79–80
East Asian economic integration, 294
economic crisis 1997–98
   see Asian financial crisis
economy, 24, 280–301
   ASEAN comparison, 287
   competitiveness, 306, 327
   drivers of growth, 287–9
   development master plan, 273, 297, 319, 328, 341
   'Ease of doing business' surveys, 296
   exchange rate, 289, 290, 291–2, 294, 329–30
   fiscal policy, 9, 119, 155, 159, 289, 290, 291, 292, 293, 304, 320, 321–2
   GDP, 27, 287, 288
   government expenditure by sector, 329
   growth, 1, 27, 35, 75, 284–7, 288, 306, 327
   inflation, 289, 291
   international comparisons, 27
   Logistics Performance Index, 297
   macroeconomic management, 289–93
   openness, 293–6
   per capita income, 285, 285n, 286
   protectionism, 294, 306
   public debt share of GDP, 290
   public sector debt, 290, 298
   structural reforms, 2, 108
   terms of trade, 294
education, 326, 328, 334–8
   basis of funding, 335
   educational attainment, 335–6
   enrolments, 336–7
   government expenditure, 293, 328
   Law 20/2003 on the National Education System, 328, 335, 337
   Law 14/2005 on Teachers, 335, 337
   Schools Operational Assistance (Bantuan Operasi Sekolah, BOS), 335, 335, 337
   teacher quality, 335, 337
Eisenhower, Dwight D., 69, 70
employment, 204, 285, 295, 303–4, 305, 306, 306, 307–11, 321
   formal sector, 300, 308, 309, 310
   informal sector, 308, 309
   wages, 300, 307, 308, 310, 310n, 318, 319
   youth unemployment, 308
   see also labour regulations
energy subsidies
   see fuel subsidies
environment, 258–75
   carbon dioxide emissions, 264
   carbon emissions target, 258
   deforestation, 259, 263, 264–5, 273–4
   environmental and social impact assessments, 261
   greenhouse gas emissions, 110, 259, 260, 263–6, 273
   indigenous peoples, 260, 268, 269, 270, 272
   Law 32/2009 on Environmental Protection and Management, 11, 259, 260–2, 275
   permits, 261
   Reducing Emissions from Deforestation and Degradation (REDD), 265, 266, 266–71
   regulations, 260–1, 275

role of district government heads, 261
Satgas REDD+, 266, 268, 269
see also forests and forestry
Estrada, Joseph, 64, 65, 68, 70
European Union, 140, 230, 289, 290

F
Facebook, 14, 50, 249, 252
Fauzi, Gamawan, 158, 167, 168, 171–2, 246, 248, 251, 255
FKUB
see Religious Harmony Forum
foreign investment, 295, 318
forests and forestry, 165–6, 258, 262, 264–5, 266–71
  agreement with Norway on deforestation, 266, 273
  community forests, 267–8
  corruption, 265, 266, 267–8, 269, 272
  deforestation, 259, 265, 266, 271, 273–4
  fires, 262, 264, 274–5
  indigenous peoples, 268
  Lapor, 272
  memorandum of understanding on the acceleration of forest gazettement, 270–1
  moratorium on new licences, 271, 272
  One Map Movement, 166, 269–70
  permits, 265
  Reducing Emissions from Deforestation and Degradation (REDD), 265, 266, 266–71
  tenure reform, 268
FPI
see Islamic Defenders Front
Free Aceh Movement (Gerakan Aceh Merdeka, GAM), 36, 137, 138, 139–43, 152
  Aceh Transition Committee, 141
  Partai Aceh, 141, 142, 143
Free Papua Organisation (Organisasi Papua Merdeka, OPM), 146, 146n
Freedom House, 17, 221, 221n, 222, 232–3, 234
fuel subsidies, 2, 9, 10, 30, 289, 292, 292n, 299, 313, 320, 321–2, 326, 327, 328, 329–30, 334, 338, 342
future Indonesia, 64, 70, 111

G
G20 nations, 1, 73, 77, 80
  Pittsburg meeting, 258, 263, 265–6
GAM
  see Free Aceh Movement
gambling, 120, 124
GAPKI
  see Indonesian Palm Oil Association
garments and footwear, 310, 311n
gender equality, 199–214
  Gender Gap Index, 200
  legal protection, 205–7
  migrant workers, 210–11
  women in poverty, 203–5
  women's political representation, 201–3
  Yudhoyono conservativism, 207–9
  'zipper' system of listing candidates, 201
  see also women
General Elections Commission, 201
global economy, 282, 286
global financial crisis 2008–09, 27, 80, 283, 284, 291, 293, 301, 310
Global Green Growth Institute, 88, 258, 275
global production networks, 291, 295
Golkar party, 5, 8, 45, 47, 98, 101, 102, 109, 202
  corrupt parliamentarian, 179
government coalitions, oversized
  see rainbow coalition cabinets
greenhouse gas emissions, 110, 259, 260, 263–6, 273
  carbon dioxide emissions, 264

H
Habibie, B.J., 24, 30, 55, 155, 305, 327
health, 27–8, 314, 330–4
  children, 328, 332, 339
  government expenditure, 329, 331, 332
  immunisation rates, 332
  Law 40/2004 on the National Social Security System, 327–8, 330, 332, 333, 334
  Law 24/2011 on Social Security Providers, 331, 333
  maternal mortality, 204, 331–2
  regional health insurance schemes, 330, 333–4

universal basic health insurance, 316, 326, 327–8, 330–4, 342
women, 328, 331, 339
workforce, 331
Helsinki peace accord, 137–40, 152
human capital, 313, 336
human rights, 11, 29, 59, 81, 128, 143, 145, 206, 211, 217–36
civil and political rights, 221, 222
domestic view, 223–5
freedom of association, 17, 225
freedom of expression, 187, 205, 206, 218, 225
freedom of expression on the internet (case study), 232–4
international perceptions, 220–3
justice for murder of Munir Said Thalib (case study), 229–30
justice for past crimes (case study), 225–8
National Plan of Action on Human Rights, 226
political prisoners in Papua and Maluku (case study), 230–2

I

ICC
see International Criminal Court
ILO
see International Labour Organization
India, 264, 312, 317
Indonesia Corruption Watch, 181
Indonesia Peace and Security Center, 28
Indonesian Armed Forces (Angkatan Bersenjata Republik Indonesia, ABRI), 115, 117, 127
dissolution, 127
Indonesian Banking Development Foundation, 180
Indonesian Communist Party (Partai Komunis Indonesia, PKI) 65, 66, 220, 227
Indonesian Council of Ulama (Majelis Ulama Indonesia, MUI), 242, 243, 246–7, 248
fatwa, 242, 246, 247, 248–9, 251
Indonesian Democratic Party of Struggle (Partai Demokrasi Indonesia-Perjuangan, PDIP), 49, 66, 97, 98, 169, 202

Indonesian Forum for the Environment (Wahana Lingkungan Hidup Indonesia, WALHI), 261
Indonesian National Army (Tentara Nasional Indonesia, TNI), 114–35
accountability, 125–6, 129
annual budget, 118
businesses, 122–3
corruption, 120
oversight and governance, 125
procurement, 121–2
relationship with Polri, 129–32
Special Forces (Komando Pasukan Khusus, Kopassus), 126
TNI Law, 119, 122, 123, 125–6, 130
Indonesian National Police (Polisi Republik Indonesia, Polri), 114–35
accountability, 127–8, 129
annual budget, 118
budget planning, 121
businesses, 123–4
corruption, 120, 128, 129, 186
oversight and governance, 125
police chief, 119–20, 121n, 128, 247
presidential oversight, 127–8
privileged under democratisation, 117
relationship with TNI, 129–32
Indonesian Palm Oil Association (Gabungan Pengusaha Kelapa Sawit Indonesia, GAPKI), 273
industrial relations, 101, 308, 309–10, 327
industry policy, 289
inequality, 2, 27, 203–4, 214, 293, 300, 303–4, 305n, 316–17, 316n, 320
gender, 199–214
urban versus rural, 318–19
wage, 318–19, 321
infrastructure, 19, 23, 75, 121, 159, 160, 293, 319, 329
deficit, 296–9
Logistics Performance Index, 297
Tanjung Priok, 298
institutions, 17, 19, 24, 93–111, 272, 341
international affairs, 1, 2, 24, 28, 79–88
International Convention on the Protection of the Rights of All Migrant Workers and Members of Their Families, 205

International Covenant on Civil and
    Political Rights, 221-2
International Criminal Court (ICC),
    226-7
International Labour Organization
    (ILO), 309, 310n
International Monetary Fund, 1, 285
International Women's Day, 204
Investment Coordinating Board
    (Badan Koordinasi Penanaman
    Modal, BKPM), 296
Islamic Defenders Front (Front
    Pembela Islam, FPI), 209, 242, 246,
    247, 248, 249, 255

J
Jakarta Anti-Corruption Court
    (Pengadilan Tindak Pidana
    Korupsi, Tipikor Court), 175, 178,
    181, 182, 183-4, 186
    appointment of judges, 182
    number of judges presiding over
    cases, 179
Jamkesda
    see Regional Health Insurance
Jamkesmas
    see Community Health Insurance
Jampersal
    see Maternity Insurance
Japan, 82, 263
Jemaah Islamiyah, 148, 151
JKN
    see National Health Insurance
Judicial Commission (Komisi
    Yudisial), 191-2, 192n
judicial integrity, 176, 182

K
Kalla, Jusuf, 5, 24, 30, 31, 45, 46, 47, 51,
    78, 98, 101-2, 148
    Aceh negotiations, 137-9, 152
Kamnas bill
    see security sector, Kamnas bill
Komnas HAM
    see National Commission for
    Human Rights
Komnas Perempuan
    see National Commission on
    Violence against Women
Kompolnas
    see National Police Commission
Korean War, 67

Korpri
    see Civil Servants Corps
KPK
    see Corruption Eradication
    Commission
KPPU
    see Business Competition
    Supervisory Commission
KUR
    see People's Business Credit

L
labour regulations, 101, 307
    Law 13/2003 on Labour, 47, 101,
    307, 308-11
labour-intensive industries, 306n, 307,
    308, 309, 310, 327
legislation, 249-51
    Forestry Law, 268
    Law 1/PNPS/1965 on Prevention
    of the Misuse and/or Abuse
    of Religion (Blasphemy Law),
    249-50, 250n
    Law 26/1997 on Military
    Discipline, 125-7, 260
    Law 39/1999 on Human Rights,
    217
    Law 26/2000 on Human Rights
    Courts, 225
    Law 21/2001 on Special
    Autonomy for Papua Province,
    143, 144
    Law 2/2002 on the National
    Police (Police Law), 119, 125, 127,
    128, 129, 130
    Law 3/2002 on State Defence, 125
    Law 30/2002 on the Corruption
    Eradication Commission (KPK
    Law), 180, 185
    Law 12/2003 on General
    Elections, 201
    Law 13/2003 on Labour (Labour
    Law), 47, 101, 307, 308-11
    Law 17/2003 on State Finances,
    121, 289
    Law 20/2003 on the National
    Education System, 328, 335, 337
    Law 24/2003 on the
    Constitutional Court, 190
    Law 34/2004 on the Indonesian
    National Army (TNI Law), 119,
    122, 123, 125-6, 130

Law 40/2004 on the National Social Security System, 327–8, 330, 332, 333, 334
Law 14/2005 on Teachers, 335, 337
Law 10/2008 on General Elections, 201
Law 17/2008 on Shipping, 298
Law 44/2008 on Pornography (Anti-Pornography Law), 205, 225
Law 28/2009 on Regional Taxes and User Charges, 164
Law 32/2009 on Environmental Protection and Management, 11, 259, 260–2, 275
Law 46/2009 on the Anti-Corruption Court, 181, 182
Law 13/2010 on Horticulture, 109, 306
Law 8/2011 on the Constitutional Court, 190, 193
Law 17/2011 on State Intelligence Agencies, 107
Law 24/2011 on Social Security Providers, 331, 333
Law 2/2012 on Land Acquisition, 299
Law 18/2012 on the Production and Importation of Food, 109, 306
Law 19/2012 on the Protection and Empowerment of Farmers, 109
Law 17/2013 on Societal Organisations, 225
Law 19/2013 on the Protection and Empowerment of Farmers, 306
Law 3/2014 on Industry, 294–5, 306
Law 5/2014 (Civil Service Law), 106, 107
Law 7/2014 on Trade, 109, 294, 306
Law 22/2014 Law on Local Elections, 166
Law 23/2014 Law on Regional Government, 164, 166
1974 Marriage Law, 188, 190
2004 Law on National Development Planning, 121
2004 Law on a Truth and Reconciliation Commission, 226
2004 State Audit Law, 121
2004 Treasury Law, 121
2006 Supreme Audit Agency Law, 121
2008 Law on Information and Electronic Transactions, 234
Lehmann Brothers collapse, 286
Lembaga Survei Indonesia (LSI), 47–8, 199
local government regulations (*perda*), 163, 206
    Aceh regulation on Islamic criminal code (Qanun Jinayat), 206–7
    discrimination against women, 206–7, 209, 225n
    revocation by national government, 163–4, 207

M

Malaysia, 151, 205, 210, 211, 275, 286n, 291, 295, 296, 297, 307, 320
Mallarangeng, Andi, 45, 46, 47
Maluku political prisoners, 230–2
Mangkusubroto, Kuntoro, 109, 266, 268–70
manufacturing, 69, 287, 288, 289, 306
    employment, 306, 311, 318
Massachusetts Institute of Technology Abdul Latif Jameel Poverty Action Lab (J-PAL), 315–16
Master Plan for the Acceleration and Expansion of Economic Development in Indonesia (Masterplan Percepatan dan Perluasan Pembangunan Ekonomi Indonesia, MP3EI), 273, 297, 319, 328, 341
Master Plan for the Acceleration and Expansion of Poverty Reduction in Indonesia (Masterplan Percepatan dan Perluasan Pengurangan Kemiskinan Indonesia, MP3KI), 316, 328, 341
Maternity Insurance (Jaminan Persalinan, Jampersal), 331
media, 23, 45, 47, 51, 53, 73, 145, 146, 147, 162, 169, 194, 208, 209, 217, 220, 244, 310, 313, 333
migrant workers, 204–5, 210–11, 309n
    memoranda of understanding, 211, 211n

military
   businesses, 122–3
   civilian trials for criminal
      violations, 126–7
   defence budget, 119, 120–1
   draft military tribunal bill, 126
   involvement in political affairs, 1,
      4, 62, 107, 115
   procurement, 121–1
   strength, 75–6
   support for Aceh peace, 140
   territorial command system
      (Komando Territorial, Koter), 130
   see also Indonesian Armed Forces;
      Indonesian National Army
Millennium Development Goals, 80,
   110, 204, 328, 338
mining and logging licences, 157, 163,
   268, 270
minority groups, 8, 49, 86, 100, 206,
   234, 235, 239–55
Mochtar, Akil, 192, 192n, 193
money politics, 25, 160–1, 202, 203
MP3EI
   see Master Plan for the
      Acceleration and Expansion
      of Economic Development in
      Indonesia
MP3KI
   see Master Plan for the
      Acceleration and Expansion of
      Poverty Reduction in Indonesia
MPR
   see People's Consultative
      Assembly
MRP
   see Papua, Papuan People's
      Council
Muhammadiyah, 242
MUI
   see Indonesian Council of Ulama
multi-partyism, 7, 12, 13
Muslim
   /Christian conflict, 147, 247
   clerics, 148, 149, 153
   communities, 242, 243, 253, 254
   deaths in Ambon and Poso, 151
   democracy/nation, 1, 73, 74, 80,
      148, 207, 252, 254
   militants, 137, 149, 243, 251

musrenbang
   see social welfare, development
      planning (*musrenbang*) process
Myanmar, 79, 81

N

Nahdlatul Ulama (NU), 242, 246
Natalegawa, Marty, 79, 81
National Agency for the Placement
   and Protection of Indonesian
   Migrant Workers (Badan Nasional
   Penempatan dan Perlindungan
   Tenaga Kerja Indonesia,
   BNP2TKI), 205
National Coalition, 98, 99
National Commission for Human
   Rights (Komisi Nasional Hak
   Asasi Manusia, Komnas HAM),
   227, 228, 230, 270–1
National Commission on Violence
   against Women (Komisi
   Nasional Anti Kekerasan
   Terhadap Perempuan, Komnas
   Perempuan), 200, 205, 206, 210,
   211
National Counterterrorism Agency
   (Badan Nasional Penanggulangan
   Terorisme, BNPT), 27, 147, 150,
   153
National Development Planning
   Agency (Badan Perencanaan
   Pembangunan Nasional,
   Bappenas), 313, 331
National Health Insurance (Jaminan
   Kesehatan Nasional, JKN), 331,
   333, 341
National Medium-term Development
   Plans, 328, 341
National Police Commission (Komisi
   Kepolisian Nasional, Kompolnas),
   128–9
National Program for Community
   Empowerment (Program
   Nasional Pemberdayaan
   Masyarakat, PNPM), 311, 313,
   314–15, 338–40
   derivative programs, 339–40
national social security council, 332
National Socio-economic Survey
   (Survei Sosio-Ekonomi Nasional,
   Susenas), 316n, 318, 336

national statistics agency (Badan Pusat Statistik, BPS), 340
National Team for the Acceleration of Poverty Reduction (Tim Nasional Percepatan Penanggulangan Kemiskinan, TNP2K), 108, 313, 328, 340
natural resources sector, 19, 23, 70, 164–6, 189, 260, 261, 263, 264–5, 272, 274, 319, 321
  commodity boom, 75, 159, 287, 293, 294, 306n, 319, 321
  commodity prices, 286, 289, 294
New Order, 3, 4, 13, 26, 27, 40, 70, 114, 115, 130, 217, 218, 219
  human rights abuses, 225–8
newly industrialising economies (NIEs), 285
Nixon, Richard, 70
Nobel Peace Prize, 140
Non-Aligned Movement (NAM), 77
non-government organisations (NGOs), 131, 210, 271
Norway, 266
NU
  see Nahdlatul Ulama

O

Obama, President Barack, 2, 50, 106, 221
oil price subsidies, 104
  see also fuel subsidies
OPM
  see Free Papua Organisation
Organisation for Economic Co-operation and Development (OECD), 286, 331

P

palm oil, 273, 293, 319
Pancasila ideology, 13, 100
Papua, 29, 131, 136, 137, 143–7, 152–3
  conflict, 143, 145, 147
  division, 143, 144
  enhanced special autonomy, 146
  Free Papua Organisation (OPM), 146, 146n
  governor election, 145, 146
  Papua Peace Network, 145, 146, 153
  Papuan People's Council (Majelis Rakyat Papua, MRP), 144
  political prisoners, 230–2
  Special Autonomy Law, 143, 144
  role of Sarwo Edhie Wibowo, 220
  splitting of districts (*pemekaran*), 146–7
  Unit for the Acceleration of Development in Papua and West Papua (UP4B), 144–5, 147
Partai Aceh, 141, 142, 143
patronage, 8, 19, 99, 156, 161, 261
PD
  see Democrat Party
PDIP
  see Indonesian Democratic Party of Struggle
pemekaran, 146–7, 157, 161, 162, 163
  moratorium and evaluation, 166–7
People's Business Credit (Kredit Usaha Rakyat, KUR), 212
People's Consultative Assembly (Majelis Permusyarawatan Rakyat, MPR), 43, 94, 95–6, 217
People's Representative Council (DPR), 3, 8, 9, 11, 94, 96, 99, 101, 102, 103–4, 106, 107, 108, 110, 167, 170, 225–6
  position of speaker, 105
perda
  see local government regulations
Pertamina, 293
Philippines, 14, 57, 58–68, 221, 285, 287, 288, 291, 295, 296, 297, 307, 308
  Ramos, Fidel V., 57, 58–63, 67, 69
PISA
  see Programme for International Student Assessment
PKH
  see poverty, conditional cash transfer program
PKI
  see Indonesian Communist Party
PKS
  see Prosperous Justice Party
PNPM
  see National Program for Community Empowerment
police
  arrest of KPK commissioners, 28, 48, 176, 184
  drive-by shooting of, 151

politicisation, 127–8
  see also Anti-bomb Taskforce;
    Detachment 88; Indonesian
    National Police
policy decisions, majority view, 10, 15,
  16, 48, 49, 233–4, 254
political parties, 8, 26, 139, 161, 154,
  149, 311
  judicial candidates and, 191, 192
  women candidature, 201–3
  see also Democrat Party; Free Aceh
    Movement; Golkar; Indonesian
    Communist Party; Indonesian
    Democratic Party of Struggle;
    Prosperous Justice Party; United
    Development Party
polls, 15, 47–8, 49
pollution, 260, 262, 299
Polri
  see Indonesian National Police
poverty, 23, 27, 159, 267, 300, 303, 305,
  306, 306n, 311–16, 342
  alleviation programs, 311–12, 326
  community empowerment,
    314–15, 338
  conditional cash transfer program
    (Program Keluarga Harapan,
    PKH), 313, 314, 328, 338
  database of poor households, 314,
    315, 328, 340–1
  Gini ratio, 305n, 316–18, 320
  income distribution, 316–20
  international poverty line, 312
  Master Plan for the Acceleration
    and Expansion of Poverty Reduc-
    tion in Indonesia (Masterplan
    Percepatan dan Perluasan
    Pengurangan Kemiskinan
    Indonesia, MP3KI), 316, 328, 341
  national poverty line, 305
  National Team for the
    Acceleration of Poverty Reduc-
    tion (Tim Nasional Percepatan
    Penanggulangan Kemiskinan,
    TNP2K), 108, 313, 328, 340
  rate, 1, 2, 312
  social protection card, 314, 315
  subsidised rice, 328, 338
  unconditional cash transfer
    program (Bantuan Langsung
    Tunai, BLT), 313–14, 314n, 328,
    338

urban versus rural, 312, 317
women, 203–5, 315
  see also inequality; National
    Program for Community
    Empowerment
PPP
  see United Development Party
Presidential Advisory Council
  (Dewan Pertimbangan Presiden,
  Wantimpres), 100, 109, 246, 251
presidential elections
  2004, 5, 24, 44, 63, 199
  2009, 5, 24, 46, 46n, 48, 141, 142,
    199, 305
  2014, 4, 15, 18, 23, 28, 48, 56, 169,
    171
presidential decrees, 226, 228
  61/2011 on greenhouse gas
    emissions, 263n
  71/2011 on taskforce on migrant
    worker legal protection, 210–11
  37/2014 on national committee
    for AEC, 79
presidential instructions, 206
  2003 on Papua, 143
  13/2003 on labour law, 101
  3/2006 on migrant worker
    training, 211
  5/2007 on Papua, 144
  5/2008 on economic
    development, 79
  10/2011 on licences in primary
    forests and peatlands, 271
  11/2011 on AEC implementing
    commitments, 79
  2/2013 on disturbances to
    internal national security, 131
  6/2013 on licences in primary
    forests and peatlands, 271
  6/2014 on Indonesian
    competitiveness in the AEC, 79
Presidential Regulation 43/2009 on
  TNI, 122–3
Presidential Working Unit for
  Development Monitoring and
  Oversight (Unit Kerja Presiden
  untuk Pengawasan dan
  Pengendalian Pembangunan,
  UKP4), 108, 109–10, 111, 166, 266,
  268, 269–70, 272
presidentialism, 7, 13, 103

Programme for International Student
  Assessment (PISA), 335–6
Propatria, 131
Prosperous Justice Party (Partai
  Keadilan Sejahtera, PKS), 9, 10,
  29, 233, 289
  jailing of chair, 179
PT Kallista Alam, 261–2

R
rainbow coalition cabinets, 3, 7–8, 45,
  97–8, 105, 110, 299
  problems of power-sharing,
  99–102
REDD
  see environment, Reducing
  Emissions from Deforestation and
  Degradation; forests and forestry,
  Reducing Emissions from
  Deforestation and Degradation
reformasi, 17, 25, 304
regional autonomy
  see decentralisation
Regional Health Insurance (Jaminan
  Kesehatan Daerah, Jamkesda),
  330, 333–4, 340
Regional Representative Council
  (Dewan Perwakilan Daerah,
  DPD), 157
regulations, 11, 100, 101, 108–9, 132,
  142–3, 144, 156–8, 165, 169, 184–5,
  191, 193, 225, 231–4, 241, 244,
  249–51, 259, 260–1, 267, 268, 272,
  275, 308, 321
  see also Aceh, local regulation
  on Islamic criminal code
  (Qanun Jinayat); deregulation;
  environment, regulations; labour
  regulations; local government
  regulations; Presidential
  Regulation 43/2009 on TNI
religious affairs, minister, 8, 29, 100,
  242, 244, 246, 251
Religious Freedom Advocacy Team,
  251
religious tolerance, 8, 12, 29, 82, 86,
  239–55
  Ahmadiyah, 8, 12, 100, 241–3, 248,
  253
  appeal to United Nations, 251
  Christians, 147, 148, 239, 241,
  244–5

  Joint Decree(s) on Houses of
  Worship, 250, 251
  Religious Harmony Forum
  (Folrum Kerukunan Umat
  Beragama, FKUB), 251
  Shi'a, 243–4
rice
  economy, 293, 312n
  imports, 104, 289, 312n
  subsidised for the poor, 328, 338
Rome Statute, 226, 227
rural communities, 204–5, 212, 272,
  293, 317, 318, 331
Russia, 80, 264

S
Said Thalib, Munir, 29
Saiful Mujani Research and
  Consulting (SMRC), 48
Satgas Bom
  see Anti-bomb Taskforce
Satgas REDD+
  see environment, Satgas REDD+
Saudi Arabia, 205, 210
security sector, 11, 59, 114–53
  budgetary accountability, 121–2
  budgets, 118–24
  businesses, 122–4
  corruption, 120, 124
  domestic security, 129–30, 131
  framework for reform, 116–18
  governance and oversight, 124–9
  Kamnas bill, 130–1
  police/military relationship,
  129–32
  'professionalism', 114–16, 117, 132
  structural reform, 115, 128
  see also Indonesian Armed Forces;
  Indonesian National Army
semi-presidentialism, 3, 6–10, 95
services sector, 287, 288, 306, 318
sharia law, 206, 209
Shi'a community, 8, 239, 241, 249
Shinawatra, Thaksin, 16, 65, 68
Singapore, 151, 275, 286n, 295
SKK Migas, 179
social media, 14, 18, 28, 50, 232, 234
social welfare, 12, 27–8, 325–42
  budget cuts, 330
  community development
  program, 338

development planning
  (*musrenbang*) process, 338–40, 341
  expenditure, 329
  social assistance, definitions, 340
South China Sea dispute, 76, 77, 79
  Declaration on the Conduct of
    Parties in the South China Sea, 79
South Korea, 307, 335
Sri Mulyani, Indrawati, 8, 105, 284
State Finance Accountability
  Committee, 122
State Intelligence Agency (Badan
  Inteljen Negara, BIN), 107, 145,
  229
  deputy director charged with
    murder, 229–30
Subianto, Prabowo, 4, 18, 23, 48n, 53,
  56, 64, 65, 68, 70, 122, 169, 192,
  227, 235
  Yudhoyono support for, 48–9
Suharto, former president, 13, 14, 40,
  44, 49, 59, 61, 62, 67, 93, 94, 95,
  96, 97, 106, 108, 110, 121, 161, 179,
  187, 190, 248, 304n
  appointment of Yudhoyono, 4
  economic record, 285, 286, 287,
    289, 291, 294, 298, 303
  foreign policy, 77
  poverty record, 2, 304, 304n, 305,
    315, 316–17, 321
  resignation, 25, 42, 115, 217, 219,
    229
Sukarnoputri, Megawati, 5, 17, 24, 30,
  44, 49, 51, 55, 62–3, 96, 97, 98, 110,
  117, 122, 127, 129, 133, 138, 143,
  147, 148, 231, 304, 305, 327, 331
Supreme Audit Agency (Badan
  Pemeriksa Keuangan, BPK), 96,
  105, 122
Supreme Court, 25, 181, 182, 187
Susenas
  see National Socio-economic
    Survey
Syria, 151–2

T
Taiwan, 79, 307, 336
taxation, 157, 157–8, 163–4, 293, 316,
  320
technology, 114, 151, 295
  see also Facebook; social media;
    YouTube

terrorism, 27, 29, 35, 107, 136
  Australian embassy bombing, 147
  counterterrorism, 27, 35, 137, 138,
    147–52, 153
  extremist clerics, 149, 153
  ISIS rally, 152
  Poso violence/bombings, 147–9
  recruitment, 149, 151
  training camp in Aceh, 150
  2002 Bali bombings, 147n, 150
  2005 Bali bombing, 148
  2009 hotel bombings, 137, 149
Thailand, 14, 16, 57, 58–68, 221, 286n,
  287, 288, 291, 295, 296, 297, 307,
  320, 331, 335, 336
  Choonhavan, Chatichai, 64, 70
  Communist Party, 66
  Tinsulanonda, Prem, 57, 58–63,
    66, 69
Timor Leste, 16, 73, 78, 331
Tipikor Court
  see Jakarta Anti-Corruption Court
TNI
  see Indonesian National Army
TNP2K
  see National Team for the
    Acceleration of Poverty
    Reduction
Transparency International, 121, 177,
  178
transport, 298, 299
Truth and Reconciliation Commission,
  226
Twitter, 14, 28, 50

U
UKP4
  see Presidential Working Unit for
    Development Monitoring and
    Oversight
unions, 101, 309–10
United Development Party (Partai
  Persatuan Pembangunan, PPP),
  29, 246
United Nations, 28, 53, 73
  Climate Change Conference 2007,
    80
  Committee on Economic, Social
    and Cultural Rights, 205
  Committee against Torture, 228
  Convention on the Law of the
    Sea, 79

Framework Convention on Climate Change (UNFCCC), 265
High Commissioner for Human Rights, 221
High-level Panel of Eminent Persons on the Post-2015 Development Agenda, 80
Human Rights Council, 221
  peacekeeping missions, 28, 42
  Security Council, 80
  Working Group on Arbitrary Detention, 231
  Yudhoyono request to ban blasphemy, 250, 254
United States of America, 2, 7, 66, 67, 69–70, 77, 80, 150
  carbon dioxide emissions, 264
  –China relations, 77
  military presence in Southeast Asia, 66–7
  9/11 attacks, 107
  presidential leadership, 56
United States-Indonesia Comprehensive Partnership, 74
UP4B
  see Unit for the Acceleration of Development in Papua and West Papua

V

Vietnam, 295, 296, 297
Vietnam War, 67
violence, 1, 25, 61, 65, 66, 98, 137, 143, 145, 147, 151
  against women, 200
  religious, 241, 242, 242, 243, 244, 248, 251
religious, 241
  see also terrorism

W

Wahid, Abdurrahman, 5, 6–7, 14, 24, 43, 55, 62, 95, 97, 98, 110, 127, 129, 133, 138, 231, 304, 305, 327
  impeachment, 5, 44, 95, 96, 97, 98, 127
WALHI
  see Indonesian Forum for the Environment
Wantimpres
  see Presidential Advisory Council

Wibowo, Sarwo Edhie, 40, 41, 42, 43, 66, 220
Widodo, Joko, 18–19, 23, 26, 28, 31, 49, 49n, 70, 152, 160, 171, 214, 236, 255, 301
  cabinet, 203n
  fuel subsidy pronouncement, 292n
  wages pronouncement, 310
Wirajuda, Hassan, 77, 79, 80, 103n
Wiranto, 62
women
  corruption and, 203
  health care, 328
  human rights, 225n
  inequality, 199–214
  International Women's Day, 204
  legal protection from discrimination, 205–7
  maternal mortality, 204, 331–2
  Maternity Insurance, 331
  migrant workers, 204–5, 210–11
  political representation, 201–3
  poor, 203–5, 315
  quota system to increase political representation, 201
  rural, 204–5, 212
  voters, 199–200
  'zipper' system of listing political candidates, 201
World Bank, 78, 203, 204, 285, 295, 330, 338
World Economic Forum
  Gender Gap Index, 200
World Health Organization, 331

Y

YouTube, 18, 28, 51, 152, 169
Yudhoyono, Susilo Bambang
  Aceh peace, 1, 11, 27, 30, 35, 46, 136–7, 152, 230
  anti-corruption record, 29, 35
  appointment to Global Green Growth Institute, 88, 258, 275
  cabinet appointments, 7–8, 29, 30, 45, 47, 97–8, 101, 125, 128, 168, 203, 246, 284, 294
  campaign style, 5
  candidacy for presidential elections, 5
  cautiousness 7, 15, 138, 226, 235, 281, 300, 301

childhood, 37–9, 51
communication abilities, 18, 81
comparison with Prem and Ramos, 58–63
conservativism, 8, 13, 57, 116, 131, 133, 207, 219, 253, 334
counterterrorism record, 27, 35
democracy record, 1, 2, 4, 15–18, 24–5, 35, 49
early political career, 4–5
economic record, 2, 27, 35, 46, 75, 281, 282, 286, 287, 292, 300
education record, 328, 338
educational background, 4, 39, 40, 42n
employment record, 308–9
environmental policy record, 259, 272, 275
family background, 4, 13, 37–9, 84
foreign policy record, 2, 28, 78–82, 88
gender equality record, 203, 212–13
human rights record, 29, 81, 219, 221, 223, 224, 225, 235, 252
indecisiveness, 2, 6, 30, 36, 44–5, 46, 49, 50–2, 82, 85, 149, 213
infrastructure record, 2, 281, 297–8, 299, 300
insecurity, 36, 50–2
intelligence, 4, 36, 39, 42, 45
international awards, 51, 83
marriage, 4, 13, 40–1, 43, 219
military career, 4, 40, 42
military links, 13, 40
moderator, 2–3, 3–4, 10–15
moral politics, 208–9, 213, 233
national unity record, 26–7, 35
policy decisions, majority view, 10, 15, 16, 48, 49, 233–4, 254
political background, 3
popularity, 6, 44
poverty reduction record, 2, 27, 303, 304, 311, 313, 321
presidential election results, 24, 44
public image, 14–15, 82, 275
rainbow coalition cabinets, 3, 7–8, 45, 97, 98, 105, 110, 299
religious tolerance, 8, 12, 29, 82, 86, 253, 254–5
retirement, 6
security sector reform, 132, 133

Selalu Ada Pilihan (2014 book), 14, 51, 82, 85, 158, 213
semi-presidentialism view, 3, 9
social media use, 14, 18, 28, 50
social welfare record, 27–8, 316, 334, 341–2
stability, love of, 7, 12
stability record, 19
vanity, 14, 35, 36, 46, 50, 50–2, 53

INDONESIA UPDATE SERIES

1989
Indonesia Assessment 1988 (Regional Development)
edited by Hal Hill and Jamie Mackie

1990
Indonesia Assessment 1990 (Ownership)
edited by Hal Hill and Terry Hull

1991
Indonesia Assessment 1991 (Education)
edited by Hal Hill

1992
Indonesia Assessment 1992 (Political Perspectives)
edited by Harold Crouch

1993
Indonesia Assessment 1993 (Labour)
edited by Chris Manning and Joan Hardjono

1994
Indonesia Assessment 1994: Finance as a Key Sector in Indonesia's Development
edited by Ross McLeod

1996
Indonesia Assessment 1995: Development in Eastern Indonesia
edited by Colin Barlow and Joan Hardjono

1997
Indonesia Assessment: Population and Human Resources
edited by Gavin W. Jones and Terence H. Hull

1998
Indonesia's Technological Challenge
edited by Hal Hill and Thee Kian Wie

1999
Post-Soeharto Indonesia: Renewal or Chaos?
edited by Geoff Forrester

2000
Indonesia in Transition: Social Aspects of Reformasi and Crisis
edited by Chris Manning and Peter van Diermen

2001
Indonesia Today: Challenges of History
edited by Grayson J. Lloyd and Shannon L. Smith

2002
Women in Indonesia: Gender, Equity and Development
edited by Kathryn Robinson and Sharon Bessell

2003
Local Power and Politics in Indonesia: Decentralisation and Democratisation
edited by Edward Aspinall and Greg Fealy

2004
Business in Indonesia: New Challenges, Old Problems
edited by M. Chatib Basri and Pierre van der Eng

2005
The Politics and Economics of Indonesia's Natural Resources
edited by Budy P. Resosudarmo

2006
Different Societies, Shared Futures: Australia, Indonesia and the Region
edited by John Monfries

2007
Indonesia: Democracy and the Promise of Good Governance
edited by Ross H. McLeod and Andrew MacIntyre

2008
Expressing Islam: Religious Life and Politics in Indonesia
edited by Greg Fealy and Sally White

2009
Indonesia beyond the Water's Edge: Managing an Archipelagic State
edited by Robert Cribb and Michele Ford

2010
Problems of Democratisation in Indonesia: Elections, Institutions and Society
edited by Edward Aspinall and Marcus Mietzner

2011
Employment, Living Standards and Poverty in Contemporary Indonesia
edited by Chris Manning and Sudarno Sumarto

2012
Indonesia Rising: The Repositioning of Asia's Third Giant
edited by Anthony Reid

2013
Education in Indonesia
edited by Daniel Suryadarma and Gavin W. Jones

2014
Regional Dynamics in a Decentralized Indonesia
edited by Hal Hill

2015
The Yudhoyono Presidency: Indonesia's Decade of Stability and Stagnation
edited by Edward Aspinall, Marcus Mietzner and Dirk Tomsa